This book, which is largely based on the Bank of England's own archives, describes the internal workings of the Bank from 1930 to 1960 under three Governors, Lord Norman, Lord Catto and Lord Cobbold.

Each chapter is devoted to the organisation and working methods of a particular department, such as Cashier's, Accountant's (now Registrar's), the Printing Works, the Overseas Department and so on. The book also includes the first full published description of how the Bank continued working during the Second World War when many of its staff were evacuated to Hampshire and elsewhere. Much hitherto private information is disclosed, covering among other topics the Bank's accounting methods and profitability, and the note issue and bank note design.

These decades were a period of enormous change for the Bank, when its working methods (many dating back almost to its foundation in 1694) were radically updated and in some cases mechanised in a progression of record-keeping from handwritten ledgers to computers. New functions such as exchange control were put into place, and there was a slow but definite expansion of the role of women. The Bank also helped many newly independent countries to set up their own central banks. New buildings, including a new Printing Works, were erected, some of which feature among the many text illustrations.

# A DOMESTIC HISTORY OF THE BANK OF ENGLAND, 1930–1960

The Threadneedle Street Entrance by Sir Henry Rushbury KCVO
CBE RA, Keeper of the Royal Academy 1949–64. This is one of a series
of watercolours by Rushbury commissioned by the Bank of England
in 1954

# A DOMESTIC HISTORY OF THE BANK OF ENGLAND, 1930–1960

ELIZABETH HENNESSY

CAMBRIDGE
UNIVERSITY PRESS

Published by the Press Syndicate of the University of Cambridge
The Pitt Building, Trumpington Street, Cambridge CB2 1RP
40 West 20th Street, New York, NY 10011-4211, USA
10 Stamford Road, Oakleigh, Victoria 3166, Australia

First published 1992

Printed in Great Britain at the University Press, Cambridge

*A catalogue record for this book is available from the British Library*

*Library of Congress cataloguing in publication data*
Hennessy, Elizabeth.
A domestic history of the Bank of England, 1930–1960 / Elizabeth Hennessy.
p.   cm.
ISBN 0 521 39140 7
1.  Bank of England – History.   2.  Banks and Banking, Central – Great Britain –
History – 20th century.   I.  Title.
HG2986.H46   1992
332.1′1′09410904 – dc20   91-15811   CIP

ISBN 0 521 39140 7 hardback

# CONTENTS

# ILLUSTRATIONS

The Bank of England, 1954 *frontispiece*

## Colour (between pages 144 and 145)

Dividend Day at the Bank of England
The 2s. 6d. and 5s. 'currency notes'
Reverse of 10s. note
Design by Stephen Gooden for £2 note in the Houblon Series
Front of the £1 series C 'portrait' note
The Picquet marching to the Bank: oil painting by H. S.
Kortright

## Black and white

# FOREWORD

Given the nature of the Bank of England's tasks, it is hardly surprising that our recent official historians have tended to concentrate much more on the development of policy than on the Bank as an institution in its own right. There has in fact been no purely domestic history of the Bank since Marston Acres published 'The Bank of England from Within' in 1931, and of the three official histories published since then only Sir John Clapham's (1944) gave our domestic affairs any real prominence.

It was at the time of our commissioning the most recent history, by John Fforde, which was published earlier this year, that we recognised the omission and resolved to correct it by inviting Elizabeth Hennessy to take the story on from the 1930s, when the Peacock Committee initiated a series of major reorganisations, right up to 1960, when Mr Fforde's history stops. The inspiration for this came from the then Deputy Governor, Sir George Blunden, whose personal and family recollections of the Bank could themselves have furnished several histories, and who indeed contributed substantially to this one.

Mrs Hennessy has produced a fascinating account of a very eventful period of our history. It was a time of rapid change, in which we began to move away from the clerical traditions of 200 years – in effect, the world of Acres – and to accept specialisation, mechanisation and modern management disciplines; in which we went to war and introduced the fearsome apparatus of exchange control; in which we began, hesitatingly at first, to see the uses of economists and statisticians; and in which large numbers of our staff went abroad to set up new currency boards and central banks in the Commonwealth countries. It was a period in which the Bank began to realise that it depended not only on its traditions and on the loyalty of its staff but also on their quality and adaptability – even if, as Mrs Hennessy shows, progress here was sometimes made only against stubborn opposition.

The Bank described here is very far from the Bank of today. Less than 5 per cent of our present staff have any personal recollection of the Bank prior to 1960. Now the old departments are gone, and in their place is the more flexible structure introduced by Lord Richardson in 1980. Exchange control is gone, too – although we have recently had to re-learn some of its disciplines to administer controls on Iraqi and Kuwaiti assets in London. Accountant's, now Registrar's, Department has finally left London for Gloucester; the New Change building is being partly sub-let. In every area our staffing is very much less generous – though without I think any loss of quality in our work; and the continuation of the graduate recruitment and training programmes established under Lord Cobbold has brought a new intellectual rigour to the Bank's policies and management. Even so there is a very pronounced tradition and culture in the organisation – one that is discernible in this volume and still present today. Duty, care, accuracy, dispassionate analysis: the Bank is a cautious and watchful institution still, but a humane one too, and a place in which the humour can sparkle through in the most unlikely places – as it does so often in Mrs Hennessy's book.

So I have no hesitation in commending this volume both to those who know the institution from inside and to those who know it only by repute. Mrs Hennessy has made an excellent and entertaining study of an eventful thirty years in the Bank's life, and explained the background to its work with commendable clarity. Like Mr Acres' work, it will be of abiding interest to staff, to pensioners and to the lay reader.

ROBIN LEIGH-PEMBERTON

# ACKNOWLEDGEMENTS

As its title implies, this account of thirty years of the domestic history of the Bank of England is based very largely on internal sources. The Archive material for the period is rich and extensive and the standard of drafting of the minutes, memoranda, committee and other reports and correspondence is outstanding. The Bank's own papers, therefore, to which I have enjoyed unrestricted access, have provided the framework of the book.

Of equal importance were the recollections of many of the people at work in the Bank during and after the period and responsible in various ways for making its history. Staff of the Bank both past and present gave generously of their time to talk freely to me and often went to a great deal of trouble to verify facts and impressions and to answer my numerous questions. Some of them, together with their wives (in several cases themselves former members of the Staff), kindly entertained me in their own homes, and these visits were an especial pleasure.

My first thanks are due to Sir George Blunden who as Deputy Governor was instrumental in arranging for the book to be written and who, in spite of the many and compelling calls on his time, read every chapter as it was written and provided invaluable encouragement, help and information.

Lord O'Brien, who was in the Bank throughout the period under review, also read the book in its entirety in MS form, talked to me at length and in detail on many of the topics and was kind enough to compile a written memoir outlining his unique career in the Bank from Probationary Clerk to Governor. He gave me a perspective – particularly on the responsibilities of the Chief Cashier and the work of the Cashier's Department – which would have otherwise been unobtainable.

It is impossible for me to thank Derrick Byatt adequately for all the help I received from him over nearly four years of research and writing. His profound knowledge of, and affection for the Bank, its people, buildings, bank notes, methods of work and (sometimes highly idio-syncratic) customs were put unstintingly at my disposal and no question was ever too large or too small for him to answer. I benefited greatly from his insistence on accuracy and the book would have been much the poorer without him.

To David Best I am grateful for his expert guidance through the thickets of the Bank's pre-1970 accounts; he provided a dossier of information on this subject and on many other financial aspects without which I could not have written chapter 6.

John Flemming supervised the project throughout and was another to read the book chapter by chapter, providing many helpful suggestions and removing several inaccuracies and infelicities.

The Archive has already been mentioned: warm thanks are due to the Archivist, Henry Gillett, and all his staff for unfailing promptness and good humour in producing all the documents I needed and for considerable help and guidance in their selection. Terry Bell, Librarian, and his staff in both Reference and Staff Libraries were a constant support and source of advice and information. John Keyworth, Curator of the Bank of England Museum, and his staff in the Museum and Historical Research Section gave me the benefit of their unrivalled knowledge and were tireless in answering a multitude of queries; the Curator, the Bank's photographer Ian McQuire and Christine Turner gave particular help with the location and choice of the illustrations.

The Bank provided me with an office and I had every assistance in contacting all the people whom I interviewed from the Secretary of the Bank, Geoffrey Croughton, and the staff of his Office who provided cheerful and willing secretarial and administrative help.

I owe a great debt to all these people and also to those whose names appear below, many of whom have read and commented on one or more chapters of the book and whose contributions have added significantly to its content and to my own enjoyment of an absorbing assignment:

The late John Atkinson, Richard Balfour, Ray Barber, Robert Barkshire, Brian Bennett, Nigel Bevitt-Smith, Eric Bilton, David Buxton, Anthony Carlisle, Hilton Clarke, Lady Hermione Cobbold, Peter Cooke, Margot Cripps (nee Young), Lionel Cunnell, Gair Drake, Charles Excell, John Fforde, John Footman, Alan Fraser, Hugh Harris, Sir Jasper Hollom, James Humphry, Alex Jarvis, Graham Kentfield, Barry Mackay, Aphra Maunsell, Joan Morris, the late Sir Humphrey

Mynors, Beryl Neatby (nee Walsh), Howard Neatby, Portals Ltd, Jon Pullinger, John Rumins, James Selwyn, David Somerset, Peter Taylor, Kenneth Thompson, William Thompson, the late Michael Thornton, Guy Watson, Herbert Weston, Kathleen Weston (nee Douthwaite).

# INTRODUCTION

The original constitution of the Bank of England was defined by its first Charter granted in 1694 (this was varied by a supplementary Charter of 1896) and the Bank's own By-Laws, which could be amended only by a vote of a General Court, or meeting, of the Proprietors (registered holders of Bank Stock). As well as by the Charters and By-Laws the powers of the Bank were later widened by a number of Acts of Parliament, relating particularly to the Public Debt and the issue of bank notes. The By-Laws provided for a Governor, a Deputy Governor and a Court of twenty-four Directors, all of whom were subject to annual election by the votes of the qualified Proprietors at a General Court held in the spring of each year. Two years as Deputy Governor were normally followed by two as Governor, although these terms of office, which were also regulated by By-Law, were occasionally exceeded. The Court was wholly amateur and recruited almost exclusively from the ranks of the merchant bankers of the City of London.

The three chief officers of the Bank appointed by the first Court were the Secretary and Sollicitor, the First Accomptant and the First Cashier, an arrangement that was to remain virtually undisturbed for nearly 250 years (although the first Secretary and Sollicitor was the only one to hold that title and was succeeded by a Secretary). The rest of the original staff of the Bank numbered sixteen, and by 1734, when the move was made into a permanent home in Threadneedle Street, had only increased to ninety-six.

The first Chief Cashier lived on the premises and most of his successors continued to do so until 1914: the Chief Accountant lived in the Bank at various times between 1699 and 1894 and the Secretary or one of his deputies did so between 1809 and 1867. There was no very rigid departmental structure – it was not until 1851 that the House List (an annual list of all employees and their positions) was divided into Accountant's, Cashier's and Secretary's Departments. With their offices located close to the official quarters of the Governors, known as the Parlours, the three senior officials were able to hold frequent and informal meetings among themselves and with the Governor and Deputy Governor. The day-to-day administration of the Bank rested on these five people; the Directors other than the Governors exercised their influence by means of the weekly Court and the Committee of Daily Waiting, a rota of Directors who were particularly concerned with discount business.

The Country Bankers Act of 1826 enabled the Bank to set up Branches in any part of England or Wales: eight had been established by the end of the following year. No new Departments were opened in Threadneedle Street until the irregularities of the Chief Cashier in 1893 provided unwelcome evidence that an independent audit was necessary. An Auditor was appointed in 1894 and his Department was, and has remained, completely autonomous, reporting directly to the Governors.

Governor Norman instituted the new post of Adviser in 1928. The basic administrative structure of the Bank, however, remained unchanged until the recommendations of the Peacock Committee were implemented. Set up by the Court in 1931 to examine the whole question of organisation in the light of the growing complexity and multiplicity of the Bank's activities in both home and foreign affairs, the Committee reported the following year and made a number of far-reaching suggestions. These included the formation of two new Departments: Overseas and Foreign, which took over the work (other than routine banking) of the Central Banking Section of the Cashier's Department; and Establishments, which relieved other Departments, chiefly that of the Secretary, of staff duties including those relating to what had become because of inter-war rebuilding a substantial Works Department. Another and most important result of the Peacock Committee was the institution of Executive Directors, the first of whom was appointed by the Court immediately after it had endorsed the Committee's report.

From this date the principal duties of the Secretary were those of the Head of the Secretariat, looking after the needs of the Governors and the Court and providing Secretaries to most of the Bank's standing and *ad hoc* committees. In 1934 Accounts (from the Accountant's Department), Costing (from the Audit Department) and Economics and Statistics (from the Cashier's Department) were transferred to the Secretary's Department. This required more formal arrangements between the Heads of Departments, who together formed a committee which met under an Executive Director from 1936 to 1939 and then, after a break, from 1941 under the Chief Cashier.

The introduction of Exchange Control in 1939 was a new and large-scale operation. By 1941 its size was such as to justify the creation within the Cashier's Department of a large group of Offices entitled Cashier's Department (Exchange Control). The former Overseas and Foreign Department was incorporated into this group as the Overseas and Foreign Office.

The nationalisation of the Bank in 1946 made no difference to the conduct of its internal affairs. The number of Directors, who since the 1930s had included representatives of industry, was reduced to sixteen (of whom not more than four were full-time Executive Directors) apart from the Governor and Deputy Governor. In 1957 the Overseas and Foreign Office became the Overseas Department; two years later this was merged with the Statistics Office to form a new Central Banking Information Department.

The Printing Works was part of the Cashier's Department until 1925 when it became a separate Department.

The post of Inspector of Offices and Branches was created in 1942 and abolished in 1958; a Supervisor of Expenditure had been appointed in 1948 but his functions were merged with those of the Inspector in 1952.

# 1

## THE BANK AT WAR

Early in 1937 it was recognised within the Bank that war with Germany was almost certainly inevitable. In February of that year the Treasury questioned the Bank about various measures that would be necessary before its outbreak,[1] and much work was done to summarise and evaluate the steps which had been taken in 1914 and the later years of the First World War. From this period onwards the Bank was engaged in continuous preparations for what was referred to as 'Zero': preparations which were so thorough and complete in almost every respect that when war was finally declared on 3 September 1939 all the various activities of the Bank were able to continue with a minimum of interruption.

Air raid precautions, or ARP, had been instituted in Threadneedle Street in the autumn of 1914, but happily the Bank had been spared any direct hit from a bomb during the first war and no civilian member of staff received any injury from bombs while on duty.[2] It was clear, however, that the danger from air raids was likely to be very much greater in any future conflict and, acting on the advice of the Home Office, the Bank began to consider the question of ARP in the spring of 1937.[3] The two floors of enormously substantial vaults were regarded as offering excellent safety to members of staff even during the daylight raids on London which were anticipated, and arrangements were made for people to move underground if necessary. The Bank's Medical Officer, Dr Donald Norris, gave courses in first aid and gas detection and de-contamination, while stretcher parties practised carrying patients down each one of the thirty staircases in the Bank. A series of lectures on air raid precautions, attended by almost every member of staff, was illustrated by grim films of the results of air raids in Barcelona during the Spanish Civil War. A first aid station and several first aid posts, a small but well-equipped operating theatre and a gas decontamination centre were fitted up in the vaults, with advice from one of the resident surgeons at St Bartholomew's Hospital. After the issue of gas masks in September 1938, everybody in the Bank wore them for five minutes each week; air raid rehearsals were held, and the Bank in its turn helped other firms and institutions in the City with their own preparations as the safety campaign in London intensified.

Once the safety of the staff had been considered, attention was turned to protecting the premises. Plans for strengthening the basements of buildings other than Head Office were prepared and submitted for approval to the relevant local authorities, and later to the Ministry of Home Security (thus becoming eligible for grants under the provisions of the Civil Defence Act 1939). Head Office building, one of the strongest in London, needed no such protection, but quantities of sandbags were procured to shelter some of the most vulnerable of its 85,000 square feet of window glass. In order that work could continue, even if the parts of the building above ground should become unusable, a subsidiary telephone exchange was installed in the Sub-Vault. Accommodation for a much increased Foreign Exchange Section was earmarked underground, extra ventilating plant installed and a large quantity of battery lamps were bought in case the lighting system broke down.[4]

Towards the end of 1938 it was decided that, in order to safeguard the production of bank notes, provision must be made for them to be printed well away from London. The notes, together with dividend warrants for all the stock accounts held by the Bank and a great deal of other material for external and internal use, had been produced for over twenty years at the Bank's own printing works at St Luke's in Old Street. If printing were to be carried out elsewhere, one obvious solution was to site it in the neighbourhood of the Hampshire paper mills of Portals Ltd, who had supplied bank note paper since 1724. At the end of 1938 some land adjoining one of Portals' factories at Overton was leased by the paper firm to the Bank who built a factory on it, known as Shadow Factory A, providing 21,000 square feet. This was conveniently close to the source of supply of paper, and the factory was also able to purchase the necessary steam, electricity and water from its neighbour. Shortly after its completion, Shadow Factory B was built on the same site to house the Dividend Preparation Office* so that this could occupy, as it had done since 1928, premises side by side with the Printing Works. Both buildings were completed and equipped by June 1939.[5] Meanwhile, further plans for evacuation were being formulated. During 1939, the Bank leased

---

* Dividend Preparation Office – responsible for the preparation and despatch of dividend warrants. See chapter 2, p. 49.

Templeton House in Roehampton from the Incorporated Froebel Education Institute for use as 'liaison Headquarters for representative bodies in the event of evacuation '.[6] The Committee of London Clearing Bankers decided early in the same year to move the Central Clearing House, on the outbreak of war, to Trentham Park in Staffordshire. This was a large house, part of which had been pulled down, formerly belonging to the Duke of Sutherland and standing in grounds which had been turned into an amusement park containing a dance hall. It was this hall which the Bankers rented, and the section of the Bill Office* which dealt with the Bank's own clearing was scheduled to go there too. In order for the staff of the Dividend Accounts Office and part of the Dividend Pay Office† to be near to the Clearing House, and thus avoid constant transport of quantities of dividend warrants, the Bank decided to look for local premises for them, ultimately renting Barlaston Hall, four and a half miles from Stoke-on-Trent, from Josiah Wedgwood‡ and Sons Ltd, who had acquired it in 1937 as a site for a new factory.[7]

But by far the most complex evacuation plans made by the Bank during 1939, and those which were to affect the largest numbers of its staff, were the arrangements concerning the Accountant's Department. This Department, which was responsible for the management of all the Bank's registers of holdings of government and other stocks, had been moved out of Threadneedle Street to offices in Finsbury Circus at the beginning of 1923 during the rebuilding of Head Office, into which it was not due to return until some time in 1940. Once the decision had been made, in conjunction with the Treasury, that Inscribed Stock should be transferable by Deed,§[8] it was possible to contemplate moving the bulk of the work out of London. A first idea was to use some of the Sports Club and Record Office premises at Roehampton for this purpose, and plans were drawn up for a considerable expansion of the Record Office building.[9] By the spring of 1939, however, it seemed likely that war might well break out before the extensions could be completed; the insecurity of the site was another decisive factor. It was then suggested that premises near Portals and the new Shadow Factories might be more suitable, and, as such large numbers of Bank staff would be involved, it was further decided that some sections of the Establishment Depart-

---

* Bill Office – responsible for collection of bills, cheques, etc. See chapter 7, p. 239.
† Dividend Accounts Office – acted as check on payments made by Dividend Pay Office, which paid coupons, dividend warrants, etc.
‡ Wedgwood, Hon. Josiah, 1899–1968. Chairman, 1947–67, and Managing Director, 1930–61, Wedgwood & Sons Ltd. Director, Bank of England, 1942–6.
§ See chapter 2, p. 55.

ment* – those dealing with salaries and pensions, income tax, the Bank Provident Society and the Branches – should also be evacuated.

The first suggestion for a Hampshire location, made in February 1939, was that the Bank should lease East Stratton Park, which was situated between Basingstoke and Winchester. However nothing came of this idea, and the house was shortly afterwards taken over by Barings. The Czechoslovakian crisis of the following month led to more urgent consideration of the whole question, and several other properties in the same district were inspected. The one that seemed most suitable was the house known as The Mansion† at Hurstbourne Priors, about four miles from Overton, which belonged to the Earl of Portsmouth and was currently occupied by Patrick (later Sir Patrick) Donner, Conservative Member of Parliament for the Basingstoke division of Hampshire since 1935. Situated just outside the village of Whitchurch, The Mansion was a large and handsome late Victorian building of red brick with gables and mullioned windows, set in extensive grounds which Charles Kingsley had described as the finest park in England.

By April 1939 the Bank had entered into negotiations with Donner to take a five year option on The Mansion for a small retaining fee, under the terms of which he agreed to vacate the house and all its outbuildings at forty-eight hours notice on the outbreak of war.[10] It was estimated that a minimum staff of 490 men and 138 women would be needed to cope with the day-to-day work of the Accountant's Department if it had to be evacuated: large as it was, The Mansion would not be able to accommodate this number, and a lease was shortly afterwards taken from the Portsmouth Estates on a piece of land adjoining the park known as Winsome Meadow. On this it was proposed to put up some wooden buildings to be used as offices and living quarters. By May 1939 work had started in the Meadow on what became known as Hurstbourne Camp: the plans were prepared by the Clerk of Works in the Bank and provided for a large office block of 50,000 square feet, sixteen sleeping huts, catering and domestic offices and a canteen. The work was supervised by a member of the Accountant's Department, acting on behalf of the Establishment Department; furniture and equipment were ordered and stacked in a store at Hurstbourne station, while a quantity of tinned food was purchased and kept in a disused laundry building at The Mansion, which provided the Bank's headquarters and office during the period of preparation.[11]

---

* Establishment Department – responsible for staff and premises. See chapter 10.
† The Mansion, built in 1894 and pulled down in 1965, stood on the site of an earlier house designed by James Wyatt, which had burnt down in 1870.

Towards the end of August it became clear that war was imminent. On Friday, 25 August the two Offices due to go to Barlaston Hall, together with the Section of the Bill Office destined for Trentham, began their final packing of equipment and papers at 4 p.m. The following day it was all loaded on to two lorries which arrived in Staffordshire in the evening, as did an advance guard consisting of the Principal of the Bill Office, F.D.V. Goodall, who had driven up with three senior colleagues. Arranging billets for the rest of his section proved a difficult and exhausting task for the Principal and two senior women clerks, but finally all was arranged, the lorries were unpacked on the Sunday and work began in both Trentham and Barlaston on Monday, 28 August: the Barlaston staff were almost all lodged in the North Stafford Hotel, where they remained for the rest of their stay.[12]

On 29 August the Chief Accountant,\* the Deputy Chief of Establishments and the Superintendent of Women Clerks† travelled down to Whitchurch. Most of the male staff from the Printing Works and forty women were to arrive the following day, with the rest of the staff – some 275 women – due four days later. Much remained to be done at both Hampshire locations: The Mansion was still occupied by Patrick Donner and his family, the canteen had not yet been built, the bath huts had water laid on but no fixtures, and the only lavatories were Elsan latrines. The sleeping huts were totally unfurnished, and the private billets which Lady Portal, the Chief Billeting Officer for the district, had undertaken to find in the Overton area for the staff of St Luke's and of the Dividend Preparation Office had in many cases proved unsuitable.

Those private billets which could be used were reserved for the men, and most of the first contingent of women were found temporary quarters in some of the larger houses in the neighbourhood. A desperate search for additional accommodation resulted in the discovery of Foxdown House near Overton Station. It was unoccupied and in the care of executors, one of whom was found in Basingstoke and was persuaded to let the house to the Bank for £1 per day. With the help of staff from the Hurstbourne estate it was cleared and the standard issue of camp-bed, three blankets and a pillow per person was installed. Donner was prevailed upon to waive his right of forty-eight hours notice, and moved out of Hurstbourne Mansion in the afternoon of Saturday, 2 September; exactly twenty-four hours later the 275 women of the Dividend

---

\* E.M. Stapley. At this date there were two joint Chief Accountants, Stapley having been appointed in May 1939 in tandem with A.M. Walker who had been Head of the Department since January 1921.

† L.A. Gash and Miss Stetton.

Preparation Office arrived, having been seen off at Waterloo by Governor Norman.* They moved into The Mansion for the time being, although the bathroom and lavatory accommodation was of the most makeshift variety.

When war was declared on 3 September the evacuation of the Accountant's Department had already begun, with staff arriving in batches over the next two weeks. Hurstbourne Camp was still in an embryonic state, but there was enough rough and ready accommodation in the huts for some hundreds of men; a marquee was hastily erected and equipped with trestle tables and duckboards to serve as a canteen. One of the huts was fitted out with a few borrowed cooking utensils, and under these very difficult and unsatisfactory conditions the staff of the Bank Club struggled for a few weeks to carry out the catering. This was subsequently taken over and continued for the rest of the war by J. Lyons and Company.

An immediate preoccupation, in the first few days of war, was to find suitable accommodation for the Dividend Preparation Office staff so that they could vacate The Mansion in favour of the women from the rest of the Accountant's Department. Luckily the Bank managed to obtain immediate possession of two good-sized houses in Whitchurch, The Yews, which included a small cottage, and The Lawn immediately opposite. This lovely house, whose gardens run down to the River Test, subsequently became the home of Lord Denning; but at this date the owner had just died leaving it in a deplorable condition of dirt and disrepair. The water supply consisted of a pump in the scullery, there was no electric light and no usable sanitary arrangements. It was speedily cleaned and within two or three days the two houses were accommodating over a hundred women, who had their meals in relays at the White Hart Hotel in the village. In the next few weeks other billets were found reasonably near, and the women working at Hurstbourne Camp could be housed in The Mansion, although still under very cramped conditions (at one time there were 309 women living there sharing seven bathrooms, and a rota was drawn up giving time off during the day for a weekly bath).

Senior staff fared rather better. The Principals lived for a time in the stable block of Laverstoke House, the residence of Lord Portal, and the Chief Accountant in Laundry Cottage at Hurstbourne.[13] There was plenty of work to do, and it began at 8.15 in the morning, usually continuing until dusk, in the large work hut. The hours of overtime clocked up were formidable, and, overtime payments having been

* Norman, 1st Baron (1944) of St Clere, Montagu Collet Norman, PC, DSO, 1871–1950. Director, Bank of England, 1907–18; Deputy Governor 1918–20; Governor, 1920–44

Plate 1.1  A sleeping hut at Hurstbourne Camp

suspended at the outbreak of war by Order of Court, were rewarded by
gratuities paid at 'suitable intervals' (and not always very gratefully
received, as they were often considerably lower than the corresponding
overtime payment would have been at the current rate). They were,
however, tax-free, and altogether in October 1939 amounted to £9,600,
mostly due on account of the work connected with evacuation. Overtime
payments proper were resumed during the same month.[14]

Gradually this almost wholly urban staff settled to an unfamiliar rural
life, lived communally and in many cases far away from family and
friends, although some of the married men did manage to find suitable
housing locally and were reunited with wives and children. The vexed
questions of billeting allowances and leave were finally settled as equitably
as possible: after various different arrangements annual, or 'Governor's'
leave was fixed at twelve days a year for all staff regardless of rank,[15] with
Principals urged to give extra days or long week-ends where feasible.
Most of the staff in Hampshire were able to travel to London on alternate
week-ends, normally being allowed to have Monday morning free for the
return to work. The fine weather of the first autumn of the war helped to
alleviate some of the more obvious discomforts, most of which were fairly
swiftly eradicated. Divans replaced the camp-beds, the sanitary arrange-

ments were greatly improved, and the canteen building was finished and included a space for recreation. One of the principal tribulations of the living quarters was the fact that there was no hanging or storage space whatsoever for clothes and possessions, so that an early priority was the provision of a small chest and hanging cupboard for each person.

This large influx of strangers to the locality meant that special provision had to be made for medical services, as the single local practitioner was quite unable to manage on his own. A full-time doctor was engaged, a dentist established in Whitchurch so that the necessity to travel to Basingstoke or Andover for treatment was avoided, and a lease taken on yet another local private house – Bere Hill House, Whitchurch – for use as a hospital. The joint Chief Accountants, Walker and Stapley, both by now in residence, decided that they were happy in Laundry Cottage and would stay there: the house taken for them before the outbreak of war, The Roos, was then allotted to the new doctor and the dentist. (By the end of the war the Bank owned or rented a total of forty properties in and around Overton and Whitchurch.)[16] The health of staff at the locations did remain remarkably good during the war years, apart from a brief epidemic of German measles and a prevalent sore throat, known as 'Whitchurch throat' and ascribed to the dry, chalky soil.

While this period of frenzied activity was taking place in Hampshire, the staff in London were themselves undergoing the inevitable traumas of the change from peace to war conditions. Many were called up into the Services, but because of the heavy recruiting policy followed by the Bank in the immediate aftermath of the First World War (subsequently much criticised as causing the so-called 'Hump' of men whose promotion prospects were severely limited)*[17] the proportion of those eligible for call-up was less than might have been expected. The top-heavy age profile meant that, of a pre-war total of 1,849 male clerks, nearly 900 were aged forty-one or older. By mid October, about 370 of the younger men had gone into the Services and a further ninety were under twenty-five years old and thus unlikely to remain at work for long, so that nearly a quarter of the male staff would be gone.[18] The banking industry qualified as a 'reserved occupation', i.e. one of vital national importance and thus allowed to retain the services of its employees, only as far as men of thirty and over were concerned. The Bank tried, unsuccessfully, to persuade the Ministry of Labour to reduce this age limit of twenty-five. But its demand for staff rose rapidly on the outbreak of war, particularly in the field of exchange control, and it was clear that action would have to be taken to fill the gaps, in most cases by stepping up the employment of

* See chapter 10.

women, but also by the recall of pensioners and an increasing reliance on part-time staff.

An early measure was the decision of the Court to suspend the rule requiring women to leave the Bank's employment on marriage (a fairly common practice in offices at that date).[19] Except in special circumstances, recruitment to the male staff was in a temporary capacity only, and those serving the requisite three years probation were told that they could not be appointed to the permanent (pensionable) staff until the end of the war. Increasing numbers of women, both temporary and permanent, full-time and part-time, were employed throughout the Bank and its Branches, frequently doing work that few – or few at least of their male colleagues – would have deemed possible for them in pre-war days. By February 1940 they outnumbered men for the first time in the Bank's history, and have continued to do so ever since.[20] The men and women who joined the Forces (some of them in the face of considerable resistance on the part of their superiors) were treated generously by the Bank. After an initial period of nearly a year during which they were paid full salary or wages, the Bank decreed that they should receive the difference, if any, between their Bank pay and service pay. Those who joined up after this first year were granted full pay for the first three months of their service.[21]

The first, relatively uneventful months of the war – the so-called 'Phoney war' – were occupied within Head Office in refining the programme of security which had been initiated during peacetime. The regular troops from the Brigade of Guards who formed the Picquet which carried out a nightly watch* were replaced, from the evening of 26 August 1939, by a detachment of the National Defence Company of the Honourable Artillery Company. Soon after the outbreak of war it was decided that a guard was necessary during the hours of daylight as well, and the numbers were increased to two officers and sixty other ranks, although this was subsequently decreased again. In July 1942 guard duties were taken over by the Corps of Military Police, and this arrangement continued until the evening of 6 September 1945, when once again a detachment of the Brigade of Guards marched through London from Wellington Barracks to take up their nightly watch duties.[22] Fire-fighting was another major preoccupation. Care was taken to ensure that there was always in the building an adequate number of people trained in this role: as they became more proficient, they formed a body known as the Bank Auxiliary Fire Brigade with clerks acting as officers and some of the non-clerical staff of messengers and porters as the rank

* First instituted as a result of an attack on the Bank during the Gordon riots in 1780.

Plate 1.2   Bank Auxiliary Fire Service and ARP teams practising on the roof, Threadneedle Street, 1940

and file. They were all volunteers, and during 1940 it was agreed that they should receive a payment, but later in the war fire duty became a statutory duty and payments had to cease.

The fall of France in June 1940 prompted the Bank, like most other major institutions in London, to review its arrangements for a total evacuation of the city. By this date the idea of using Templeton House had been abandoned, and it was decided that essential work – primarily government and bankers' accounts – could if necessary be transferred to what was dubbed 'Location O', attached to Birmingham Branch. 'O' concealed the identity of the Overbury estate in Worcestershire, which included a large Georgian house set in what a local guide book, without mentioning the identity of the owners, describes rather mysteriously as 'a banker's garden'. It was indeed a banker's garden, because the estate belonged to the family of Edward Holland-Martin.* An option was taken on Overbury Court, and various smaller houses and buildings on the estate were leased and fitted out as office and sleeping quarters for the 130 men and forty women considered necessary by the Chief Cashier to carry on essential banking services; but in the event only about thirty

* Holland-Martin, Edward, 1900–81. Director, Bank of England, 1933–48.

Probationary Typists and one senior man from Establishments used the location. The typists lived there for three months before going to Threadneedle Street: they took dictation in Lady Holland-Martin's bedroom, where she presided wearing a mauve nightcap, and practised typing in the village hall. The senior man had custody of certain confidential banking records for which a strong-room was constructed in the Court, but he only remained there for a year, after which the duty devolved on the senior typist. This arrangement lasted until December 1942 when the women moved back to London.[23]

At the same time as the Bank was engaged in making arrangements for the use of Overbury, preparations for further evacuation were also under way. The Bill Office was destined to go to Trentham, while 'Location K', Perrystone Court at Ross-on-Wye in Herefordshire, was to be taken over from its owner for the use of the Bank Note Office,* although neither of these plans had to be put into execution.

Once the German bombing raids began in earnest, in September 1940, the wisdom of the Bank's detailed safety precautions in the London premises was swiftly confirmed. In the middle of that month Waterloo Station was hit by a bomb and put out of action for some days, which meant that for large numbers of staff travel became almost impossible. In order to ensure that enough people were present in the Bank each day to carry on with the work, emergency rotas were organised in as many Offices as possible whereby staff slept in the Bank for three nights and then went home for two days. In other Offices, a skeleton staff stayed in the Bank on one night each per week so that work could begin promptly in the morning, whatever the disruptions to the travelling arrangements of the others. By now almost all the work in Threadneedle Street was being done underground, and many people slept next to their desks on camp-beds in the vaults. Bunk beds were also put up in some of the security vaults and even in the vault corridors, where sleep was disturbed by the noise of the tube trains; a room was fitted out for the use of the Court (the colours of the Bank Volunteers during the Napoleonic Wars were hung on its walls),[24] the Directors had their own quarters and Governor Norman now began his practice, which continued for nearly three years, of spending two or three nights each week sleeping in the Bank, where his juniors occasionally caught a glimpse of his spare figure in a dressing-gown emblazoned with a dragon.[25] The atmosphere of the time was evoked many years later by one who remembered all too clearly 'those airless vaults it was part of our fate to endure, on one of those nights

---

* The Bank Note Office kept registers of higher denomination bank notes. See chapter 4, p. 136.

which were a mixture of extended hours of work, interrupted by meals, with an occasional spice of danger but mostly made up of hours and hours of empty boredom'.[26]

These meals, eaten in an emergency underground canteen, were spiced with rather more danger than anybody realised at the time; it was not until the raids had abated considerably that somebody patrolling the vaults during the course of his nightly watch (carried out by a senior official), worked out that the canteen – formerly the theatre and later turned into the Reference Library – was in fact situated immediately below the Garden Court. Mercifully this was spared a direct hit, but other parts of the Bank were not so fortunate. The first damage was done by two bombs, believed to be about 500 pounds each, on the night of 9 September 1940: one fell in Threadneedle Street, the other on the roof north of the Garden Court. The first caused a huge crater nearly 40 feet in diameter and 12 feet deep, which severely damaged water, gas and other services, as well as hurling a piece of concrete weighing about a third of a ton through a skylight into the Bank and chunks of road surface on to the highest point of the roof. The balustrade facing the street was shattered for a length of fifty feet. The other bomb hit a beam which supported the roof over the telephone room on the seventh floor; it knocked a large hole in the floor, broke quantities of glass throughout the Bank and bent a number of bronze window sashes, as well as destroying a section of the roof and putting the Directors' kitchen out of commission. Luckily there were no casualties, and the emergency telephone installation was brought into service.[27] 'Much disorganised' noted Governor Norman in his diary the following day;[28] a week later he wrote to John Martin*, a Director and close friend:

> I am not going to give you a history of recent German plane visits nor of our so-called barrage – which is just about as deafening as bombs – nor about the prospect of immediate invasion. A good deal of this you can read in the newspapers and what you can't read there I don't know, except that a week ago a bomb fell in Threadneedle Street a few yards from our outside wall ... Another bomb fell on our roof, happily at a very strong point close to the corner of Lothbury and Tokenhouse Yard, which smashed the telephone exchange, kitchens and a bit of the two top storeys on that side. And a shell which was fired at Ealing – or some such friendly spot – but never exploded, came through the roof near the corner of Princes Street and Lothbury and smashed the ceiling and the water pipes and made a mess but did no other harm. These accidents and the continuous raid

---

\* Martin, John, 1884–1949. President, Transvaal Chamber of Mines; Chairman, Argus South African Newspapers; Director, Bank of England, 1936–46.

warnings are gradually converting us all into moles, for most of us live a greater part of the day underground and many sleep there too. I am longing for the time when we shall have a working telephone system and can get a decent meal and shall have some glass in the 80 % of windows which were broken...[29]

A month later Norman wrote to Martin again:

You may not realise it, but for us one of the great troubles now is travel. The stations in London are for ever being bombed and closed for some days or else the tracks and perhaps bridges are busted – or again the bus roads in and out of London become unusable. Instead of an hour morning and evening from door to door many of our folk take 2 or 3 hours and have to walk a good step: troublesome and hard on individuals and getting worse with the shorter days and blackout.

Our higher floors are hardly used and most work is done below ground where mercifully there are, as you remember, several floors of huge desolate vaults. And soon perhaps as many as 1,000 men and women will be working 2 or 3 days running and sleeping here the one or two nights and then going off and staying at home for a couple of days. In this way travel should be ever so much reduced and along with it, weariness and wet skins and all the ills and miseries of winter...[30]

As the bombing campaign intensified further ARP works were instituted at Head Office. Sky-lights were protected with sand bags after the incursion of concrete from the first bomb, and air raid shelters in the basements were completed. 'Bomb-bursting platforms' of reinforced concrete were put up over all the courtyards except Garden Court, and over lift shafts and light wells, and anti-blast walls were erected in front of some of the ground floor windows.[31] One of these belonged to the Office of a Deputy Chief Cashier, H. B. C. Yeomans, who, declining to spend his days facing a blank wall, commissioned one of the Bank's many talented artists to paint on it a *trompe l'oeil* picture of the Garden Court in summer. This was done very successfully by Hilton Clarke, a future Principal of the Discount Office.[32]

The incendiary bombs dropped by the Germans at the end of 1940 and the beginning of the following year caused only slight damage to the Bank, the worst occasion being on 10 May 1941 when a total of eighteen fell on the building and were speedily dealt with by the Auxiliary Fire Brigade.* The Bank's Fire Brigade, Light Rescue Service and Mobile First Aid Post all rendered invaluable service over quite a large area of the

---

* The Chief of this organisation wore a splendid uniform, the sight of which caused a woman he had helped to rescue from a burning building in the City to wonder audibly 'if a sixpence tip would be enough?'.[33]

City, a service which was greatly increased in value by the presence of the Bank Medical Officer who accompanied them to many 'incidents'. The Mobile First Aid Post was formed as a result of experience gained on the night when Bank underground station was hit and was considered to be one of the most efficient in London.[34]

St Luke's Printing Works in Old Street was hit by incendiary bombs almost every night during the Battle of Britain, but here again the resulting fires were all successfully dealt with by the staff fire-fighting force and production was never interrupted for more than a few days at a time. The worst damage was caused on the same night as Head Office suffered its principal attack, 9 September, when a high explosive bomb hit the boiler house, wrecking it and shattering many glass roofs in the building. The incendiary bombs were at their height the following April and May, when St Luke's on some nights received as many as twenty-seven hits: casualties were light, and the fabric of the building remained remarkably unscathed except for the loss of a charming eighteenth-century wooden clock tower which had once adorned the chapel of the hospital from which the Printing Works had been converted.[35] Both St Luke's and Head Office operated highly effective 'spotter' systems under which staff observers were on duty during all daylight hours while people were at work. Relatively pleasant during the summer months, this became a most disagreeable operation in winter; in Threadneedle Street it was carried out at first on the third floor balconies, but during the autumn of 1942 a new observation post was built and centrally heated. This was a great improvement, and, by the end of the year, the system was operating so well that very few of the staff had to go below ground on the sounding of the public sirens but waited until the observers could actually see the approach of enemy aircraft. On days when these failed to materialise it was difficult, as one of the observers noted at the time, 'to keep up interest and enthusiasm when the only visible activities, apart from the traffic and the pigeons, are the movements of the balloon barrage and the arrival on neighbouring roofs of sundry resident housekeepers to hang out their week's washing'.[36]

Sport at the Bank's Club in Roehampton had naturally been curtailed by the call-up of most of its active male members and the departure of the Accountant's Department. In the autumn of 1940 the Club suffered two direct hits; the first, on 17 October, caused only minor damage, but the second, on 29 November, almost completely destroyed the men's pavilion and did some damage to the women's.* From that date regular games became impossible, but the Bank kept up the playing fields as well

* See chapter 10, p. 363.

Plate 1.3    Bomb crater at Bank underground station, January 1941

as it could so that members of the Forces could use them. Various local schools and youth organisations also played cricket and football in the grounds, but during 1941 the Club began to hand over sections of the playing fields to Barnes Council for allotments. The Costing Section of the Secretary's Department was moved to the Record Office for a time, and the Local Defence Volunteers, or Home Guard, used part of the building as its headquarters. The undamaged portion of the women's pavilion was used as a canteen throughout the war to provide meals for staff working at the Record Office, where shelters were constructed in both wings – one used by the Bank, and the other handed over to Wandsworth Borough Council for public use.[37]

Windows and doors were blown out in the Law Courts Branch in the Strand, but the majority of the Bank's seven country Branches were relatively fortunate as far as bomb damage was concerned. Newcastle escaped entirely, and Leeds suffered only a few broken windows. Plymouth Branch remained untouched during some of the worst raids in March 1941, and was the only bank open for business on 21 March when half the city was ablaze. That night it suffered a direct hit, and although the banking premises were only slightly damaged the house of the Agent (the Manager) collapsed and both the Acting Relief Agent and a porter were buried in rubble and seriously injured. Bristol Branch escaped the effects of the worst of the severe raids which flattened parts of the city between November 1940 and April 1941, largely because of the vigilance and prompt action of all the staff in putting out fires; many near neighbours of the Branch, including the Guildhall, Corn Exchange, Council House and Post Office, were wholly or partially destroyed. Only very slight damage was done to Manchester Branch, despite several heavy raids in 1941 and 1942. Birmingham lost almost all its windows and part of its roof when a land mine exploded on the roof of a nearby building on 19 November 1940, and some further minor structural damage was done in July 1942, but again it was extremely lucky compared with many of its neighbours and at one time opened part of the premises to another bank whose building had been destroyed. The newest Branch of all, Southampton, which had only been opened in April 1940, survived a series of heavy raids which demolished most of the buildings in its immediate area, suffering nothing more than blast damage. At one period in September 1940 it was without water, electricity and telephones for some weeks: water was brought from Romsey and some food was provided by Whitchurch.

Most seriously affected of all the Branches was Liverpool. The Branch building was badly damaged by fire on the night of 3/4 May 1941, during which the Bank fire fighters helped the local fire brigade, and the fire was thought to be under control by the morning of 5 May. It broke out again, however, a couple of days later, doing much further damage during which the roof collapsed. Happily the main walls stood firm and the Branch did manage to continue to function under very trying conditions which included being without gas and electricity for some time.[38]

In common with people on the 'Home Front' all over Britain, Bank staff naturally did what they could to further the war effort by subscribing to savings schemes and such activities as knitting garments for those in the Forces. When news was received in the spring of 1940 that six members of staff had been captured as prisoners of war, a fund was immediately established to send them extra comforts such as tobacco and cigarettes. At that particular time transport conditions were too chaotic to allow any goods to be posted, but by the end of the year parcels costing £1.13s. 6d. each and containing 1,000 cigarettes and one pound of tobacco were sent to every prisoner once a month.*[39]

A major effort was the Bank Spitfire Fund, which was started at the suggestion of the Deputy Secretary, W.H. Nevill, in July 1940. A

---

* Letters were also sent to the POWs using an ingenious code, e.g. 'Anne's pub' – The Rising Sun near the Bank, where Anne was the barmaid – denoted Japan.

Spitfire fighter aircraft cost £5,000: a committee was formed with the object of raising this sum and the total was passed by February 1941. A letter was sent to Lord Beaverbrook* together with the cheque requesting that the aircraft should be christened 'The Old Lady'. This was duly done, and a reply from Beaverbrook to the Fund's treasurer assured the contributors in Churchillian tones that the plane will 'win honour and glory for its donors in defence of our home, our civilisation and all that we hold dear'. Although doubtless useful to swell the overall number of aircraft, 'The Old Lady' unfortunately did not have a very distinguished service life after its initial use at 266 Squadron at Wittering, from where it took part in strikes on the Dutch coast. The aircraft was transferred to 277 Squadron, on Air Sea Rescue duties, where it remained until March 1944. It then moved to an Operational Training Unit, finally meeting its end in April in a collision with another aircraft.[40]

One practical venture took the form of munitions work in the vaults. During 1942 there was a particularly acute shortage of rubber and copper, urgently needed for manufacture of armaments, and an appeal by the Director of Salvage for these materials was met within the Bank by an undertaking to process cable from crashed or obsolete aircraft. Work started in September 1942: it was tough and laborious, involving stripping rubber coated cables to free the fine copper wire inside. People worked in lunch breaks and slack moments, entertained by the wireless and helped – with permission from the Governors – by the Works Department. They were the first to devise a really satisfactory method of carrying out the work, and altogether a hundred miles of cable, weighing three tons, were dealt with in this way, enough to wire an entire squadron of Spitfires and provide a set of tyres for a bomber.[41]

In Hampshire, housing problems remained acute after three months of war. A few women from the Dividend Preparation Office were still living at Hurstbourne, while the rest were scattered around the countryside and had to be taken by bus each day to Overton: at one time there were thirteen buses in regular use by the Bank. About half a mile away from Overton a camp was in course of construction, and on enquiry it was found to belong to the National Camps Corporation and destined for use by about 300 young boys from poor families as a summer holiday camp. Six dormitories each containing fifty-eight beds in double tiers had

* Beaverbrook, 1st Baron of Beaverbrook, New Brunswick, and Cherkley, Surrey, William Maxwell Aitken, 1879–1964. When Beaverbrook wrote to the Bank he was Minister for Aircraft Production; ironically, at exactly this date Norman was involved with Lord Trenchard in efforts to remove him from that position, which he left for the Ministry of Supply in June 1941. See *Montagu Norman*, by A. Boyle, pp. 318–19.

Plate 1.4   Head Office staff on munition work – an impression by J. Neck.
*Old Lady of Threadneedle Street*, March 1943

already been built, and the camp seemed to provide a possible home for
about 150 women. After some difficulties with the owners, who were
reluctant to let it, a successful appeal was made to the Treasury and a
temporary lease was granted, starting in November 1939, of what became
known as Overton Chalets. Other accommodation rented at this time
included Major-General Guy Dawnay's house at Longparish, which was
used by senior male members of staff, and, in February 1940, Sir

Alexander Gibb's house, Tangier Park. (This proved too far away from the offices to be very convenient, and was later used as an isolation hospital.) A further house, The Gables in Whitchurch, involved the Bank in some unfavourable publicity. It had originally been a Poor Law Institution and at this date was occupied by seventy aged and mentally handicapped women; by arrangement with the Ministry of Health, the Bank undertook to restore and make habitable a disused workhouse at Stockbridge, a few miles away, and here the old women were transferred while women from the Bank were moved into The Gables. The Stockbridge Institution was made as comfortable as possible but still compared poorly with the former quarters, which aroused a good deal of adverse comment locally.

There remained the problems of overcrowded conditions, especially for the women clerks, at Hurstbourne. All nearby possibilities had been exhausted, even though Bank staff were usually seen as a considerably better option than the alternative of having to take in soldiers or evacuee children from London. A search was instituted further afield and resulted in the discovery that the George Hotel in Winchester was empty, having been bought by the Ministry of Transport for demolition under a road widening scheme, now in abeyance. The Bank arranged to rent it from the Ministry for the duration of the war, but before it could be used it needed much cleaning and restoration work. This was finished by May 1940, and, as at that time enough other accommodation had been found for the women working at Hurstbourne, it was used for a few months as a holiday hotel for the families of staff. (Later another hotel, the Elderfield at Otterbourne four miles outside Winchester, was used for the same purpose.) More space had also been found in Winchester in various houses and hotels, and a special train service was run from the city to Whitchurch station, with buses from there to Hurstbourne Camp.

Meanwhile the Bank was under strong pressure to vacate Overton Chalets, a question even being asked in the House of Commons on the subject. As Foxdown at Overton stood in six and a half acres of grounds, the Bank decided to buy the whole property, plus a further two acres of adjoining land, and build another camp which was originally intended for the printing staff but eventually made over to women staff of the Dividend Preparation Office. The contractors who had been putting up the chalets undertook this work, and built a camp consisting of eleven sleeping huts, a canteen, recreation room, sick bay and other buildings, twenty in all, constructed out of cedar wood. By March 1940 all the Dividend Preparation women were at last housed together near their place of work. The Printing Works staff, a number of whom were still in

private billets of varying degrees of unsuitability, were finally accommodated properly during 1940, many of them in hostels in Basingstoke.

By the end of the first year of the war the housing problems of the
Hampshire locations – whose inhabitants reached a maximum of well
over 2,000 in 1942 – were largely solved. Efforts were now concentrated
on a continuing improvement of the conditions under which the staff
lived, and of the facilities for their recreation. In the first months there
was almost nothing to do and nowhere much to go except to the local
pubs. Sitting rooms and games rooms were an immediate priority in
camps and hostels, and two new office blocks and a cinema were built at
Hurstbourne in early 1940. (The camp here eventually consisted of as
many as fifty buildings covering a good seven acres of ground.) Laundry
Cottage in the village of Whitchurch was altered and extended so that it
provided not only the residence of the Chief Accountants but also an
officials' lunch room and rooms for visiting directors including Governor
Norman who slept here on a visit to both Hampshire locations in August
1941.[42]

The distance of sixty miles from London gave a considerable feeling of
safety and ARP precautions were at first fairly slight and consisted
mainly of the issue of gas masks and concentration on black-out
regulations, the latter proving a constant source of vexation to all
concerned and difficult to enforce over so many different buildings close
together with continual comings and goings between them. Fire was one
of the chief dangers, as the majority of the buildings were constructed of
wood, but luckily one of the clerks at Hurstbourne was an enthusiastic
amateur fireman. Seconded to the Establishment Department he formed
and directed a small brigade, which later in the war was merged with a
section of the National Fire Service and took part in duties beyond the
immediate premises. An unofficial police force was also enrolled, whose
main duties were to enforce the black-out regulations.[43]

When the Home Guard was started in June 1940 it met with great
enthusiasm, and a Bank section of fifty men was formed who manned
three posts in the park. Later a platoon of over 160 men from the
camp was attached to the local organisation, carrying out among
other activities a nightly armed guard watch all round the grounds. Bank
members living outside the camp joined their own local detachments. A
blood transfusion service was formed and many members of staff from all
the locations volunteered for first aid and Red Cross duties, including
some nursing at hospitals in Winchester and Basingstoke.[44] Many hours
of war work were also carried out by staff at factories in Winchester, to
which they went after a full day's work in the office: it was hoped to

Plate 1.5    The Bank of England Home Guard Section on parade outside The Mansion, Hurstbourne Priors

extend the scheme to include factories elsewhere, but opposition from the Amalgamated Engineering Union prevented this.[45]

Many of these activities came under the aegis of the various Sections of Establishments which had been evacuated from Head Office. Considerable difficulties were faced in the early days of the war by the Attendance Section in particular: a number of staff, on what was known as the 'A' list, were told to remain at home and wait until they were summoned and told where to report. Others joined the Forces at irregular intervals and the Attendance Section had to keep track of them in order to notify the Payments Section. At the end of 1939 over half the entire clerical staff of the Bank were at locations other than London; later, when the swelling numbers in Exchange Control meant that those in London were more numerous, the greater part of the Attendance Section returned to Head Office.

The Branches Section was evacuated because it seemed that contact with the Branches would be easier from the country if bombing or other enemy action seriously disrupted communications between London and the provinces, but it returned to London at the end of the blitz in 1941. Payments, dealing with all salaries, wages, pensions and allowances, had its work greatly increased not only by the continual adjustments made necessary by changing rates of service pay, but also by the addition of numbers of temporary staff for Exchange Control and other work.

Three Sections of Establishments came into being entirely for the purpose of location work: Equipment and Transport, Premises and Location Accounts. The first of these was originally known as the Camp Supervisors' Office, and was housed in Laundry Cottage until the whole of Establishments removed to The Lawn in August 1940. It was responsible for the acquisition, distribution and maintenance of all household stores and furniture, looked after the increasing number of cars and other vehicles – which included several rather unreliable ambulances – and kept a check on details of petrol and mileage, duties which became especially complicated after the introduction of petrol rationing. The Section also looked after laundry, for which staff were allowed four shillings a week.

Leases, tenancy agreements and the management of gardens and food rationing were the responsibility of the Premises Section. Food, for obvious reasons, was rather less of a problem in the country than in towns during the war, and the experiences of the staff in Hampshire were no exception to this rule.* Many allotments were cultivated at both locations (as well as small but flourishing gardens round the sleeping huts), and at The Lawn in Whitchurch some livestock including pigs, hens, goats, bees and a pony plus trap were introduced. This venture was so successful that the Bank took over the stock; all labour was voluntary and all the produce was given to the canteens. Poultry keeping was subsequently extended to every hostel, and the combined efforts produced around 75,000 eggs, 350 gallons of goats' milk, 300 pounds of honey and two pigs – two other pigs, under food regulations, had to be given to the Ministry of Food. Soft fruit, such as peaches and strawberries, grown in the Park in quantities insufficient for canteen use, constituted an extra treat which was sold from a stall to an eager queue. The complexities of Emergency Ration Cards, necessary for weekend and other leaves, meant that a Branch Food Office had to be established in the camp for their issue.

The Premises Section was also responsible for a successful venture which represented an entirely new departure for the Bank. The pre-war population of Whitchurch was about 2,600, and this figure was nearly doubled by the influx of Bank staff and some of their families. Apart from a number of pubs, there was little in the way of refreshment: no tea-shop or cafe where friends could meet for a light meal or a snack away from Bank premises, and the need for such a place soon became pressing.

---

* Staff at Threadneedle Street, however, benefited from the generosity of Directors who often provided salmon and duck from their country estates.

The terms of the Bank's Charter prohibited it from trading on its own account, but an ingenious way round the difficulty was provided by the acquisition of The Bay Tree. A picturesque old house in the London Road, Whitchurch, which had been in use as a grocer's shop, came on to the market at the end of 1939 at the price of £700. It appeared ideally suited for adaptation as a tea-shop or restaurant and it happened that two women who had been temporarily acting as housekeepers in one of the Bank's hostels had in fact arrived in Hampshire just before the war with the intention of starting up a tea-shop. They readily agreed to run the business, but were unable to raise the necessary finance themselves. So the Bank bought and renovated the house for a total of £1,200, and leased the premises to the two women for £60 per annum, making an unsecured loan of £600 to cover the cost of furniture, equipment and stock. The cafe was named The Bay Tree after one which grew in the front garden, and opened for business in November 1940. It could serve fifty-two at a time, and proved an immediate success not only with Bank staff but with the public too. Its accounts were submitted to the Establishment Department, who also helped with general advice, but the venture was so rapidly profitable that within a year the tenants were able to repay their loan and Bank supervision could be relaxed. In 1944 the house was sold, but the new owner undertook to continue the business on similar lines.

The payment of local wages and accounts, billeting fees and allowances, travelling allowances (a certain number of return fares to staff's homes were allowable per year) and catering charges for hostels were all carried out by the Location Accounts Section, which maintained close liaison with the Accounts Office in London – visits from the Audit Department were frequent as the book-keeping activities grew in scope and complexity. The Bank used the local branches of Lloyds, keeping a deposit account of £30,000 with them to 'recompense for work done'.[46]

There was little disturbance from enemy aircraft in the Whitchurch area during the war. Two bombs were dropped at Overton on 16 August 1940, apparently quite deliberately aimed at Printing Works staff leaving the factory *en masse* to catch a train: one exploded on Portals' factory and another hit a bungalow nearby, causing several casualties, none of them Bank staff. After this incident staggered hours of work were arranged to avoid having large numbers of people on the exposed roads between the office, camp and station. Local opinion, which with regard to the huge body of strangers plumped down in their midst was in any case, and quite naturally, mixed, felt that blackout failure had contributed to these bombs, and the regulations were accordingly tightened up. Several air raid alarms and bomb explosions within earshot followed, and the Principal of the Dividend Preparation Office himself expressed some disquiet about the adequacy of the Foxdown blackout arrangements on 23 September: his staff, he noted, were 'more important to the Bank than any other section of the community – we have to get the dividends out...but here we are congregated at night in one camp, situated on an exposed position on the side of a hill, an absolute target to hostile aircraft, and our only defence is the "Blackout"'. His feelings the day after this communication, when two unexploded bombs were discovered in ground adjoining Portals' cooling plant, are unrecorded. Throughout the whole war Whitchurch received only one bomb, which exploded harmlessly in a field.[47]

The first few months at the locations were spent, as already noted, almost entirely in working, and it is true to say that the Accountant's, or 'Stock side', was far busier during the war years than the 'Cash side' at Head Office – always excepting Exchange Control which came under the umbrella of the Cashier's Department. Norman, in one of the few references in his wartime correspondence to the day-to-day activities of the staff, contrasted the two in June 1940: 'the Banking Department hardly employed, the Government's [sic] Department continuously overworked'.[48] But the immediate pressure on the Accountant's Department did ease off during 1940 and the staff in Hampshire began to organise and enjoy their leisure hours. Many had bicycles (the Bank bought up a large quantity early in the war and sold them to the staff at cost price) and enjoyed rides in the countryside which surrounded the camps; the extensive grounds of Hurstbourne Mansion, with walled gardens, lily-ponds, and woods of oak, beech, chestnut and lime, provided a multitude of pleasant walks. Swimming was possible in summer at Sawmills, part of Lord Lymington's estate on the River Bourne; a member of staff bought a horse, Kashmir, who was soon joined by Prue, Turk, Little Jane and others, leading to the formation of a good riding school which rapidly recruited 350 members for whom the Bank employed a groom. Golf was another sport which proved very popular – there was a long disused nine-hole course in the park, which was restored and a professional installed. Later in the war much of the course had to be ploughed up and used to grow vegetables, but the game was able to continue on a smaller scale. Tennis courts were built at both Hurstbourne and Foxdown, and at several hostels, and cricket was played on the delightful village ground at Hurstbourne Priors.[49]

Many of the staff helped the local farmers, Mr Gray at Manor Farm and Mr Bomford at Tufton Warren, during the harvest and at other times of year: the former is on record as saying that the labour provided by the Bank was some of the most willing help he ever had. Some of those concerned had, as he noted, never seen a farm before, but they came down after a full day's work and would hoe and 'even pick up stones', so that the occasional mistake, such as hoeing up an entire field of beet in mistake for charlock, was more readily forgiven.[50]

One of the most memorable facets of the social life in Hampshire was that provided by the Bank of England Operatic and Dramatic Society, known familiarly as BEODS. BEODS, temporarily suspended in London, was revived with great vigour at Hurstbourne largely through the enthusiasm and abilities of Frank Coldicott, a clerk in the Accountant's Department. Actor, producer, general organiser, Coldicott was responsible for some excellent shows, some of which went 'on tour' in neighbouring towns and military camps to raise money for war charities. He also wrote topical sketches, including a long-remembered monologue based on names and addresses taken from stockbrokers' covering letters and entitled *Victorian Virtue Assailed and Triumphant*, whose heroine was Miss Angel Court.[51] Foxdown, too, was responsible for a good deal of amusement with such productions as the Chalets Revue and the Foxdown Follies.

Serious music lovers were catered for by the activities of the Musical Society among whose concerts and recitals there figured some eminent performers such as the pianists Eileen Joyce and Louis Kentner. Many of these activities are described in the pages of the Bank's magazine *The Old Lady of Threadneedle Street*, which had been started in 1921 and whose editorial offices were moved down to Hampshire in November 1940 in order to free some much-needed space in Head Office. This proved a happy move as it meant that the wartime editor, Beryl Langford, who had previously been the editor's secretary in London,[52] was on hand to chronicle much location life which might otherwise have gone unrecorded.

One form of entertainment which was enjoyed by almost everybody at some time during the war was the cinema. A Film Society had been organised in the Bank in December 1936, with the object not only of showing films but also of allowing members – who by the outbreak of war numbered nearly 600 – to learn all aspects of cinema production, visit studios and listen to lectures from prominent members of the industry. The interest and enthusiasm of such large numbers of staff had encouraged the Bank to consider installing a full-sized projector in the new lecture theatre in Head Office, but, on the outbreak of war, this plan had had to be shelved.

Within a day or two of arrival at Hurstbourne, permission was sought from the Chief Accountant for a return to London to fetch apparatus for

showing films in the camp, permission which was readily granted. As a
result films were shown almost every night to an enthusiastic audience in
one or other of the huts or in The Mansion, on 16 mm. equipment
belonging to Gilbert Peake who with his brother Richard formed the two
mainstays of the society. During this period, too, Gilbert Peake took
films of life in Hurstbourne Camp, the Bank paying for the cost of the
film.

By the beginning of January 1940 a regular show on a 16 mm. Bell
and Howell sound machine provided by the Bank had begun, and this
gradually developed into an approximation to a real cinema show with a
set programme given one night at Hurstbourne and the next at Overton.
The organisers, nobly stifling their own preference for the more *avant
garde* productions with what they considered to be 'genuine filmic
merit', appreciated that for their increasing audiences the weekly show
provided a blessed escape from the many difficulties of daily life, and
attempted to cater to popular demand, which was mostly for comedies
and gangster films. Some of the best received items of the first year were
the regular slices of camp life provided by Peake's film, accompanied by
a caustic and witty commentary delivered by Coldicott and which on the
first anniversary of the arrival in Hampshire was shown as a full length
feature.

When the new office building was put up at Hurstbourne one of its
wings was given additional height to allow for its use as a cinema. Here
35 mm. equipment was installed and the weekly shows consisted of two
'shorts' – one of the excellent Ministry of Information films on a vast
range of topics from allotment cultivation to the manufacture of tanks,
plus a cartoon – and a full length feature. The cinema could accommodate
480 people, was the subject of a licence from the local county authority
and usually played to an audience of around 300, but was full to
overflowing for such smash hits as *Dangerous Moonlight.* All the
considerable amount of labour involved was voluntary, including
selecting and obtaining the films via a London agency, projection, the
provision of usherettes in uniforms of their own devising, and preparing
and clearing the hall, which in busy periods was in office use until shortly
before the performance. Shows were given to American and Canadian
troops stationed nearby, and towards the end of the war the American
Office of War Information provided some films, of which the Frank
Capra series of war documentaries were an outstanding success.[53]

Films, music, sports and all the other leisure pursuits went some way
to assuaging the loneliness and boredom which formed the obverse side
of the communal camp life where privacy was almost impossible

Plate 1.6   The main office block at Hurstbourne Camp

(something which the older staff members found particularly trying) and rumour, gossip and intrigue flourished in a fertile soil. Romance, and sometimes marriage, naturally did so too, in spite of an unwritten but quite definite discouragement on the part of authority (two married male clerks who transgressed this to the mild extent of taking two of the girls out for an evening found themselves swiftly transferred back to London). Dances, however, were permitted and became extremely popular both in the recreation hall at Hurstbourne and at local army camps to which the girls were taken in buses, with a strict curfew for the time of return laid down according to age. Small wonder that one homesick youngster on arrival at Whitchurch in 1942 found the atmosphere 'a mixture of school, hotel and military camp'[54]: and the humorist Basil Boothroyd, who was married to Phyllis Youngman, a Bank girl who worked in Hampshire during the war, remarked in his autobiography[55] on the 'Boredom, privations, separation from loved ones, feuds, jealousies, unlikely liaisons' established in 'that outcast Bank society'.

Their very distance from Threadneedle Street did, none the less, bring some definite advantages. One was quite simply the improvement that sprang from the fact that, in the camp, almost all the work of the Accountant's Department was carried out under one roof. The different Offices occupied one vast floor area, which meant that the work flowed much faster when it had to go from one another. In Finsbury Circus documents had been carried up and down stairs by a large body of messengers and porters; staff from different Offices rarely met except perhaps at lunch in the basement canteen, and many of them had never set eyes on the Chief Accountants, whereas at Hurstbourne Stapley and Walker were far more visible – even to the point of eating in the marquee that preceded the dining hut in the first chaotic days of the location. This enforced breakdown of some of the rigid pre-war behaviour patterns was particularly noticeable in the general and unavoidable mingling of the sexes, who had been kept apart in the London Offices and the sports and eating clubs to an extent which was remarkable even at that date. Such fierce segregation was no longer possible, and few people seemed to lament its passing. The work got done with some necessary economies (described in chapter 2) but no fall in the high standards of accuracy that have always been the special pride of the Bank, by men and women working side by side as they had rarely done since women had first been employed in the Bank in 1894.

Clothing was another area in which relaxations soon had to take place. The women staff of the Bank had always been subject to regulations, rigorously enforced, as to colour and style of their dress, which prohibited among other things any pattern of 'stripe, sprig or spot' on the white blouses which were allowed with dark blue, grey or black skirts: any infringement of the rules meant that the offender had to spend the day shrouded in a navy blue holland overall. Hats and gloves had always to be worn on arrival and departure. Male staff also dressed with an almost uniform sobriety, but were allowed as a concession to wear tweed jackets and grey flannel trousers (certainly not plus-fours) on Saturday mornings. Clothes rationing and the vagaries of the weather – more noticeable in a hutted camp in the middle of the countryside than in the centre of London – combined to make such traditions impossible to maintain. Women were given permission to wear trousers in the work hut, which was heated by electric stoves but remained obstinately draughty, and could also wear jodhpurs in the morning if they were going riding at lunch-time. Everybody needed thick jerseys, and wellingtons in wet weather which turned the camp-site into an expanse of mud; the male clerks habitually wore sports jackets and flannels to work in and even, during spells of particularly hot weather, shorts.

Few of these freedoms in fact survived the end of the war (although the Draconian rules on women's wear were not re-introduced), but they were appreciated at the time and were no doubt taken into consideration when the staff of the Accountant's Department were asked in 1942 for their views as to whether the Department should be based permanently outside London once the war had ended. Not surprisingly for a body composed almost entirely of Londoners, most people voted for a return to the City as early as possible; but many spoke up for the newly discovered pleasures of country life and 18 per cent said that they would be prepared to go to a new location provided it were 'near a large town'.[56] Vigorous debate on the topic continued for the remainder of the sojourn in Hampshire, but the overwhelming preference was always for a return to the homes and families from which all but a fortunate few were parted.

In London, there were few raids during 1942 and 1943, and the Bank's ARP arrangements could remain virtually unaltered. In June 1944 a new and sinister menace began with the arrival of the pilotless V1 and V2 missiles, which caused lengthy periods of alert during the night and many short ones during the day. The latter made it impossible for the staff to keep moving back and forth to their shelter accommodation, and as it was judged that a flying bomb could do little damage to the Threadneedle Street premises they soon ceased to do so. When the signal was given, only a few particularly exposed places were evacuated, and all other offices had their curtains drawn as a protection against flying glass. At a further signal, indicating that a direct hit was likely, staff had to take cover immediately under desks, in strong rooms or wherever else was possible. This procedure probably saved some lives when a flying bomb fell on one of the Bank's offices at 19, Old Jewry, at 9.15 a.m. on 19 July 1944. Windows and partitions were broken by the blast, lifts were put out of order and there were several fatalities. About twenty people who received minor injuries were treated at the Bank First Aid Post. The building, which was leased by the Bank to the Commissioners for the Reduction of the National Debt, was uninhabitable and temporary accommodation for the National Debt staff was provided in Head Office. The same bomb caused heavy damage to Nos. 1, 2 and 3, Bank Buildings, including the complete destruction of the flat on the top floor of No. 3, occupied by the Head Gate Porter who was badly injured. Some of the tenants of these buildings, including offices of the Board of Trade and the City of London Savings Committee, had to find premises elsewhere, but the staff of the exiled Bank Polski were moved across the street into Head Office.* Nearly three months later another flying bomb fell close to the first one, hitting the offices occupied by the Bank's solicitors, Messrs Freshfields, Leese and Munns in Old Jewry. Luckily this incident did not result in

---

* In gratitude for their accommodation in Head Office, Bank Polski made in 1947 what Governor Catto called 'a sumptuous acknowledgement' in the form of a suite of over 300 pieces of crystal engraved with the Britannia medallion.

any casualties, but there was a good deal of broken window glass on the side of the Bank facing Princes Street. Freshfields were provided with temporary shelter in Head Office.[57]

The last year of the war brought two important events in the Bank's history, one national and one domestic. In January 1944 Governor Norman was injured in a fall on a foggy evening at his brother's home in Hertfordshire: he only made a partial recovery from the subsequent serious illness, and never returned to the Bank. He had been Governor for very nearly twenty-four years and before his illness had been actively concerned in the discussions about who was to succeed him, Lord Catto* emerging as the eventual choice.[58] Catto, who had been a Director of the Bank for a brief period in 1940 – he had to resign from Court on appointment to the post of Financial Adviser to the Treasury – succeeded Norman as Governor in April 1944, and was thus at the helm during the celebrations, necessarily muted because of the war, of the second of the year's major events. This was the 250th anniversary of the granting of the Bank's Charter in July 1694, and the 100th anniversary of the Bank Charter Act of 1844.†

With customary thoroughness the Court had initiated preparations for this occasion well in advance by commissioning in 1938 the historian John (later Sir John) Clapham‡ to write the first major history of the Bank from its foundation up to 1914. An earlier work, *The Bank of England from Within*, had been published in 1931 by a member of its own staff, William Marston Acres, who avowedly set out to 'write a book wherein financial matters were subordinated to the main purpose of bringing into prominence the human element in the Bank's history', a purpose which he delightfully and effectively fulfilled. Clapham, who had been professor of Economic History at Cambridge until his retirement in 1938, was concerned less with the human element than with a full-scale economic and financial account of the operations of the Bank. Despite delays occasioned by new commitments undertaken by the author on the outbreak of war, his two volumes tracing the Bank's history up to 1914 were completed in time for publication as scheduled

* Catto, 1st Baron (1936) of Cairncatto, Thomas Sivewright Catto, 1st Bt. (1921), PC, 1879–1959. Director, Bank of England, April–June 1940; Financial Adviser to the Chancellor of the Exchequer, 1940–4; Governor, Bank of England, 1944–9.

† A piece of legislation of vital importance in the Bank's history, this Act first separated the Banking and Issue Departments (see chapter 6) and prohibited other banks from issuing notes unless that had been their previous practice, thus eventually eliminating from circulation all except those of the Bank of England.

‡ Clapham, Sir John H., Kt. (1943), CBE, 1873–1946. Professor of Economic History, Cambridge, 1928–38.

in the anniversary year, forming a magisterial and scholarly contribution to economic literature.[59]

What further steps should be taken to mark the anniversary date proved more difficult to determine. A six-man Committee under the chairmanship of John (later Sir John) Hanbury-Williams* was appointed in September 1943 to consider and report 'whether and if so in what manner' the Bank should celebrate.[60] They concluded, in a report made three months later, that 'the Bank should not seek to belittle the significance of 250 years; and in considering what forms of celebration to recommend, we are agreed that the anniversary should not be treated as of purely private concern. The opportunity should be taken to indicate the character and responsibility of the Bank as a public institution and to dispel some of the ignorance and misunderstanding that may exist of its aims and functions.' The Committee appreciated that the uncertainty of wartime conditions must mean that the celebrations would probably have to be quieter than if they were to take place in peace, suggesting a lunch (rather than a dinner) to which the King and Queen might be invited, as the principal festivity, plus a Service of Thanksgiving in St Paul's Cathedral, and lamented the fact that circumstances prevented the floodlighting of the building in Threadneedle Street. A shorter and more popularly accessible history of the Bank as an accompaniment to Clapham's work was also mooted; this project was pursued for some months but finally collapsed because of wartime shortages of paper and manpower which the different publishers who were approached were unable to overcome.† Ready co-operation with the Press in what the Committee rightly foresaw would be widespread interest in the event was another recommendation; various proposals for the benefit of the staff, including some form of special or sabbatical leave and a scheme of educational endowment assurance for children of staff members, were referred to the Staff Committee for further consideration. Finally, there was the question of a permanent memorial. A building or 'other physical monument' was felt to be inappropriate, and the Committee recommended a capital benefaction to the Bank Clerks' Orphanage, together with some form of endowment for research. It was suggested that this should be research into monetary and business conditions, 'to which the Bank has so far made little overt contribution although they cannot fail to be interested in and often influenced by its results'.

---

* Hanbury-Williams, Sir John Coldbrook, Kt. (1950), CVO, 1892–1965. Chairman, Courtaulds Ltd, 1946–62; Director, Bank of England, 1936–63.

† However a Temporary Clerk, Reginald Saw, did produce an unofficial history entitled *The Bank of England 1694–1944 and its buildings past and present*, Harrap, 1944.

The Committee of Treasury,* to whom the original report was submitted, felt constrained to rule out, as unsuitable in wartime, the suggestions of the service in St Paul's and of inviting Their Majesties, and possibly the Prime Minister, to the luncheon party; however both questions continued to be discussed for some months but were eventually abandoned, as the Governor mentioned in Court at the beginning of June that he had taken 'informal advice in Whitehall which gave a definite hint against inviting Their Majesties and the Prime Minister'.[61] The other recommendations went forward to the Governors and were largely followed. Clapham was asked to prepare some short articles on the Bank's history for use by the British Council, which he did,[62] and a large amount of further material suitable for use by a wide range of newspapers and periodicals was prepared internally, including a series of 'Strange Facts' about the Bank, such as the Bank giant, the Bank nun, the cholera cure, the first pound note and so on, which were written up by the staff of the News Summary.†[63] Much of this information, as well as some provided in special press briefings which were given to individual publications, was used in the thousands of column inches in which the event was celebrated in the world's press in due course.

A donation of £25,000 was made to the Bank Clerks' Orphanage, together with further sums amounting to £1,000 to various charities connected with the staff of the Printing Works.[64] The vexed topic of what, if anything, to do for the direct benefit of the staff as a whole was never resolved and appears to have been allowed to peter out on rather vague grounds of the unsuitability of a bonus or gift and the difficulties, in wartime conditions, of allowing 'special leave' (an idea which was to be put forward again at intervals over the next fifty years). In the event the staff received no material recognition. The most important, because most permanent, memorial was the establishment of the research fund, which the Committee decided at the end of 1943 might be called the Houblon-Norman Fund after the first and present Governors. Governor Norman agreed to this suggestion and the name was adopted in spite of one objection to its 'Alpha-Omega' effect. Lord Keynes‡ was closely consulted as to the form the endowment should take, approving the Committee's first thoughts that fellowships should be awarded without being tied to the production of a particular piece of research and

---

* The senior and most important of the Standing Committees of the Bank, concerned with financial matters both internal and external and with staff affairs.

† The News Summary was begun in about 1925 by the Governor's Secretary at first solely for the use of the Governor. It grew in scope and circulation – see chapter 11, p. 378.

‡ Keynes, 1st Baron (1942) of Tilton, John Maynard Keynes, CB, MA, FBA, 1883–1946. Economic Adviser to the Treasury during WW2. Director, Bank of England, 1941–6.

suggesting that the proposed sum of £300 a year was 'not very adequate' and ought to be £500.[65] There was much further discussion of details of terms, conditions and administration of the fund, and in particular of its practicality. A note to Governor Catto from Sir Otto Niemeyer* in June 1944 expressed the writer's feelings that 'it would surely be inconceivable that a Fellowship should be given to somebody who is just going to sit about and think ... there must be some approved programme of research'; an opinion with which Humphrey (later Sir Humphrey) Mynors† concurred, adding that without such a programme the candidate 'might just fiddle about (as I did myself with a University Research Scholarship)'.[66]

The fund, for the 'promotion of economic research', was finally established with a capital sum of £100,000 drawn from the Bank's undistributed profits. The Bank administered the fund via three trustees, the first of whom were the Deputy Governor Basil Gage Catterns,‡ Lord Eustace Percy§ and Samuel Courtauld,‖ but otherwise remained outside the management of the trust. A Committee was set up to make the actual awards, consisting in the first instance of Sir Henry Clay,¶ Sir Hubert Henderson,** and A.M. Carr-Saunders.†† As well as the major Fellowship, fixed initially at a sum of £800 annually, there were several minor disbursements of £100 and £150 each year for foreign travel or other special needs in pursuit of specific pieces of research. Topics in the first few years of the fund's existence included the external relations of insurance companies, country banking in the eighteenth and early nineteenth century, and the economics of investment trusts. Two future historians of the Bank, Professor R. Sayers‡‡ and John

---

* Niemeyer, Sir Otto, 1883–1971. Joined the Bank 1927; Adviser to the Governors, 1935; Director, 1938–52. Chairman of BIS, 1937–40; Vice-Chairman, 1941–64.

† Mynors, Humphrey, C.B, 1st Bt. (1964), 1903–89. Joined the Bank in 1933; Secretary, 1939; Adviser to the Governors, 1944; Director, 1949–54; Deputy Governor, 1954–64.

‡ Catterns, Basil G., 1886–1969. Chief Cashier, 1929–34; Director, Bank of England, 1934–6 and 1945–8; Deputy Governor, 1936–45.

§ Percy, 1st Baron (1953) of Newcastle, Eustace Percy, PC, 1887–1958. Rector of Newcastle Div. of University of Durham, 1937–52.

‖ Courtauld, Samuel, 1876–1947. Chairman, Courtaulds Ltd, 1921–46.

¶ Clay, Sir Henry, Kt. (1946), 1883–1954. Economic Adviser to the Bank, 1930–44; Warden of Nuffield College, Oxford, 1944–9. Author of *Lord Norman*, Macmillan, 1957 (posthumous).

** Henderson, Sir Hubert, 1890–1952. Economic Adviser to the Treasury, 1939–44.

†† Carr-Saunders, Sir A.M., 1886–1966. Director, London School of Economics, 1937–56.

‡‡ Sayers, Professor Richard S., 1908–89. Emeritus Professor of Economics, University of London; author of many economic works including *The Bank of England 1891–1944*, Cambridge University Press, 1976.

Fforde,* were among the early beneficiaries, most of whom produced books, pamphlets, papers or articles in learned journals as a direct result of the financial aid they received.

On 27 July 1944, the actual date of the 250th anniversary, seventy people sat down to lunch in the Court Room on the first floor of the Bank. Because the flying bombs were frequent at this date, some consideration had been given to having the meal in the lecture hall in the Sub-Vault, it being apparent that should a 'Crash Warning' sound 'it would not be easy to accommodate them all quickly and conveniently under the tables or in the alcove at either end of the Court Room'.[67] The Court Room was the final choice, however, and happily no such occurrence disturbed the guests who included the Governor and Deputy Governor, all the Directors except Lord Keynes and John Martin, seven ex-Directors, five Advisers and eleven members of staff including the Controller of Women Clerks,[68] Miss Margery Baldwin, who was the only woman present.† Twenty-three outside guests were headed by the Chancellor of the Exchequer, the Rt Hon. Sir John Anderson (later Viscount Waverley)‡ and included the Lord Mayor of London, Sir Frank Newson-Smith,§ the Bishops of London and Stepney, senior Treasury officials and representatives of all the principal City banks and institutions. The Governor and the Chancellor both made speeches; the former read out a telegram from his predecessor whose illness prevented him from attending: 'My thoughts are with you on this unique occasion. I send affectionate and respectful greetings to the Old Lady and pray for her increasing youthfulness and prestige.' Four wines accompanied the meal, whose menu had necessarily been drawn up with wartime restrictions in mind but still managed to strike an appropriately celebratory note by starting with Clear Turtle Soup. The Court Room was decorated with some fine arrangements of roses from Wills & Segar, the royal florists, which were despatched that evening to the Matron of Guy's Hospital for distribution among the wards. The public was included in the celebrations by a radio broadcast given by Governor Catto after the 6 o'clock news – at that date the main vehicle for

* Fforde, John S., 1921–. Joined staff of Bank, 1957; Adviser to the Governors, 1964–6; Chief Cashier, 1966–70; Executive Director (Home Finance), 1970–82; Adviser to the Governors, 1982–4; Official Historian, 1984–91.

† The Women Clerks were also celebrating the fiftieth anniversary of the appointment of the first women to the staff of the Bank in 1894.

‡ Waverley, 1st Viscount (1952) of Westdean, John Anderson, PC, GCB, OM, FRS, 1882–1958. Chancellor of the Exchequer, 1943–5.

§ Newson-Smith, Sir Frank E., 1st Bt. (1944), Kt. (1941), 1879–1971. Lord Mayor of London, 1943–5.

information about the progress of the war, and a fixed point of evening listening in almost every household in the land.[69]

On the same day it was announced that Norman was to be created a baron: he took the style of Lord Norman of St Clere, his house in Kent. He had earlier refused to consider a title, but according to his biographer Andrew Boyle finally agreed to accept ennoblement as a result of the persuasion of his old friend and colleague Holland-Martin, and it was certainly a fitting tribute in this anniversary year to his long period of Governorship.[70]

The Directors of the Bank wished to mark the anniversary by a presentation to the Bank, and decided that it should take the form of a specially commissioned piece of silver. Each of them contributed £10 towards the gift, but it proved impossible at the time to find someone to carry out the work; the project was shelved until 1950, when on the recommendation of the Goldsmiths' Company Leslie Durbin* was chosen to make an inkstand, which he completed the following year. Designed to stand on the table of the Court Room, it is a massive piece of plate measuring 17 inches by 10 inches, richly embossed with a central medallion based on designs on the earliest ledgers and records of the Bank, and other decorative features echoing details of stonework and mosaic floors in the Threadneedle Street building. Both the medallion and the cornucopias on top of the twin inkwells are worked in gold, and one of the two silver pen trays is inscribed with the names of all the donors.[71]

By the time of the birthday celebrations in the summer of 1944 some of the 'outcast Bank societies' were beginning to return to London. The staff of the Dividend Accounts Office had come back in March[72] (although their neighbours at Trentham remained in Staffordshire for nearly two more years) and small sections of the Establishment Department were also sent back during the year, while other provisional locations were given up as the need for them was obviously not going to materialise. As the tide of war turned in favour of the Allies, the staff of the Hampshire locations became increasingly anxious about their future. It had been decided in principle that the Accountant's Department should return to London without prejudice to a move at a later date, but the general feeling was that it would have to stay at Hurstbourne for at least eighteen months after the end of the war. The Royal Army Pay

---

* Durbin, Leslie, 1913 – . Apprenticed to Omar Ramsden, who did much work for the Bank. Durbin made part of the decoration of the Sword of Stalingrad, the gift of King George VI on behalf of the British people to the people of Stalingrad for their defence of that city during the war.

Corps had taken over the offices in Finsbury Circus, and it was evident that the rooms originally intended for the Department in Head Office would continue to be needed by the staff of Exchange Control.

The following chapter details the various courses that were pursued to try to solve the problem. Failing all else, the Bank was anxious to regain occupancy of Finsbury Circus, and in April 1945 Governor Catto took a hand, writing personally to Sir Edward (later Lord) Bridges* to ask him for help in pressing the military authorities 'forthwith' to find other quarters for the Pay Corps.[73] Two days later there was a meeting at the War Office between representatives of the Bank and the Army, at which the latter agreed to make a direct exchange of premises, with the proviso that the changeover should be simultaneous and take place within a month.[74] The reason for this urgency was that demobilisation, which would begin as soon as the war in Europe was officially ended, would involve the Pay Corps in an enormous amount of work during which a change of location would be impossible.

The date for the move was fixed as 28 May; the suddenness of the announcement came as a shock even to those most anxious for a return to London and the packing up of desks, files, office equipment and all the personal accumulation of five and a half years proved a gigantic task within the short span of time allotted. In addition to the practicalities at the Hampshire end, many of the staff had pressing domestic preoccupations of their own concerning accommodation for themselves and their families once the move had been made. It was understood at first that the Pay Corps would be taking over the Hurstbourne Camp, The Mansion and Laundry Cottage only, but it soon emerged that they wanted The Lawn – home of Establishments – as the Officers' Mess. So, in addition to organising the move, Establishments had also to cope with a temporary transfer of its own, to Redleaf, a house in Whitchurch which the Bank had taken in 1943, adding considerably to the problems of the whole exercise. A total of 260 miscellaneous lorries, cars and vans were required for the move, which also involved the disposal of mountains of surplus equipment, termination and disposal of leases, dismissal of local and temporary staff and many other considerations. The winding up of local affairs meant that a skeleton Establishment staff had to remain behind, moving out of Redleaf to Foxdown Camp. There were various claims for dilapidations and repairs to settle, and the elderly women had to be returned to The Gables, while all the spare furniture and stores were piled up in the vacated Dividend Preparation Office quarters at Overton

---

* Bridges, 1st Baron (1957), Edward Bridges, KG, PC, GCB, GCVO, MC, 1892–1969. Secretary to the Cabinet, 1938–46; Permanent Secretary to the Treasury, 1945–56.

and catalogued before removal to London. Large amounts of domestic furniture were sold to staff at prices usually below cost. The main removal was successfully accomplished by 28 May, but it was not until the end of October that the last of the Printing Works staff finally departed for London and the life of the location was officially at an end.

The expenditure involved in Hampshire (excluding amounts applicable to the Printing Works) during the evacuation period has been estimated at a little more than £1.25 m. Capital expenditure on buildings was £231,152, and on furniture and equipment £60,826, while current expenses included £450,000 for wages and food.[75] Inevitably, the question was asked at the end of the war whether the whole exercise had been justified: the Finsbury Circus offices had not been bombed, so perhaps there had been no need for evacuation? But, as the Deputy Chief of Establishments pointed out in his commentary on the Hampshire locations,[76] the lack of damage to the London home of the Accountant's Department was a matter of chance only – the corresponding block at the other corner of Finsbury Circus was completely wrecked. It was doubtful, he felt, that the work carried out in Hampshire could have been accomplished in London during the blitz. Head Office had only been able to carry on by arranging for large numbers of people to sleep in the vaults of a building extremely safe in itself, whereas similar arrangements and the elaborate catering involved would have been very hazardous, if not completely impossible, in offices such as Finsbury Circus and the Dividend Preparation Office at St Luke's. On the other side of the argument the Deputy Chief was constrained to add that both records and staff were still at risk, possibly at even greater risk, 'in temporary buildings, mostly constructed of wood, had a determined attack been made on the location'. A direct hit on the Camp would have been a disaster of major proportions, and while the records, which were photographically duplicated, could in theory have been reconstructed this would have been an enormously lengthy and difficult operation even if the entire staff had escaped injury. No doubt, he concluded wryly, 'the enemy was aware of the Location and did not think it worthy of attack …'.

The chronic shortage of accommodation in the immediate aftermath of war in and around a London which had lost a considerable proportion of its housing stock through enemy action meant severe difficulties for many of the staff. These the Bank did its best to soften by a variety of measures, firstly by continuing to pay the billeting allowance for some time with periodic reviews. Some members of staff continued to live in Hampshire, commuting daily to the Bank, and they were given temporary help towards travelling expenses, while dormitories were fixed up, again temporarily, on the sixth floor in Head Office. A longer-term solution was found in the provision of a number of hostels, which were managed by the Bank in a similar fashion to that adopted in Hampshire. After the inspection of a number of potential houses and hotels it was decided to acquire three properties: a large house in Hampstead, the Star and Garter Hotel in Richmond and the Astor Hotel in Princes Square, Bayswater.

The Hampstead house, 42 Redington Road, was occupied in August 1945 by about forty women, and the Astor (known as 43 Princes Square) three months later by fifty men. The Star and Garter Hotel needed extensive repairs and alterations and was not ready until December, when it was able to house 100 women. For a while it was known as The Mansion, a name chosen to provide a link with Hurstbourne, but the Bank was approached by the Richmond Georgian Group and asked to re-name it Nightingale Hall after Nightingale Cottage, which had once stood on the same site and was the home of a celebrated pair of blue-stockings known as the Cultivated Ladies. The YWCA took over the management of the women's hostels in 1948 and by 1952, when accommodation in London was less difficult to find, all three had been discontinued.[77]

At the outbreak of war the total staff of the Bank, male and female, clerical and non-clerical, numbered 4,120: two years later it reached its wartime peak of 6,285, of whom 814 were away on active service. In February 1946 over 600 were still awaiting demobilisation, and the total actually working in the Bank was 5,080, so that effective numbers had increased by less than 1,000 during the war. In all 2,209 staff were released to the services, of whom fifty-five were killed, and there were thirteen civilian fatalities as a result of enemy action including one Director, Lord Stamp.*[78]

---

* Stamp, 1st Baron (1938) of Shortlands, Josiah Charles Stamp, GCB, GBE, KBE, 1880–1941. Economist. Director, Bank of England, 1928–41. For details of Bank War Memorials, see chapter 10, p. 365.

# 2

## THE ACCOUNTANT'S DEPARTMENT*

From its very beginning the Bank of England had responsibilities as a Registrar. The original Charter of 1694 entrusted the Bank with the management of its own newly created Capital Stock, and directed 'that there shall be constantly kept in the public Office of the said Governor and Company of the Bank of England, a Register, or Book or Books, wherein all Assignments and Transfers shall be entered'. Maintaining the registers was the duty of the 'First Accomptant', and trade in the new stock was quite brisk from the start: Acres notes that many prominent Whigs disposed of their holdings within a year or so of the foundation of the Bank, and that the £10,000 which had been subscribed in the names of King William and Queen Mary was transferred to William Lowndes of the Treasury, who sold it in May 1695.[1] The sum of five shillings was payable to the Bank by the transferor on every transaction, towards the cost of 'Books, Accountants, Law Duty, and other like expenses'.

The work proceeded on this footing for the next two decades, but one of the earliest Acts of King George I, the Ways and Means Act of 1715, not only enlarged its scope, leading ultimately to stock registration activities on a gigantic scale, but also had more far-reaching effects with regard to the Bank's power and influence in the country's financial affairs. The 1715 Act confirmed the Bank's current legal position in various consolidating clauses and then provided that subscriptions for a new issue of 5 per cent annuities, designed to raise £910,000, should be paid to the Bank, whose responsibility it would be to manage the stock in the same way in which it managed its own, by keeping books to record transfers and by paying dividends. A fee was payable to the Bank for receiving the subscriptions, and the Chief Cashier and Chief Accountant

---

* Under a general reorganisation of the administration of the Bank, the Accountant's Department was renamed the Registrar's Department with effect from 1 March 1980.

were allowed an annual grant for undertaking the duties prescribed for them by the Act. (They were not permitted to keep this for themselves, however: they were firmly told by the Court that the money was 'at all times to be in the disposal of the said Court, to which they both assented'.)[2]

This was a new departure, because up until that time all subscriptions for new issues had been made to the Exchequer, but, as the economic historian P.G.M. Dickson has pointed out,[3] the medieval processes of the Exchequer were not well suited to this type of business; in particular their methods of transfer were slow and laborious. The newly created concept of public debt was also putting considerable pressure on the Exchequer just at a time when the increasing size and complexity of government revenue was straining its capacities of machinery of receipt, account and audit. A possible answer to the problem would have been to create a new State Department to carry out the management of the loans, but a simpler and more obvious solution was that which was chosen – to entrust the entire business to the Bank. In addition to the effective management of its own stock, it had in the intervening years since its foundation gained relevant experience by acting as receiver in the majority of state lotteries held between 1710 and 1714. The Bank had also begun to acquire a central position in short-term finance via its management of exchequer bills and loans on security of departmental tallies; the assumption of these new responsibilities was thus a logical step.

The act of 1715 was effectively the beginning of the Bank's role as manager of the National Debt, and two years later, when a Sinking Fund was established, the management of various government securities was also passed from the Exchequer to the Bank. At first the Bank had no monopoly of lending to the government, who also borrowed from the East India Company and, after its inception in 1713, the South Sea Company. The collapse of the latter in 1720 discredited the practice of borrowing from the Corporations, and from that date onwards the government relied on loans from the public, in almost all cases subscribed to the Bank. From this it was a natural step for the Bank to give advice on the terms of the new issues, a function whose importance was increased by two world wars and which itself is closely linked with the Bank's regulation of the domestic financial system. However these major developments, which are in any case well beyond the scope of this volume, could hardly have been foreseen in 1715.

Once the pattern had been established, it suffered little disturbance over the next two centuries. As the capitalisation of such things as transport, power and public utilities has tended in this country to be undertaken by private enterprise, government borrowing was usually occasioned by the needs of war. The 1914–18 war saw a steep increase in such borrowing, and the amount of government stock at the Bank went up from £700 m. to £4,000 m., while the number of accounts expanded from 150,000 to 2.5 m. The tasks and responsibilities of the Accountant's Department increased with them to a new degree of magnitude and complexity. In the Second World War government borrowing was heavier still: the amount of stock rose again, this time doubling in value from £6,000 m. to £12,000 m., but the rise in capital did not produce a proportionate rise in the number of accounts. The large institutional investors, rather than the private investors who had replied to the government's appeals in the previous war, were the principal subscribers in 1939–45, and they continued to be the largest holders of government stock at the Bank in the post-war period.[4]

From the outset Bank stock was held in inscribed form and the 1694 Charter gave detailed instructions as to how it should be transferred, including specimen wording. Provision was also made for transfer by Attorney 'in case the person assigning be not personally present'. Inscribed Stock gave the holder no documentary proof of his ownership, the sole evidence of which was the entry of his name, address and occupation in the Bank's books; stock issued in this form, principally by government and later by local authorities, was considered by the Bank to give wholly adequate security of title and unequalled simplicity of transfer. When it was sold or transferred, the holder had to come to the Bank in person or be represented there by his appointed Attorney, and sign a transfer in the Bank's transfer books, assigning his rights to the transferee whose name was then inscribed in his stead.

In order to guard against fraud, both transferor and transferee (whose presence or representative was also required, until the end of the eighteenth century) had to be identified by someone already known to the Bank, usually a member of the Stock Exchange. When the transaction was carried out the stockbroker prepared in advance a stock receipt which was signed by the transferor in the presence of the Bank clerk witnessing the execution of the transfer, who himself signed the document after he had checked over all its details. This receipt was, however, only a memorandum and it was not necessary for it to be produced at any subsequent transaction.

As stock ownership widened from its original base, largely composed of people working, and often living, within the City, it was not always so convenient for owners to turn up at the Bank in person and transfer by duly accredited attorney became more common. Powers of Attorney were drawn up, appointing certain members of stockbroking firms to act for the stockholder; later the Bank issued its own special form of Powers of Attorney. If a stockholder died, the Bank required proper evidence of the fact: a death certificate was usually acceptable in the case of a joint stockholder but, if the dead person was a sole or surviving holder, specimen signatures of the legal personal representatives, together with addresses, were required. These were filed by the Bank and referred to when action was taken on the account.

During the nineteenth century another method of transfer, by deed or written instrument, was developed. The deed was signed by both buyer and seller and was found to be better suited in many ways to the needs of the investing public, its chief attraction being the issue of a certificate of title held by the owner. Many of the new securities which financed Britain's industrial growth were of this kind, and investors grew used to certificates: as they began to invest in British government stocks a demand arose for those, too, to be transferable by deed. The growth of the demand, and the delaying tactics pursued by the Bank, are described in detail by the Bank's internal historian of Inscribed Stock[5]: in spite of the opinion offered to HM Treasury in 1906 by the Chief Accountant that 'to substitute transfer by deed for transfer in the Bank is practically impossible', and that, if it were possible it would be 'strenuously opposed by Bankers, Brokers and many large holders of Consols', it eventually became evident that concessions would have to be made. By 1911 the Governor, in a graceful volte-face, was telling the annual dinner of the Country Bankers' Association that the Bank 'had always been prepared to make arrangements for transfer by Deed should the government think it desirable... it would have to be in addition to the present system'. Nine days after this speech the Chancellor of the Exchequer, Mr Lloyd George, announced that parliament would introduce legislation to make Consols transferable by deed, a promise which was implemented by a clause in the Finance Bill of 1911 under which the Bank was empowered to draw up the necessary regulations with the concurrence of the Treasury.

Number 11 of these regulations gave the Bank ten days' grace after a transfer had been lodged before it was required to provide a 'Register Certificate' – a name proposed by the Chief Accountant. At first the Bank (who had had experience of Transfer by Deed since 1884 when it had undertaken management of the first of the Indian Railway debenture stocks) refused to allow transferees in any circumstance to deal with stock until the certificate had been issued; the method of Transfer by Deed was thus slower than the transfer of Inscribed Stock. This fact gave rise over the ensuing decades to a good deal of complaint on the part of stockbrokers and jobbers, and the Bank gradually allowed relaxations in the rule. But Registered Stock, as it was known, did not replace Inscribed Stock and existed side by side with it for nearly thirty years.

The payment of dividends was, naturally, a prime responsibility of the Bank for all the stocks, of whatever type, under its management. The first dividend on a stock managed by the Bank was paid on 25 March 1695, on £1·2 m. Bank Stock. The first Dividend Book in the Bank's possession is for the fourth dividend on the stock which was paid on 25 December 1697; bound in white vellum, it contains about 1,700 accounts grouped according to initial letter, and then arranged in order of amount. There was no Income Tax at this date, so the book only shows, in addition to the name of the stockholder, the amount of the principal and the interest on it.[6]

In 1752 an Act consolidated the various sums of Annuities, the entire management of which was entrusted to the Bank, who by then administered almost the whole National Debt with the exception of South Sea Company stock (although further loans were not raised by the government through the South Sea Company after 1720, it remained in existence as a corporation until the middle of the nineteenth century). In order to facilitate the preparation of dividends, the early practice within the Bank was to close the ledgers for transfers for about a month before each dividend payment date. An Act of Parliament in 1861[7] reduced this period to fifteen days, but in the same year the Governors decided that the books should be closed only nominally to allow a balance to be struck; a further provision of the supplementary Charter of 1896 enabled the Bank to close its books nominally for this purpose on any day not more than thirty-seven days before the payment of the dividend was due.

Each half year – or each year for government stock administered by the Bank – a dividend list was prepared from the ledger accounts, showing the names of the owners of the stock, the amount held and the dividend due. The proprietor or his representative came in person to collect the money and was given a payment warrant to present to the cashier. These methods ensured that the right people were paid, and not merely the owners of pieces of paper (as at the Exchequer), and that the Bank knew at any time who was the owner of the stock, how much was held and what transactions had taken place in it over a given period. Warrants were addressed by the Chief Accountant to the Cashiers of the Bank, directing them to pay to bearer the amount of dividend due; they were obtainable only by personal attendance at the Office dealing with the particular stock either of the holder himself or his appointed attorney and then only after identification had been made. The holder or attorney signed the dividend book as a receipt for his warrant, the signature being verified from a previous dividend book by the clerk issuing the warrant. (Bankers or brokers had to attend at the Bank to identify stockholders or attorneys claiming dividends for the first time.) The warrants were subsequently presented for payment over the counter in the Dividend Office – the subject of two delightful paintings done by G.E. Hicks in 1859, both in the Bank's collection[8] – or through a banker in the normal way.

Subsequent changes from the initial practices of the Bank included the printing of the dividend warrants, the delivery of warrants by post and various arrangements for the deduction and reclaim of Income Tax from holdings where this was necessary.[9]

All this work of registration, transfer, dividend payment and other aspects of stock management necessitated a large and growing amount of book-keeping under the auspices of the Chief Accountant. From the foundation of the Bank all the stock, whether that of the Bank itself or of government issues, was accounted for by a double-entry system – in contrast with the much less satisfactory single-entry practised by the Exchequer at that date – based on the Italian system which spread throughout Europe during the seventeenth century. Some methods from other countries were adopted too: for example the transfer books of the Bank are almost identical with those of the Dutch East India Company, founded in 1602.[10] As the work grew in scope and complexity, so did the number of clerks employed on the 'Stock Side', and the organisation of the Accountant's Department soon began to assume the pattern which endured, with minor variations, until the advent of computers in the early 1960s brought about a reorganisation on more functional lines.

A look at the structure of the Department in the inter-war years shows how it had developed in response to the tasks entrusted to the Bank by the government. The records of stock holdings and the process of transfer were in the hands of four large Offices named for the principal stocks they handled – Bank Stock, Colonial and Corporation Stocks, Consols, and $3\frac{1}{2}\%$ War Stock – plus two Transfer by Deeds Offices.[11] A Transfer by Deed Office had originally been opened to the public in the Consols Annexe in April 1912, after the new regulations relating to Deed Stock had been passed, but after six months the Chief Accountant had reported that he felt it was unnecessary to have a separate Office: the Governors had concurred with his suggestion that it should be closed, and the work undertaken in the appropriate Inscribed Stock Offices. The vast expansion of Deed Stock work occasioned by the 1914–18 war, however, led to a reappraisal of the question, and the Court approved the formation of one central office for the transfer of Deed Stock in December 1917. For various domestic reasons this was not immediately implemented, and the Deeds work remained the responsibility of the Consols Office, but was moved, under the charge of a Principal, to 50 London Wall early in 1918. A Deeds Office as a separate entity was eventually established under a Court Order on 19 June 1919.[12]

The Dividend Office dealt with dividend mandates, changes of address, investment of dividends under the Accumulative Dividend Scheme (described below), and with any dividends which might be returned to the Bank for various reasons. The Register Office dealt with proof of death and recording and implementing court orders, and the Power of Attorney Office prepared and registered Powers of Attorney for the sale and transfer of stocks. Two Offices carried out further aspects of dividend work: the Dividend Preparation Office, which was situated within the Bank's Printing Works at St Luke's in Old Street, prepared and despatched the warrants, and the Dividend Accounts Office acted as a check on payments made by the Dividend Pay Office (which came under the jurisdiction of the Chief Cashier). In addition to these was the Chief Accountant's Correspondence Office which handled all the correspondence in connection with the management of the stocks.

The decision taken in the early 1920s to rebuild Head Office in Threadneedle Street\*, together with the continual expansion of the work of the Accountant's Department at that time, led to the search for new accommodation for the Department, which, early in 1922, began a gradual removal to premises sub-let to the Bank by Finsbury Offices Ltd, comprising 18/21 Finsbury Circus and the contiguous 18/25 Eldon Street. The Deeds Office was the first to move from its address in London Wall, and on arrival was split into two.[13] At this time, and indeed until the outbreak of war in 1939, it was assumed that the Department would move back into Head Office to quarters specially prepared for it, once the rebuilding was completed, but the transfer to Finsbury Circus in fact marked the beginning of an odyssey which was to last for nearly forty years.

The methods of work pursued by the clerks in the Accountant's Department, until the advent of mechanisation of some of the processes in the 1930s, would have been quite comprehensible to the sixteen men who made up the staff of the Bank when it was founded over 200 years earlier. The double-entry system of book-keeping was basically un-

---

\* The rebuilding is described in Sayers, R.S., Vol. 3, pp. 338–43.

changed, although it had naturally become subject to later accretions, including an amount of checking, double and even triple checking of the work of one clerk by his colleagues and superiors which ensured that Bank standards of accuracy and thoroughness were unrivalled. The ledgers, of which a virtually unbroken series since 1694 is still in existence, were all written up entirely by hand: every clerk entering the service of the Bank had to undergo a simple examination which included a hand-writing test set by the London Chamber of Commerce. Entries were made in the ledgers in Bank ink, mixed from a powder specially formulated for its blackness and enduring qualities, but which had a fiercely corrosive effect on steel nibs – each clerk was issued every month with two pencils, an eraser, a pen-holder and twelve nibs. The ledgers themselves were of formidable size, the majority measuring about 15 inches by 18 inches by 7 inches thick and weighing some twenty-five pounds apiece; anyone who could carry three of them down the length of an office was highly respected, and there are many enjoyable stories, some no doubt apocryphal, of pranks involving such things as kippers being concealed in their spines. The total ledger weight in the Department by the mid 1930s was estimated at about thirty tons, and all of them had to be locked away each night by a small army of porters, who then got them out again the next morning.[14]

Hours were shorter on the 'Stock' than on the 'Cash' side; most of the Offices finished work at 4.30 p.m., and there was a generous amount of extra leave granted at the discretion of Principals or Head of Department. Even so, the days unenlivened by kippers must often have seemed very long. There was no disguising the fact that the majority of the work was dull, repetitive stuff, yet by its very nature it demanded concentration and care and an often finicky precision. Those whose progress and handwriting merited it were given the responsibility of actually writing up the ledgers, for example with the particulars of new stockholders or changes of address of existing ones, and a retired editor of *The Old Lady of Threadneedle Street* recalled the slow pace of the task: 'I used to inscribe in beautiful copper-plate four new accounts in the £5 % War Stock ledgers every afternoon, half an hour to each set of names and addresses. And if one finished before time one risked being reported as "hasty, and probably careless".'[15] Other jobs were still more tedious, such as ruling red lines in the Bond ledger (for Bearer Bonds, largely done away with in the Second World War as an exchange control measure). Even worse was the pointless re-doing of work already done in order to fill slack moments – and there were many of those, because of the Bank's contemporary policy of over-staffing in order to be able to cope

Plate 2.1  Mr J.P. Greig in the Record Office at Roehampton in 1942, with some of the early ledgers kept by the Accountant's Department

with the highly seasonal busy periods. A former Chief Cashier, who memorably described such work as 'turning swans into geese', spent many weary hours filling in income tax slips (sent to the Inland Revenue as evidence of deduction of tax at source, whence it could be reclaimed by the stockholders if appropriate) only to see them torn up and the list handed on to another clerk to do exactly the same work all over again. Similarly a clerk who had worked in the Bearer Bond Section recalled that 'sorted Bonds were taken away, unsorted and given out again to be resorted. Failing all else one was expected to be seen writing something – even with the wrong end of one's pen.'[16]

Work in the Dividend Preparation Office at the Printing Works was carried out by a staff largely composed of women, many of them quite young (a 'Young Person', in Bank terminology, meant a girl under the age of eighteen). The names of stockholders and the money due to them had to be entered clearly in ink on the printed warrants; the paper was thick and expensive and mistakes much frowned upon by the women supervisors. Like all the clerks in this and other banks at this period, the 'Div Prep' girls had to be able to add columns of pounds, shillings and pence rapidly and accurately in their heads, in order to total up the sums of money due, entered again in various ledgers, one for each bank. In some respects the girls were rather luckier than their male counterparts in Finsbury Circus: 'Whenever work was slack, we read or knitted, but if anyone was visiting the office, we added trip sheets from old ledgers, proved them, rubbed out the totals and began again.'[17]

By today's standards, this seems little short of drudgery; but by the standards of the time, it did not differ very greatly from work in other banks and commercial firms, except perhaps in the stringency of the standards of accuracy and neatness required. What is questionable, and what was questioned frequently at many levels in the Bank in the period between the wars and later, was whether the educational level required from entrants to the Bank's staff was unnecessarily high. The suggestion of a 'second division' of less well-educated workers to carry out some of these monotonous, routine tasks was frequently canvassed (and is discussed in detail in chapter 10), but never actually put to the test. In the meantime the Bank did all it could to palliate the situation by authorising the shorter hours of the Department and also by turning a blind eye to some of the activities the clerks engaged in while theoretically working. It was frequently said, not wholly in jest, that you could find an expert in the Bank on almost any subject except banking, and certainly some of that expertise was acquired in banking hours and in the Accountant's Department. A sorrier aspect of the whole situation was the amount of quite heavy drinking which went on at lunch-time and after office hours by bored and frustrated men, whose salaries in some of the worst cases were even paid directly by the Bank to their wives.

These were, however, only a very small minority, and the concentration on the checking processes within all the Offices of the Bank was strong enough to provide a safety-net to catch any errors. The majority of the clerks, whatever their true feelings about spending their days proving balances, posting information to ledgers or passing transfers, carried out their duties carefully and reliably, but the inherently routine nature of most of the tasks did mean that much of the work of the Department was highly suitable for the early processes of office mechanisation which were first available in Britain in the 1920s.

That the Bank was keeping a sharp eye on the progress of office mechanisation is evident from Departmental files which contain pub-

lished literature on the subject including detailed documentation of
ledger posting by machines in the Post Office Savings Bank (POSB),
which was the first instance in this country of the application of such
methods to bank accounts on a large scale – ten million POSB accounts
had been mechanised in this way by 1928. Two years before that the
POSB had begun replacing the old, hand-written ledgers with machines
and cards, and had also initiated the use of what it referred to as a
'remarkable machine' for automatic calculation of balances.[18] The
machine companies, too, kept the Bank informed of new developments,
and on 1 January 1930 loose-leaf transfers for Inscribed Stock were
introduced. Sixteen varieties of these replaced the separate transfer
books previously kept for every stock, and a similar number of stock
receipts superseded the 400 types, in various colours, then in use. The
change involved new methods for stockbrokers: instead of first making
out applications, they were asked to complete the specified transfer form
which, if it was found to be in order, was then at once executed by them
in the presence of a Bank witness.[19]

This experiment was an unqualified success, and paved the way for the
introduction in the same year of accounting machines, the very first
within the Bank, to deal with the posting and balance-book work in
connection with the active accounts in the War Stock Office and, later, in
other Transfer Offices. Meanwhile the Cashier's Department was making
similar studies and in 1932 the Drawing Office* introduced book-
keeping machines for the work of preparing Bankers' Accounts and passbook statements. Many different types of machine were by now on the
market and the Bank made careful evaluation of several of them before
the Governors authorised the extension of mechanisation with Mercedes
accounting machines (made by the Daimler-Benz Company) to all
banking accounts in the Drawing Office and, in 1935, to active stock
accounts (other than jobbers' accounts) in the Accountant's Department
with the aid of Burroughs equipment. At the same time mechanisation of
some of the processes of dividend preparation was instituted using
similar methods.

By this date it had become apparent that punched cards were most
likely to form the basis of future developments in accountancy. They had
already proved their capabilities in the fields of census and statistical
work, but for accountancy purposes were not yet far enough advanced to
compare favourably with the standard of work produced, if more
extravagantly, by the manuscript plus printing methods employed by the
Bank. For this reason the keyboard type of accounting machine was

* The Drawing Office is responsible for the management of all current accounts.

adopted, causing various problems within the Accountant's Department. New staff (primarily female) had to be engaged and trained to operate the machines; more exacting was the requirement of transferring 3 m. stock accounts from bound ledgers to loose-leaf format and setting up a similar number of records for dividend preparation purposes, as well as embossing – by hand – 3 m. stencil plates to replace the printers' type. A five-year plan was introduced, both to safeguard the employment of the printing staff and to allow the clerical staff, who might otherwise have been redundant, to devote their time to the work of the transfer of the accounts. The General Works Manager of the Printing Works played a major role in this reorganisation, and even designed a machine, the Logograph, for printing the amount in words on the postal dividend warrants. However the special Protectograph machines, built to the Bank's design, had already been purchased, so use of the Logograph was deferred until they needed to be replaced.[20]

A further development was the use of the fanfold voucher system. Efforts had been made within the Department to find some method of producing in one operation the several abstracts of transfer details required for the various registration processes. Handwritten carbon copies proved unsuccessful, but by the end of 1931 the idea of the typewritten fanfold system was developed and was first used within the Bank for 5% War Stock in February 1932. It was now possible to produce at one time a transfer acknowledgement, a form of certificate receipt, a journal record, and debit and credit abstract vouchers, all of which had up until then been produced separately by hand. New additions to the staff of copy typists were recruited, and special fanfold typing machines, using continuous stationery, were installed. The system was extended to all other deed stocks at the beginning of 1933. Two years later the development of punched cards was far enough advanced for the Bank to undertake protracted experiments (firstly within the Dividend Pay Office in the Cashier's Department) with Hollerith and Powers-Samas systems, the former being the final choice on account of its 'exceptional flexibility'. In 1936 Recordak machines were introduced into the Accountant's Department, photographing the accounts as they were prepared on 16 mm. film which could be easily and safely stored and which would allow a full reconstruction of the accounts should the original records be destroyed. Use of Hollerith machines was extended throughout the Bank, especially in the Dividend Pay Office and the Bullion Office,[21] and by the time war broke out in 1939 the principles of mechanisation were thoroughly understood and accepted by both 'Cash' and 'Stock' sides.

Plate 2.2   Women clerks operating Addressograph machines in the Dividend Preparation Office, 1936

As soon as the decision had been taken by the Bank and the Treasury that the evacuation of the Accountant's Department from London would be advisable in the event of war, to safeguard the registers, the question arose of how to carry on the work of stock registration away from the City. Transfer Deeds were not a problem as they could be lodged by post, but the transfer of Inscribed Stock required, as noted above, the personal attendance of the stockholder or his representative; and the entire process of the transfer of Inscribed Stock, as well as the dealer's part in that of Registered Stock, required close daily contact between the Bank and the Stock Exchange.

In April 1939, when the Bank was beginning its detailed planning for the event of war, an initial suggestion was made to the Treasury that a Bill should be prepared to legalise the transfer of Inscribed Stock 'by instrument in writing'. The Stock Exchange and the clearing banks were consulted, and the Bank felt that the provisions it had outlined to the Treasury should be made compulsory for all Inscribed Stock, whether or not the various registers remained in London. There were few who disagreed: the case for change was made all the stronger by the fact that one of the earlier benefits of Inscribed Stock, that it offered swifter marketability, had already disappeared with the acceptance in 1935 of the principle of payment on delivery for Registered Stock.[22] By August 1939

the Bill was in the hands of the draftsmen, and the Treasury agreed
verbally to write to the Bank asking it to carry out the programme
immediately and promising indemnification in the event of the Bill not
being passed into law at once.[23] However the Bill was shortly afterwards
ratified as the Government and Other Stocks (Emergency Provisions)
Act 1939; and the Bank was able to anticipate its provisions from the date
on which the Stock Transfer Offices in London were closed, 4 September
1939.

There appears to have been, at this stage, no definite intention of
interfering with the principle of Inscribed Stock, and indeed a clause in
the Act provided that no register certificate should be issued on the
completion of any transfer of it: instead a certificate of inscription was
provided as a memorandum of the transaction.[24]

On 4 September the Bank issued a press statement to the effect that its
Stock Transfer Offices were being moved to Whitchurch, in Hampshire,
and that legislation was being passed through parliament to 'provide that
Inscribed Stock shall for the time being be transferable by deed'. A small
office remained open in Threadneedle Street, under the management of
the Deputy Chief Accountant, to deal with enquiries from the public and
the Stock Exchange; in the early days of the war it was besieged by
crowds of people anxious to learn about the new procedures, almost all of
whom could be answered satisfactorily from the detailed manual of
operation prepared in the Department in the preceding months and
known as the 'War Book'.[25] This, with necessary alterations to cover
subsequent legislation, remained the basis of Departmental practice
throughout the war.

The new procedures worked so smoothly – although certainly necessitating long hours of overtime at Whitchurch in the early months of the
war – that it soon became evident that the days of Inscribed Stock were
numbered. Before the end of the year Governor Norman, writing to Sir
Richard Hopkins* about the forthcoming conversion of the $4\frac{1}{2}\%$
Conversion Loan, added that 'we feel the time has arrived to consider the
possibility of abolishing transfers of stock in books, i.e. by the inscribed
method, which in these days is regarded as an anachronism...The
adoption of one universal method of transferring stock should, moreover,
in the long run be conducive to more economical working...'[26] The
Treasury agreed; from then onwards the main consideration was how
best the changes might be brought about. British government stocks
were the first to be affected, and eventually the passage of the 1942

* Hopkins, Rt Hon. Sir Richard V.N., PC, GCB, KCB, 1880–1955. Second Secretary to
the Treasury, 1932–42; Permanent Secretary to the Treasury, 1942–5.

Finance Act, with its provision for what became the Government Stock Regulations of the following year, ended (with a handful of exceptions) the 249 year old practice of inscribing stock in the books of the Bank.[27]

This was the most important of the changes in Departmental practice brought about by the war. There were many other developments and simplifications, most of which would probably have taken place sooner or later in any case but which were of necessity compressed into a few years instead of being spread over a much longer period. The disposition of the staff at Whitchurch all on one floor played a significant part in this, with its elimination of the hundreds of daily journeys up and down stairs which had been necessary between the offices in Finsbury Circus. Some of the changes were also beneficial financially: the practice of verification of signatures to transfers, for instance, had to come to an end because the ledgers in which the handwriting was checked were simply too bulky to be transported to Hampshire, and this saved the Bank the £6,000 a year which was its pre-war cost as well as some 28,000 sheets of paper (wartime paper economies in the Department resulted in the saving of over a million foolscap sheets annually). Most documents used or issued by the Bank were reduced in size, and reductions in the length of time for which records were retained liberated large amounts of paper for salvage. Not without misgivings, it was decided to use 'multigraph' forms for much routine correspondence, containing set replies and space for short remarks, and not requiring a signature.

Despite such simplifying measures the work of the Department increased rather than decreased during the war, largely because of new loans. Work on $2\frac{1}{2}\%$ National War Bonds 1945/7, the first tap issue, was begun in London, but because of the bomb damage caused to St Luke's on 9 September 1940 the work was transferred to Whitchurch and all future issues were handled from there. Issue on tap, rather than by allotment, was more easily managed and by a smaller number of clerks, but the average number of subscription forms rose sharply during the various 'Savings Weeks', on one occasion topping 15,000. The frequent wartime fluctuations in the standard rate of Income Tax, and thus to amounts of net dividend payable, also accounted for many thousands of man-hours, as did the large numbers of redemptions and conversions.

Considerable difficulties were experienced with the constantly changing numbers of staff. At the outbreak of war, there were 1,377 people working in Finsbury Circus, including nearly 500 women. By October there were in Whitchurch only 445 men, 128 permanent women and a handful of temporary clerks, and recruiting of temporaries on a large scale began in December. A year later the staff of the Accountant's

Department numbered 990, and it was estimated that if all the work were to be completed in a nine-hour day – doing away with some of the massive amounts of overtime worked in the early stages of the war – a staff of 1,050 would be required, a figure reached in the summer of 1942. After that date numbers declined, until there were 900 in December 1944.[28]

In 1942 the Department was subjected to a new and unfamiliar type of investigation. F.W.R. Laverack, a Principal in the Cashier's Department (Exchange Control), had by the beginning of that year been engaged for some months in looking into the whole administration of the Exchange Control Offices with the aim of effecting economies in staff and material as its work rapidly expanded. The results of this were found to be very valuable, and it was proposed to Court that his position 'should be given more permanence and the field extended to cover the other Departments of the Bank', by the creation of an extra-departmental post of Inspector of Offices and Branches. To this suggestion Court assented,[29] and Laverack was duly appointed. One of his earliest duties in the new post was to carry out a searching examination of the Accountant's Department, which lasted from September 1942 to September 1943. Terms of reference included consideration of the general staff position, the possibility of economies and of carrying out the work more speedily and efficiently, the elimination of any duplication of work, the potential extension of mechanisation and the replacement 'where possible and without loss of efficiency' of men by women.

In the course of his enquiries Laverack unearthed a great many instances of what he considered to be unnecessary amounts of double, triple and even greater amounts of checking – as many as eleven sets of initials, for example, were to be found on the back of each Transfer, to identify individual responsibility at different stages of the work. Statistics relating to staff and work in the Transfer Offices could, he thought, be centralised, and other aspects of the work simplified. The work of the non-Transfer Offices, in contrast (Stock Returns, the General Card Index,* Power of Attorney, Dividend Accounts at Barlaston, and the Chief Accountant's Offices at Whitchurch and at Head Office), had largely been 'pruned of non-essential processing'. Laverack's recommendations included the installation of a 'more comprehensive system of mechanisation ... and the use of more up-to-date types of machines as

---

* Stock Returns Office – responsible for making extracts of relevant particulars of individual accounts to enable the Chief Accountant's Office to reply to correspondence and queries. The General Card Index (see below, p. 67) was attached to the Stock Returns Office.

soon as production is again possible', plus the further employment of women on much of the routine clerical work currently undertaken by the Permanent Male Clerks: 'Alternatively, the introduction of a Second Division Male Staff is practicable.' The most far-reaching of his suggestions was for a total reorganisation of the work of the Transfer Offices 'by means of a functional set-up', in other words putting like activities together as against the current system of dividing the work into Offices concerned with particular stocks, each with its own local administration and organisation. The Inspector was further moved to note his impression 'that a somewhat leisurely atmosphere exists in the (Transfer) Offices which contrasts with the quicker tempo noticeable in the larger Offices at Head Office', and to comment on a 'negative attitude' on the Stock Side where the staff were 'bound up in ... traditions and methods of work procedure of many years standing: there is an inclination to defend the status quo rather than to explore with an unbiased mind new suggestions for dealing with the work'.[30]

The status quo appears to have been successfully defended as far as his suggestions of the possibility of a second division staff and of the functional reorganisation of the Transfer Offices were concerned; the former question was not pursued at the time and it was only the advent of computerisation, a couple of decades later, which effected the latter. Many of his other recommendations bore fruit, particularly those which related to unnecessary checking procedures; and the further employment of women, together with a continuous process of mechanisation, were to be two of the most important features of the post-war era.

By the time the Inspector had produced his four reports on the various segments of the Accountant's Department the question of where it was to go after the war was over was exercising the minds of many among the highest echelon of the Bank. There had never been any intention to make the evacuation to Hampshire, described in the previous chapter, a permanency. Henry Clay, visiting the locations in October 1941, felt that the Whitchurch arrangements were 'the most impressive improvisation to meet a wartime need' that he had seen, but that they did not seem to 'offer the basis for a permanent transfer of work from London'.[31] The staff, consulted as to their preferences for the future location, had voted overwhelmingly for a return to homes and families in the London area. By the beginning of 1943, a City of London Reconstruction Advisory Council was about to begin work, and complaints were already being voiced, during the debates on a Town and Country Planning Bill, about delays in post-war planning. Noting this, the Bank set up a special committee of Directors, under the chairmanship of Edward Holland-

Martin, to make recommendations to Court about the future permanent location of the Accountant's Department in the post-war period.[32]

The deliberations of the Committee were complicated by the need to take into account a report on future dispersal from London which was made by the National Council of Social Service, partly at the Bank's instigation; however this proved an indeterminate document disappointing to Governor Norman who had hoped to 'give a lead on decentralisation... if anybody could afford to pioneer from the point of view of their public position and their financial resources it was the Bank'.[33] His colleagues were less certain that moving the Department away from London was a good idea, and when the Committee made its first report, in November 1943, it was in favour of bringing the Accountant's Department back 'as soon as possible to premises in or near London without prejudice to plans for permanent location'. Not only did they feel that many of the staff might leave if asked to continue to lead a communal life in the country for any longer than was strictly necessary, they also took into account the permanent staff returning from the Forces, who would naturally wish to rejoin their homes and families. The Stock Exchange was consulted in the persons of Messrs Woodrow and Willows of Mullens and Co., the government brokers, who conceded that the abolition of Inscribed Stock had made a difference but still felt that the location of the Department in the country was 'an inconvenience' and that the City in general would prefer it to return to London.[34]

As the Finsbury Circus offices were occupied by the Army Pay Corps, the Bank now began an active search for alternative London accommodation for the Accountant's staff, in case the former premises could not be repossessed. Many possibilities were examined, including Classic House, a modern office block in Old Street; in December 1943 there was considerable enthusiasm for the idea of taking over the Royal Exchange, owned jointly by the Mercers' Company and the City Corporation. The building was felt to be 'a white elephant', impossible to let except for one large block which was held on a seventy-year lease by the Royal Exchange Assurance, and the Bank for some time seriously entertained the idea of pulling it down and rebuilding on the same site. The architect Victor Heal, who had built the Southampton Branch before the outbreak of war, drew up plans, but it was recognised that this was a long-term solution. Other possibilities were constantly under review, and in June 1944 the Bank acquired Market Buildings, on a site between Mincing Lane and Mark Lane. It had been badly damaged by bombs and needed extensive repair work: a notice to the staff in September telling them that because of this 'some considerable time may elapse after the cessation of hostilities in Europe before the Department is returned to London' was reported to have caused 'widespread concern and despondency', and the clerks lodged a formal complaint of their dissatisfaction at having been away for nearly five years.[35]

Soon afterwards all work stopped on Market Buildings because building trade labour was directed to repair destruction done by the 'flying bombs' – damaged houses, of which 870,000 were awaiting attention, had to take priority. Then the Governor received a letter from the Chancellor of the Exchequer, urging that 'in view of the housing position in London, all possible measures be taken to postpone for the time being the return of evacuated staff'.[36] The Market Buildings project eventually had to be abandoned, occasioning the review of still more possibilities, some of which, like the Olympia Exhibition Halls, seem to have been born of desperation. (The same may be said of the feelers put out by Holland-Martin with regard to the City Road premises of the Honourable Artillery Company, which elicited a reply from the Army that to entertain any such idea was 'a complete waste of time'.)[37]

In the spring of 1945, after intervention by the Treasury, the Department did return, as described in the previous chapter, to its former offices in Finsbury Circus. The Bank continued to cherish hopes of the Royal Exchange, but the scheme collapsed the following year, apparently on the grounds of the considerable compensation which would have been required by the principal lessees.

Nationalisation of the Bank, proposed under the Bank of England Bill which was one of the first measures introduced by the new Socialist government in the autumn of 1945 (receiving Royal Assent on 14 February 1946) had two aspects with which the Department was intimately concerned. The Bill's first main clause related to the transfer of Bank Stock to the Treasury Solicitor and the compensation of the former Proprietors (holders of the stock) by an allocation of an amount of stock created by the Treasury for the purpose – 3 % Treasury Stock, 1960 or after – which would yield them the equivalent income. Bank Stock thus disappeared as a marketable security, bringing about the renaming of the Bank Stock Office which had existed since the building of the various Transfer Offices by Sir Robert Taylor* between 1765 and 1770. Its new name was the Funding Stocks Office. Two years later, in July 1948, all the Offices were rearranged and the Funding Stocks Office

---

* Taylor, Sir Robert, 1714–88. Architect to the Bank of England, 1765–88.

Plate 2.3   Trucks used in the move of the Stock Transfer Offices from Hampshire back to London in May 1945. By chance they parked overnight on the site later chosen for the New Change building

was merged with the Colonial and Corporation Stocks Office. At this date also the two Transfer by Deed Offices were abolished, there being no longer any need for separate registers for 'Deed' and 'Inscribed' Stock. A further change of name took place in April 1954 when the word

Colonial, which had begun to acquire new implications, was dropped and the Office became the Commonwealth and Corporation Stocks Office.[38]

Bringing the Bank into public ownership made virtually no difference to its internal organisation and administration, which were pursued, as both Bank and Treasury had intended, on the same lines as before. The nationalisation of industry, however, to which that of the Bank had been merely a curtain-raiser, meant that the owners of stock in corporations taken over by the government were in their turn compensated by allocations of newly created government stocks corresponding in value to the shares they had surrendered. This naturally implied a huge expansion of accounts in the stock registers maintained by the Bank, and of all the attendant work. It was obvious from the start that there would not be room for this in Finsbury Circus: new premises would have to be sought elsewhere, pending the final decision about the Department's permanent home.

It was estimated that a building of some 50,000 square feet would be necessary, and first efforts were concentrated on finding somewhere suitable in the City, but this proved impossible even with the help of the Treasury.[39] In February 1947 representatives of the Department viewed Regent Arcade House, a building in Argyll Street with a frontage also on Regent Street, where all the office accommodation above the ground floor on two sides of the building was available. 'I much dislike the idea of having a large staff in the West End', minuted Governor Catto the following month,[40] but he acknowledged that the Bank's need was 'desperate', and negotiations were already in train for a lease of forty-two years from the owners, Land Securities Investment Co. Some of the office space had been requisitioned by the Ministry of Works on behalf of the Ministry of Supply, and once more the Treasury was approached, this time by the Deputy Governor, Cameron Cobbold*, for aid in de-requisitioning it: the Ministry countered by suggesting that the Bank should move the work 'to the outskirts of London or the Provinces'. In June, Sir Wilfrid Eady† of the Treasury put the Bank's case most eloquently to Sir Harold Emmerson‡ in the Ministry of Works:

> the location at Regent Arcade House is a pis-aller, and is already as far away from the City as the work can be taken if the Stock Department is not

---

* Cobbold, 1st Baron (1960) of Knebworth; Cameron Fromanteel Cobbold, KG, PC, GCVO, DL, 1904–87. Entered Bank as Adviser, 1933; Executive Director, 1938–44; Deputy Governor, 1945–49; Governor, 1949–61.
† Eady, Sir Wilfrid G., GCMB, KCB, KBE, 1890–1962. Joint Second Secretary to the Treasury, 1942–5.
‡ Emmerson, Sir Harold C., GCB, KCVO, 1896–1984. Permanent Secretary, Ministry of Works, 1944–56.

to break down. And that is a risk we simply cannot afford. For if the Stock Department breaks down, the gilt-edged market breaks down, with the most serious consequences to Government credit. It also means that the socialisation programme comes to a standstill. In your letter you spoke of the demands of the socialised industries as though they had priority over the Bank. But have you not overlooked the fact that the Bank is the first of the socialised industries and, further, that all the other socialised industries depend on the Bank for their compensation arrangements?

... I must be frank and warn you that ... the Bank are likely to report to the Chancellor that, for want of this accommodation, they cannot issue and manage the compensation stocks by the due dates. This will immediately create a political issue of the first importance. For it will mean that the Government must amend the Transport and Electricity Bills to postpone the vesting dates.[41]

The strength of these arguments prevailed and the Ministry of Supply vacated the building at the end of September 1947. Much rebuilding and adaptation was necessary before any staff from the Department could move in, and extra space in the Arcade itself was earmarked for kitchen premises, although this work was held up for some time by supply difficulties; indeed the delays owing to problems over building permits and shortage of materials drove the architect 'nearly to despair'. But at length staff began to occupy what became popularly known as 'Spiv House', the move being completed in stages between January and April 1948: before the kitchens were built some of the earliest branded frozen food, called 'Frood', was supplied by J. Lyons and Co. Another novelty was fluorescent lighting, which proved very successful.[42]

Edward Stapley, who had been Chief Accountant for nine years (six of them jointly with A.M. Walker, who had retired after twenty-four years in 1945), retired in June 1948 and was succeeded by Cyril (later Sir Cyril) Hawker,* Deputy Chief Cashier to K.O. Peppiatt since 1944. To Hawker fell the major task of administering the Bank's manifold responsibilities in connection with the government's nationalisation programme. It was essential, for political reasons, that dealings in the new Transport Stock issued to railway stockholders should begin on the vesting date, 1 January 1948, but as the terms of the issue could not be fixed until that date no preliminary work could be done by the railway companies on the 1·25 million holdings in their registries. The position was made worse by an unexpected wave of selling after the vesting date, which involved

---

* Hawker, Sir F.C., Kt. (1958), 1900–91. Entered Bank 1920; Deputy Chief Cashier, 1944–8; Chief Accountant, 1948–53; Adviser to the Governors, 1953–4; Director 1954–62.

those at Regent Arcade House in a total of 133,000 hours of overtime in the first seven months of 1948. The vesting date for electricity undertakings was 1 April 1948, involving some 300,000 accounts, but fortunately the owners of new stock were not prompted to sell as eagerly as the railway stockholders had been. The nationalisation of gas, iron and steel followed.

The work was complex and detailed, involving large numbers of different companies (forty in the case of transport, 120 for electricity with additional complications in the shape of composite gas and electricity companies and holding companies). Valuation procedures in many cases provided for the value to be agreed for the lowest transferable unit and rounded off to the nearest (old) penny, which unless prices were at par introduced unwelcome fractions. The Bank consulted the Secretaries of some of the largest electricity companies, who did their own registry work, but found them largely unhelpful and 'only interested in finding jobs for their own staff'[43]; a plea to the Stock Exchange for help in carrying out the technical provisions of the Electricity Act (with whose drafting two senior members of the Department had assisted) proved more fruitful and resulted in the loan of four people plus a secretary. Even so, it was obviously impossible to carry out all the necessary work on the vesting date itself. The old stock or share certificates had to be treated as applicable to the new stock until certificates for the latter were issued, which in most cases was done within six months. The transactions were taking place on constantly changing registers, continually being built up from advices received from the former registrars, who themselves were not always able to keep up with the immense volumes of paperwork.

In total the stocks guaranteed by the government and issued in compensation to holders of securities in the various companies – railway, electricity, gas and iron and steel – amounted to £2,000 m. The number of accounts with the company registrars was itself nearly 2 million, but so many holdings were sold and so many were found to be in the same names that the overall number of accounts at the Bank for nationalisation stocks was only about 500,000.[44]

In spite of the Governor's misgivings about the new premises, this section of the Department stayed uneventfully in Regent Arcade House until the management of nationalisation stocks was transferred to St Luke's in October 1956. However, in one unexpected way his apprehension was well-founded, because the owners of an adjacent restaurant proved tireless litigants who involved the Bank in a lengthy series of legal arguments over compensation claimed for loss of business during the rebuilding, heating costs and cleaning exterior stonework, which were not finally settled until the end of 1953.[45]

Since its earliest assumption of registrar duties the Bank had of course been charging a fee to the government for such service, and its own nationalisation plus the extra work involved in the nationalisation stocks made it especially anxious to dispel any idea that other registrars gave better value for money in this respect. This consideration, together with a desire to keep abreast of all possible developments in mechanisation which might prove useful to the Department, gave rise to a major investigation of its work which began in the summer of 1948. The Governor asked Sir George Abell* and S.B. Chamberlain† to carry this out in co-operation with the Chief Accountant and to report to him on 'the possibilities of reducing operating costs by further mechanisation or otherwise'.[46] The terms of reference did not actually set up a committee but the scope of the work proved so extensive that Abell and Chamberlain 'found it convenient to proceed on committee lines', and it was nearly a year before the report appeared.

During its preparation the Governor sanctioned four journeys abroad by a special team consisting of the Deputy Chief Accountant, W.D. Simpson, L.J. Attridge from the Central Mechanisation Office (set up in September 1945 as a special office in the Establishment Department to centralise, as far as possible, the use of machines throughout the Bank)[47] and F. Compigné-Cook from the Accountant's Department. It was apparent from the outset that France and Switzerland and particularly the USA were all well ahead of Britain in the field of office mechanisation, and the three men visited a total of forty-two banks, financial institutions and business equipment manufacturers in those countries. Their chief concern was the needs of the Dividend Preparation Office, where an experiment to replace the Burroughs Protectograph machines with Hollerith cards, used in conjunction with the existing Addressograph plates, had been tried after two years' planning in 1947 but found to be too complicated a system.[48] Further work which had taken place on the continent and in the USA seemed to promise possible solutions in the future to the Bank's problems in this area, one of the principal difficulties, as mentioned earlier, being re-taxing of dividends on a change in the rate of Income Tax. The importance of this point can be judged from the fact that during the preceding thirty-five years there had been twenty-three

---

* Abell, Sir George E.B., KCIE, OBE, 1904–89. Joined Bank as Adviser, 1948; Director, 1952–64.
† Chamberlain, S.B., CBE. Joined Bank in 1904. Works Manager of Printing Works, 1931–48.

changes in the standard rate of Income Tax, each of which under the existing system entailed the alteration of the tax and net interest, manually, on nearly 1·5 million balance slips.

The team was impressed by the large sums of money being invested in electronic research: the Burroughs Adding Machine Co., for example, had allotted $5 m. to this and undertook to consider the Bank's dividend problem in its research department. In view of all these developments the recommendation of the Abell Committee was to delay any changes in the system of dividend preparation for at least two years. The word 'computer' is not mentioned – it was still, at this date, used only by specialists – but it was evident to the Bank's investigating team that electronic data processing was likely to supersede the electro-mechanical punch card handling equipment then in general use.

An equally searching examination of the other points specified by the Governor, including the overall costs and staffing policy of the Accountant's Department and possible improvements in working methods, satisfied the Committee that there was 'no need for the Bank to feel vulnerable about the cost of the Department'. The volume of work handled was 'immensely greater' than that undertaken by other registrars, many of whose figures are cited for comparison, and while this was a factor in lowering the costs per million stock managed, it was also true that the ratio of transfers to accounts was much higher in the Bank than elsewhere, which tended to increase the cost. In such qualities as efficiency and standards of precision and security the Department was assessed as, in many cases, far superior to other registrars, some of whose costs were admittedly lower. The Committee made special reference in this connection to the General Card Index, which housed over 4 million cards with the full name and address of every stockholder, executor, administrator and nominee for the receipt of dividends, together with the reference number of every account, both open and closed, in which these names appeared in any of the 155 securities managed by the Bank. The cost of maintaining this index, which was at the heart of the Department's structure, was about £40,000 a year, but if it were abolished, the Committee felt, the savings in labour costs would be offset 'to an unpredictable extent' by the extra work of consulting the separate indexes of the various stocks and by handling the greatly increased number of communications which would be returned by the Post Office as undeliverable. 'Here is a conspicuous instance of the Bank being forced, by the volume of work undertaken, to maintain a large and expensive organisation...the smaller registrars do not consider it necessary to keep such an index...'[49]

The question of a 'second division' staff was again mooted and again dismissed. Labour costs of the Department were shown to have been cut by nearly 25 per cent since 1939 if allowing for changes in salary scales, and the Chief Accountant was reported to be taking 'special steps' to ensure a close control over staffing levels in future. (Hawker's own recollection of this, given in an interview in *The Old Lady* over thirty years later, was succinct: 'When a Principal came to me and said he needed more staff, I'd just say "Sorry, there aren't any". It meant overtime on some days, but on others I simply said "When the work's done, everyone can go home". This led to fewer hours worked and fewer teas taken!')[50] The Committee advocated a greater use of women clerks, who could be paid less money: from a pre-war total of 46 per cent of the Department the proportion of women had risen to 55 per cent by the time of the report in 1948 and Abell suggested a new aim of two-thirds permanent women and one-third permanent men, once the extra temporary staff needed for nationalisation work could be released.

Another question was the amalgamation of the Dividend Pay Office and the Dividend Accounts Office, but the Committee decided to endorse the ruling of Edward Holland-Martin, made three years before, that any such amalgamation should await a decision on new mechanisation in the Dividend Preparation Office. Similarly the organisation of the Transfer Offices on functional lines rather than by stock, which had recently been urged afresh by the Committee of Principals, was again considered and rejected, the Committee's view being that, although the correspondence work in the Department had been successfully centralised in special offices, the transfer work at present was 'well-balanced and efficient' and any re-organisation was unlikely to produce greater economy.

One small but important technical change proposed by the Abell Committee was the abolition of the Accumulative Dividend Scheme. The Bank had on request re-invested dividends, where holdings were less than £2,000 (except in certain special cases), since 1890, the idea having been first broached by a member of the Stock Exchange in a letter to *The Times*.[51] The Treasury had welcomed the idea as offering the small investor an incentive to save, and also increasing the numbers of people directly interested in public funds. By 1948 the number of accumulative dividend accounts, which had been falling steadily for some years, formed less than one half of one per cent of the total, and the Bank's charges for administration, at the rate of 1d. for each £1 or part of £1 invested, brought in an income of only about £300 p.a. This sum entirely failed to cover the expenses incurred, and Abell recommended the abolition of the scheme, except where the 'sole surviving and competent stockholder' was a minor. A month later the Deputy Governor, Dallas Bernard,* told the Chief Accountant that he had spoken to Sir Wilfrid Eady on the subject and the latter had been 'loth in principle to take any action which might reduce the attractiveness of Government securities for small investors, but he was quite prepared to consider it if we could show that the requirements or the demands for the facilities were gradually becoming less...'. This the Bank was easily able to do and shortly afterwards the scheme was discontinued for new issues.[52]

The Abell Report, without making any very dramatic changes in the structure or work of the Accountant's Department, proved a useful exercise in its function of providing an authoritative overview of the Department as a whole in a period when the Bank was still greatly concerned with the vital question of its future location and when very considerable changes were afoot in areas of mechanisation which would affect the Department's practices. The overseas contacts which Simpson made proved valuable in forthcoming years – he succeeded Hawker as Chief Accountant when Hawker became an Adviser in 1953 – and were built upon by successive visits to the United States and elsewhere throughout the 1950s.[53] The enquiries made by the Committee had resulted in a clearer view of what it was the Bank ultimately required for dividend preparation: the electronic calculation of interest, tax and net, at the same time as the printing process took place, and the reproduction by a printer of both alphabetical and numerical data on the interest documents in the same process and at a speed consistent with that of calculation.

In 1947 the government, after a certain amount of wavering, had finally declared itself in favour of a policy of dispersal of offices from London, and began to move some of its own departments and offices out of the capital – the Post Office Savings Bank went to Sheffield, for example, part of the Inland Revenue to Worthing, and part of the Ministry of National Insurance to Newcastle. Pressure was brought to bear on the nationalised industries to do the same, and the Treasury asked the Bank to consider to what extent the government's policy might be applicable to its organisation, particularly having regard to the experience gained by the removal to Hampshire and elsewhere during the war. This led to yet another investigation of the possibilities of locating some of the work away from London, from which it became clear that the only large part of the activities which could possibly be separated

* Bernard, Sir Dallas G.M., 1st Bt. (1954), 1888–1975; Director, Bank of England, 1936–49; Deputy Governor, 1949–54.

from the rest was the Accountant's Department.[54] But the Bank emphasised, in a letter from Deputy Governor Cobbold to Sir Eric Bamford* of the Treasury on 26 June 1947, that it was not prepared to make any immediate move:

> With a return to more normal housing conditions and with less difficulty in finding and keeping suitable staff, it might at a later stage be reasonable to reconsider, as a long term policy, the possibility of moving the Accountant's Department from the centre of London. But in present conditions and with the tremendous burden of new work which is to be placed upon the Bank as a result of the Government's policy of nationalisation, we cannot contemplate such upheaval. Close contact with the banks, the Stock Exchange, brokers and solicitors will be essential and facilities must be maintained for the interchange of staff between the different offices and Departments at short notice. Finally a large proportion of the work of the Accountant's Department is carried out by women staff, many of whom, particularly the young girls, would find other employment rather than face travelling difficulties or domestic upheavals consequent on a move of the Department to the suburbs or the provinces.[55]

There, for the moment, the matter of dispersal officially rested, but a search for a new site continued and it was not confined to London. Laverack investigated the Development Corporations of the infant New Towns;[56] later Walton-on-Thames was for some time a favoured option, and the possibility that some part of the work of the Bank could be located outside London was under internal and virtually continuous review for a further six years.[57]

At the beginning of 1949 St Quintin Son & Stanley, chartered surveyors who carried out much work for the Bank, drew the attention of the Chief of Establishments to a site to the east of St Paul's Cathedral. The Cathedral itself had been almost miraculously spared serious bomb damage, but in this area of nearly two acres divided roughly in half by Friday Street, which ran south from Cheapside across Watling Street to Cannon Street, there was little left above ground except the shattered doorway of the Livery Hall of the Worshipful Company of Cordwainers.[58] The Corporation of the City of London was anxious that the site should be restored as soon as possible, and had designated it 'Redevelopment Unit No 1', but there were many inherent problems including the obligation to re-house former tenants. None the less, the Chief Accountant liked the site, and in the absence of any serious alternative it gradually became the favourite. The Corporation was

---

* Bamford, Sir Eric St J., KCB, KBE, CMG, 1891–1957. Third Secretary to the Treasury, 1946–8.

known to be considering a compulsory purchase order, so that development could be speeded up, and this was confirmed in January 1951;
a promise was made that the Corporation would 'do its utmost' to see
that existing owners and occupants of the site would be re-housed in any
buildings which might be erected.[59]

After further efforts by the Treasury to get the Bank to agree to move
out of London, the Governor was finally successful, at the beginning of
1951, in obtaining a promise from Sir Edward Bridges that the Bank could
go ahead in putting in an application for what was now referred to as the
Friday Street site, and that this would not be queried on dispersal
grounds; Sir Edward intimated that he had 'had a great deal of trouble
in the Treasury on this subject'.[60] Even at this late stage, however, the
Governor himself was not finally convinced; he tended to think that the
government's policy was the right one, and he was backed up by Sir
George Abell. But at a meeting with the Deputy Governor, Abell, the
Chief of Establishments and the Chief Accountant in September 1951,
the Governor accepted the arguments of his Deputy and the two Chiefs,
which were primarily based on the recruitment problems associated with
an out of town location, and with the agreed policy of switching staff
between Departments.[61]

It was now definitely agreed to continue to negotiate for the purchase
of the Friday Street site. There were several other interested parties, and
the fact that the Corporation at first wished to grant only a ninety-nine
year lease put a question mark over the whole project, but this was
resolved amicably and 'in the exceptional circumstances' the Bank was
granted a 200 year lease, to commence when building was finished. The
Bank had to undertake to re-house any former tenants from the site who
wanted new premises, and it was decided that building would take place
in two phases, the first for the Bank itself, the second mainly for tenants.

While the legal aspects were under discussion, Heal was occupied in
drawing up plans for the new building. There were many constraints on
his design. The site was subject not only to the views of the City
Replanning Committee (who were said by the Town Clerk to regard the
Bank 'as just another government department', questioning its need for
so much space), but any building had also to comply with the
requirements of the St Paul's Preservation Act of 1935, which laid down
strict regulations as to height and the safeguarding of different views of
the Cathedral. All the neighbouring buildings had to be faced in Portland
stone (of which the Cathedral itself is built) to the ground floor, and in
brickwork, with the minimum of stone, above, and Heal was very
conscious that the elevation along the new road planned opposite the east

end of the Cathedral needed special treatment as it would form a 'backcloth' to Wren's masterpiece.

He had finished his preliminary designs by the middle of 1952, and suggested to the Bank that it would be better to consult the Royal Fine Art Commission at this stage, rather than for that body to express its opinions unasked after the plans had been finally approved. The Bank agreed, and the drawings were duly submitted to the Commission's Technical Committee at the end of the year. They were approved, although some alterations were suggested by Professor Richardson,[*] who told the Deputy Governor that, as the Commission's 'oldest member and only real expert', he had 'told Heal how the building should be modified so as to fit in with St Paul's and make one large harmonious whole. He says that Heal is very good but requires a little teaching in these great artistic designs.'[62] Heal took this in good part, and made the suggested alterations to his design for the facade.

By this date a considerable number of people were deeply involved in the interior and exterior planning of the building. Within the Bank those most closely concerned were naturally representatives of the Accountant's Department itself and of the Establishment Department;[63] the Governors and members of the Court were keenly interested and progress was monitored by the Committee of Treasury and the Special Committee on Bank Premises.[64] Legal aspects were handled by the Bank's solicitors, Freshfields, and Bank personnel had to hold a protracted series of meetings with the Corporation Surveyor, the Surveyor to St Paul's, the London County Council and the City Planning Officer, one of whose many concerns was that the proposed building would comply with the overall recommendations of the official plan for post-war London, drawn up by Charles Holden[†] and Professor William (later Sir William) Holford.[‡] The Stock Exchange and many other banks and City institutions were applying for licences to rebuild at this time, and there were some doubts as to whether the fact that the Bank had obtained licences for other building projects including its new Printing Works might prejudice the application for this one. But widespread criticism of slow progress in the rebuilding of the City – where large areas were still a chaos of rubble and weeds – caused Winston Churchill, who found it a

[*] Richardson, Professor Sir Albert, KCVO, 1880–1964. Professor of Architecture, London University, 1919–46; President of the Royal Academy, 1954.
[†] Holden, Charles, FRIBA, 1875–1960. Town planning consultant to City of London, 1944–54.
[‡] Holford, Baron (1965) of Kemp Town; William G., RA, 1907–1975. Professor of Town Planning, University College London, 1948–70. Town planning consultant to City of London.

'shocking sight', to promise an improvement in the licensing arrangements for rebuilding.[65] In the event the Bank had no difficulty in obtaining the necessary licences, which were granted in May 1953.

The designs for what was still known as the 'Friday Street site' in spite of efforts to rechristen it 'St Paul's Precinct' were given their first public display at this time, when the Bank allowed Heal to show them in the Royal Academy's Summer Exhibition. To the Bank's surprise and no little chagrin, they provoked some fierce criticism. The early reaction was quite favourable, *The Times* contenting itself with the observation that the building appeared as 'a tall red-brick structure in modified Georgian style differing little from the conventional office buildings of the 1930's'.[66] But a few days later the same newspaper carried a sharp attack in the form of a letter from ten art scholars, headed by Professor Anthony Blunt* and including William Coldstream, Ben Nicolson and Nikolaus Pevsner (whose *Buildings of England*, published a few years later, was to be less than complimentary to Sir Herbert Baker's remodelling of the Bank's premises in Threadneedle Street as well as to this building).[67] Much correspondence in *The Times* and other papers followed, largely unfavourable and critical of the size and bulk of the building, although some of the fire was drawn by the plans for Bucklersbury House which were also unveiled at this period. Fourteen storeys and 150 feet high, this was another office block considered enormous at the time, although lower than the Bank's building whose final height varied from 121 feet – well below the 234 feet of the stone gallery below the dome of the Cathedral – to a maximum of 185 feet on the Bread Street side, furthest from St Paul's.

The Bank took possession of the site in August 1953 and clearance and excavation work began in November, a first necessity being to seal off or divert the numerous services running under Friday Street. During this work a macabre discovery was made of some headless skeletons, thought to date from the days of Newgate gaol nearby.[68] Difficulties arose almost immediately over the terms of the building agreement and lease, still not finalised; when the City Solicitor made some amendments which were considered quite unjustified, the Bank felt obliged to give the Corporation a curt reminder that they were not dealing with 'speculative builders' but with 'one of the best architects in London and a leading firm of building contractors' – Holland & Hannen and Cubitts – after which the altercation was settled in the Bank's favour.[69] A strike by steel erectors, or 'spidermen', held up progress during twenty-one weeks at the end of

* Blunt, Professor Anthony, 1907–83. Professor of History of Art, University of London and Director of the Courtauld Institute of Art, 1947–74.

1954 and early 1955: Mynors wrote to Harold Watkinson, Parliamentary Secretary to the Minister of Labour, to ask him to intervene, but the men returned to work before Watkinson had time to do more than acknowledge the letter.[70]

Soon after the building work had got under way, a further campaign to change the exterior design was mounted. Duncan Sandys,* Minister of Housing and Local Government, wrote to the Governor on 2 May 1955 to say that the whole area round St Paul's was being 'reconsidered', and Sir William Holford was about to prepare fresh proposals for it. These would advocate 'a single homogenous, though not necessarily uniform' architectural treatment of all surrounding buildings, and Sandys expressed his disquiet about the presence 'of one large building which was altogether out of keeping with the others'. Governor Cobbold replied that Heal would contact Holford, but that the Bank's plans were now at a very advanced stage and had been agreed for some time 'with all the authorities concerned'. Holford, when consulted, pressed for replacing brick facings with stonework on the frontage to the Cathedral, greatly annoying Heal who considered that the proposal, coming at this late stage, presented 'insuperable difficulties... this has been designed as a brick and not a stone building'. It shortly emerged that the suggestion had in fact originated with Sandys, Holford's own views coinciding more with those of Heal and the Bank: a compromise was eventually reached, with no fresh stonework at first floor level but the tops of the second floor windows 'accentuated' by Portland stone.[71]

Decisions about the interior design of the building were less taxing. The Governor, writing in early 1953, had made his own views clear: 'I assume that in the internal planning of the new building all the emphasis will be on useful, practical office accommodation and that we shall avoid grandeur, showiness and waste of space.' It was necessary also to bear in mind the possible disappearance of exchange control, and changes, either enlargement or reduction, in the nationalisation programme – 'We ought to make provision for the maximum of flexibility with the minimum of structural change.'[72] The architect adhered to these guidelines, but even so the spaciousness of the building (341,000 square feet in all, of which the offices took up some 221,500) gave the staff considerably more elbow-room than they were used to in Finsbury Circus, as well as providing some pleasant extras in the form of a lecture hall which could be used by BEODS as a theatre, and an underground range for the use of the Bank's Rifle Club. Lyons, who had provided such excellent service in Hamp-

---

* Duncan-Sandys, Baron (1974), Duncan E. Duncan-Sandys, CH, PC, 1908–. Minister of Housing and Local Government, 1954–7.

shire during the war, were called upon to advise on kitchen and dining room layout: 600 people could be served in the dining rooms, 450 in the coffee rooms and a quick lunch counter in the basement seated seventy-five. There was much discussion as to whether a separate dining room should be provided for Principals, who themselves put up a strong case for such a room with waitress service; the room was agreed, but not the special service.[73] J.G. Rains Bath acted as adviser on decoration and furnishing, using a handsome Nigerian walnut for most of the wood furniture, and the staff were encouraged to make suggestions on all aspects of the building: all the ninety-one points they raised were carefully examined and thirty-five of them incorporated.[74]

Two flats were built on the eighth floor, one for the use of the Governor and one as official accommodation for visitors. This was given no official publicity (those within the Bank who were concerned with it were requested to refer not to the 'Governor's flat' but to 'living quarters'),[75] but the news inevitably leaked out and was accorded a nod of approval by *The Financial Times* who stated that 'nothing could be more desirable or more appropriate' in view of the excellent old tradition of merchant bankers living above their premises.[76]

The naming of the new building posed a delightful problem giving full scope to the abundance of classical and archaeological knowledge within the Bank, although the main concern of the Chief Accountant was directed to the practical question of the large amount of printed stationery used by his Department, most of which had to be ordered months in advance. The Deputy Governor was anxious to 'hit upon a title now [April 1954] thus avoiding a drift towards a name which might be inappropriate or colloquial and which might be difficult to change'.[77] 'Friday House' was ruled out 'for reasons which are obvious', and indeed part of Friday Street had from the beginning been scheduled to disappear in the redevelopment of the site. (The Corporation stipulated that a public footway must be made 'on or about the line of Friday Street' and this was incorporated in the plans.) The street was so named because of the fishmongers living there and serving Friday's market in the Middle Ages; it had an interesting association with the Bank which seems to have been overlooked during these discussions. William Paterson, one of the founders of the Bank, presided here over the 'Wednesday's Club in Friday Street', whose meetings in the early 1690s were devoted to political and economic topics such as public debt: later the Club discussed another subject with which Paterson was intimately connected, that of the union of England and Scotland.[78]

J.A. Giuseppi, the Bank's archivist and historian, produced a list of various courts, taverns and private houses with historical associations on or near the site, and favoured the name of Chepe Cross, which had been placed in Cheapside by Edward I to mark one of the resting places of the coffin of Queen Eleanor in 1290. The famous Mermaid Tavern had entrances in Cheapside, Bread Street and Friday Street. John Milton was born in Bread Street, and Milton and Pepys had both attended a school situated just to the east of the Cathedral.

None of the possibilities suggested by these names found favour. The Chief Accountant suggested Norman, Houblon or Mercer House, the latter commemorating Thomas Mercer, the 'First Accomptant'. A year later, in August 1955, the question had still not been decided; Simpson by then favoured Ariel House, but shortly afterwards the Bank learnt that the road between the Cathedral and the new building was to be called New Change. This was in counterpoint to the narrow street between St Paul's Churchyard and the site, called Old Change, which in turn was named after 'the King's Exchange at London', situated in medieval times near the Cathedral. Mynors roundly declared that the name New Change was 'a nonsense', but it proved decisive. By September 1955 it had been agreed that, on the analogy of 'The Bank of England, Threadneedle Street', there should be no specific name or number, and the new building would simply be known as 'The Bank of England, New Change'.[79] Some anxiety was caused in the ensuing months by wavering on the part of the Corporation, who changed their minds several times about whether there should be a road there at all, and if so, whether it should be a carriage road or perhaps a private, gated road, but in the end the original scheme prevailed, and Holford's new plan, published in May 1956, provided for a traffic link between Queen Victoria Street and Cheapside, duly named New Change.

The position of the building had in large measure dictated its architectural style – there was no scope, in the shadow of the Cathedral, for the adventurous attitude which the Bank was able to take so successfully in its other major building project of the 1950s, the new Printing Works at Debden in Essex. Equally the interior layout and furnishing, while handsome enough, were circumscribed by the practical necessities of modern office procedures as well, perhaps, as a desire to avoid the opulence of some parts of the Threadneedle Street premises. But the Bank did permit itself a few grace notes to the purely functional theme when it came to the choice of the decoration of the building both by exterior sculpture and, inside, by the flooring of the entrance hall.

The Threadneedle Street building is particularly rich in sculpture and decorative carving, almost all of it allusive or symbolic in character, and much of which was executed by Charles (later Sir Charles) Wheeler,* who had enjoyed a long and fruitful association with the architect of the 'new' Bank, Sir Herbert Baker. Wheeler was thus a natural choice to provide some of the sculpture to ornament New Change. He was initially engaged to provide statuary for the exterior of Phase I and his first suggestions were of two naked female figures representing Wealth and Mineral Ores respectively. Models for these were shown to three members of the Special Committee on Premises, Sir Charles Hambro,† Sir George Abell and W.J. Keswick,‡ who felt that they were 'more realistic than they had anticipated'. Wheeler produced further models, this time clothed in formalised drapery, but these too were rejected and the Committee opted for their replacement by two figures of St George, Combatant and Triumphant. He was asked to make changes in his first models of these, the former being privately considered to look 'extremely bored' while the latter 'looks rather like a benevolent yokel': finally the Committee expressed itself satisfied with the remodelled figures into which Wheeler injected more vigour and movement.

Wheeler also provided, for Phase I, a new statue of the 'Old Lady', which was a replica of the design over the Southampton Branch of the Bank, and half a dozen keystones including three which symbolised the London rivers of Thames, Fleet and Walbrook. All these are placed on the New Change frontage. The Bank had decided to commission other, younger sculptors to provide further decorative work on this phase of the building, and chose Donald Gilbert, David Evans and Esmond Burton, whose work is seen in the South Court and on the Watling Street and Bread Street frontages, all of it symbolic of various aspects of the work of the Bank and its situation in the City.[80]

Some of the finest decorative work in Threadneedle Street is the mosaic flooring of the main corridors, carried out by the Russian mosaicist Boris Anrep§ during the pre-war rebuilding of the Bank. By a happy chance some more of his work which had been executed for the Bank, but not used, was still in existence; it had been intended to replace the original floors at the Bartholomew Lane entrance, laid in 1928 but

---

* Wheeler, Sir Charles T., KCVO, CBE, 1892–1974. RA, ARA, President, Royal Academy, 1956–66.
† Hambro, Sir Charles J., KBE, 1897–1963. Chairman of Hambros Bank Ltd. Director, Bank of England, 1928–63.
‡ Keswick, Sir W.J., Kt. (1972), 1903–1990. Chairman, Matheson & Co. Ltd, 1949–66. Director, Bank of England, 1955–73.
§ Anrep, Boris, 1884–1969. Born in St Petersburg, Anrep lived in Paris from 1908 onwards. He began work as a mosaicist in the early 1920s and carried out a number of major commissions in England including the floors of the National Gallery.

found some years later to be badly worn.[81] Anrep had designed a figure of Ariel, medallions representing the countries of the Commonwealth, and two larger medallions of William and Mary and of George VI; the work was completed in 1939, but the outbreak of war prevented it being laid. It survived the war in his Paris studio and in 1948 was transported to Threadneedle Street where, as Mynors pointed out in 1955, the stones were 'cluttering up the vaults'. New Change provided the ideal home for it, but it was obviously necessary to substitute a portrait of the new Queen Elizabeth II for that of her father who had died in 1952. Permission to do so was accordingly sought from Buckingham Palace and granted by the Queen, and as well as carrying out this portrait Anrep turned the faces of William and Mary so that they faced to the left, while the Queen looked to the right.

In the autumn of 1955 Anrep came to London and with his assistants laid out the new designs in the Museum at the Bank, subsequently taking 15 cwt. of marble pieces back with him to Paris for further work. He now began to grow very anxious at the idea of people walking about over the Queen's face, a prospect which, he wrote, 'schocks (sic) me greatly', and proposed that four bronze posts should be placed round the medallion, joined with a velvet rope, to prevent such disrespect. He was assured that the Queen had seen his design, approved it, and was quite aware of the purpose for which it was intended, but the position of the medallion, which he considered 'one of my best works', continued to trouble him. When he came in April 1959 to see it *in situ* he plaintively enquired 'Could not something be done about it?', but the Bank took a more robust view of the matter and refused to accede to his wishes.[82]

The sculpture for Phase II of New Change, which housed those tenants whose interests in the site the Bank had undertaken to safeguard, involved the Bank in an unhappy situation *vis-à-vis* Wheeler, who was by now President of the Royal Academy. There had been a certain amount of criticism of his work for Phase I, including the opinion voiced by *The Scotsman* which had hoped for a 'Young Lady of New Change' and thought that Wheeler's Old Lady 'looked like Stalin in certain lights'.[83] The Premises Committee, while not overtly dissatisfied, had made no final decision that Wheeler should carry out any work for the second phase, but a letter to him in November 1955 from the contractors, who were unaware of this, gave him some grounds for supposing that he had been commissioned to do so; he continued to act on this supposition in spite of letters from Victor Heal attempting to persuade him that the final choice of sculptors had not been made. After much anxious consultation with Freshfields the Bank had perforce to pay him a substantial fee 'on account of sketches for Phase II and in termination of contract '. Wheeler himself suggested that the official reason, if one should be required, was that 'owing to my duties as P.R.A. I have "withdrawn"''; the whole matter was handled on the Bank's behalf, and with a good deal of tact, by Heal.[84]

Negotiations with the other sculptors for Phase II proceeded smoothly. The largest piece was by Esmond Burton, and took the form of a group symbolising the granting of the Bank's Charter: the first Governor, Sir John Houblon, holds the Charter, accompanied by Michael Godfrey, first Deputy Governor, with King William and Queen Mary above them. Donald Gilbert provided a statue of St George as a Roman Centurion, which he probably was,* for the north side of South Court, over the pedestrian way. The Friday Street motif was emphasised in this work by keystones representing the prow of a boat below, leaping salmon on either side and a lobster above, Heal considering the representation of the lobster 'superb'. A 'fortress of gold' and a lion with its key, both in Newgate Street, are the work of Alan Collins.[85]

For a city of its size London has surprisingly few fountains, and it was accordingly decided to place one in the sunken garden in South Court; Heal knew of a pleasant fountain, sculpted in the form of a water nymph by the late Ernest Gillick, who had designed the original Antarctic Medal and the Lord Mayor's Seal. This had been shown at the Royal Academy in 1938, but remained unsold, and his widow Mary had kept it in their Chelsea studio. Members of the Premises Committee visited the studio and liked it, and Mary Gillick arranged for a new bronze casting to be made for New Change.[86] A final and most pleasing touch was the decision of the Committee to honour the architect Heal, who was seventy-three in 1957 and 'at the end of a very valuable period of service with the Bank'. In view of the size and importance of the New Change project they felt it was suitable to commemorate him there with a plaque bearing his portrait. This was designed by Mary Gillick, whose portrait of the Queen had been chosen for the new coinage, and was put up in the main entrance hall.[87]

The necessary concentration by many people in the Accountant's Department on the physical aspects of the new building had not been allowed to interfere with progress in the areas of Departmental organisation and practice. One milestone of historical interest during these years was the combination, from 1 July 1955, of the Power of Attorney Office with the Register Office. This move ended 150 years of

---

* St George, martyred for his adherence to the Christian faith in c.303, seems likely to have been a member of the Praetorian Guard of the Emperor Diocletian.

separate existence for the PAO, although no warrant for it can be traced. The original terms of reference were given to the Committee of Inspection of the Stock Offices in March 1805, when it was decreed that 'instead of the present practice of registering wills and making out and examining Powers of Attorney in each of the several Stock Offices, an Office be constituted for combining the said business regarding all the Stock and Annuities transferrable (sic) at this House...' However, when in November 1807 the premises were completed and clerks appointed from among those who had previously done the work in the 'Corners'* of the various Transfer Offices, two Offices, not one, were set up: so that the 1955 reorganisation at last brought matters in line with the original intention of one and a half centuries earlier.[88]

The mid 1950s had introduced a period of intensive discussion and research into computerisation throughout the whole of the UK banking industry. The development of calculation in £sd at this date was of particular interest to bankers, because until then virtually all the most sophisticated machines were designed for the US market. All five of the major companies in the field – Addressograph-Multigraph, National Cash Register, British Tabulating Machine, Burroughs Corporation and Powers-Samas – kept in close touch with the Bank and its requirements, and in the last quarter of 1955 a small party visited the US to hear at first-hand from two of the companies concerned their plans for the remechanisation of the work of the Department, and to have a further look at new developments. Subsequently all five put forward their ideas and proposals, all of which introduced electronic equipment. Two years were spent in the Bank in evaluating the plans, at the end of which period it was decided to carry out an experiment using Powers-Samas equipment. The advantages of this company's equipment from the Bank's point of view lay in the fact that the capacity of its punched cards was much greater, alterations to the file of cards could be applied periodically and mechanically instead of daily and manually, and the calculation of interest and tax could take place at the time of interest preparation, simultaneously with printing.[89] A further benefit was that the whole installation could be acquired without dollar expenditure, an important consideration at this period.

The scheme was described by the Chief Accountant in a note to the Governors as 'a revolutionary departure from present methods and habits of thought'. By this date, March 1957, the word 'computer' was in general use and the pilot installation included a computer as well as

---

* The Corners were responsible for staff matters and sometimes for other functions such as the collection of statistics, etc.

Plate 2.4 New Change – the Watling Street frontage, looking west, in 1958

another device which calculated the gross interest and the income tax to be deducted, including fractions of a penny in each case, established the net dividend payable and submitted all the information to a high-speed printer producing warrants at the rate of some 50/60 per minute. These were 'not quite as good as at present, because diphthongs, accents, small letters etc.' were not available: but the Chief Accountant noted that the warrants – 95 per cent of which were for less than £50 – were usually only in circulation for a few days, after which they returned to the Bank for payment, recording and eventual destruction. The Chief Cashier agreed with him, he assured the Governors, that the proposed warrant 'may be regarded as a suitable document to come from the Bank'.[90]

The pilot system, which constituted the Bank's first direct experience of computers, was installed in New Change, because with the completion of Phase I of the building it was at last possible, after thirty-six years, to house the whole of the Accountant's Department under one roof. (The author of an appraisal of the building in *The Old Lady* worked out that it was feasible for a current member of staff to have worked in as many as a dozen buildings.)[91] A move on such a vast scale, involving some 2,000 staff – two-thirds of them women, as the Abell Committee had recommended – and the documentation necessary for the management of around 160 securities, took many months of careful planning. It was accomplished with a minimum of disruption in less than a month, between 15 February and 10 March 1958; a comic note was struck by the mock funeral cortege which accompanied the departure of the Dividend Preparation Office from St Luke's where it had been, except for the war period, since 1929.[92]

Two and a half years later, in August 1960, Phase II of New Change was completed. The cost of the whole building, which was the City of London's biggest single post-war building project at that date, was very close to the £6·25 m. approved by the Committee of Treasury in 1956. A small part of the second phase was used by the Bank itself, the remainder being let to tenants including shops, offices and branches of three of the clearing banks.[93]

# 3

## EXCHANGE CONTROL, 1939–1957

There was little exchange control in Britain during the First World War, as both the Bank and the Treasury were extremely anxious to preserve the freedom of the exchanges and maintain a normal free gold market in London. Some trade restrictions were imposed and gold exports discouraged but not prohibited; there was no systematic attempt at control until the formation of the London Exchange Committee in November 1915. This was given wide powers, but was in some respects unable, in others unwilling to exercise them, and the cost of the war to the national reserves was certainly greater than it need have been.

After the war, in spite of great efforts to maintain free markets, various forms of control had to be adopted, again with little or no attempt at co-ordination. In 1926 the Bank set up an Exchange Section for the first time, within the Chief Cashier's Office; valuable experience was provided by C. P. Mahon and L. Lefeaux* who had each been seconded at different times to act as Secretary to the London Exchange Committee. The operations of the Section expanded rapidly after the 1931 crisis and Britain's departure from the gold standard, and the following year the Exchange Equalisation Account (EEA)† was established in order to 'check undue fluctuations in the exchange value of sterling'. During the 1930s applications of exchange control became widespread overseas, and included the requisition of foreign exchange earnings, prohibition of exports of capital and various types of compensatory and clearing agreements. Germany was the chief exponent of these last, and the German controls were among the most rigidly structured and enforced.[1]

---

* Mahon, Chief Cashier, 1925–9, retired as Comptroller in 1932. Lefeaux became Assistant to the Governors and was released to be the first Governor of the Reserve Bank of New Zealand, 1934–40. See chapters 10 and 11, pp. 352 and 373.
† For a full account of the EEA see QB, December, 1968, pp. 377–87.

While there was distaste in the Bank for any idea of imposing a similarly Draconian system, a definite opinion had been formed as early as the winter of 1936 as to the possibility of war and hence the need that would arise for exchange control in order to conserve and increase the gold and foreign currency reserves and to ensure their use for the maximum national benefit. The earliest recorded communication with the Treasury on the subject is in a long letter written on 8 July 1937 by the Deputy Governor, B.G. Catterns, to Sir Frederick Phillips* on the subject of a number of steps to be taken in the event of war.[2] Catterns recalled the exchange restrictions imposed at the time of the 1931 crisis and then proceeded to outline measures to be taken immediately on the outbreak of war. These measures, very little modified, in fact became the basis of the regulations which were ultimately imposed, but a lengthy dialogue now ensued between Bank and Treasury as the latter resisted many of the Bank's arguments. The Treasury was particularly averse to the idea of blocking foreign balances, and felt that the system described by Catterns would imply 'a very great interference with the existing free institutions of the City of London'. There were fears of disturbing international confidence in sterling, and apprehension that any offence given to the US might prejudice American help in the event of war. The Bank was naturally aware of the dangers, but the Governor remained convinced, as he said on 10 August 1938, 'that statutory control would prove inevitable on the outbreak of war'. The experience of the Munich crisis in the following weeks confirmed these convictions – in August the EEA lost £26m. and in September £36m. in gold, entirely on account of sales in New York – and the Bank pointed out to the Treasury that the same thing would almost inevitably happen in the event of another crisis.

While this debate continued, the Bank, the clearing banks and the Treasury itself were proceeding with numerous drafts of regulations and public announcements, and very reluctantly the Treasury came round to accept most of what the Bank viewed as necessary when and if war broke out, although the question of non-resident sterling remained a point of contention right up until September 1939. From the beginning, the Bank had made it clear that its involvement with exchange control would be almost entirely technical and monetary in scope; it would administer the country's gold and foreign exchange reserves and act as the agent of the Treasury (at one time a governmental Foreign Trade Control Office was envisaged but this idea was abandoned). To avoid delay in commercial transactions the Bank would in turn delegate to specified commercial banks a considerable degree of authority to handle routine business for

* Phillips, Sir F., KCMG (1933), 1884–1943. HM Treasury, 1908–43; Under Secretary, 1932.

their own customers, referring any difficult cases to the Bank of England. These banks were known as Authorised Banks, and by the outbreak of war fifty-four had been selected. More limited powers were given to stockbrokers and solicitors, known as Authorised Depositaries, to allow them to deal with the large amount of work involved in security transactions.[3]

Professor Sayers has described how Governor Norman put his Adviser Harry Siepmann* in overall charge of exchange control, 'because Siepmann hated any controls and would therefore see that administration was kept within sensible bounds'; and how Siepmann put the famous notice on the wall of his room: 'Freedom is in danger. Defend it with all your might.'[4] It was in this spirit, of avoidance wherever possible of bureaucratic complexities, and seeking always to be helpful rather than obstructive while applying the rules in good faith as agents of the Treasury, that the Bank approached the problem of exchange control, and it was this attitude that predominated in all the years of control that lay ahead.

By the summer of 1939 the form of the Defence (Finance) Regulations, very largely embodying the proposals of the Bank, had been finally agreed and drafted to suit the requirements of Parliamentary counsel. The necessary forms, instructions to banks and public notices were ready. Arrangements were co-ordinated with the other countries conducting the majority of their trade in sterling, and holding their reserves predominantly in that currency, which were known at this date as the sterling bloc. The Colonies had been requested to introduce similar regulations, the Dominions asked to co-operate: both New Zealand (which already had a control) and Australia introduced satisfactory regulations at the outbreak of war. South Africa agreed in principle to introduce control, but in the event did so only gradually. Canada, Newfoundland and Hong Kong were not part of the bloc.

There was no intention at this stage of building up a large staff within the Bank to administer exchange control. Neither Bank nor Treasury wanted to follow the German example, where a huge bureaucracy (believed to employ as many as 20,000 people) had grown up around the complex system of regulations, and it was felt preferable here to begin with a relatively simple system which could be tightened up as experience was gained.

During the last months before war broke out the Bank was busy not only in framing the first batch of regulations but with its own internal arrangements for their physical implementation. Certain members of the

---

* Siepmann, Harry Arthur, 1889–1963. Entered Bank 1926 as Adviser to the Governors; Executive Director, Bank of England, 1945–54.

Permanent Male Staff working in various 'Cash Side' Offices – principally the Chief Cashier's Office, the Trade and Payments Section, Branch Banks Office and the Bullion Office – who were considered to be 'suitable men and to have the right kind of experience' were earmarked to move into the Foreign Exchange Section and form the nucleus of the new operation. This Section existed until the outbreak of war as a more or less self-contained unit within the Chief Cashier's Office, with an Assistant to the Chief Cashier (who signed all work arising in the Section), two Principals, and a staff of twenty-six divided almost equally into dealers, foreign exchange routine and gold routine. In addition the Section had its own typists and filists.

The chief function of the Section was to carry out gold and foreign exchange transactions – the latter in collaboration with the Bullion Office – either arising out of the management of the EEA on behalf of the Treasury or initiated by or on behalf of central banks and other customers. It was the focal point in the Bank for all matters concerning the London market in foreign exchange and gold, relying on an extensive network of information both internal and external, and it was also closely in touch with foreign markets. As the summer of 1939 progressed the Section was abnormally busy with the task of intervention and the shipment of national gold reserves to places of safety. It was envisaged that the Section would, after the outbreak of war, continue to carry out gold and foreign exchange transactions on behalf of customers, as far as regulations permitted, and also operate for the country's gold and foreign exchange resources. The same system and books of account would be used; the EEA, currently concerned with only a proportion of the country's reserves, would take over responsibility for them all (including some £280m. of gold still held by the Issue Department, leaving only a nominal amount in the currency backing). In order to cope with the vast increase of work that this would imply, a number of London banks were nominated to act as Authorised Dealers in foreign exchange, and six bullion brokers were appointed Authorised Dealers in gold.[5]

The Principal of the Foreign Exchange Section at this date was George (later Sir George) Bolton,* a man of vast experience in the foreign exchange market and also of considerable vision. It had been clear to him for some time that the foreign exchange market would have to close down immediately war broke out, and further, that, in order to 'maintain peace in the Market, it would be necessary to eliminate [the foreign exchange brokers] as a body'. There were altogether about 120 of these brokers including partners and staff, each with his own nexus of connections and

---

* Bolton, Sir George L.F., KCMG (1950), 1900–82. Entered Bank to assist in management of EEA, 1933; Adviser, 1941–8; Executive Director, 1948–57; Director, 1957–68.

loyalties with the foreign departments of the banks in the market: Bolton feared that, if they were deprived of their livelihood and left with no occupation, 'they would become a breeding ground for discontent and criticism' and might well affect the co-operation of the banks.

Bolton accordingly approached J.K. Jones, chairman of the Foreign Exchange Brokers' Association, and told him in strict confidence of the general plans for exchange control in the case of war, and of his own views about the closure of the market. Jones provided him with a list of all the brokers and they went through it together, picking out likely candidates for positions in the Bank, based on a 'mixture of character and ability'. About seventy-five were selected. Some weeks later Bolton discussed another plan with Jones, which was that the Bank might take over certain brokers' offices for decentralisation purposes, should bombs damage the Bank. The grounds on which these were chosen were the Post Office telephone exchange with which they were connected, the quality and spread of their system of private lines to the banks, and the existence of a substantial building and/or adequate ARP.[6]

By this time the Bank had roughed out an administrative plan for Exchange Control and had split up the Department into a number of Offices and Sections. An attempt had been made to define the functions and responsibility of each Office; the Bank staff likely to be available had been provisionally allotted among these various Offices but it was accepted that Temporary Clerks, brought in from outside, would also have to be employed in responsible positions.

An Emergency Staff Committee was already established under the chairmanship of Edward Holland-Martin, and was consulted from an early stage. It was agreed that these temporary assistants should be graded into three categories according to knowledge and experience, paid respectively £400 p.a., £700 p.a. and £1,000 p.a. upwards. During August, Jones called a meeting of his Association to advise brokers that in the event of war their livelihood would be endangered, but that the Bank of England might well be prepared to engage a number on a temporary basis. He was in a difficult position: he was besieged with applicants in person and by letter, from men growing more desperate by the day as they had to accept the unpalatable truth that the exchange would indeed close down. Many of the brokers, particularly the partners, were very highly paid and committed to a wealthy life style: even those who were ultimately taken on by the Bank were in almost all cases offered salaries, on the scales referred to, which were far lower than they had been receiving.

The Sub-Offices project ultimately gave rise to a good deal of misunderstanding. Bolton was quite clear on the point that it was not a question of keeping a few favoured firms of brokers in existence – they were being taken over for a definite purpose associated with the possibility of air raids and to relieve pressure on the Bank's dealing boards, although this did not preclude the Bank from using them for exchange control work if necessary, even if the bombs did not materialise. However the brokers whose offices were retained in this connection undoubtedly did believe that their business and goodwill was going to be kept alive. Each Sub-Office was left under the control of a partner of the original firm, paid £700 per year; four were taken over quickly at the beginning of the war (later reduced to two by amalgamation), which led to considerable friction with the partners of other firms who thought that their offices might be required. Much later in the war, after the death of Jones, who himself came into the Bank, these resentments came to a head when brokers who always somehow expected that 'things would be put right later' realised that there was to be no question of any substantial salary increases or compensation. But such problems lay in the future, and in any case had no effect on the work of the Control which could certainly not have operated so smoothly or efficiently without the expertise and loyalty of the large body of men who came in from outside. These included commodity brokers as well as foreign exchange men, and a few members of the Stock Exchange.[7]

To rehearse all the financial regulations imposed as a result of the war is impossible here, and there are in any case many internal and external accounts available, covering both their general scope and particular aspects.[8] However a brief résumé of the more important restrictions will help to give an idea of the complexity of rules with which the Bank had to deal.

The first regulations, relating to the registration and acquisition of various securities marketable outside the UK, were brought in on 25 August 1939. On 3 September a further batch of instructions was issued involving:

Control over dealings in all currencies
The requisitioning of gold and balances in specified ('hard') currencies in the hands of residents and an obligation to surrender any acquired in the future
Control of the export of British and foreign bank notes and securities
Control over the crediting of non-resident accounts by residents
Control over credits and of the granting of overdrafts to non-residents

The chief effect of these initial regulations was to put an immediate stop to capital transfers by residents and to bring exchange speculation to an end. The Treasury, acting through the Bank, became the ultimate dealer in gold and all hard currencies – American and Canadian dollars and other currencies of which Britain was, or was likely to become, short – at rates which were officially fixed and maintained.

While day to day administration of the enforcement of these regulations was delegated by the Treasury to the Bank, high level policy and administrative decisions were taken by the Exchange Control Committee (ECC), which was set up in September 1939. It met weekly at the Bank (which provided the chairman and secretary) and was composed of representatives of both Bank and Treasury and one representative of the commercial banks. The latter came from the Foreign Exchange Committee (FEC), a separate body which comprised the clearers and other major banks engaged in foreign banking activities, and which had been formed in 1931 to oversee restrictions on currency speculation when Britain left the gold standard. The ECC without the FEC member also met weekly at the Bank to deal with particular aspects of policy and special cases; during these sessions the Committee was referred to as the Exchange Control Treasury Committee but it was not regarded as a separate, formally constituted committee.[9]

The organisation of the Offices of the Control which had been mapped out before the war by Bolton in collaboration with Cobbold and Cyril Hawker (Deputy Principal of the Foreign Exchange Section), was put into action immediately war broke out. The new Control remained, as the Foreign Exchange Section had been, within the Cashier's Department, rather than being granted independent departmental status. There was at this time a distinct feeling among the senior officials of the Bank that exchange control was a temporary measure which would disappear with the ending of the war: as Siepmann put it some years later: 'Exchange Control is thought of as an accrescence, or kind of fungus which one day will be lopped off'[10] (a view to which he personally did not subscribe). Even when those expectations faded there remained a distaste for the whole operation, as an intrusive activity all too likely to tarnish the image of the Bank in the eyes of the City and of the public. This attitude was undoubtedly partly responsible for the way the subject of its administration was approached during the war and for some time after it.

Those picked to staff the Control assembled in the Bank on Sunday 3 September (after a false air raid alarm) for a final run-through. A public enquiry counter was set up on the fourth floor, but nobody had foreseen the huge flood of applicants for information which besieged it immediately it opened for business the following morning. Stockbrokers, solicitors and ordinary members of the public swarmed in, crowding the small office sometimes thirty or more at a time, all anxious, some belligerent. It was an entirely new experience for Bank staff, few of whom apart from the senior members of the Discount Office ever came into contact with the outside world during working hours unless to cash or receive cheques in the hushed atmosphere of the Drawing Office. After the initial shock, many of them, particularly the younger ones, came to enjoy it.

The men in charge of each Section of the Control were fully occupied in dealing with the technical direction of their groups, and as Sub-Sections came to be formed, the most experienced or otherwise suitable men available were put in charge of them irrespective of rank or status. This, too, was highly unusual in the rigidly stratified Bank hierarchy. For once seniority gave way to capability, and many of the younger men in the Control were swift to seize the opportunities which came their way. In the words of one of them:

> Suddenly everyone was on our doorstep with questions of bewildering complexity. The rule-book was sketchy and of precedent there was none. We made up rules as we went along and we made them fast under the pressure of insistent enquiry and the threat of unjustified loss for the enquirer. To those in the Bank who liked the challenge, and that was most of us, the exchange control was highly stimulating. Many of us excelled ourselves, even over-reached ourselves, as never before. Long hours meant nothing in such a vibrant community which for some years worked and slept in Threadneedle Street. As the machine necessarily expanded with new offices being created, promotions and appointments came thick and fast and they caused some uneasiness, if not jealousy.[11]

Thirty of the seventy extra men allotted to Exchange Control at the outbreak of war were added to the Foreign Exchange Section's existing staff to form the Dealing, Books and Statements, Foreign Exchange and Gold Sections of what was almost immediately promoted from a Section to the Foreign Exchange Office in Cashier's Department.[12] By the time this Office was created, in November 1939, the Control comprised fairly well-defined Sections: detailed descriptions of the work of each group and of the Offices which most of them became, are extant in the Bank's archives and it must suffice here to give a brief outline of the scope of their activities.

The Sections of the Foreign Exchange Office just referred to (which in 1941 were together designated the Dealing and Accounts Office – see below) were at the beginning of the war overwhelmed with work. The original wartime staff of sixty was rapidly augmented until by April 1940 there were around 100 people carrying out between 400 and 600 transactions a day. A vast amount of work was generated by the rupture of banking relationships with the continent, leaving over 1,000 forward contracts outstanding in the books of the Bank. The Gold Section had a period of intense activity following the German invasion of France and the Netherlands, when gold was shipped to New York and Ottawa for safety on all available naval vessels and liners; this included both customers' gold and that belonging to the EEA which went to the United Kingdom Security Deposit in Montreal, as described below, and a total of some £210m. had left by the end of 1940. In 1941 the Bank took over the responsibility for the sale and purchase of silver, including the marketing of Indian silver previously carried out by the India Office. Other new undertakings for the Bank were extensive dealing in foreign notes and coin, and, later, the provision of foreign notes, under conditions of the utmost secrecy, for various military operations.*

The Bank's involvement in the control of securities began before the outbreak of war. As mentioned above, the first Treasury Order relating to the control of securities was made on 25 August. This prohibited all UK owners of any security payable or optionally payable in certain specified currencies from dealing with them in any manner without the prior permission of the Treasury (or, in practice, of the Bank as agents of the Treasury). In addition, owners were required to make a return of all such securities within one month. The Securities Registration Office was established on 28 August, under the supervision of the Bank's Auditor, A.S. Craig; altogether well over a million registration forms were received, relating to some 2,000 securities and arriving at the Bank literally by the truck-load. Many of the titles of the securities were shown inaccurately on the documents, and sorting them out proved to be like solving a 'super jig-saw puzzle'. The Office was also responsible for the administration of the Acquisition of Securities Order, under which owners of the securities specified in it were required to surrender them against payment of the sterling equivalent of their market value on the date of the Order. Some of the securities (or the proceeds of their sale) were given outright to the government or alternatively lent interest-free for the duration of the war. Sums ranged from touchingly small amounts ('...my sister and I have been discussing what we can do towards the War Effort...') to substantial gifts such as the £50,000 donated by an Indian Prince from the sale of New York Central Railroad stock. He asked for the money to be sent to the Ministry of Aircraft Production for the purchase of 'a flight of Spitfires'.[13]

General Regulations, whose name was shortly switched to Regulations General, was and remained one of the largest Sections. The introduction

* See chapter 4, pp. 132–3.

of control into such a highly industrialised and trade-oriented country and international financial centre as the United Kingdom naturally gave rise to innumerable problems, and the initial task faced by the Control was answering a vast number of enquiries about the general effects of the regulations. Regulations General handled these plus applications to make payments abroad in foreign currency and sterling, to export bank notes, foreign currency securities or gold, and for exemption from the obligation to surrender specified currencies and gold. The Section was divided into two main parts, one dealing with correspondence and one with forms, and these parts again subdivided to provide a fair amount of specialisation. The original staff consisted mainly of men from different Offices of the Cashier's Department who had some previous experience of foreign exchange or of the Overseas and Foreign Department as it then was. They were supplemented by Temporary Clerks from the collapsed Foreign Exchange Market whose experience was of particular value in this Office. The pressure of work was inordinately heavy from the start and the staff had to be steadily augmented not only by the Temporary Clerks but by men drawn from elsewhere in the Bank, particularly the Accountant's Department. But as the staff increased, so did the regulations as the loopholes in the original provisions were one by one pulled tighter. The technical nature of this aspect of the work called for a high degree of intelligence and initiative and it became necessary to build up a team of technicians with considerable weight at the top.[14]

The function of the Trade Control and Investigations Section was, broadly speaking, to supervise exchange control. The General Section maintained liaison with HM Customs for imports and scrutinised applications passed by the authorised banks, and was also responsible for seeing that currency proceeds of authorised sales of foreign securities were duly received. The Investigations Section dealt with enquiries which resulted from submissions by the Censorship, usually in the form of photostat copies of suspect letters or documents. When breaches of the regulations were detected, it was obviously necessary to pursue the offender. If the case was considered to be likely to end in prosecution, the Control passed the results of its investigations to the Treasury, who proceeded from there (with Bank personnel, if necessary, in court as witnesses) but the greater part of the efforts of the Section was directed to educating the public. It was the investigations aspect of the work of exchange control which caused especial heart-searching on the part of the Bank as being very much contrary to its normal ethos and functions, and the Principal confessed to the 'haunting thought that the investigation side of the work should have been undertaken by some outside body'.[15]

Acceptance Credits was one of the smaller Offices of the Control: its full complement throughout the war was never more than ten. Its function was the authorisation of all commercial credits, guarantees and overdrafts under which a resident incurred a direct or contingent liability to make payment in foreign currency or transfer sterling to a non-resident account. Acceptance Credits also dealt with the authorisation of bail bonds for ships, and names appearing on all these applications were checked with the Ministry of Economic Warfare's Black List of specified persons and Grey List of suspected persons. These lists were kept in the form of a card index and in 1942 the Office became a central enquiry bureau for enquiries of this nature which could be referred to it by other parts of the Control. (By 1944 there were 22,000 names on the index, which was finally abolished at the end of the following year.)[16]

Two other pre-war Offices were immediately brought into the orbit of Exchange Control. The Overseas and Foreign Department* provided an intelligence service to the Bank generally regarding economic, financial and monetary conditions throughout the world, and was naturally drawn into advising on the wider aspects of exchange control and payments agreements, working closely with the Advisers. Parts of the Economics and Statistics Sections of the Secretary's Office were seconded at the outbreak of war to form the Statistics Office within the Control. This rapidly became engaged on work relating to exchange control on behalf of both the Bank and the Treasury. It compiled a statistical commentary on the gold, foreign exchange and restricted security assets of the Sterling Area which together with other material available enabled it to analyse the payments made outside the Area as a whole and by each of its members, and to forecast the balance of payments of the Area with the rest of the world. These forecasts were of vital importance in the formulation of exchange policy.

The early growth of the Control along these broad lines was astonishingly rapid and gave rise to staff problems which were quite outside the Bank's experience and which were intensified by the constant departure of the younger men for the Forces and the removal of the Accountant's Department to Hampshire. The Principals and all the staff were so overwhelmed by the pressure of events and the volume of work that no-one could be spared at first to attend to such matters as registering the new Temporary Clerks with the Establishment Department, dealing with premises matters, and obtaining stores, furniture and necessary equipment. The Staff Director, Holland-Martin, soon realised that the situation was getting out of control and on Monday,

* For an account of the history and functions of this Department see chapter 9.

18 September he directed an Assistant Principal working in the Drawing
Office, A.E.G. Payton, to report to Bolton, Principal of the Foreign
Exchange Office, and take over the staff and all matters connected with
stores and equipment. He was also authorised to have direct access to the
Staff Director and report to him each day. Payton started a new Section,
which he named the Staff Register because of his long association with
the Drawing Office where the section dealing with staff matters had that
name. (In most Offices it was known as the Staff Post.)

The Staff Register swiftly became involved in the recruitment of new
personnel to the Bank's staff – an inevitable task because the work of the
Control was unlike any previously undertaken by the Bank and it was
obviously essential for applicants to be interviewed by someone able to
assess whether their experience and temperament were suitable. The few
senior members of the Permanent Staff who had any previous experience
of staff administration were all more than fully occupied on the technical
organisation of the Control.[17]

The Foreign Exchange Filing Section had been run by two Senior
Women Clerks before the war, and extra women were added to the
Control from an early date. The first batch started clerical duties in the
Staff Register on 2 October 1939; on the same day a Section was formed
to index all the applications for currency and sterling transfer forms
submitted to the Control, and this was also staffed by women. A Principal
(Woman) Clerk, as the title then existed, was allocated to the Control by
the Controller of Women Clerks on 18 December and soon most of the
indexing and virtually all the sorting and distributive duties were carried
out by women whose sphere of usefulness and influence was steadily
extended throughout the war.[18]

It had always been the intention of those planning the Control that the
Bank's Branches should play a part and in November representatives
from the Manchester, Birmingham, Leeds, Liverpool, Bristol and
Newcastle Branches spent a minimum of a week at Head Office to
familiarise themselves with the regulations. Exchange Control sections
were set up in those centres on 11 December 1939 and work continued in
all of them throughout the war, staff attending Head Office for instruction
when necessary.

As the war progressed, an edifice of further regulations began to arise
on the foundations of the early measures, and the instructions, definitions
and arrangements essential to their full enforcement were continually
refined. There was a good deal of press criticism in the early months on
the subject of various loopholes and 'the undue leniency with which
exchange regulations have been devised and enforced'; this came as no

surprise to the Bank where it had always been accepted that imperfections were inevitable. In December 1939 the Deputy Governor, Catterns, wrote to Sir James Taylor,* Governor of the Reserve Bank of India:

> 'Control' of an international currency system, operating over a vast area, can not and should not mean quite the same thing as the hideous, but technically admirable, juggernaut which the Germans, in their need, contrived and invented. Moreover, if our conception were the same as theirs, we should be wasting one of our greatest assets – the loyalty and adaptability of those who, instead of being the passive victims of a machine, are prepared to co-operate with us and make it work. We are all very conscious of the fact that our so-called 'control' is neither logical or complete, and we are constantly being criticised for permitting anomalies. But I rather think that I am content to plead guilty and still try and maintain some semblance of economic life instead of aiming at a mechanised efficiency...[19]

Despite these words, there was one particular area about which the Bank had felt considerable anxiety since well before the war. The Treasury had refused to agree to bring in any control over the proceeds of exports, maintaining this attitude until it was clear that sterling was being lost as a result of it. At the end of the year it accepted that exports would have to come under control regulations, and in January 1940 the Export Permits Section was set up in the Bank. The actual work of supervision began in March, when a limited control was introduced which required payment within six months, in certain currencies, for particular goods, all of which were potentially useful dollar earners. On 13 May the Securities Dealing and Control Office was started, when new regulations were brought in to prevent the sale in the United Kingdom of securities looted by the enemy from occupied territories; this proved intricate work which called for close collaboration with the Stock Exchange. At the end of the same month, the Foreign Exchange Office was amalgamated with the Securities Registration and Vesting Office to form the Exchange Control Office.[20]

Further action was taken in the next few months to prevent continued leakage and eventually all but the smallest loopholes were successfully closed. The greater part of the tightening up regulations was imposed well within the first year of the war, the last fundamental changes being those of 17 July 1940 dealing with special accounts and blocked sterling. (It was at this juncture that the term 'Sterling Area' was officially used for the first time.)

---

* Taylor, Sir James B., KCIE (1939), 1891–1943. Governor, Reserve Bank of India, 1937–43.

Early in 1940, when plans were being made in case it proved necessary to evacuate further parts of the Bank, consideration had been given to decentralising the Control in the event of 'a general breakdown of communications'. The Treasury and the clearing banks were consulted, the latter via the Foreign Exchange Committee, and a plan eventually agreed under which the Control would be split up, if necessary, into independent regional units co-ordinated from a location outside London. The centres were chosen to conform to the National Civil Defence plan for dividing the country into twelve regions each under a Commissioner. Regional Controls would be established at the Branches already carrying out exchange control work and also at Cardiff, Nottingham, Glasgow and Belfast; teams of clerks proficient in all aspects of the regulations would be sent to each from Threadneedle Street. A branch of a clearing bank was nominated in each area to provide a Superintendent, which at once gave rise to discontent. Chairmen of several of the banks which had not been selected sought interviews with Catterns to ask for reconsideration on the grounds that their own bank would be 'more appropriate'. None of these applications was successful.[21]

Bolton decided to anticipate the decentralisation plan (which was destined not to be implemented in any other respect) by starting an Area Control at one selected centre. He thought this should be Glasgow, because as he noted on 12 June, 'Scotland is badly served already from the point of view of exchange control'. A few days later a Principal from Exchange Control went to Glasgow with a member of the Works Department and, having made contact with the Royal Bank of Scotland, inspected various premises suggested by the bank's factors, or estate agents. They encountered considerable difficulty in finding office space, because most that they saw was too small, in too poor a state of repair, too high up in buildings without lifts or with inadequate ARP to conform with what the Bank felt was acceptable. The Bank was also in competition with various other firms and institutions from London who were searching for offices in Glasgow for similar reasons. Suitable offices were eventually found, however, although split between two buildings, and the Bank took leases on accommodation at 145 St Vincent Street and in the North British and Mercantile Insurance Company's building almost opposite. The two men also visited a large number of hotels in the city with a view of billeting Bank staff, and eventually decided on the Beresford in Sauchiehall Street as the best of what was plainly considered a poorish range of possibilities.

An advance party led by Hawker travelled to Glasgow by the night train on Sunday, 23 June and the Glasgow Control opened for business on 29 June. The Royal Bank of Scotland was appointed as an Agent for the Bank, which again prompted grumbling by competitors until a successful appeal was made by Cobbold for 'all rivalries to be set aside' in the national interest. Principal of the new Control was W.P. Waller, who soon discovered that 'the observance of the Defence (Finance) Regulations in Scotland left much to be desired'. The first objective was to start the education of the Joint Stock banks, which, as Waller observed, involved 'a certain amount of discretion in order to overcome the somewhat sceptical curiosity with which the arrival of the Bank of England in Scotland was viewed locally'. The Bank's contacts with the managers and other local officials soon became harmonious, and Waller and his team turned their attention to spreading abroad in the rest of Scotland the knowledge that the Control's Office had been opened for the convenience of bankers and others in the region and 'not merely – as some people thought – for their correction'. The 'others' included the legal profession (in many cases a solicitor in a country town acted as Agent of a local bank), and both brokers and solicitors were found by Waller to be 'particularly ill-informed and in some cases recalcitrant' when dealing with securities forming part of decreased estates. He set out on a tour of all the local Stock Exchanges to explain the responsibilities and answer members' questions. The lawyers proved more difficult, and the profession was much fragmented into different societies such as Writers to the Signet, Solicitors to the Supreme Court and many others. However the tact and determination of the Principal eventually ensured friendly and useful co-operation with the majority, helped by contact with the lawyers' General Council.

At the end of September 1940 Northern Ireland was added to the area for which the Glasgow Office was responsible, and visits were made to Belfast every two weeks or so, by air whenever possible. Special problems were encountered because all except one of the Northern Irish banks had branches in Eire: in three cases only the Head Offices were north of the border, and one bank had no office in Belfast although there were six branches in other parts of Northern Ireland. Thus the majority were subject to two entirely different controls. At first all liaison with the Control authorities in Dublin was via Threadneedle Street and Whitehall for 'political and diplomatic reasons', but after the autumn of 1941 it was arranged for Waller to meet directly with officials of the Department of Finance in Dublin, as well as the representatives of the chief officers of the various banks in Eire. This made for much smoother working.[22]

Like the other locations described in chapter 1, the Glasgow Control kept in almost daily contact with Threadneedle Street by post, telephone and visits in both directions. Another group of Bank personnel, not directly part of the Control but whose movements were dictated by its existence, formed a unit very much further away from home, where communication was more difficult. This was the United Kingdom Security Deposit in Montreal, Canada. In June 1940, following the invasion of France, it was decided by the Treasury and the Bank that private holdings of gold and negotiable foreign securities should be shipped abroad for safe custody and to be more readily available to pay for desperately needed war supplies or to act as security against a dollar loan. The first 448 boxes were taken to Scotland and left the United Kingdom on 23 June in the cruiser HMS *Emerald* in the charge of A.S. Craig and three other members of Bank staff. The *Emerald* was escorted by the destroyer *Cossack*: the Atlantic was extremely rough and there were large numbers of U-boats about, but they arrived safely in Halifax on 1 July. There they boarded a special train for the 700-mile journey to Montreal, where office space had been reserved for them and their cargo in a vault in the third basement of the Sun Life Assurance Co. building. This was soon threatened by flooding and was judged too insecure, so an inner vault, 80 feet by 75 feet, with ceilings and walls of steel and concrete, a massive steel door and remote microphone control, was built in four weeks by men working continuously day and night.

Further shipments of gold and securities followed, one in the charge of Sir Otto Niemeyer who visited Canada for a short period to oversee the arrangements. Early in August the boxes – between two and three thousand of them – which had been under the temporary guard of Royal Canadian Mounted Police, were moved by night to their new home. The securities then had to be verified, classified and recorded in a card index system, during which activity over 6,000 'Query Slips' were despatched to England drawing attention to various discrepancies (and over seventy miles of tape was used to tie up the parcels of securities). The total value at this time was about £2,000m.; about one third of this was gold, mostly in the form of bullion although at one period in the Deposit's existence it held thousands of sacks of coin issued by countries around the world.

On 26 October 1940 the first vesting order after the Deposit's establishment in Canada was made. Under this all holdings of certain Canadian securities belonging to residents of the United Kingdom were acquired by the Treasury, and three further orders, covering American securities, were made before the end of the year. The transfer of many thousands of holdings to the account of the Treasury in one continent and the payment for them as promptly as possible in another involved a complex system of working. To avoid heavy cable costs a special code was prepared, and this worked well in practice with the staff finding they were able to deal with as many as a thousand holdings a day. Craig and the other members of the Bank's staff remained in Canada for the whole of the five year existence of the UKSD; the work connected with the Deposit also required a staff of about 100 recruited locally in Canada plus twenty-eight in London.[23]

By November 1940 it was clear to Siepmann that the departmental administration of the Control within the Bank would have to be reconsidered, for it was growing so swiftly that it was in danger of getting out of hand. With the agreement of the Chief Cashier his Deputy, E.N. Dalton, was accordingly released from his current work in order to report to the Governors as to how this new and unwieldy function should best be positioned 'as an integral part of the Bank's departmental organisation'. It was also explicitly stated that his report should take into account the Overseas and Foreign Department and the Trade and Payments Section of the Chief Cashier's Office.

By this date the staff of the Exchange Control Office numbered approximately 1,200 and, as Dalton pointed out in his report, dated 16 December 1940, the various activities of the Control, although directed to the same end, 'are widely different and would be better conducted by appropriate Offices, each under a Principal'. What he saw as the 'cleanest solution' was the creation of a group of Offices in the Cashier's Department under the general heading of Exchange Control.

The potential argument that exchange control was a specialist activity which had no real connection with the form of banking carried out by the Chief Cashier's Department, Dalton forestalled by noting that the Chief Cashier's interests as a banker were 'deeply affected by the activities of the Exchange Control, not only in their effect upon the figures with which he is concerned, the accounts in the Drawing Office and the accounts upon which he signs, but upon Markets... The absorption of the new growth into a department whose general organisation is well established and has been well tried should prove of mutual benefit.'

As for the Overseas and Foreign Department, Dalton viewed that 'as a Corporate Adviser': he saw no benefit in making any radical changes but recommended the definition and co-ordination of the duties of certain Sections of the Exchange Control Office, which made use of the Department, 'in order to avoid overlapping and the supply of different sets of figures by the Bank in connection with the same subject'. The Trade and Payments Section had its roots – the negotiation of agreements with foreign countries – in the Exchange Control Office but its work came to fruition in the working of the agreements in the Cashier's

Department. Dalton felt it immaterial from the point of view of efficiency whether the Section was in the CCO or in EC, but decided on balance it might be more expedient to continue to include it in the former.

Dalton cited what he considered the pre-eminent reason for the changes he proposed: the fact that it had been found necessary for the heads of Sections to hold a weekly meeting to discuss problems. 'Such a procedure should not be necessary in a properly organised Department where decisions would be obtained from the Head of Department who would, if he thought it necessary, seek the guidance of an Adviser or refer to a Governor or Executive Director.' The current Principal of Exchange Control, Bolton, he thought was 'unsuited by temperament and training to fit into a departmental organisation, an opinion which I am glad to feel may be regarded by all concerned, including himself, as a compliment rather than adverse criticism'.

What Dalton now proposed was the creation of a group of Offices in the Cashier's Department under the general heading of Exchange Control and the appointment of a Deputy, Assistants and Assistants to the, Chief Cashier (Exchange Control). Secondly, he recommended the maintenance of the Overseas and Foreign Department in its present form for the moment, and thirdly the continuance of the Trade and Payments Section of the Chief Cashier's Office and the appointment of its Principal to be an Assistant, or Assistant to the, Chief Cashier. 'The abilities of the existing Principal of Exchange Control would doubtless have fuller and even more profitable scope if he were appointed to some extra-departmental position in connection with the Exchange Control.'

The Governors accepted this report with the exception of the recommendation on the subject of the Overseas and Foreign Department. The other proposals were all put into practice with effect from 3 March, 1941, on which date the Cashier's Department (Exchange Control) officially came into being. It comprised the following Offices:

| | |
|---|---|
| Dealing and Accounts | Statistics* |
| Regulations General | Glasgow |
| Export Permits | Securities Regulations (and Vesting) |
| Trade Control and Investigation | including UKSD |
| Securities Dealings Control | Staff register |

The Overseas and Foreign Department was also to be absorbed into the Cashier's Department (Exchange Control), with the title of the Overseas and Foreign Office. Bolton, the former Principal of the

* The Statistics Office returned to the Secretary's Department in 1942.

Plate 3.1    The Exchange Control Dealing Room, probably late 1941. F.L.S. Barnes is second from the left; Jack Lee fourth from left; D.M. Stokes third from right; C.C. Lockitt second from right

Exchange Control Office, was appointed Adviser. At the same time a small internal committee, the Defence (Finance) Regulations Committee,* was created by the Governors to supervise the future policy and administration of the Control. Cobbold and Siepmann were Chairman and Deputy Chairman, and the other members were Henry Clay, George Bolton and a Deputy Chief Cashier.[24]

Six months later, on 1 September, the Filing Section of 144 women, which dealt with the 44,000 Control files raised by this date (plus 2 million forms, 2·5 million other documents and 300,000 index cards) but had previously been separate from the Control proper, was amalgamated with it and the staff of the Control reached its wartime peak of 1,330.[25] From this point on numbers declined; the outlines of the wartime control had been firmly drawn and subsequent alterations and amendments were largely concerned with administrative questions rather than the framing of any new or complex legislation requiring an increase in staff numbers.

The question of what controls, if any, would be necessary or desirable

* The Committee's title became the Exchange Control Offices Committee in April 1948, the Exchange Control and Overseas Committee in March 1949 and the Overseas Committee in April 1957.

after the war was over was never far from the minds of those concerned
with the formulation of exchange control policy, and this topic formed
the chief focus of the so-called 'Post-war Committee', a small ad hoc
committee which was set up in 1942 by Governor Norman to study all
aspects of Britain's post-war exchange policy. A precis of its findings
written by Leslie (later Lord) O'Brien* – a future Governor of the Bank
who had previously served as the Assistant Secretary of the League
Loans Committee† – noted:

> They [i.e. the Committee] regard a conscious return to the international
> monetary chaos of 1918/39 or to a system similar to that which functioned
> in the 19th century as alike impossible, and *envisage a continuation and even
> extension of control* not merely as a pis aller to be dropped as soon as
> conditions improve but as a deliberate and constructive policy calculated to
> prevent a recurrence of the mass capital movements of the pre-war period
> and to build up a system which will fit into a world in which exchange
> control will have become the almost universal rule.[26]

In the light of the very carefully considered findings of the Committee
Cobbold, who chaired the regular Exchange Control Committees,
decided that the time was ripe for what he called a 'sit-down' review of
Exchange Control practice. 'We have been on much the same lines for
two years now', he minuted to the Governors in July 1942, 'and although
we are always revising and modifying I do not think we should disregard
the possibility that more fundamental changes may now be desirable than
can appear in the ordinary run of administration'. He preferred to stand
aside from such an examination himself, and suggested Dallas Bernard as
chairman, with Isaac (later Sir Isaac) Pitman,‡ who was a non-executive
director, Sir Kenneth Peppiatt§ and Dalton to represent Exchange
Control. O'Brien was chosen as Secretary.[27]

This was one of the most far-reaching of the committees which
examined exchange control practice. It was not the first: Laverack, the
Inspector of Offices and Branches, had embarked in May 1941 on a review
of each Office with the purpose, *inter alia*, of making recommendations as
to the number of staff required to cope with existing conditions. (These

---

\* O'Brien, Baron (1973) of Lothbury, Leslie Kenneth O'Brien, GBE, PC, 1908–. Entered
Bank of England, 1927; Deputy Chief Cashier, 1951–5; Chief Cashier, 1955–62;
Executive Director, 1962–4; Deputy Governor, 1964–6; Governor, 1966–73.

† Constituted in 1932 to protect the rights of bondholders of loans made under the
auspices of the League of Nations to six eastern European states to restore their financial
stability after the First World War. Four had defaulted in the service of their loans by
early 1932.

‡ Pitman, Sir Isaac James, KBE (1961), 1901–85. Chairman of Sir Isaac Pitman & Sons
Ltd, 1934–66. Director of Bank of England, 1941–5.

§ Peppiatt, Sir K.O., see note p. 224.

basic staff figures were subsequently reviewed at intervals and amended as conditions changed during the war.)[28] Laverack had only just finished his survey when the new one began with much wider terms of reference:

> To review existing exchange control practice and consider whether, subject to the overriding necessity of conserving our exchange resources for the war effort, any changes should be introduced, bearing particularly in mind –
>
> (a) the need to economise in man-power dealing directly or indirectly with exchange control, both in the Bank and elsewhere;
>
> (b) the present restricted and controlled basis of world trade and exchange movements;
>
> (c) the desirability of moving towards a system more suited to post-war conditions.

The Committee set to work immediately and continued to hear evidence for the rest of the year. It interviewed those in charge of policy, including Cobbold, Hawker and Siepmann, as well as listening to each Principal in the Control give an outline of the work of his Office, after which he was subjected to rigorous questioning on all its aspects. Three interim reports were produced, in September, October and December 1942, each dealing with specified Offices and suggesting various modifications of practice, many of which echoed the conclusions of Laverack as to the desirability of paring down the number of documents kept and saving both paper (vitally important at this stage of the war) and manpower. For example, work connected with the forms B and D which had to be completed by buyers and sellers of securities, in order to reveal whether any person resident outside the Sterling Area had any interest in the security before or after the transaction, took 126 man-hours a day and nearly 2 million sheets of paper annually. Yet over 90 per cent of all transactions on the Stock Exchange were between residents and the Committee felt the changes in this area were most desirable. There were a number of other such recommendations, but the Committee made no fundamental criticism of the system 'which appears to be well adapted to the special conditions resulting from war and to be administered efficiently'. They were particularly impressed by the way in which policy and practice, and the work of each Office within the Control, were continually under review by the Defence (Finance) Regulations Committee and modified or extended where necessary. As far as it was possible to foresee what would happen after the war, the Committee visualised an expansion of overseas trade and a revival of British financing of overseas development. Efforts were already under way to remove or modify the present restrictions on the transfer of sterling between countries outside the

Sterling Area, and moves were being made to unify the many types of non-resident sterling into one 'external' sterling.

In the light of these developments the Committee felt that it was vital that control should be 'as little irksome and obtrusive as possible to all but the deliberate evader'. This was important at the time, but would become more so after the war, when with the removal of other restrictions, those relating to exchange control would be less readily tolerated. Irksomeness was partly the result of excessive formality and undue delay – the Committee found some examples of both and recommended changes of practice but in general there was 'little of either of these evils in the control at the present time'. Much in fact had been done to avoid them by decentralising the control through the banks, and the Committee noted approvingly the 'remarkable infrequency of errors by the banks or improper conduct by traders or others to whom concessions had been made'. Finally the clarity of the evidence given (which ran to many hundreds of pages) 'bears impressive testimony to thorough knowledge of intricate subjects'.

Four months after this final report the Deputy Governor was able to tell the Committee of Treasury that the Defence (Finance) Regulations Committee had concurred with the recommendations contained in it and with the approval of the Governors had taken action where necessary.[29]

From 1942 onwards there were few significant changes in the administration of the Control. As Bernard's Committee found, the machine was well-oiled and in excellent running order; staffing problems became less acute and most of those working in the Control became expert in one area or another. An Exchange Control School was set up early in 1942, under a 'schoolmaster': courses at first lasted four weeks but were later cut down to three, and were initially followed by an examination. The Securities Dealings Control Office was merged with Securities Registration (and Vesting) in January 1942 as a result of Laverack's findings, the chief benefit being economy of staff numbers. In August of the same year the work of the Staff Register Office was decentralised and each Office undertook the bulk of its own staff work, again as a result of recommendations made by Laverack. This brought the work of the Principals of the Control Offices in line with that of Principals of 'Cash Side' Offices outside the control – they made their staff returns directly to the Chief of Establishments and kept their own staff records. A Central Office was created, on the lines of the Chief Cashier's Office, which did much of the work of preparing material for departmental committees and 'promulgating decisions to the offices of the control'.[30]

Plate 3.2    Securities Control Office, Exchange Control, at Roehampton in 1942

The work of many of the Offices of the Control tended to decrease in the second half of the war, although there were sudden flurries of activity occasioned by war developments. For example the Regulations General Office experienced a considerable upsurge of work in 1942 when large contingents of US Forces arrived in the United Kingdom and required special banking and remittance facilities. Individual authority was needed to open many thousands of US registered accounts in their names and to examine the returns supplied by banks of numerous credits made to these accounts other than the holders' pay and allowances. During this year too the Office was much preoccupied with applications for remittances to children – mainly in Canada – who had earlier been evacuated from Britain because of fears of a German invasion. In 1943, however, the work load was considerably reduced, largely because of bulk purchasing by government departments, lease lend, and the greater experience of the banks which allowed them to use their delegated authority more fully. As the war drew to its close, the liberation of the occupied territories involved the RGO in many ways, most importantly the relief of the population of the countries concerned and the development of commercial relations with them. The re-establishment of full banking facilities with Belgium in October 1944 and France in

March 1945 gave rise to numerous enquiries about trade and about the sterling accounts of people resident, or formerly resident in those countries. And as firms prepared to resume their peacetime activities, the Office received an increasing number of applications for expenditure abroad for such things as advertising, the establishment or re-opening of branches or agencies, business travel and holding stocks overseas.

The special problems posed by films, oil, cotton and insurance were all handled by the RGO, who had a section of 'Gimlets' (a Bank term for a researcher who prepares summaries of difficult subjects for submission to higher authority) devoted to enquiries on these topics. By the end of the war each of the four categories was under the individual supervision of a Principal.[31]

The difficulties facing exporters as the war progressed were reflected in the numbers of staff in the Export Permits Office. These reached their peak of forty-six in 1941 when the government export drive of the previous year was having its maximum effect; subsequently numbers dwindled to around thirty by the end of 1943 because of the shortage of raw materials and the increased diversion of manpower from industry to munitions. Lack of shipping, the intensification of the U-boat campaign and the bombing of London and other ports all had their effects and Japan's entry into the war meant the loss of Far Eastern markets. After July 1942 only essential exports were permitted and by the end of the following year nearly three-quarters of our export trade had vanished, sacrificed to the needs of the war effort.[32]

By this date, too, the regulations were better known and understood by the banking and legal fraternities and by the general public. The work of 'educating' the public in the existence and meaning of exchange control was greatly assisted by the keen interest shown in the prosecution of various well-known people, notably Noel Coward, Gracie Fields and George Arliss, for breaches of the regulations. The Principal of the Trade Control and Investigations Office noted in 1942 that 'it is believed that a large number of people after reading these cases appreciated the existence of the regulations for the first time', although as late as the end of 1943 an old lady living in a Welsh village assured the Control that she was exempt from the regulations regarding securities as she had a letter to that effect from the Dollar Securities Committee dated 3 December 1917. The diamond, fur and textile trades were the most troublesome to the Office, but many other types of company came under scrutiny ranging from world-wide groups to one-man firms, and so did individuals from 'keepers of houses of ill-repute to high Church dignitaries'. The Office found that qualified accountants were necessary to assist with company control, and by 1945 was employing four of them. During the war it dealt with 730,000 submissions from HM Customs, of which 43,000 cases were followed up; 500 were forwarded to the Treasury, 117 people were prosecuted and fines amounted to £307,540.[33]

The domestic affairs of the Glasgow Control proceeded smoothly enough for the duration of the war. A few people were recruited locally, mostly women and non-clerical staff, the others being seconded from Threadneedle Street; many of these, like the staff at the other wartime locations, appreciated the unfamiliar benefits of country life, which here included playing golf, visiting the coast and climbing Ben Lomond. During 1942 the arrival of consignments of Russian gold at Scottish ports, for sale in London or shipment on to the United States, involved the Glasgow Control in new duties. A panel of four escorts was formed to accompany the gold on the train to London and Head Office, occasionally having the pleasure of a trip out to a warship on a tender and drinks in the wardroom before superintending the unloading of the gold at the dockside.

Much diversion was provided by a running battle with the Beresford Hotel, many of whose wartime occupants were felt by the Principal to be most unsuitable neighbours for Bank staff. In order to lessen contact with these undesirables he wrested a private sitting room from the management for the use of his flock. He also pounced instantly when he detected any slackening in the standards of food or service, which usually occurred when the hotel was fully occupied. The proprietors (who changed several times during the war) sometimes felt obliged to refer in justification to the discount on the normal hotel rates which had been negotiated by the Bank in 1940.[34]

By the end of the war the staff of the Control numbered 877. It was clear that exchange control in some form or another would continue, but the impossibility of knowing how much and for how long was a major difficulty for those concerned with recruitment policy in the Bank (indeed this continued to be the case until the end of all controls in 1979), as well as giving rise to constant anxiety among the Control staff itself. This was particularly acute among those employed as Temporary Clerks, although the Bank gave them assurances of continued employment for periods varying with age and date of appointment. The immediate effect of the end of the war in Europe was an upsurge of work in many areas, as various transactions which had been in complete abeyance during the war years became once again permissible. More authority was now delegated to the banks – the list of Authorised Dealers was increased in July 1945 to include a number of merchant banks, acceptance houses and

Dominion and eastern banks. Authorised Dealers were further empowered to give permission to open credits for the finance of trade to and
from the United Kingdom and to finance exports from the rest of the
sterling area. Foreign banks with offices in London were allowed to
sanction exchange operations between the UK and their own countries:
measures which made possible the vigorous growth of trade financing
through London which was a notable feature of post-war international
business.[35]

The future of Glasgow was especially problematic at this date. Legal
and political considerations precluded it becoming a Branch,* which it
resembled in its relative autonomy although without the security of
tenure which was enjoyed by Branch staff. Its continuance post-war had
been under discussion since 1943, when Cobbold and Hawker had
agreed with a representative of the Treasury that 'the office would not
cease suddenly the day the Armistice was signed'; nonetheless the
Principal felt distinctly uneasy about its future and gave much time in
1945 to correspondence with Threadneedle Street on the subject. In
November it was finally decided that Glasgow should remain a 'location'
(i.e. not a Branch) but staff would have greater security of tenure than
before. The so-called 'Glasgow Charter' was adopted the following
month, giving staff privileges in accommodation and travel allowances,
which did much to settle the previous unrest. A year later, in November
1946, better and more convenient premises were found at 24 Vincent
Place, in the centre of the city and close to the principal Glasgow banks.[36]

By the autumn of 1945 the plans for returning the securities from
Montreal to the United Kingdom were in operation. In the week
beginning 6 September some 1,200 boxes weighing 75 tons and
containing upwards of 5 million documents and other securities were
brought by warship to Rosyth and delivered to the Bank. Over the
weekend of 15/16 September, fifty representatives of twenty of the larger
banks and 200 Bank of England staff checked about 75 per cent of the
securities, after which they were physically delivered to the 'owner'
banks. The remaining thirty-three banks checked and took delivery of
their securities during the following week.

In addition to checking the securities returned to it as an owner bank,
the Bank of England had also to deal with 60,000 individual holdings
comprising about 250,000 separate pieces of security against which
Security Deposit receipts had been issued during the previous years in
Montreal. The whole of this gigantic task, from packing to redelivery,
was accomplished within a seven week period, eliciting a letter from the

* See chapter 8, The Branches.

Chancellor to the Governor appreciative of the Bank's 'hard work and ingenuity'.[37]

The thoughts on the shape of post-war exchange policy of those within the Bank concerned with policy formulation – chiefly Cobbold, Bolton, Siepmann and Hawker, and later Lucius Thompson-McCausland* – had in many cases been shared with the Treasury in the form of various papers and memoranda. One on 'Sterling after the war' sent to the Treasury in April 1943 suggested among its conclusions that action might be taken to draft permanent legislation to replace the Defence (Finance) Regulations which were essentially temporary in character. The following September Sir Wilfrid Eady wrote to Cobbold suggesting detailed examination of the regulations, with a view to deciding exactly how much of them needed to be retained and how they could be enforced in post-war conditions under the assumptions (a) that there would be a censorship, even if it did not cover more than a percentage of correspondence, or (b) that the censorship ceased to exist. Cobbold agreed, and at the 237th meeting of the ECC on 9 November 1943, it was resolved to set up a small Sub-Committee to examine the future of the regulations in relation to post-war policy. Its members were Ernest (later Sir Ernest) Rowe-Dutton,† who was the Treasury's chief exchange control expert, his colleague Brooks, and Bolton and Hawker from the Bank. The Sub-Committee did a large amount of work and it was from this that the 1947 Exchange Control Act finally resulted.

The background against which the Act was framed was naturally quite different from the crisis period of 1938 and 1939 when the Defence (Finance) Regulations had been drafted. In many ways the problems increased rather than the reverse: censorship was abolished, there was greater freedom of movement and an ever-widening area to be covered. Efforts were almost immediately directed towards making sterling freely convertible, but Britain had been left with a large liability in the shape of sterling balances accumulated as a result of the war (notably by India and Egypt). The problem of the liquidation of these balances was linked with the negotiation of dollar credit. Britain's obligations to the International Monetary Fund and under the Anglo-American Financial Agreement of December 1945 were not inconsistent with the policy of exchange control – Article VI, Section 3 of the Bretton Woods Agreement begins:

* Thompson (later Thompson-McCausland), Lucius Perronet, CMG, 1904–84. Joined Bank as Temporary Clerk, 1939; Assistant Adviser, 1941–9; Adviser to the Governors, 1949–65. Consultant to H.M. Treasury on International Monetary Problems, 1965–8; Chairman Tricentrol Ltd, 1970–6, Moody's Services Ltd, 1970–5.

† Rowe-Dutton, Sir Ernest, KCMG (1949), 1891–1965. Treasury, 1919–51; Third Secretary, 1947.

'Members may exercise such controls as are necessary to regulate international capital movements...' and the new Act was a necessary condition of the fulfilment of these obligations. The restrictions imposed by the Act were intended not to hamper world trade but to assist it, and particularly to maintain the value of sterling by preventing speculative attacks on it.[38]

The Bank had much say in the wording of the Act and was consulted by the Treasury at every stage. The first draft, largely the work of Percy Beale,* was produced in July 1945. The Chancellor became very troubled by the length and complexity of the early efforts, and pressed continually for it to be shortened; he personally favoured the idea that the Act should be an enabling one only, allowing the Treasury to bring in regulations imposing the necessary prohibitions, rather than having all these set out in the Act itself. This was successfully resisted by both the Bank and the Parliamentary draftsmen.

The Act, which came into force on 1 October 1947, showed some significant changes from the preceding legislation. Chief among these was the abandonment of the power to require foreign securities owned by British residents to be sold to the Treasury. All references to 'enemy' interests were dropped. The term 'Scheduled Territories' was substituted for 'Sterling Area'. One important new control was introduced to safeguard against the transfer of British-owned securities to foreign ownership, except for value received: all securities other than those on a UK register had to be lodged with an approved bank chosen by the owner. The bank would keep the document of title until it was presented for redemption or sale.[39]

While the final wording of the Act was being hammered out between Bank and Treasury, much thought was being given by the former to the machinery of exchange control administration, and especially of the way policy was now to be shaped. Cobbold was insistent on the need for ensuring that exchange control policy as a whole must be primarily a matter for the Treasury, and in January 1945 Governor Catto wrote to Sir Richard Hopkins on the subject of the future of the ECC. After outlining the way the Committee had worked during the war, with its two sessions, one attended by representatives of Bank and Treasury and the other joined by a representative of the Foreign Exchange Committee, he continued:

> In so far as the work of the committee is concerned with the allocation of exchange and permission to 'export' sterling (both in laying down rules

* See note p. 225.

and limits of general application and in considering the difficult individual cases) we feel it would now be better done by a committee at the Treasury. Our principal reason for this belief is the following.

During the war, or at least until quite recently, the work has been mainly negative and concerned to prevent any expenditure not immediately necessary. It is however, already taking a different turn and becoming more positive and selective. It therefore needs more and more to be closely aligned with Government policy in other fields. In case after case, and increasingly as time goes on, the overriding consideration is not an 'exchange' point but a matter of Government policy, it may be in development of exports, in oil, in films, or in emigration, to name but a few. In all these cases there is an exchange factor, but we suggest that the questions could be handled with more expedition and in better perspective if representatives of the Departments concerned could attend as and when required, a regular meeting at the Treasury at which the Bank could be represented.

I think it would be useful to maintain a regular meeting at the Bank (perhaps once a month) between Treasury, Bank and Market representatives to survey the general working of the exchange control machine (but not questions of exchange allocation) and oil the wheels where necessary. This would provide a useful means of contact and review and would supplement the regular contact through the normal channels between the Treasury and the Bank and between the Bank and the Market...[40]

Hopkins agreed with this suggestion which was put into practice from the beginning of April onwards, when the meetings took place at the Treasury under Treasury chairmanship. The Committee as newly constituted was named the Foreign Exchange Control Committee (FECC). The material on the FECC's agenda was prepared by the Bank, and the Bank supplied the secretariat; but the changeover represented an overt distancing of itself by the Bank from the responsibility of policy formulation.[41]

In the years immediately following the end of the war the volume of work undertaken by the Control continued to increase as a result of the resumption of world-wide trade and of travel for both business and pleasure. The number of forms received in 1945 was 937,000: the following year the figure was nearly three and a half million. During the same two years the number of letters to the Bank on exchange control matters amounted to 93,000 and 177,000 respectively, while letters written jumped from 65,000 to 141,000. In spite of these increases, the number of staff employed in the Control only rose during the same period by around eighty, and the Bank had constantly in view the necessity to try to counteract as far as possible the increasing costs of

Exchange Control while maintaining its reputation for efficiency.[42] From the middle of 1946, however, staff numbers began to rise sharply, and on 28 January 1947 the Inspector of Offices and Branches was again asked to carry out an inspection of all the Exchange Control Offices, by this date employing some 1,300. The task took him almost exactly a year, and in the course of his review he prepared a Job Analysis of the work done by the Control and recommended revised basic staff figures for all the Offices, to be reviewed quarterly.

In his final report in January 1948, Laverack noted the particular complexities of control work and the special needs for training:

> The Control is a large and complicated organisation, the internal work processes of which are continually changing to give effect to new policy decisions and adjustments in the incidence of existing controls. This changing aspect of the work is not a feature of other Departments and demands an administrative staff with high qualifications and a personnel skilled and adaptable in handling the varied day to day problems. Most of this skill has been acquired as a result of experience and training within the Control during the last eight years. The technique and thoroughness of training is therefore of the utmost importance in handling new recruits who are the technicians of the future. Another factor which is uncommon in its degree of application is the varying volume of work – particularly of correspondence and forms for authorisation – handled daily by a fixed number of people, giving rise, as a result of new regulations, changed policy and procedure rulings, to peak 'loads'.[43]

The period of this review included the financial crisis of the summer of 1947: in July of that year the obligation to make sterling convertible was implemented, but a month later the drain on reserves and near exhaustion of the dollar credit forced the suspension of convertibility. The problems arising from the transferability of sterling remained; and the strains inherent in the effort to preserve sterling as an international currency, and the need to conserve Britain's dwindling reserves, necessitated an increasing measure of control and supervision by the Bank. At the same time the Bank was under pressure from the Treasury on the subject of the costs of the Control, and two months after the completion of Laverack's final report in January, Cobbold and Siepmann decided that another internal committee should be set up to review Exchange Control practice and 'see whether we are making the best possible use of manpower available for the purpose'. This Committee, which consisted of Bolton in the chair, Sir George Abell, Beale, J.L. Fisher (Deputy Chief Cashier, Exchange Control) and R.N. Kershaw* (Adviser), was

* Abell, Sir George, see note p. 66. Fisher, J.L. see note p. 305. Kershaw, R.N., see note p. 294.

asked to carry out an examination comparable with the work of the 1942 Committee. Bolton's memorandum to his colleagues before they embarked on their review noted that the pattern of exchange control, fashioned for war, might need to be redesigned if it were still to be serviceable in time of peace. He continued:

> The procedures of our exchange control administration may have become obsolete and wasteful. They imply a distribution of authority and responsibility, between the Treasury and the Bank, which does not correspond to the facts as known to everyone. The Bank does the work, gets the credit and the blame, but the procedures imply that the Bank is a kind of junior partner. Broad lines of policy are laid down in Whitehall, as they should be; but the Treasury also maintain, at low levels, a pretence of control in the petty details of administration of which no more than a negligible proportion ever reach them. We are ourselves partly responsible for this because we have insisted on being 'merely' the agents for the Treasury. A more realistic recognition of the facts might now require the liquidation of Treasury authority over detail and a delegation of full administrative control to the Bank, with a consequent saving of time and manpower. On the other hand, Treasury control over policy needs to be highly concentrated so that exchange aspects of policy may be treated as a whole, at high level only, with the Bank as assessor in a purely advisory capacity.

The original pattern of control had become, Bolton said, a patchwork, where weak spots were recognised but had to be ignored as being beyond the resources of the administration 'but no one asks or knows what the unassessable losses amount to in the aggregate as compared with the savings which result from what is still admitted and achieved'.[44]

The Committee began its work with some basic questions in mind: is the practice of control sound in principle? does it give results which justify the work involved? has it been rendered wholly or partly out of date by changes in conditions since 1939?

The findings of the Committee were embodied in a series of interim reports dealing with every Office in turn. The Committee took full note of Laverack's recent report, and were able to endorse many of his recommendations as to the scrapping of certain forms and some checking procedures, although other suggestions of his, mainly relating to reorganisation of work within the Offices, were not accepted. Destruction of old forms, correspondence, index cards, files and other documents was encouraged wherever possible. It was also noted that there was a serious shortage of women clerks in the Control, and that every effort should be made to recruit them, possibly even by advertising (the Bank had never advertised for clerical staff, and in fact did not do so for some years). But these were all relatively minor points. After addressing the fundamental questions cited above, the Committee reported that the structure had stood the test of time and that it did not consider that any major reorganisation of the Control could improve its efficiency.

It did feel, however, that some strengthening of the upper ranks was desirable, recommending the appointment of an additional Assistant Chief Cashier and two additional Assistants to the Chief Cashier (the next most senior position). There was concern too over the pressure of work falling on the Principals, who at that time numbered thirty-four. It had been the Control's aim to force down the responsibility as much as possible to the levels of Senior and Principal Clerks, and this had been achieved so successfully that men in those ranks enjoyed considerably more authority in the Control than their equals had elsewhere in the Bank. However as both the volume and the complexity of the work were increasing, the Principals themselves were felt by the Committee to be seriously overworked. An immediate increase of seven was suggested, to bring the total to forty-one.

The effect of all the Committee's recommendations, therefore, was on balance to bring about a net increase in costs rather than the reverse: Bolton remarked that its inability to suggest any means by which a major economy could be achieved 'is due basically to this country's economic position which renders necessary a close supervision over all exchange transactions and to the government's tendency towards increasing regulations'.[45]

In one important area the Committee was overtaken by events. Quite early in their meetings some of the members had expressed unease over the apparently anomalous position of the Overseas and Foreign Office. Kershaw in particular was aware that its existence as an Office within the Control did not correspond to its place in the total of the Bank's work on external affairs. The Office was divided into Groups each with special responsibility for an area of the world or for some particular activity: Group X, dealing with multilateral transfers, and Group XII, Dominion and Colonial Exchange regulations, worked almost wholly on exchange control matters. The Control made many calls on other groups, but the work of the Office as a whole went a long way beyond its exchange control functions. This had been a highly controversial issue ever since its absorption into the Control in 1941 and now in peacetime was more so, and the Committee had accordingly begun to discuss whether the Office should remain within the Control, be attached elsewhere within the Bank, or become an independent Department with its own Head.

Even as Bolton's Committee pondered the question, Cobbold decided that the matter was too pressing for further delay. In October he addressed a note to the Governor noting the necessity

> whilst keeping its work close to that of Exchange Control, to give O & F more independent existence and in particular to have it under the direct charge of senior officials who could give it undivided attention. At the same time there is need for consolidating and coordinating the services available to the Advisers on the foreign field and for supervising and directing the work of the Assistant Advisers etc...

Cobbold considered the creation of a separate Section of the Cashier's Department under a Deputy Chief Cashier, but thought the time not yet ripe for this although it might eventually prove the right solution. Meanwhile, he recommended 'experimentally' a half-way house, under which Overseas and Foreign (O & F) should remain within the Cashier's Department (Exchange Control) which could be renamed Cashier's Department (Exchange Control and Overseas). An additional Deputy Chief Cashier should be appointed, who would work in close contact with and under the general authority of the Deputy Chief Cashier (Exchange Control and Overseas) but relieving him of direct responsibility for O & F work and having direct access to the Governors. For this new post he suggested A.P. (later Sir Anthony) Grafftey-Smith, who was currently an Acting Adviser, with Guy Watson* and Roy Bridge† (both Assistant Chief Cashiers, Exchange Control) directly under him, Watson to supervise the day to day work and Bridge free for special duties and negotiations. Cobbold also recommended the creation within the Office of new ranks of Senior Assistants and Assistants, for men engaged on special duties. These ranks would be comparable with those of Principal and Assistant Principal but without administrative status.

These suggestions of Cobbold's were accepted and the change of title and Grafftey-Smith's appointment were effected on 1 November 1948.[45] Six of the seven additional Principals were also appointed within a short period.[46]

The pressures on the Bank to make the working of the Control as efficient as possible were both internal and, as described in chapter 6, external: the Treasury was constantly anxious that its costs should be regularly and stringently monitored. This became especially urgent early in 1951 when the Bank's forecasts of the costs of the Control for the

---

\* Grafftey-Smith, Sir A., see note p. 302; Watson, G.M., see note p. 297.

† Bridge, R.A.O., CMG, 1911–78. Entered Bank 1929. Asst. Chief Cashier, 1946–51; Acting Adviser 1951–3; UK Alternate Director, Managing Board, EPU, 1950–2; Principal, Dealing and Accounts Office, 1953–7; Deputy Chief Cashier 1957–63; Adviser to the Governors 1963–5; Asst. to the Governors 1965–9.

period September 1950–August 1951 showed an increase of more than £100,000 over the previous year. Although there had been several relaxations in control regulations, these had the effect of increasing rather than decreasing work – only complete abolition of any regulation did that. Staff costs had risen too, largely because of wage increases.

Sir Edward Bridges wrote to Governor Cobbold expressing the Treasury's disquiet at the proposed increases, coming as they did at a time when the Chancellor was facing extreme difficulties 'in framing his 1951 budget, having regard to the increased provision which will be necessary for Defence expenditure'. All possibilities of economy should be rigorously pursued, and he asked Cobbold to try to cut the current year's costs of the Control by £130,000. Cobbold, in turn, asked Grafftey-Smith to study the possibility of reducing the staff of the Exchange Control by 100 men.[47]

At this date there were 102 Temporary Male Clerks in the Control, most of whom had been recruited from the Foreign Exchange market at the outbreak of war. Sixty-eight of them were aged over fifty, and twenty-one of those were over sixty-five and due to leave within the coming year. Grafftey-Smith concentrated his examination on this body of men, partly because the numbers fitted in with the Governor's query and partly because they were 'at risk to a greater extent than the rest of the male staff of the Bank'. He listed the steps necessary to cope with such a reduction, including reducing the scrutiny of bankers' certificates to a minimum, abolishing the check of Overseas Control forms, discontinuing various records and increasing delegation to Authorised Depositaries. The dismissal of the whole of the Temporary Male Staff in the Control would result in savings of about £80,000 in a full year. 'Assuming our normal practice of giving three months' notice to all temporary men, if such notice were given to them all at the same time, say, the end of February, the full effect would not be apparent in the charges payable by HM Treasury during the fiscal year 1951/1952.'

A further possibility suggested by Grafftey-Smith, which would cause in his opinion the least dislocation to the services provided by the Bank, would be to dispense not only with the Temporary Clerks but with another hundred composed of thirty Supplementary Staff and seventy-five Women Clerks, effecting a saving altogether of £140,000. This would still imply drastic cuts in the Offices with the least contact with the public: he ruled out O & F and thought 'our most likely field of action would be to do away with certain sections of the work done in TC & I'.[48]

The decision to dismiss a large number of clerks in the Control was not an easy one to make; mass redundancy of the kind now being contemplated had only occurred once before in the history of the Bank, when the services of 127 men were dispensed with in 1821 after the issue of £1 and £2 notes was discontinued.[49] The question of the status and permanency of the Temporary Clerks had in any case been under constant review since the end of the war. In 1950 a staff of Supplementary Clerks had been been formed, to which selected members of the Temporary Staff were offered appointment, the chief benefit being a pension. But even then the appointments were made 'dependent on a suitable amount of work continuing to be available'.[50]

The discussion with the Treasury on the possibilities of economies continued, but the fate of the Temporary Clerks was sealed: by 2 February, Bernard was able to tell Bridges that 'As from the 1st February , all our Temporary Clerks working in the Exchange Control have received notice of the termination of their employment in the Bank. Some of these will be leaving within the next three months and the remainder within the following three months.' Further cuts in the work processes were possible, to effect savings of some £20,000 in a full year, but if the Bank were pressed to move beyond this point by economising still more Bernard said that it would have 'a definite effect on our foreign currency receipts'.[51] This admonition was apparently effective, for there appears to have been no further demand from the Treasury for economies at this date.

The dismissal of the Temporary Staff was a painful episode which left lasting scars in spite of the Bank's efforts to help them find new employment, which many of them did as their exchange control experience was valuable to banks and other financial institutions. A gradual scaling down of Exchange Control staff followed, including the final disbandment of the remaining Supplementary Staff in 1956. This was the result of a dwindling of work in many areas of the Control, although others burgeoned. The early 1950s marked the beginning of a second and more gradual approach to the objective of making sterling convertible into any other currency. The government's policy during these years was to move towards liberalisation of payments and, as trade began to open up throughout the world, organised UK markets in primary commodities were re-established, most of them having been closed throughout the war. The first to re-open was the coffee market in 1946, when commodities were dealt with by a Section of the Trade Control and Investigations Office, whose accountants inspected the books at regular intervals. The work expanded as the opening of other markets followed, and was transferred to the Central Office in 1952. In 1954 an independent Commodities Office was formed.[52]

Before this date, however, the essentially uneasy relationship of control with Britain's foreign trade efforts had been the cause of another searching examination of the work. There were signs of restlessness in the summer of 1952 in both the City and Whitehall, arising out of the difficulties in aligning current policy on credit with that on exchange control. In August the Hon. Hugh (later Lord) Kindersley,* a member of the Court, wrote a personal letter to Siepmann in which he expressed his

> firm conviction that the City houses and their industrial clients are not only frustrated by the eternal delays which they meet once they have crossed the threshold of the Bank of England but they are at a loss to understand how it is that business passed by the E.C.G.D.† and through the F.E.C.C. can be suddenly stamped on by the Bank. The Chancellor publicly encourages us to compete for exports on lines of extended credit, he tells us E.C.G.D. facilities will be widened to help meet this type of foreign competition and, in spite of all that verbiage in the House, once the door of the Bank of England is reached it seems to be partially slammed in our face. The inevitable reaction is to wonder whether the usual channels for the City to approach the Treasury (through the Bank) are not a snare and a delusion and whether some alternative of short circuiting the Old Lady would not be possible and better.
>
> The technicalities and difficulties faced by the Bank are not appreciated nor understood so that inevitably faith in the Bank as the leader and parent of the City becomes progressively shaken. In other words I believe the reputation of the Bank is at stake and unless something can be done to improve matters and to put things on to a more businesslike footing, also to guide the City as to what is or is not wanted of it, the great regard in which the Bank has been held will gradually diminish and it will come to be looked on as just another Government Department with wheels that turn just as slowly as any other Department. In other words the result of nationalisation as foretold by many in the early days...[53]

These were harsh words from one of its own Directors and they struck home, giving substance as they did to some of the Bank's deepest apprehensions on the subject of exchange control. Bernard's private opinion was that 'HK has not heard of the ninety-nine sausages that pass through the machine normally but is told about the one which is delayed by bone or gristle clogging the machine and regards it as normal'; but the accusation could not be dismissed lightly. Siepmann drafted a reply in

---

* Kindersley, 2nd Baron (1954) of West Hoathly, Hugh K.M. Kindersley, CBE, MC, 1899–1976. Director, Lazard Brothers & Co., 1965–71 (Chairman, 1953–64, Managing Director, 1927–64). Director, Bank of England, 1947–67.
† Export Credits Guarantee Department.

which he said that the subject was never far from their thoughts 'but when it elicits a cri de coeur from such as you, it needs to be taken even more seriously'. He answered the criticism of delays, and of the administrative efficiency of the Control, by citing various statistics showing the comparative numbers of forms and letters dealt with by the Regulations General Office in 1946 and 1952, the daily output of work of the staff and the speed with which they replied (80 per cent of all letters were answered within eight days of receipt, and 50 per cent of forms dealt with within twenty-four hours). The work was also becoming much more complex, and where possible routine work had been delegated to Authorised Dealers so that the Bank was left 'with all the difficult cases'. As to the fact that the Bank did not seem to be able to do anything to speed up the passage of these cases, Siepmann continued with a definitive version of the problem as the Bank viewed it:

> The short answer is that the Bank is an agent in these matters, not a principal. Whether in law, or in ethics, an agent should be responsible for the actions and inactions of his principals I do not know; but it is quite certain and inevitable that for the shortcomings of the 'Control' we shall be blamed, now that we have become part of the authorities. But the fact remains (I think) that the amount of blame we do incur is surprisingly small. When one considers how arbitrary and tyrannous, how intrusive and impertinent, the foreign exchange control is bound to seem to those who suffer from it, the surprising thing, to my mind, is that we are not more hated and execrated. Partly this may be due to the fact that in some domains we are financially ineffective, i.e. that personal suffering can often be prevented by evasive action. But I believe it is also due to our having realised at the Bank from the very start, that what you do matters, very often, less than how you do it. Dilatory we may be, where we have not the authority to be prompt and decisive; but if you were to tell me that we are inconsiderate, tactless, rude, or even curt, and that we take sides with the Sheriff of Nottingham rather than with Robin Hood, I should feel deeply hurt...

Siepmann concluded by saying that he felt that the very existence of the controls tended to 'loosen the contacts between industry and the banking system, especially when the predominance of financial consider-ations is so commonly called in question as it is today'. His experience with the newly freed commodity markets had led him to hope that 'we were working our way towards a new pattern of responsibilities, in which the Bank is seen as an essential link between the interests of business and the demands of officialdom. If that were so, we ought actually to be gain-ing in authority and prestige; and (as you know) we have gone to great trouble and expense on that assumption in order to build up a staff which can more than hold its own in Whitehall.'[54]

A good deal of the matter needed, in Cobbold's opinion, 'to be sorted out at the Whitehall end' but he was anxious to get a clear view on two points: whether there was need for alteration in the Bank's own arrangements and what, if any, suggestions and advice should be given to Whitehall.

To answer these questions he set up a small informal Committee in October 1952 to advise the Governors, consisting of Peppiatt as Chairman, Sir Charles Hambro, Siepmann, Kindersley and Michael Babington Smith.* They had the following terms of reference:

> To review the Bank's administration of the exchange control regulations from the aspect of
> (a) relations with the City of London and applicants for foreign exchange generally
> (b) the link between exchange control and credit control and
> (c) the machinery for aligning decisions given by Whitehall, ECGD, CIC† and the Bank of England and
> (d) to advise the Governors on any internal steps which may be judged advisable and on any submissions which might be made to HM Treasury.[55]

The Committee, which became known as the Liaison Committee, met frequently during the autumn, at first discussing the questions among its own members and then calling in evidence from Bolton, Niemeyer, the Chief Cashier, and Maurice (later Sir Maurice) Parsons.‡ Bolton attested with vigour to his views on 'the incompatibility of the policy of planned production and programmed exports and limitation of the amount of credit which we wished to see passing into the monetary machine'. The two systems were mutually exclusive, he said, but had to operate side by side: tiresome as this was, the City would just have to suffer it. Bolton also mentioned that he believed there were now about a million different regulations in all.

The Committee's twenty-two page report, dated 24 December 1952, confirmed what Siepmann had originally claimed to Kindersley – that 'the frictions commonly attributed to the operation of the system are

---

* Hambro, see p. 77n. Babington Smith, Michael James, CBE, 1901–84. Deputy Chairman, Glyn Mills & Co., 1947–63; Director, Bank of England, 1949–69.
† Capital Issues Committee.
‡ Parsons, Sir Maurice H., KCMG (1970), Kt. (1966), 1910–78. Entered Bank of England 1928; Deputy Chief Cashier, 1950–5; Assistant, 1955–7; Executive Director, 1957–66; Deputy Governor, 1966–70.

more properly attributable to the system itself…'. The Committee concluded that the relations of the Control with the City were good, and that the day to day administration by the Bank was satisfactory. The machinery for aligning decisions by the various authorities was adequate 'but can only be expected to function smoothly if bankers and their customers understand the accepted procedure and comply with it; every effort is made, and should continue to be made, to help them to do so'. Closer administrative association between the Bank and the CIC had been considered but was not thought desirable; however, although Exchange Control should not undertake to give rulings as to whether application to the CIC was called for, approvals should where necessary be 'qualified and limited, so as to forestall possible misunderstanding'. Finally the authority and independence of the Bank in the Discount Market was a matter of paramount importance with which the agency functions of the Bank must not be allowed to interfere. The Committee had no concrete suggestions to make as to any submissions to the Treasury but thought that the Treasury might well be informed 'whether officially or unofficially' that it had carried out such an examination and reported its findings.[56]

Exchange Control shrank further as the 1950s progressed. Offices were closed or merged: the Acceptance Credits Office was disbanded in 1954 and its little remaining work taken over by Regulations General.[57] Trade Control and Investigations and Export Permits were both abolished from the beginning of November 1956 and their functions distributed between Securities Control and Regulations General.[58] There was less prosecution of offenders, enforcement tending to become 'more a matter of stern admonition'. The chief preoccupations of the remaining Offices were emigration and applications for business and holiday allowances: the need to fill in a form for travel abroad was the most constant reminder to the general public that exchange control still existed and in the mid 1950s such applications totalled about 140,000 a year. Staff numbers fell from a peak of 1,634 in the half-year ended August 1950 to 843 by October 1956.[59]

The natural apprehensions which were aroused in the staff by the falling workload were to some extent offset by the varied nature of the problems that did occur, and the fact, first evident during the war but still valid, that even the more lowly members of the Exchange Control Offices found scope for initiative and judgement. This kept interest alive and morale good. The Principal of the RGO noted in July 1954 that he thought it 'undoubtedly true that the staff found the work of EC far more congenial than the duties they had to perform before the war',[60] and

Plate 3.3    The post-war Securities Control Office, in 1958. The office is in one
of the banking halls built by Sir Herbert Baker to replace those of Sir John Soane.
Baker used the original Coade stone caryatids and freely adapted much of Soane's
classical decoration to his own design. (Watercolour drawing by Sir Henry
Rushbury)

while this was probably true of most of the Bank's Offices it was
particularly noticeable in the Control. The Control also offered extra
chances of promotion and an improved career structure together with a
wide range of experience which its staff would certainly not have gained
elsewhere in the Bank, in such areas as foreign trade, investment,
takeovers, shipping, films, oil, insurance and many others. Conversely,
as it gave the Bank the opportunity to extend its knowledge of commerce
and industry, exchange control also gave the world and the City in
particular a chance to look into the Bank – something which had scarcely
been possible before, and which would stand the Bank in good stead in
the years to come.

Towards the end of the 1950s it seemed as if the imposition of
exchange controls must be approaching the end of its term. In January
1957 the reorganisation of the whole structure within the Bank was under
fresh consideration, and a month later it was announced that the group of

Offices designated Cashier's Department (Exchange Control and Overseas) would cease to exist as a separate organisation. The Overseas and Foreign Office was to become a separate Overseas Department such as existed before the war; the Central Office was abolished, and staff responsibilities would be taken over by those who supervised such matters in the Cashier's Department as a whole. The five remaining Control Offices – Dealing and Accounts, Regulations General, Securities Control, Commodities and Glasgow – were transferred to the Cashier's Department.[61] The process of dismantling controls continued for another four years, until the sterling crisis of 1961 reversed the position and gave new strength to what had become known as 'the Bank's withered arm'.

## Appendix

In addition to the internal committees mentioned in chapter 3, the Bank was represented on several external committees dealing with various aspects of the exchange control regulations during the war. The more important of these are listed below.

Exchange Control Conference. This was a Committee composed of senior officials from the Treasury and the Bank which met between August 1940 and February 1943. It was formed to deal with exchange control policy matters and foreign exchange problems at the highest level: during the critical period 1941/2 it met constantly but thereafter only occasionally until it ceased to function after February 1943. The Bank was represented by Cobbold; J.M. Keynes (later Lord Keynes) and Lord Catto, Governor of the Bank from 1944–9, were members.[62]

Exchange Control Credits Committee and Securities Restrictions Committee. These were composed of representatives of the Bank, Treasury, clearing and other banks, Ministry of Economic Warfare and Trading with the Enemy Department.

Committee on Direct Investments in the USA. This was set up to discuss the possible liquidation of direct investments in the USA. Lord Catto was Chairman and the other four members were Directors of the Bank.

Import Licensing Committee. This was a Board of Trade Committee dealing with miscellaneous imports, and was attended by representatives of other Government Departments and the Bank of England as occasion demanded. After Lease-Lend it lapsed but was revived shortly before the end of the war.

There was also considerable liaison between the Bank and HM Customs (over the proceeds of goods exported), Censorship, Passport Office, Board of Trade, Ministry of Supply and Petroleum Department (later Ministry of Fuel and Power) on various cases. An official of the Bank attended the weekly meetings of the Foreign Exchange Sub-Committee of the Clearing Banks and Accepting Houses, which advised on exchange control questions.

# 4

## THE NOTE ISSUE

The first depositors with the Bank of England had a choice of three methods by which they could later obtain repayment. The amount of the deposit could be entered in the books of the Bank, and drawn upon by the depositor, who held a passbook; he could receive an 'acceptable note' as a receipt, and draw on that; or he could receive notes payable to bearer, like the notes issued by the goldsmith-bankers which passed freely from hand to hand in the localities where they were recognised. The bearer, or running cash note – which could be cashed in part if required – formed, as Sir John Clapham noted, 'the bank note *par excellence*' and is the direct antecedent of those in circulation today. It is clear that William Paterson and his supporters fully intended their new bank to be a bank of issue, although neither the Bank of England Act of 1694 nor the Bank's Charter make specific mention of such activity, doubtless because Paterson's first scheme had foundered on this very question which had aroused opposition from the government. Within a few hours of the sealing of the Charter the Court of Directors at its first meeting decided on the repayment methods outlined above, and the Bank has issued notes without a break since that time.

Although the Directors ordered that 'the Running Cash Notes be printed', and copper plates were engraved for notes of £5, £10, £20, £50 and £100, there is no evidence that these plates were ever used. A few days later, on 6 August 1694, the Court decided that the running cash notes were too liable to be counterfeited, and directed that they should be 'done on marbled paper Indented'. No specimens of these survive, but they were presumably written by hand, with perhaps a few lines of engraving.

Meanwhile preparations for a more secure printed note went ahead and the first 12,000 were ordered in June of the following year in seven denominations from £5 to £100, each denomination bearing a distinguishing letter from A to G. Within two months a counterfeit £100 note was presented for payment, whereupon use of the printed notes was discontinued and some of the cashiers were given the duty of writing notes. The Bank lost no time in seeking a remedy against such forgery and further enquiry into different sorts of paper resulted in the idea of a special watermark, which in various forms has been a feature of all Bank of England notes since. Three years after the Bank's foundation one of its first Directors, Sir Theodore Janssen,* while admitting that 'giving out Notes payable to Bearer...(is) liable to many dangers and Inconveniences', observed that the custom was by then so prevalent that 'the Bank could hardly carry on business without it'.

The handwritten notes were succeeded at some date between 1696 and 1699 by partly printed notes, which themselves gave way to notes in mainly printed form after 1725. In 1720, the year of the South Sea Bubble, the total value of the Bank's notes in circulation was about £3 m.; the Bank's credit successfully withstood that crisis and its notes continued to grow in popularity and acceptability until by 1795 the circulation had risen to £13·5 m. Two years later, in 1797, the economic difficulties associated with the war against Napoleon gave rise to a shortage of specie and an Order of the Privy Council authorised the Bank to stop paying notes in gold and silver. Notes for £1 and £2 were issued as an alternative form of payment. This was the beginning of the notorious 'Restriction Period' which lasted until payment in specie was resumed in 1821: counterfeiting became more prevalent as the new low denomination notes circulated more widely among people previously unaccustomed to handling paper money and in many case illiterate. The penalties for forgery and 'uttering' (passing) a counterfeit note, or merely being in possession of one, included hanging and transportation, and considerable odium attached to the Bank as the originator of notes which were too easily reproduced. Its efforts to rectify the current position and produce the 'inimitable note' were considerable and lasted for twenty-five years.[1]

When payment in gold and silver was resumed the note circulation, which had risen by 1815 to some £26 m., began to decline and in 1822 stood at £17 m. The Bank ceased to issue notes for less than £5 and, apart from a brief emergency issue of £1 notes in the financial crisis of 1825–6, did not do so again for over a hundred years. But that crisis had another and much more lasting effect on the note issue. Private banks failed

---

* Janssen, Sir Theodore, Bt., 1658–1748. Director, Bank of England, 1694–9, 1700–1, 1707–11, 1718–19.

throughout the country, many of them banks of issue which had produced their own notes. Their bankruptcy was a contributory cause of the passing of the 1826 Country Bankers Act, following which the Bank of England established Branches in some of the principal cities of England and Wales. These were able to provide the provinces with a secure note circulation, and their foundation marked a crucial stage in the Bank's progression towards a monopoly of the note issue in England and Wales. Country Branch notes, which bore the name of the town in which the issuing Branch was situated, were payable either at the Branch or in London: their usefulness led to a steady decline in the circulation of provincial bills of exchange. Some country banks which had weathered the crisis and continued to issue their own notes subsequently ceased to do so because of the Bank's policy of refusing rediscount facilities to banks which declined to circulate Bank of England notes.[2]

The Bank's issue was further strengthened by the Bank of England Act of 1833 which made Bank of England notes legal tender in England and Wales for denominations, and for all sums, over £5, on condition that the Bank continued to pay its notes in legal coin on demand. The 1833 Act also debarred any joint stock bank from being established in London or within sixty-five miles of the capital unless it undertook not to issue its own notes.[3]

Eleven years later the passing of the Bank Charter Act of 1844 provided the final piece of legislation necessary to remove any competitors of the Bank of England note. No banker not at that date issuing notes could do so in the future; any banker who ceased to issue notes, for no matter what reason, was prohibited from resuming issue. Existing banks of issue were not allowed in future to exceed their average issue for the twelve weeks ending 26 April 1844. Even more effective, in the long term, was the provision that, if an amalgamation of two or more private banks of issue brought the number of partners to more than six, then the right of issue was forfeited. Banks in Scotland and Ireland could continue to issue their own notes, as they still do,* and moreover do not lose their rights if they amalgamate, but all except a very small amount of their issues, which are not legal tender, have to be covered by holdings of Bank of England notes, gold or silver coin.

Until the passing of the 1844 Act the backing of the Bank's liabilities on demand, i.e. deposits and notes, consisted of about two thirds securities and one third bullion. As described in chapter 6, the Act required the Bank to set up a separate Issue Department to handle all note issue business in distinction to that carried out in the Banking

* The legislative authority now relates to Scotland and Northern Ireland.

Department. The Issue Department was now authorised to issue notes against gold to an unlimited extent; against silver to a maximum of one quarter of gold holdings; and against securities – the fiduciary issue – to an amount limited to £14 m., of which the government debt of £11 m. was to form the main part. If any private bank ceased to issue its own notes, however, the Bank was empowered by the Act to obtain an Order in Council to take over two thirds of the lapsed issue. At the time of the passing of the Act the aggregate issues allowable to the joint stock and private banks were about £8·5 m.[4]

The second half of the nineteenth century was marked by a decline in the importance of bank notes owing to the expansion of joint stock banking, a greatly increased use of cheques and the growing circulation of gold coin. By 1900 the Bank's note circulation was less than 50 per cent greater than it had been at the time of the 1844 Act, although the national income had risen by some 300 per cent in the same period.[5] The outbreak of the First World War, and the withdrawal from general circulation of gold coins the following year (although they remained legal tender), brought about a sharp increase in the demand for other currency. An Act of 6 August 1914 empowered the government to issue notes for £1 and 10s. which it rapidly proceeded to do. This pre-empted the Bank who had also worked swiftly to prepare a £1 note, a miniature of the £5, which was never issued.[6] The government issue of Currency or Treasury notes were soon dubbed Bradburys after the Permanent Secretary to the Treasury, Sir John Bradbury,* whose signature was reproduced on them. They were legal tender for any amount throughout the United Kingdom, whereas the Bank's notes were still regulated by the 1833 Act which made them legal tender in England and Wales only for amounts over £5. During the war years the note circulation began a rapid increase which was to continue with varying intensity for more than half a century, bringing practical problems in its train which are described later in this chapter and in the next; between 1913 and 1916 the Bank of England's note circulation went from around £28 m. to over £70 m. and the circulation of Currency notes was, by the latter date, more than £300 m.

In 1921 the last of the country banks to issue its own notes, Fox, Fowler and Co. of Wellington in Somerset, was taken over by Lloyds Bank.[7] Bank of England and Currency notes circulated side by side until the issue of the latter ceased with the passing of the Currency and Bank Notes Act of 1928. By its provisions the Bank assumed liability for the

---

* Bradbury, 1st Baron (1925) of Winsford, John S. Bradbury, KCB (1913), 1872–1950. Joint Permanent Secretary to the Treasury, 1913–19.

payment of Currency Notes together with responsibility for the issue of £1 and 10s. notes which were given full legal tender status in England, Wales, Scotland and Northern Ireland; the Act also conferred legal tender status on the £5 note in England and Wales, which it had not previously possessed. The backing for the Currency notes was entirely composed of government securities, and these were transferred to the Bank's Issue Department, which had the effect of making more than 60 per cent of the Bank's note issue fiduciary. A ceiling of £260 m. was fixed for this fiduciary issue, although it could be varied at the discretion of the Treasury.[8] The 1928 Act required the Bank to pay to the Treasury the net profits of the Issue Department.*

The Bank moved swiftly to put its own £1 and 10s. notes into circulation; the former denomination had not been issued by the Bank for over 100 years and it had never previously produced a 10s. note. The designs had been approved the previous year and were a joint effort by the artist W.M. Keesey (he was also an architect) who was responsible for the reverse of both notes, and other people both inside and outside the Bank. The obverse of both showed Daniel Maclise's medallion of Britannia, which had been used on all the Bank's notes since 1855;[9] the colour schemes, green for the £1 and red-brown for the 10s., with variegated colours of the same basic shades on the reverse, were the work of J.S. Blunt, RBA.[10] Both were issued in November 1928, and were known as 'low sum' notes in distinction from the higher denominations of £5 to £1,000, all printed in black on white paper, which the Bank was already producing.

With the passing of the 1928 Act the Bank assumed for the first time in its history responsibility for the entire note issue of England and Wales, and has retained it since that date. This involves design, production, distribution and eventual cancellation and destruction of millions of pieces of paper annually, each individual note having to be accounted for at every stage of its life under conditions of the greatest possible security. The actual mechanics of issue have changed little: the notes are printed, as described in chapter 5, at the Bank's own Printing Works and transferred in bulk to the custody of the Issue Office in Threadneedle Street, where a store is maintained of enough notes to satisfy projected demand for some months taking into account seasonal fluctuations or any possible interruption to production. This stock is held for the Issue Department which will sell them to the Banking Department as the latter's holdings decline (at which point they become 'live', i.e. a liability

---

* The 1939 Currency and Bank Notes Act directed the Treasury to pay sums thus received into the Exchange Equalisation Account.

Plate 4.1   The Maclise Medallion

of the Issue Department, although – as the Bank Return makes clear –
Banking Department holdings are not regarded as in public circulation).*
At certain times the flow will be in the opposite direction. The
commercial banks obtain their supply of new (or on occasion re-issued
– see below) notes and dispose of their holdings of worn or dirty notes by
transferring them from or to the Bank of England, either in London or at
the Bank's Branches, against settlement through their accounts with the
Bank.

From the late nineteenth century to the mid 1970s the principal
method of transport of the notes was by rail, although some cancelled
high sum notes were returned to Head Office from Branches by registered
post and the General Post Office High Value Packet Service was used for
consignments of notes between London and Northern Ireland. When
going by rail the 'Treasure', as the notes were called in this context, was

* Changes in the fiduciary issue are necessary when fluctuation is greater than can be
  accommodated by the Banking Department's store.

escorted to its destination by a clerk from the Branch Banks Office accompanied by a Messenger.*

From the mid 1930s onwards, as described below, the Bank was working on a new design for the £1 and 10s. notes, and consideration was being given to making a new issue either in 1944, the 250th Anniversary year, or in 1948, twenty years after the 1928 Act. But the approach of war introduced a new dimension: the possibility of large-scale forgery. In June 1939, after consultation between the Deputy Governor, Catterns, and Sir Frederick Phillips† at the Treasury, it was decided that active measures should be taken to guard against any move by the Germans to flood the country with counterfeit notes and thus undermine confidence in the currency. The first priority was to create a reserve stock of some £40 m. of £1 and 10s. notes of the existing design and colour, and secondly, in the event of war, to print notes lithographically instead of by the plate printing process, in order to save both labour and money.[11] The lithographic notes would be of the same design but different colours, and would embody a safety device of a metal thread woven into the paper. This had been invented some years earlier by S.B. Chamberlain, General Works Manager of the Bank's Printing Works, and had already proved successful in trials of notes produced for the South African Reserve Bank.[12]

The experience of 1914–18 forewarned the Bank that a sharp increase in the note circulation was likely if war did break out and the 1939 Currency and Bank Notes Act was passed to increase the fiduciary issue to £300 m.[13] The new lithographic notes were put into circulation at the end of March 1940. The reserve stock which had been planned before the start of the war was not in fact complete at its outbreak, but nearly £12 m. in notes of £1 and 10s. had been deposited at various provincial centres of the Big Five banks (Barclays, Lloyds, Midland, National Provincial and Westminster) and a further store of notes (paid but uncancelled‡ and suitable for re-issue) was gradually built up in the vaults of Threadneedle Street. This store was considerably reduced in May 1940 when the danger of invasion seemed a distinct possibility: about £120 m. of uncancelled notes were burnt at Battersea Power Station and the remaining stock was cancelled. A further distribution of store notes took place at the same time, so that by the middle of August 1940 over

---

* For description of 'Treasure journeys' see chapter 8.
† Phillips, Sir Frederick, GCMG, CB, 1884–1943. HM Treasury, 1908–43; Under Secretary, 1932.
‡ Cancellation of paid notes was usually effected by 'milling', i.e. punching or cutting holes (discontinued in 1987). Some high sum notes were cancelled by tearing off the corner bearing the signature of the Chief Cashier.

£162 m. of low sum notes and some £77 m. of high denominations had been deposited with branches of the clearing banks throughout the country, plus £1 m. in low sum notes with banks in Northern Ireland.

Another aspect of the note issue with which the co-operation of the clearing banks had been secured before the war was the question of re-issue. They had all agreed to re-issue soiled notes of all denominations if necessary, and to tell branches to supply currency even to competitor banks in cases of real emergency. This worked well in practice with the result that the life of the low sum notes was considerably extended in comparison with pre-war standards and despite persistent demands on the banks for new notes made by government departments, the Forces and industrial firms. The 10s. note, which had lasted for an average of four months in 1938, was in circulation for two and a half times as long by the end of the war, and the life of the £1 note was extended from five months to nearly two years in the same period.[14]

The fears of a vast incursion of German forgeries, perhaps dropped by air, were never fulfilled, but in September 1942 the Bank received from Tangier some skilfully executed counterfeit £5 notes. They were classified as type BB in line with the Bank's practice of assigning a letter code to each distinguishable series of counterfeits, and were so good that the only method of detection, at this early stage, was the 'feel' of the paper; later, other methods were introduced, such as the use of a quartz lamp which showed up differences in colour according to the type of paper used for the note.

Denominations of £5, £10, £20 and £50 were produced in the BB type, and nearly 10,000 of them had been received in the Bank before the end of the war in Europe. It had soon become apparent that they were being produced in Germany; the details of their manufacture, by specially selected artists, printers and engravers who were confined in Sachsenhausen concentration camp near Berlin, are well documented.[15] They were used for various purposes such as Skorzeny's rescue of Mussolini after the Badoglio coup, the purchase of British arms from warring factions of Yugoslav partisans, and paying agents for overseas operations. The Germans made desperate efforts to destroy the evidence of their counterfeiting activities before surrendering in 1945, but the Allied occupying forces took possession of some 1·75 m. notes of this type and a further cache, plus some of the plates used in their manufacture, was recovered from the lake at Toplitzsee in the Austrian Alps in 1959. In spite of the excellence of the BB notes, however, the Germans were never able to have them made in sufficient quantity to carry out successfully any efforts to debase the British currency, although knowledge of their existence was certainly one factor in the unpopularity of the £5 note for some years after the war.

As well as catering for the ever increasing demand for notes on the home front, the Bank of England carried out other note printing activities during the course of the war. A suggestion apparently originating with the clearing banks before the war was for the issue of notes of smaller denominations than 10s.; plans for the production of 5s. and 2s. 6d. notes were made although neither Bank nor Treasury were keen to issue them. Shortage of silver, however, was a problem of varying intensity throughout the war, and in the autumn of 1940 production of coin ceased entirely for a short time owing to bomb damage to the Royal Mint and to the gas supplies on which, at that time, the Mint was entirely dependent. The Bank therefore proceeded to put into production 'silver notes' with an initial printing of 8 million each of 5s. and 2s. 6d., coloured pink and light blue respectively. These were all distributed around the country, and a further 8 million of each printed for holding in London. The total stock therefore only amounted to £6 m. at face value, and in fact was never issued. Reasons given by the Chief Cashier early in 1941 included the fact that German propaganda would certainly allege a shortage of silver in Britain (which was true), or of foreign exchange: inflation was a further possibility. The Treasury cited shortage of paper, additional labour necessary for counting wages and the danger of the hoarding of silver coin. The public was unlikely to have welcomed the silver notes, which would have been subject to considerable wear and become quickly torn and dirty; few people outside the Bank ever saw them although they did receive some publicity in October 1940 as the result of a leak of information. *Whitaker's Almanac* mentioned them in 1941 but the editor removed the reference in subsequent editions at the request of the Secretary of the Bank. In 1947 it was decided that they should be destroyed, apart from a few specimens to be retained in the Bank's archives; a small number escaped during the pulping process at the paper mill at Snodland.[16]

Still more secret, and of immense practical importance, was the Bank's involvement with the War Office in producing the quantities of notes required for various military operations, and the co-ordination and supply of currency notes of various countries for 'special purposes', such as sabotage, financing underground movements and the preparation of purses of money for airmen in case they were shot down over enemy territory. The first Wavell offensive in the Western Desert in the winter of 1940/1 prompted the Bank to consult the Treasury about what money should be paid to the troops in the Italian African colonies. Sterling was impossible for obvious reasons, Egyptian pounds were also considered undesirable, and it was finally decided in January 1941 that a special issue of notes was to be prepared for use not only in the Western Desert but in other invaded territories as necessary. Printed with the words 'Issued by the British Military Authority', these notes became known as BMA notes; they bore the Lion and Crown emblem of the General Staff, and were issued in denominations of £1, 10s., 5s., 2s. 6d. and 1s., to which a 6d. note was later added.

BMA notes were used in many theatres of war, and a large emergency reserve was kept partly in this country and partly in the Middle East. They were also used extensively on troopships in the Mediterranean. Altogether over 259·5 million notes were issued of a nominal value of £59·8 m., all printed at the Bank's Printing Works, St Luke's in Old Street.

In addition to these over 7,000 million notes for some sixty different currency authorities were printed between April 1942 and the end of December 1944, in over 300 different denominations. (Unprinted bank note paper was also exported by Portals to eleven different countries including India who received more than 3,000 tons.)

One of the most taxing operations for the Bank was the work concerned with the Normandy landings, starting in January 1944 and continuing, with the exception of three Sundays only, every day until 14 May. Quite apart from the production of the notes this involved the packing of 2,700 boxes for UK troops; making up 2,200 packs in cardboard boxes for the airborne troops; waterproofing 1,500 boxes to prevent the notes getting wet when the lorries landed from the landing craft; the use of nearly three miles of rope and string and over that quantity of banding iron. Military working parties were employed within the Bank throughout the period, clocking up some 7,000 man hours.

The notes required for 'special purposes' posed particular problems of their own. After considerable pressure from the Bank, the various users were persuaded to co-ordinate their requirements, and monthly meetings took place in Threadneedle Street at which representatives of the Foreign Office, the War Office and the two principal Secret Service organisations would make their forecasts of what notes they required. The actual procurement of notes, many of them from occupied Europe, was largely carried out by the Secret Service, who managed to get adequate supplies into the vaults of the Bank for distribution when needed for various undercover operations. From the summer of 1943, purses were made up for Allied air crew containing notes of all the enemy or occupied territory over which they were about to fly, thus enabling them, if they crashed or had to bale out, to pay their way in local currency until they got in touch with an underground repatriation organisation. This involved large scale importation of marks, guilders, Danish crowns and Belgian and French francs. Some of these imports were paid for by means which were, as the Bank's internal war history puts it, 'outside the normal practice of a Central Bank' and included saccharine and collections of postage stamps.[17]

Among the most important of the decisions affecting British bank notes during the war was that to withdraw all those over £5 from circulation. It first surfaced in the interim report of the Bank's Post War Committee,* made in July 1942 and sent to the Treasury the following year, after consultation with the clearing banks.[18] The original suggestion was made primarily because of the almost certain abolition of the postal Censorship after the war, but there was also evidence that high sum notes were used in the black market, for hoarding and to avoid tax. Forgery was prevalent on the continent, and in any case the use of cheques was becoming more common, making such notes less necessary; but these considerations were secondary to the exchange control aspect. In April 1943 it was announced by the Chancellor that the Bank of England would issue no further notes of denominations of £10 and above, and would withdraw those already issued as the opportunity offered. The Bank knew that many of the notes were actually in the tills of the clearing banks, and indeed, largely because of the return of these, the value of high sum notes in circulation fell from £65·7 m. in April to £43·6 m. three months later.[19]

The next step was to call in the notes and demonetise them, in other words to declare that they were no longer legal tender – although such a step never frees the Bank of England from its obligation to pay the notes which, however old, can always be exchanged there by application either in person or via a commercial bank. The Bank hesitated for some time about calling them in, but at length Cobbold wrote to the Treasury in September 1944, urging that notes of £10 and above should be demonetised as soon as possible. From the exchange control point of view, he added, 'it would be an advantage if the £5 note could be similarly demonetised. But it is felt that in view of the large numbers of this denomination in the hands of the public and its wide use for commercial transactions ... the balance of advantage lies in retaining the £5 note; moreover if it were not retained early demonetisation of high sum notes would not be physically possible.' The Treasury agreed, and, after some legal discussion as to whether amendments to previous

* See chapter 3.

Banking Acts might be necessary, the Bank issued a notice on 23 March 1945 calling in the notes on 30 April.[20] By the time the notice came into effect there were about £25·8 m. in circulation, most of which were believed to be abroad.

As a result of this measure there was naturally a rise in the number of £5 notes issued in replacement. The design of this note had been under discussion within the Bank for some time, for the current note was virtually unchanged from 1855 and printed, as its higher value brethren had been, by letterpress from electrotypes in black on white paper. The German BB and other forgeries had demonstrated that this was no longer adequate protection against counterfeiting, and in November 1944 the Bank began to prepare a new note. Identical in colour and size to the old one, it was produced by lithography instead of by letterpress on metal-threaded, mould-made paper which was thicker than the hand-made paper previously used. The distinctive crackle of the old paper was much missed, and the Chancellor, shown the new production, said he had seen it 'with a twinge of regret'.[21] The new notes were issued in October 1945 and circulated side by side with the old type until these were withdrawn the following February. Within a short time the skill of Portals' papermakers enabled a thinner threaded paper to be produced and this was used for the £5 note from September 1948.

During the war years the note circulation rose from £507·3 m. in 1939 to £1,284·2 m. in 1945.[22] There were various reasons for this: full employment, higher earnings, and a tendency to hoard notes to an extent which the Bank found decidedly puzzling. Prices, in spite of some governmental control, inevitably rose, and this in turn meant that people kept a larger amount of their disposable income in notes (and coin) in order to pay for consumer goods. Notes were slower to return to the Bank, because of shorter banking hours, dispersal of workers and the Forces to places remote from banks, delays in the post and divided households. Air raids and the numbers of Allied troops stationed in this country in 1943 and 1944 all had their effect.

The German forgeries, although they had never been dropped by air or otherwise entered the country in bulk, had certainly had an effect on the British people's perception of the £5 note. Since some were known to be counterfeit, all tended to be looked on with a certain amount of suspicion. In the years immediately following the end of the war, its popularity underwent a continual decline. A further reason for this was the practice, common since Victorian times, of asking anyone tendering a £5 (or larger) note to endorse the back of it with their name and address. There was no legal obligation to do this, and some people refused: Bank

Plate 4.2    Posters, prickers and stampers marking the Bank Note Registers, 1942

of England clerks paying the notes over the counter requested a signature but never insisted on it. The use of the signature, provided of course it was genuine, helped the Bank in its provision of a service to a degree probably unique among banks of issue – the ability to keep track of high sum notes with the aid of the Bank Note Registers.

The Registers had their origin in the Note Books instituted from the first days of the Bank's establishment in 1694. The number and date of every note were entered in a ledger and when the notes had returned to the Bank and been paid and cancelled (either in Threadneedle Street or at a Branch) and scrutinised for forgeries by the Issue Office, they were handed to the Bank Note Office. Here they were first subject to a secondary cancellation – in addition to that carried out by the Issue Office – and machine-stamped with a number, again additionally to the number by which it was issued and paid. Notes were then sorted into numerical order and listed in a form suitable for posting, or entering, in the Note Register. Posting involved stamping the Register, against the relative note number, with the date of payment: this information was condensed into a figure for the day and a code letter for the month. The pricker, or checker, then took over the lists, turned up the relevant volume of the Register again and added the year against the payment date previously posted. The notes were kept for reference in the Bank Note Library for a period which was occasionally varied, but was usually for five years. A vastly detailed book-keeping system, involving by 1942 thirty-six ledgers, was maintained in addition to the records kept in the various sections of the Office. At the outbreak of the Second World War the Bank Note Office employed a staff of ninety-four, including forty-eight Non-Clerical workers (posters and stampers), dealing with an average of 62,000 high sum notes a day.[23]

The maintenance of the Registers, to the high standards of accuracy and completeness demanded and achieved by the Bank, together with the detailed records kept by the Issue Office, meant that precise information about the beginning and end of the life of the majority of high sum notes was available. The Issue Office knew to which bank any individual note had originally been delivered, the Bank Note Office knew when it had been returned to the Bank and usually by whom. This enabled the Bank to pay on notes which had been lost, stolen or destroyed, if the numbers were known – sometimes immediately, sometimes, if there was doubt as to the circumstances, after a certain period and under indemnity by a bank or insurance company in case the note should subsequently turn up. Information about the provenance of specific notes believed to have been stolen was given on request and in confidence to Scotland Yard, and occasionally Bank clerks appeared in court to testify details of issue or payment (the Bank would only allow them to do this if the Chief Cashier were subpoenaed). Individuals requesting payment of lost or destroyed notes could also be informed if notes of that number had been previously paid, and occasionally information was provided to the Inland Revenue on the date of issue of notes, which could prove crucial in cases where a claim was made, for example, that a large amount of cash had been won at a race track on a particular date. If the notes in question proved to have been issued at a later date, the story was obviously a false one.

The value of preserving this extremely expensive operation (which also took up a great deal of space) was frequently queried from the time of the 1933 Economy Committee* onwards but after deliberation it was always decided to keep it during the lifetime of the black and white notes of £5 and above. Naturally the volume of the £1 and 10s. notes issued from 1928 precluded the maintenance of similar Registers in their case, and where low sum notes were lost, stolen or totally destroyed the Bank declined to replace them. Mutilated notes, however, were a different matter. Their payment depended (and still does) on the extent to which they are damaged, and the qualification for payment at banks or post

* See chapter 6, p. 200

Plate 4.3    The Bank Note Library of Cancelled High Sum notes, 1942

offices has varied slightly over the years; it has most commonly been demanded that the note must consist of more than half the original area and contain the 'promise to pay' with at least one third of the signature and one complete number plus a portion of the other.

Notes more heavily mutilated must be submitted to the Bank of England where, at first within the Issue Office and since the mid 1970s at the Newcastle Branch, a vast body of skill and expertise has been built up in dealing with and assessing charred, soaked, torn and otherwise damaged notes, notes that have been chewed by children or animals, dug up from underground caches, rescued during the war from bombed buildings, or collected from unsavoury locations such as the clothes of a corpse long dead. (Special procedures are carried out to protect staff dealing with notes liable to carry infection.) Even the ash from totally burnt notes can be scientifically weighed and analysed, and in several cases it has been discovered that more notes were involved than had been claimed for, and payment made accordingly.[24]

In parallel with the care given to the payment of notes there runs the problem of disposal, involving the destruction of tons of paper annually and again under conditions of complete security. The original method was burning, followed by pulping in the machine installed in the Bank under the control of the Printing Department, which was replaced during the First World War by a guillotine with an automatic shaving attachment. The large store of notes which accumulated during this war (because of a decision by the Governors to extend the period of storing notes from three to seven years) were burnt at Messrs Peak Frean's biscuit factory in early 1915 under the supervision of two representatives of what was at that period known as the Accountant's Bank Note Office.* Notes were then pulped for a while, and later burnt at the Bank's Record Office in Barnes, as always under a system of dual control which ensured that, whatever the method employed, it was closely supervised by at least two clerks who had to make certain that the notes had been entirely destroyed.

During the 1920s the method changed to pulping in machines known as Miracle Mills, installed at St Luke's, which were capable of converting used notes into dry pulp at the rate of around 1,200 pounds per day apiece. Some of the pulp could be sold for small amounts for re-use in paper manufacture, and this became a more practicable proposition after methods of de-inking the pulp were developed. After the Second World War, when paper was in short supply and the note circulation rising, various paper and board mills were persuaded to pulp the notes, but the stringent security conditions the Bank was forced to impose were a constant source of irritation to them.[25]

The enormous security organisation which attended the bank notes at every stage of their life thus constituted a major preoccupation for the Chief Cashier and his Department, and practical considerations were

---

* The Bank Note Office was in the Accountant's Department from 1853 to 1935. It was then transferred to the Secretary's Department, and was renamed Accounts and Bank Note Office in 1958. In 1963 its responsibilities were transferred to the Printing Works at Debden.

under constant review as the note issue continued to increase. The Treasury, meanwhile, was more concerned with the problems of the fiduciary issue. In July 1949 P.L. Smith, a Principal in the Treasury, wrote to H.G. Askwith, then Acting Deputy Chief Cashier,* notifying him that the Treasury had obtained authority to introduce into the 1950 session of Parliament a Bill designed to 'tidy up' the fiduciary issue and the power to call in and demonetise Bank of England notes:[26] in other words to rationalise and put on a permanent footing the provisions of the 1928 and 1939 Currency and Bank Notes Acts together with subsequent Defence (Finance) Regulations 7AA and 7AB which had been passed during the war.

With regard to Regulation 7AA, which dealt with alterations to the fiduciary issue, the Treasury asked for the Bank's opinion on two possible alternatives. One was that the Treasury should be left to determine from time to time what the total fiduciary issue should be, with no basic statutory figure and no time limit. The other was a perpetuation of the current method, whereby a statutory figure was laid down and could be exceeded, following representations from the Bank, by authority of a Treasury Minute to be laid before Parliament and to be valid for not more than six months. Whereas pre-war legislation laid a limit of two years during which continuing increases could be authorised by the Treasury by successive Minutes, it was now proposed to abolish the limit which had in any case been in abeyance under the wartime regulations.

Regulation 7AB empowered the Bank to call in any of its notes of any denomination of not less than £5, after which they would cease to be legal tender. The Treasury now suggested replacing the Regulation by a clause on the same lines and drafted to include demonetisation also of £1 and 10s. notes called in. This was considered advisable because the Regulation, which only spoke of 'calling in' the £1 and 10s. notes, had created a distinction between calling in and demonetisation; the new wording would remove any possible ambiguity.

Reaction within the Bank to the first suggestions was swift and uncompromising. The Secretary, Mynors, minuted to Sir Kenneth Peppiatt and the Governors: 'I feel strongly that the Treasury should not have the power to fix the size of the Fiduciary Issue – the printing press should not appear to be under their unfettered control. This reinforces the advantage of leaving the constitutional position as it is.'[27] Governor Cobbold agreed, saying that he would press strongly for the perpetuation of the present method 'and would take up at top level if necessary'.[28]

---

* Askwith was subsequently Deputy Chief and then Chief of Establishments. See chapter 10.

This view was conveyed to the Treasury by Askwith, who added that since the distinction had been created between calling in and de-monetisation, the Bank agreed that it would be advisable to clarify the situation. For this purpose, he concluded, 'we would suggest that the provisions in existing legislation relating to issue and calling-in of Bank notes be so amended as to give the Bank power to issue, and call in, notes of such denominations (not being less than 10/-) as may be approved by the Treasury from time to time on the recommendation of the Bank'.[29]

The draft Bill which was submitted by the Treasury in October for the Bank's further observations overlooked, whether deliberately or not, Askwith's reference to 'issue' in the passage just quoted and omitted to include in the Bill any amendment to the denominations in which notes might be issued.[30] Although unwilling at this juncture to say so outright, the Bank was already contemplating the issue of a £2 note, a project ultimately doomed but which occupied, as described below, almost a decade. It was with this in mind that the altered wording had been proposed, and subsequent correspondence with the Treasury and the Parliamentary draftsmen secured it in accordance with the Bank's wishes. The true purpose of these wishes remained discreetly veiled throughout the negotiations.

By March 1950 a new draft had been prepared and received the approval of Freshfields, the Bank's solicitors. It retained the general scheme of earlier Acts in that a figure for the fiduciary issue (to be fixed at a later stage, immediately before the introduction of the Bill) was named and fluctuations above and below such a figure could be authorised by the Treasury after representations by the Bank. The procedure was simplified by making any new figure 'such specified amount as may be agreed between them [i.e. the Treasury] and the Bank', rather than repeating the existing wording which might have led to ambiguity.

The provisions relating to the issue and recall of bank notes were made general. The Bill said the Bank could issue bank notes 'of such denominations as the Treasury may approve' and gave the Bank power to call in any notes, which thereupon ceased to be legal tender; P.S. Beale, who had succeeded Peppiatt as Chief Cashier in March 1949, pointed out to the Governors that: 'These general provisions... will enable us to issue without further legislation, but subject to Treasury approval, notes of, for example, £2 or 5/- should the need arise.' He also remarked on the lack of any provision whereby notes of £5 and upwards would have legal tender in Scotland and Northern Ireland (thus continuing the status quo); in fact the Bank, as well as the Treasury, would have preferred to have legal tender status of £5 and any future higher denomination notes extended to both countries, but feared that this would lead to controversial questions about the powers of Scottish and Northern Irish banks to issue notes and the still more delicate area of fiduciary issues in Northern Ireland.[31]

In the same month, March 1950, a General Election returned the Labour government to office with a slender majority, and almost immediately the Attorney General, Sir Hartley Shawcross,* and the Lord President of Council, Herbert Morrison,† expressed their unease about the draft Bill; they felt that Parliament would baulk at the powers given to the Treasury to increase the fiduciary issue and considered that any increase over the statutory figure extending beyond six months should be subject to an Affirmative Resolution. The Treasury tried, through the Financial Secretary, to persuade them otherwise and said that if this approach failed the Chancellor would have to be consulted.[32]

Morrison, additionally, was known to be indignant at the amount of 'trouble and embarrassment' the government was currently experiencing from some of the nationalised industries, and saw in the Bill 'the Bank, as another nationalised industry, trying to contract out of Government control'.[33] The Bank for its part felt, as Beale remarked, that it was unnecessary and undesirable to insist that each and every increase should require such a Resolution with an attendant debate and 'opportunities for all the cranks to say their pieces'. The discussion continued for some weeks, with various alternatives suggested by the Bank, but the Lord President and the Attorney General stood firm, apparently in part because they feared that some unscrupulous future government might, if freed from the trammels of Parliament, print notes at will and plunge the country into wholesale inflation. In fact the Bill gave no such powers; but it was evident that the political climate was generally unfavourable to the Bill as it stood. Cobbold had all along made it clear that he was anxious to avoid controversy over the Bill, and the Treasury ultimately decided not to proceed with it during the current session. It was agreed that, for one more year at least, Defence (Finance) Regulation 7AA should stand.[34]

A year later, in the spring of 1951, the Treasury re-opened the debate once more, this time with two alternative compromise suggestions on the vexed topic of how and when changes in the fiduciary issue should be brought about – although it had been tacitly agreed, by this date and by

---

* Shawcross, Baron (1959) of Friston, Hartley W. Shawcross, PC, GBE, Kt., QC, 1902–. Attorney General, 1945–51.
† Morrison, Baron (1959) of Lambeth, Herbert S. Morrison, PC, CH, 1888–1965. Lord President of the Council and Leader of the House of Commons, 1945–51.

all concerned, that as a matter of pure economics there was no virtue at all in Parliamentary control over the note issue. The Bank agreed that it was content that alterations of the issue above the statutory figure, or the extension of a period during which such alteration was authorised, should be by Treasury Minute except at the end of a continuous three year period. A fresh draft incorporating this proposal was duly laid before the Legislation Committee of the Cabinet, but, as the Treasury subsequently informed Beale, the relevant Clause 'again met with opposition and it became clear that nothing short of a complete return to the 1928 system – which in present circumstances would automatically mean fresh legislation every two years – would be likely to get through'.[35] The Treasury felt strongly that this was going too far and therefore decided once again to drop the Bill for the present.

In October 1951 the Labour government fell and was followed by a Conservative administration under Winston Churchill. This provided the opportunity for the Bank to renew the discussion with the Treasury, and, simultaneously, to revert to the question of the profits of issue. These had, until 1939, remained in the Exchequer, but since the outbreak of war had been transferred to the Exchange Equalisation Account (EEA). The Bank had proposed early in 1951 to revert to the pre-1939 scheme, suggesting that the net amount accumulated in the EEA (representing income less net depreciation on securities) should be transferred to the Issue Department and remain there as a reserve to cover realised losses and fluctuations in value. It had subsequently been agreed between the Governor and Sir Wilfrid Eady to drop this proposal: but the Bank had not departed from its standpoint that it was correct in principle.*[36]

The Treasury found the new ministers somewhat more amenable than their predecessors to the provisions of the Bill, of which fresh drafts were made, embodying the current procedure whereby variations were made by means of a Treasury Minute which could in no instance be valid for longer than six months. The 1928 provision, that a series of Minutes authorising increases (if necessary of varying amounts) could continue for two years, also appeared, but instead of legislation at the end of any such continuous period of Minutes the new Bill provided that the two year period could be extended for a further two years at a time by Treasury Order, subject to Negative Resolution of either House of Parliament. The process could continue indefinitely.[37]

---

* Net profits of the Issue Department continued to be paid over to the Exchange Equalisation Account until 1968, after which they were credited to the National Loans Fund.

The Bill passed its First Reading in the House of Commons in January 1952, but the Parliamentary timetable of the new government was so crowded that it proved impossible to have a Second Reading during the succeeding months. In October of that year Edmund (later Sir Edmund) Compton* told Cobbold that the Treasury had been warned that opportunity would be taken to press once more for tighter Parliamentary control over the note issue and that there was 'no certainty that the Bill would in effect get on to the Statute Book. His guess was that the Bill would not be proceeded with in the immediate future ...'.[38] In fact it died with the current session at the end of October, and was pigeon-holed once more.

The Bill finally achieved its Second Reading in December 1953, introduced by the Financial Secretary to the Treasury, John Boyd-Carpenter.† The fiduciary basis for the issue was fixed at £1,575 m. (the level at which it stood on the day of the Bill's introduction). One of the main opponents of the Bill, as both Bank and Treasury had expected, was the Labour Member for Nottingham South, Norman Smith,‡ who was greatly interested in the topic of currency reform and held strong views, in particular, on bank note design. He and other Members had much to say on the question of whether the Monarch's head should appear on bank notes, on the necessity or otherwise of the phrase 'I promise to pay' and on the dirtiness of the notes currently in circulation (all of which considerations were of course under regular review within the Bank). However the Bill successfully passed its Second Reading and moved on to the Committee stage. This was achieved with only minor changes in the wording, and after a smooth passage through the House of Lords it received Royal Assent on 10 February 1954, coming into operation on 22 February nearly five years after its inception.[39]

Among the critics of dirty notes during the Second Reading of the Currency and Bank Notes Bill was James MacColl,§ who advised that if sterling were to be able to 'look the dollar in the face ... [the Financial Secretary] should take good care that sterling's face is washed, because the £1 will never have the reputation which it should have if it appears in the debased state of many notes'. The grubbiness of the notes had been a complaint for several years, as the Bank sought to alleviate some of the problems of the rising circulation by putting a certain amount of pressure on the clearing banks both to re-issue notes themselves more readily and

---

\* Compton, Sir E.G., GCB, KCB (1965), 1906–. Third Secretary, Treasury, 1949–58.

† Boyd-Carpenter, Baron (1972), John A. Boyd-Carpenter, PC, 1908–. Financial Secretary, Treasury, 1951–4.

‡ Smith, H. Norman, 1890–1962. MP (Lab. Co-op), Nottingham South, 1944–55.

§ MacColl, James E., 1908–71. MP (Lab.), Widnes Division of Lancashire, 1950–71.

Dividend Day at the Bank of England: oil painting by George Elgar Hicks. This was painted c. 1850 and exhibited at the Royal Academy in 1859

The 2s. 6d. and 5s. 'silver notes' prepared for use in the Second World War but not issued

Unissued design by Stephen Gooden for the back of a 10s note, 1954/5

Design by Stephen Gooden for £2 note in the Houblon Series, which was not issued

Design by Robert Austin for the front of the £1 Series C note, first issued in 1960

The Bank Guard leaving the Bank at sunrise: oil painting by H. S. Kortright, 1936. Kortright worked in the Dividend Office from 1917 to 1935

to accept parcels of re-issued notes from the Bank. This was by no means a new problem: the Bank itself had come under pressure from the Treasury during the First World War when the General Post Office, at that time responsible for the destruction of Treasury notes, had complained about the large number of clean notes among those sent for destruction. The Bank started sorting £1 and 10s. notes for re-issue on a small scale in 1917 and extended it in 1925, when the process, known as 'garbling' (in its original meaning of sorting), was carried out by hand; two years later machine garbling was introduced.[40] During the war, as mentioned above, the Bank successfully secured the co-operation of the clearing banks to extend the life of the notes, but the problem became acute in 1948. At the end of that year it was realised that the estimated production of notes for 1949 might fall short of the estimated issues for the same period. In March 1949 so-called 'packet garbling' of the intake of £1 and 10s. notes began, those that could be re-issued being set aside to form a special store: the condition of the notes paid in by the banks at that time was such that 65 per cent could be set aside for re-issue. Both the clearing banks and the Scottish banks were approached via the Committee of London Clearing Bankers and asked to refrain from paying in any of the new plate printed notes, unless really dirty, and also to continue to re-issue any lithographic notes in reasonable condition. This appeal went largely unheeded at first, and repeated approaches to the 'Big Five' had to be made as well as to the smaller commercial banks before the Bank's conditions were satisfied. Re-issuable notes were first issued to the banks in London in June 1949, and at the same time the Bank initiated garbling of individual notes, rather than packets, at first by hand under a system suggested by the Inspector of Offices and Branches, and shortly afterwards by the pre-war method using machines, which proved more satisfactory.[41]

The Bank did not like this practice any more than the clearing banks and the public liked to receive used notes, but it was inevitable if the overall demand were to be satisfied. Various requests for special treatment were made to the Bank, most of them from firms with large work forces where the filling of pay packets by machine was considerably hindered if new notes were not obtainable, and these received sympathetic consideration wherever possible. Garbling, however, had to continue, and in April 1952 even more stringent measures were initiated. Each of the clearing banks undertook to circularise its branches in an attempt to reclaim a further 10 per cent of notes and at the same time to explore the possibility of extending interchangeability of notes between local banks within larger areas than was currently practised. Towards the end of the year a further step was taken after consultation with the

Committee, whereby a pool of bankers' surplus re-issuable notes was held in Threadneedle Street.[42] This, although it naturally involved considerable administrative problems for the Bank, proved satisfactory in practice, and the effective life of £1 and 10s. notes was gradually extended until by 1957 the average life of the 10s. note was six months, of the £1, nineteen months, and of the £5, nearly twenty months; but from this date these periods began to shorten once more.[43] The clearing banks re-issued £5 notes, but the Bank of England never did so until after the replacement of the white 'fiver', although the possibility was several times explored.

Within two years of the amalgamation of the note issue in 1928, the Chairman of the Committee on St Luke's recommended to the Committee of Treasury that alternative designs for the existing £1 and 10s. notes should be prepared. This was agreed, and the Bank approached the Royal Mint Advisory Committee for a recommendation as to a suitable artist. Of various names put forward, three were selected in 1930 to submit designs – Stephen Gooden,* Kruger Gray and Frederick Griggs. Arthur Whitworth,† who was chairman of the St Luke's Committee from 1925 to 1946, strongly favoured Gooden who was finally selected.[44]

Gooden, whose artistic career began with etching and woodcuts, had switched to engraving in 1923, and was one of the artists responsible for the revival of this art which had fallen out of popularity since the previous century. During the early 1930s he completed a number of excellent designs for £1 and 10s. notes (including some which were two directional, in the manner of playing cards) and of these it was decided to proceed with notes bearing a portrait of Sir John Houblon, the first Governor of the Bank. A portrait, instantly recognisable and posing serious difficulties to forgers, gives valuable security to a bank note, and Houblon seemed a particularly suitable choice for the new note which, as mentioned earlier, the Bank thought could be issued either in 1944, its 250th anniversary, or in 1948 which would mark the 20th anniversary of the 1928 Act.

In 1936 proofs of the Houblon design were submitted to the Committee of Treasury, and then to the Court, and were approved. The advent of the Second World War, and the emergency measures which were forced upon the Bank's note production, made it impossible to issue the new note in 1944. In that year the designs were shown to the Treasury

---

* Gooden, Stephen, CBE, RA, 1892–1955.

† Whitworth, Arthur, 1875–1972. Director, Bank of England, 1919–46. Chairman, Brazilian Warrant Co. Ltd.

and were seen by Eady, Bridges, Barlow and Henderson; in a letter to Governor Catto approving the design, and the choice of Houblon, Eady wrote that all four had agreed 'that in so far as the prestige of sterling notes is affected by their appearance an elegant note possibly illustrating the long history and great traditions of the Bank would be as effective as one that shows a portrait of a blowzy Britannia'.[45]

After the war the question was re-opened, but production difficulties made a 1948 issue of the Houblon note impossible. The Bank was still anxious to begin a new issue, not least because this would enable the profits of 'dead' notes to be paid to the Treasury,* but it became evident that production of the Houblon note would make intolerable demands on a Printing Works already stretched to full capacity. During the enforced period of delay, doubts began to be felt about the suitability of the Houblon design itself. Questions had already been asked, in the House of Commons and elsewhere, as to whether, now that the Bank was nationalised, it should not represent the head of the reigning Monarch on the notes. This the Bank was unwilling to do, largely on the traditional grounds that the notes were Bank of England and not Government notes – a feeling which if anything had been intensified by the recent nationalisation. The Bank was also very conscious of the fact that any design, however good, would meet with criticism, and was most anxious, as Cobbold told Sir Edward Bridges, 'that the design of the Monarch's head should not be exposed to criticism'.[46] Despite these sentiments, however, there was growing unease within the Bank: it was felt that to produce a new note with a portrait of the first Governor could well expose the Bank itself to just the sort of criticism it was anxious to avoid.

As well as questions of design, the Bank was much exercised over possible new denominations. A £2 note had not been produced since the Restriction Period, but there was a body of opinion within the Bank that the issue of such a denomination might prove popular enough to wean the public from its strong attachment to the £1 – an attachment which had survived the war and consequent inflation and which was one of the underlying reasons for the size of the note issue and the fact that British consumption of notes per head of the population was so much greater than that of other countries. The £5 note, even in 1949 when wages were increasing, still represented an inconveniently large amount for many people, and Chamberlain, in the course of the lengthy internal debate about the desirability of a £2 note, mentioned that on many occasions he had found that 'a call for a specimen £5 from the pockets of both Directors and high officials of the Bank has drawn a blank'.[47] The final

* See appendix A, 'Dead Notes'.

Plate 4.4    One of the last famous 'white' five pound notes, printed to this design from 1793 to 1956

decision to proceed with plans for a £2 note was based chiefly on the preponderance of £1 notes, which indicated 'possible scope for a higher denomination', but was also influenced by the possibilities of economy in production and management of the note issue and in handling notes in quantity throughout the country. By October 1949 a design for the note was being prepared by Gooden in the Houblon series.

The unpopularity of the £5 led a growing number of employers and of the public to write both to the Bank and to their Members of Parliament, as well as on occasion to the Treasury, complaining about the 'flimsy and cumbersome' note, the difficulties associated with its negotiation and its size which often would not fit into standard wallets. It also caused complications in making up pay packets, either because employers wanted large quantities of £1 notes in order to avoid using it, or because workers who did receive £5 notes immediately changed them in local banks and Post Offices for lower denominations. By early 1950 the Bank had decided that it could delay no longer. On 10 February Beale wrote to D.W. Tilley, the General Manager of the Printing Works, to tell him that the Governors wished him to proceed with the preparation of an alternative design for the £5 'to form one of a series with the existing Houblon design'.[48]

In spite of this, there were still reservations about the suitability of Houblon, and Gooden was now asked if he could change the design, incorporating a different portrait. He replied decidedly that he could not:

the notes had been designed with the Houblon portrait as their main feature and to change that would mean altering many other elements of the note. He felt that it would be preferable to re-design them altogether, a process which would take at least two or three years; the question was further complicated because by this time it had been decided to build a new Printing Works outside London and it was thought to be unlikely that a new note could be produced until the move had been made. After much discussion at the highest level within the Bank it was finally decided in November 1950 that the designs for the proposed Houblon £1 and 10s. notes should stand, but that Gooden should also be asked to begin work on a new design for these denominations, which would be 'held in reserve or be issued instead of the Houblon if it is decided not to proceed with the latter'. Because of the value of a portrait as a protective device, the new design would certainly incorporate one, perhaps of Britannia, and for the backs of the notes Gooden suggested a Doorkeeper in traditional dress, or 'Bank Guard in full dress but without indication of regiment'.[49] Preparations for a trial run at the Printing Works of the Houblon £1 and 10s. were suspended.

The slow and complex work of design and engraving a bank note with all its attendant security devices was, in Gooden's case, further extended by long periods of illness. By October 1952 he had completed the engraving of the Houblon series £2, and preliminary proofs had been received from Bradbury Wilkinson, the firm of engravers and printers which had been able to supply the necessary expertise (and security) for the highly complex process of engraving the portrait.* Work on the alternative design for the £5 had not begun, but Gooden had submitted, the previous year, a preliminary drawing for the completely new 10s. note, which he had then been asked to amend. Questions continued to be asked as to when the notes would incorporate a portrait of the sovereign, and these increased after the accession of Queen Elizabeth II in February 1952. In July Gooden suggested that to have a portrait of Britannia, which he had earlier favoured, might be 'muddling' now that a new Queen was on the throne, and he suggested a portrait of the Queen or of the Queen dressed as Britannia. The Bank, however, remained unconvinced, but was still anxious to replace the existing £5 as soon as possible with the new multi-coloured Houblon design which Gooden produced in the middle of 1953. This was approved by the Governors and Committee of Treasury but Gooden himself was dissatisfied with it and in September 1953 he suddenly produced an entirely new design for the £5 with a head

---

* The Bank had also employed 'outside' engravers on the 1928 designs, one French and one Spanish.

Plate 4.5   Watercolour design by Stephen Gooden for Britannia on Series B £5
note

of Britannia on the front and a revised version of an earlier 'Lion and
Key'* design for the back.[50] This met with great approval within the
Bank, where it was initially known as the Series III note, the Houblon
designs being Series II.

Further delays were occasioned by the lengthy passage of the Currency
and Bank Notes Bill, because the Chancellor (one of the few outside the
Bank who knew anything of the plans for a new issue) asked for Houblon
to be held up until it was successfully through Parliament. Gooden, by
nature a slow and painstaking worker, was ill again. Meanwhile in
January 1955 L.K. O'Brien succeeded Beale as Chief Cashier and almost
immediately put up a strong case for having a design prepared with the
Queen's head. This was a particularly attractive proposition now that
Britain had a young and beautiful monarch, he pointed out, adding that
the Governors and Directors were after all appointed by her. By March

---

\* The lion, symbolising strength, is the traditional guardian of treasure; the double-
warded key represents the dual responsibility of the Bank to protect and safeguard the
nation's treasure and to release it when necessary.

1955 the Houblon design had finally been abandoned. It had come to seem, not least to its designer, old-fashioned and unsuitable, and the excellence of Gooden's Britannia £5 note sealed its fate. It was hoped at this date to issue the £5 in two years time. On 1 April 1955 O'Brien wrote: 'The Governor suggested this morning that it might be as well to proceed at once with a new design embodying the portrait of HM the Queen. I would greatly welcome a decision to do this. The present Britannia designs for the £1 and 10s. notes are not considered to be acceptable from the technical printing point of view...'[51]

Gooden's illness worsened during the spring and summer of 1955 and it became evident that he would not be able to work on any further notes: he died in September without having seen the issue of a note in any of the many designs he had produced while under contract to the Bank. By this date it had been definitely agreed to proceed with notes bearing the portrait of the Queen, for which an engraver specialising in portraits would obviously be necessary, perhaps chosen by competition as Gooden had been in 1930.

Several names were mooted but in the opinion of Malcolm Osborne,* the President of the Royal Society of Painter-Etchers and Engravers, only one was 'in the Gooden class' and that was Robert Austin† who had recently retired as Professor of Engraving at the Royal College of Art. Austin was appointed in Gooden's place in December 1955 and unlike his predecessor was to work closely with the technical experts at the Printing Works. This, noted O'Brien, would ensure that his designs were not only aesthetically satisfactory but would also have all regard to the security and printing considerations.[52]

It was settled that Austin would begin work on the £1, as this still formed by far the largest proportion of bank note circulation. An immediate preoccupation was with the proposed portrait of the Queen. It would naturally be necessary to approach her at a later date, to obtain her permission for the use of a portrait, but certain details had to be discussed at once. Austin said that he would prefer to work from an 'original, artistic portrait' rather than a photograph, but it was realised that the latter would give greater scope for choice in such matters as style of dress, whether the Queen wore a crown or tiara and whether she was shown full-face or in profile.[53]

---

* Osborne, Malcolm, CBE, RA, PPRE, 1880–1963. President, Royal Society of Painter-Etchers and Engravers, 1938–62.

† Austin, Robert S., RA, RWS, 1895–1973. Professor of Engraving, Royal College of Art; President, Royal Society of Painters in Watercolours, 1956; Royal Society of Painter-Etchers and Engravers, 1962.

After much indeterminate discussion among the handful of people in the Bank who were privy to the subject, it was decided to approach the Royal Mint to have the benefit of its recent experience of producing coins bearing the portrait of the Queen. From Sir Lionel Thompson* it was learnt that this was based on an original photograph taken by the well-known society photographer Dorothy Wilding.[54] By now another design consideration had become urgent, that of the watermark. Recent developments in the printing field, which had been closely monitored and indeed furthered by the Bank since 1951, meant that future note printing was likely to be carried out by the web process using a continuous roll of paper rather than individual sheets. This in turn would necessitate the use of a continuous watermark designed in a panel running the length of the roll, and the original suggestion of having a second portrait of the Queen as a watermark was turned down because it would be impossible to ensure that each reproduction would appear in full. Many of the notes would inevitably carry incomplete sections of the watermark at either top or bottom, and it therefore seemed 'disrespectful' to use the portrait of any living person.

Austin was already beginning to find his close involvement with the Printing Works somewhat restrictive, in spite of his own enthusiasm for the task and their efforts to be as accommodating as possible. G.C. Fortin† noted in March 1956 that the artist 'appeared to be getting a little restive and to be finding the rather deliberate pace of the Bank rather tiresome '... I can see him getting a little difficult if and when he is required to retrace his steps over this [i.e. the watermark] or any other part of the design...'.[55]

Much retracing of steps did indeed prove necessary over the watermark and many other aspects of the design, and soon someone else was chafing over the restrictions placed on her by the Bank. Dorothy Wilding had been chosen, under stringent conditions of secrecy, to take an original photograph of the Queen who had graciously agreed that her portrait should be used on a forthcoming series of £1 and 10s. notes when the subject was mentioned to her by the Chancellor, Harold Macmillan,‡ early in 1956.[56] Austin, on being told that the photographer was 'a female genius', merely remarked 'Heaven help us'; but it soon transpired that the actual picture was to be taken by Mrs Wilding's senior assistant. This

---

*  Thompson, Sir L. Lionel H., CBE, 1893–1983. Deputy Master and Comptroller of the Royal Mint and *ex officio* Engraver of HM's Seals, 1950–7.

†  Fortin was at this date supernumerary Principal in the Chief Cashier's Office; previously Staff Manager at St Luke's Printing Works, he returned to the new Printing Works at Debden and became General Manager in 1964.

‡  Stockton, 1st Earl of (1984), Maurice Harold Macmillan, OM, PC, FRS, 1894–1984.

lady at first categorically refused to take any directions from Austin as to how he wished his royal subject to be posed, or how the photograph was to be lighted – both vitally important points on which Austin naturally held strong views. However under the intimation of 'possible alternatives' her co-operation was assured and the actual sitting was harmoniously achieved, the photographer meekly accepting that her role was 'merely [to] squeeze the bulb when told'.[57] The Queen posed as Austin had requested, in 'a slightly off the shoulder gown...plus coronet, necklace and ear ornaments', wearing the Garter Ribbon with a diamond brooch on the shoulder. The coronet was in fact a diadem made originally for George IV, it having been decided at an early stage that a crown would take up too much height in the portrait.[58]

In spite of the cloak of secrecy in which the Bank shrouded all the varying bank note projects now in train, details inevitably leaked out as more people had to be involved. In April 1956, a month before the sitting at Buckingham Palace, Fortin noted that 'the press barrage seems to be closing in' on the £5 note, and in July the Bank publicly announced that it would be issued 'early in 1957', and also that notes of a future series, which was unlikely to be issued for several years, would bear the portrait of the Queen.[59] This would be the first time that the reigning monarch had appeared on a Bank of England note, although the Treasury notes produced between 1914 and 1928 had pictured George V. By this time Austin was embroiled in further problems over the watermark, both his first effort, a girl with plaits, and his second, of stylised leaves, having proved unacceptable. Bank note design was proving such a time-consuming affair at the Printing Works that a special Design Section was established there during the summer of 1956.

The wording of the traditional phrase 'I promise to pay' was a further cause of discussion. It had long been recognised that, since notes had ceased to be payable in gold, this was something of an anachronism. Fun had been poked at it during the passage of the 1954 Act through Parliament, when F.J. Erroll* had speculated as to what would happen 'if I went to the Bank of England, asked to see Mr. Beale, handed him the [£1] note and asked him to give me £1. Presumably he would give me another note – and so on we should go, backwards and forwards, until closing time, and then we might go on after that...'[60]

A valid point lay behind this jesting, and the Bank decided to consult its solicitors, Freshfields, on whether or not to retain the phrase. The

---

* Erroll, Baron (1964) of Hale, Frederick James Erroll, PC, 1914–. MP (Con.), Altrincham and Sale, 1945–64. Economic Secretary, Treasury, 1958–9; Minister of State BoT, 1959–61; President, 1961–3; Minister of Power, 1963–4.

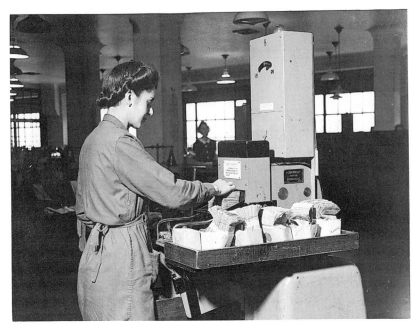

Plate 4.6   Cancelling bank notes in the Issue Office, 1942

legal opinion was that the character of the note as a promissory note made its retention advisable, and the Bank's final decision not to change or omit the wording was 'partly because it underlines that the note is a Bank of England note'.[61]

Gooden's £5 note was first issued on 16 January 1957. O'Brien had decided that it should be referred to as the Series B note, rather than Series III, because the former Series II, the Houblon note, had been scrapped. Austin's notes thus became Series C, often called the portrait notes.

The new £5, bearing a 'powerful, confident design exhibiting extraordinary draughtsmanship',[62] was printed on the same type of paper, plus metallic thread, as the £1. Britannia, in a helmet, sat on the left, with a window watermark of Britannia on the right. Under the Chief Cashier's signature was a drawing of St George killing the dragon, and on the back was the best of Gooden's several versions of the Lion and Key, on a ground of geometrical lines in blue over a mauve and green background. It had been produced with exemplary speed in scarcely two years in spite of the upheaval caused by the move of the Printing Works to Debden in the summer of 1956, but although its design was generally admired the note did not meet with unqualified approval. Britannia was variously criticised as having too much hair, looking too severe, and having 'too matronly' a bustline, while the note was described in Parliament in July as 'looking like a cross between stage money and the £1 Scottish bank note'. Those professionally involved with the handling of notes, such as cashiers and shop assistants, also complained that its colour, predominantly blue, was too similar to that of the £1 issued by the Commercial Bank of Scotland. But the public certainly approved of it.

The practice of writing the name and address of the tenderer on the back of the note died a natural death with the advent of the coloured £5, removing one of the chief obstacles to its ready use, and within nine months of its issue O'Brien was able to report to the Governors that the total of the new notes in circulation exceeded that of the old type, and that it was helping to overcome 'the traditional prejudice against the use of high sum notes'.[63] The issue of the new note was also the occasion of an almost complete discontinuance of the Register. It had been agreed three years before, with the concurrence of the Treasury, that there should be no Register for the new £5, which was then expected before the end of 1954; it was the intention that the Register should be worked out for the old-style note, a process likely to take some two and a half years. However, because of the delays and the increase in circulation which had since occurred, it was later estimated that it would take nearer three and a half years, and for that reason, as well as because of the 'much diminished value of the Register compared with pre-war days' it was felt by the Bank that the upkeep on its expenditure was no longer justified. Its costs were approaching £200,000 a year: it comprised some 4,000 volumes. The views of the Treasury were canvassed once more, and it was decided to close the Register with effect from 28 May 1956.*[64]

The progress of Austin's Series C continued to be slow and at times decidedly troublesome. Portals confessed to being 'at the end of their tether' over the continual re-designing of the watermark, which of course they had to incorporate in the bank note paper itself. Austin's first attempt at the Queen's portrait had been rejected and O'Brien in November 1957 expressed his dissatisfaction with the replacement even after six months alteration, although by this stage a successful watermark, in the form of a head crowned with laurel leaves, had finally been achieved.

The procedure followed by Austin was much the same as that adopted by Gooden, except for the fact, already noted, that he was working much

---

* There were two exceptions: a Register for notes of £10 and upwards, and an 'unofficial' Register for letterpress £5 notes dated earlier than September 1944. This covered the German wartime counterfeits, and was finally discontinued from 1 March 1960.

more closely with the Printing Works than Gooden had done. After he had produced a rough sketch showing size, position of numbers, portrait and watermark, with an indication of the necessary lettering, this was discussed at the Printing Works and preliminary engravings of a detailed portrait made in accordance with the artist's requirements. These engravings were done, as they had been for Gooden's note, by the firm of Bradbury Wilkinson. It had been recognised by all concerned from the beginning that the portrait of the Queen was likely to prove extremely difficult and so indeed it was. Every alteration, however slight, involved considerable delay and several fresh dies had to be prepared by Bradburys in the course of getting the design exactly right.

In all Austin prepared three versions of the Queen's portrait, the third and final version being finished and engraved by June 1958. Nobody was entirely happy with it but after a few further alterations it was suggested that the note might be shown to the Queen; the following month the Governor showed it to the Chancellor and the Prime Minister who had no very serious criticisms.[65]

The Queen, shown the note by Sir Michael Adeane,* her Private Secretary, had only minor alterations to suggest.[66] But the history of difficulties and delays that had attended its progress, centred on the objections made to the portrait during a period of more than two years, suggested to the Chief Cashier that an informal committee composed of two or three Directors should be set up so that he could consult them from the outset over new issues 'on matters of taste and design'. The three chosen were Sir John Hanbury-Williams, Sir William Keswick and Michael Babington Smith.†[67]

It was now time to consider the extension of Series C, and the Bank's first intention was to produce £10, £5, £2, £1 and 10s. notes all incorporating the current portrait and all of the same size (like American dollar bills) but of different basic colours. The £1 would be the first to appear but Austin was already at work, before the end of 1958, on the design for a £2 note. The success of the £5 in reducing the number of £1 notes in circulation seemed to endorse the Bank's expectations of the usefulness of this new denomination, and in the summer of 1959 the Bank decided to seek the approval of the Treasury for its issue. Work on the £2 had pride of place at Debden, where there were hopes that it would be the next after the £1 to be issued, and it was even thought possible it might be issued simultaneously with the £1. Unfortunately

---

* Adeane, Baron (1972) of Stamfordham, Michael Edward Adeane, PC, GCB, GCVO, 1910–84. Private Secretary to the Queen and Keeper of HM's Archives, 1953–72.
† See notes, pp. 35, 77 and 120 respectively.

Macmillan, Prime Minister since January 1957, had doubts about it from the first, fearing that it might be seen as an indication of inflation. Ernest Marples,* the Minister of Transport, was also known to be strongly against it. By August 1959 the Chancellor, Derick Heathcoat Amory,† had agreed that the proposal should be 'left on one side for the moment and considered again later in the year';[68] Debden was warned to stop work on it. The Chancellor himself favoured the idea, and in November pointed out to his colleagues the significant savings to the Treasury if two out of every ten £1 notes currently in circulation were replaced by a single £2 note, which would mean a reduction of the number of notes in circulation by over a hundred million and a fall by about the same number in the total issued each year. But on 17 November the Cabinet decided against it, a decision greeted with intense disappointment within the Bank and especially at Debden.[69]

The announcement by the Bank, later that month, of the forthcoming note series stated that there would be two sizes: the £5 and £10 notes would be slightly larger than the £1 and 10s. This at once caused an outcry, as the difficulty that the blind would experience in distinguishing between the notes was forcibly expressed both by members of the public – blind and sighted – and by interested bodies, such as St Dunstan's and the Royal National Institute for the Blind. It was estimated that there were, in addition to 120,000 blind people in Britain, a further 20,000– 25,000 who were partially sighted, and added to this agitation on their behalf were complaints from bank cashiers and one of their unions, the Central Council of Bank Staff Associations. After consultation with representatives of some of the associations for the blind, the Bank revised its plans once more and agreed to produce each denomination in a different size. This was announced in March 1960.[70]

The new £1 was first issued on 17 March 1960.‡ There were some reservations even within the Bank as to its design, which immediately drew forth a barrage of criticism from all over Britain. The banking unions, the CCBSA and the National Union of Bank Employees, protested about the 'very unsatisfactory' position of the numbers (placed top left and bottom right) which they claimed made counting difficult: a rather peremptory demand that the Bank should consult them about future note design met with polite but firm refusal. Television, press and

---

* Marples, Baron (1974) of Wallasey, Alfred Ernest Marples, PC, FCA, 1907–78. Minister of Transport, 1959–64.

† Amory, Viscount (1960), Derick Heathcoat Amory, KG, PC, GCMG, TD, DL, 1899–1981. Chancellor of the Exchequer, January 1958–July 1960.

‡ Almost 20,000 million of its predecessors had been printed. Annual production rose from 356 million in 1929 to 975 million in 1958.

Plate 4.7    Women clerks examining used notes in the Bank Note Office, 1942

radio were alike hostile to the artistic merits of the note, the cartoonist
Osbert Lancaster saying that it reminded him of 'a picture in an old-
fashioned medical book of the stomach of a child who had recently
swallowed a penny'. The portrait of the Queen was widely condemned as
a bad likeness, and Austin in order to avoid a posse of reporters anxious
to interview him set off on a desperate chase around the countryside. The
Chief Cashier took the unusual step of being interviewed about the note
for radio and television and was treated with deference; there was no
such inhibition in Parliament where Anthony Barber,* Economic
Secretary to the Treasury, had the task of defending the note in answer
to such criticisms as 'weak, shabby and unimpressive' and, from Harold
Wilson,† 'more like a ticket or a detergent voucher than a bank note'.[71]

   The Bank took these criticisms fairly philosophically, realising that a
new note 'invariably (had) a hostile reception ... its merits being noted in
a shining obituary when its successor appears'. A letter from the banker
Ferdinand de Goldschmidt Rothschild in *The Daily Telegraph*[72] pointed
out that there had been 'uproar' in Switzerland two years previously

---

\* Barber, Baron (1974) of Wentbridge, Anthony P.L. Barber, PC, TD, DL, 1920–.
   Economic Secretary to the Treasury, 1959–62.
† Wilson, Baron (1983) of Rievaulx, J. Harold Wilson, KG, OBE, PC, FRS, 1916–. MP
   (Lab.), Huyton, Lancs., 1950–83. Leader of Labour Party, 1970–6, Prime Minister and
   First Lord of the Treasury, 1964–70.

over the new franc note, but now no-one took the notes 'for anything else than what they stand for, i.e. the face value'. Even so, there was a consensus of opinion that outside professional expertise might be of value in future, and a critical letter from the Council of Industrial Design prompted Governor Cobbold to write to Lord Bridges,* Chairman of the Royal Fine Art Commission, to ask who – if the Bank did decide to seek help from outside – might be the best source. In May 1960, after discussions with Bridges and Sir Duncan Oppenheim,† the Design Council's Chairman, the Bank decided to ask two people with recognised competence in the design field to 'advise generally' on future notes. These were Sir Gordon Russell‡ and Professor Anthony Blunt.§[73]

In July 1960 Austin produced his designs for the Series C 10s, which were well liked within the Bank. Blunt, who was ill at this time and was to recuperate abroad for some months, took little part in the discussion over the 10s. note, but Russell was unimpressed by his first sight of it which he found 'a curious assortment of unrelated shapes'.[74] One element of the design of the £1 which had come in for criticism from the typographer Sir Francis Meynell‖ was the lettering: he complained particularly of the arbitrary mixture of upper and lower case. Some changes in this respect were made to the 10s. note, which was first issued on 12 October 1961, but were still not enough to satisfy Meynell who felt that the design remained 'ignominious'.[75]

General reactions to the 10s were, however, much less hostile than to its predecessor. By this date Austin's association with the Bank was nearing its end. He had done a considerable amount of work on other denominations in the portrait series, including of course the ill-fated £2, but even before the appearance of the £1 the Bank had decided that a younger artist should be chosen to prepare alternative designs for the £5 and £10, with a different portrait of the Queen. The delicate task of telling Austin of this decision was left to the General Manager of the Printing Works, who managed with admirable tact to enlist Austin's support in the search for his successor. A favourite soon emerged in the person of Reynolds Stone,** who, although primarily a wood rather than a steel engraver, was keen to try his hand and was 'not put off by the need

---

* Bridges, Baron, see note p. 40.
† Oppenheim, Sir Duncan, Kt. (1960), 1904–. Chairman, Council of Industrial Design, 1960–72.
‡ Russell, Sir S. Gordon, CBE, MC, 1892–1980. Managing Director (1926–40) and later Chairman (1967–77) of Gordon Russell Ltd. Director, Council of Industrial Design, 1947–59.     § Blunt, Sir Anthony, see chapter 2, p. 73
‖ Meynell, Sir Francis, 1891–1975. Director, Nonesuch Press Ltd. Typographic Adviser to HM Stationery Office, 1945–66.
** Stone, Reynolds, CBE, RDI, FRSA, 1909–79. Designer and Engraver.

to use mechanical aids like geometric lathes'. In early 1961 he and Austin both showed their design for the £5 note, Stone's – a version of which was eventually used – finding much more favour.[76]

Austin ceased to work for the Bank at the end of October 1961. He had, he wrote to O'Brien, enjoyed the 'superb challenge…but the puzzling frustrations were often disturbing'. Timetables had often seemed more important than the job; but he had been conscious of the 'enormous honour' of working for the Bank. 'I had been designing in the printing industry since I was 13…but this coming to me at 60 years led me to think that at last here was a round peg fitted into a round hole.'[77]

As well as the absorbing questions of design, many other aspects of the note issue had naturally engaged the attention of the Chief Cashier and his Department during the 1950s. The important task of estimating future note requirements became increasingly complex as the circulation figures continued to rise. As the paper situation eased, the reluctance of paper mills to purchase the cancelled notes grew, until in the autumn of 1957 the Bank had to tell the Treasury that no mills were prepared any longer to take notes under adequate security conditions. Other means of destruction had to be sought, the best proving to be burning at power stations, which meant that the small income which had been realised from the mills was replaced by an expense which was included in the overall charge made to the Treasury for the issue, custody and payment of notes. Burning, primarily at Battersea and Fulham power stations, was carried out until the Bank was able to undertake the work itself after the completion of the Paid Note Building at Debden in 1961. Inevitably there were occasional episodes, much relished by the popular press, when partially burnt notes escaped via a flue or were detected in loads of ash and clinker destined for use by the construction industry, but the security measures insisted on by the Bank and accepted with good grace by the power stations kept such accidents to a minimum. Gratuities were paid by the Bank to the stokers involved for what was a considerable disturbance to their normal routine, and Bank staff who supervised the burning under extremely hot and dirty conditions were also paid an allowance in compensation.[78]

Forgeries mercifully dwindled and after the production of the multi-coloured £5 fell away still further. Problems were experienced at various dates over defacement of the notes; in 1953 many were returned to the Bank over-stamped with the words 'Home Rule for Scotland', and in the same year the perforation by a major football pool promoting company of the notes received by post, for internal accounting purposes, caused considerable annoyance until after several representations from the Bank the firm agreed to stop the practice.[79]

Interest was aroused by the report, which later proved false, that the United States was experimenting with nylon notes, and the Bank later became engaged in a protracted law case concerning a patent for a coated bank note. A Dutchman, Hendrik van Houten, had invented a method of coating bank note paper with a protective plastic covering which was used experimentally for a short time by the Netherlands Bank, which had taken out a patent in an attempt to prevent any use of similar material in the United Kingdom without payment of a royalty. Several bank note printers in Britain, including the Bank of England, considered that the patent was unfairly wide and restrictive in its application and acted together to try to have it revoked. Eventually, on a lapse of time basis, van Houten was successfully precluded from applying for a renewal of the patent at the end of 1961.[80]

The issue of the new £1 note in February 1960 was instrumental in bringing about a slight relaxation in the Bank's attitude towards reproduction of its notes. This was, and indeed remains, a sensitive area, because of the inherent danger that any photographic reproduction might itself be used to defraud, or that the plates or negatives involved might be used wrongfully. Until 1946, almost no reproduction of notes was permitted at all under the relevant legislation: the Forgery Act 1913 Section 9 and the Criminal Justice Act 1925 Section 38. The Bank was aware that several reproductions produced for quite innocent purposes had subsequently got into the wrong hands and been used fraudulently: some of them although very poor imitations had been accepted folded and in bad lighting conditions by taxi drivers and bartenders. Whenever documents or articles bearing reproductions of all or part of a Bank of England note came to the Bank's notice, it was invariable practice to take immediate steps to stop publication and to obtain the surrender of the blocks or dies and of the stocks of the goods in question.

Difficulties did arise, however, because of the wording of the relevant parts of the Acts, and Counsel's opinion was on more than one occasion sought by Freshfields on behalf of the Bank. Opinion was divided as to whether 'intent to defraud' was essential before a prosecution could be brought under Section 9 of the Forgery Act and if Section 38 of the Criminal Justice Act amounted to a complete ban on all reproductions or whether it was necessary to establish that the resemblance was 'calculated to deceive'. These problems were not resolved by various judgements in the courts, and under increasing pressure from advertisers it was decided in 1946, in agreement with the Treasury, that the Bank would not in future raise objections to reproductions of bank notes for use in advertisements where it was plain that these could not be passed off as real notes. The Advertising Association was advised accordingly in

August 1946 and requested to refer all doubtful cases to the Bank. General guidelines were that the notes should be shown either larger or smaller than actual size, at an oblique angle, and preferably curled and partly over-printed in order to avoid the presentation of broad areas of note. They should appear if possible in black and white rather than in colour, should form part of a larger design, and all blocks, dies and negatives were to be destroyed after use.

At the same time film producers were informed that a similar attitude would be adopted regarding the filming of genuine notes except in cases where it was represented to the Bank that the production of the film would be seriously prejudiced if the rules were not further relaxed. Before the war, the Bank had supplied dummy notes to film producers but this practice was discontinued during the war and never reinstated. Film producers sometimes asked the Bank to see films before release in order to say if the presentation of the notes was acceptable, and for this purpose representatives of the Issue Office attended advance viewings of, among others, *The Ladykillers* and *Murder by proxy*. 'Flash' or imitation and burlesque notes (the latter bearing such legends as 'The Bank of Funland promise to pay...') were both regarded as objectionable and permission was never given for reproduction of the notes on any commercial items or souvenirs, because it was likely to lower the dignity and prestige of the currency.[81]

These rules remained in force during the 1950s and advertisers became accustomed to consulting the Bank at an early stage with their designs, which provided they kept to the guidelines were usually sanctioned. The Bank continued to move swiftly to stop the production of any object or pictorial representation considered objectionable and also refused permission for notes to be photographed for inclusion in books or other publications unless overprinted with the word 'Specimen' or in some other way. In August 1959 the Bank successfully summonsed a building society and its printers and distribution agents for production of advertising material in the form of wallets which, when opened, appeared to have £1 and £5 notes sticking out of the pocket. The summonses did not allege any dishonesty, but were brought, in the words of the prosecutor Mervyn Griffith-Jones,* because the Bank took the view that if the documents fell into unscrupulous hands they would constitute a source of danger; the Bank had a responsibility to the public for maintaining the dignity of the notes it issued. All three firms pleaded guilty.[82]

---

* Griffith-Jones, Mervyn, CBE, MC, His Honour Judge Griffith-Jones, 1909–79. Counsel to Crown at Central Criminal Court, 1950–64.

In 1960 the Bank looked afresh at its rules on the subject of reproduction and decided, because of the intense interest shown in the first new £1 note to be issued for over thirty years, to allow it to be reproduced photographically in the press. The Bank provided photographs of the note for publication (overprinted twice with the word 'Specimen') and requested that all blocks and negatives should be destroyed and confirmation of their destruction sent to the Bank.

Freshfields approved this measure as 'a reasonable and proper thing to do'; it was apparent that there were really no legal or defensible grounds for differentiating between reproduction for advertising and other purposes.[83] After this date the Bank viewed such requests for reproduction in books and magazines more favourably, subject to the usual provisos to ensure that reproductions were not likely to deceive, but the use of the note in any political pamphlet or other publication was not allowed.

## Appendix A: Dead Notes

Under the Bank Charter Act of 1844 all outstanding notes issued more than fifteen years previously were written off as 'dead' notes; the Bank Act of 1892 gave the Bank continuing powers to write off all unpresented notes which had been issued more than forty years previously, with profits accruing to the Banking Department. The 1928 Currency and Bank Notes Act reduced the period to twenty years in respect of Bank of England £1 and 10s. notes and provided that the amount of any notes thereafter written off under the 1892 Act, as amended, should form part of the income of the Issue Department. 'Dead' notes presented for payment became part of the expenses of the Issue Department.

The profit arising from the Transferred Currency Notes was thus due to be paid to the Treasury (via the EEA) in 1948, but that on the Bank's own £1 and 10s. notes – which were undated – would only become payable twenty years after the start of a new series, and was in any case likely to be exceptionally large because of notes lost or destroyed during the war. Hence the Bank's anxiety to bring out a new issue so that the Treasury might receive the profit arising from dead notes at as early a date as possible.

Appendix B. *Bank of England Notes, 1939–1960*

| Last Wednesday in November | 10s. | £1 | £5 | Other notes[a] | Total |
|---|---|---|---|---|---|
| Value of notes in circulation (millions) | | | | | |
| 1939 | 61 | 340 | 40 | 88 | 529 |
| 1940 | 71 | 401 | 41 | 80 | 593 |
| 1941 | 79 | 494 | 45 | 92 | 710 |
| 1942 | 87 | 623 | 53 | 107 | 870 |
| 1943[b] | 92 | 763 | 72 | 92 | 1019 |
| 1944 | 98 | 905 | 92 | 95 | 1190 |
| 1945 | 102 | 1060 | 81 | 85 | 1328 |
| 1946 | 99 | 1106 | 79 | 82 | 1366 |
| 1947 | 94 | 1070 | 97 | 79 | 1340 |
| 1948 | 91 | 967 | 104 | 71 | 1233 |
| 1949 | 87 | 989 | 120 | 70 | 1266 |
| 1950 | 87 | 997 | 132 | 70 | 1286 |
| 1951 | 89 | 1050 | 149 | 76 | 1364 |
| 1952 | 90 | 1121 | 168 | 82 | 1461 |
| 1953 | 93 | 1180 | 190 | 87 | 1550 |
| 1954 | 94 | 1253 | 213 | 92 | 1652 |
| 1955 | 97 | 1362 | 240 | 97 | 1796 |
| 1956 | 99 | 1439 | 265 | 103 | 1906 |
| 1957 | 100 | 1393 | 400 | 108 | 2001 |
| 1958 | 101 | 1314 | 521 | 108 | 2044 |
| 1959 | 102 | 1266 | 666 | 110 | 2144 |
| 1960 | 103 | 1199 | 843 | 113 | 2258 |

Appendix B. (*cont.*)

| Last Wednesday in November | 10s. | £1 | £5 | Other notes[a] | Total |
|---|---|---|---|---|---|
| Number of notes in circulation (millions) | | | | | |
| 1939 | 121 | 340 | 8 | 2 | 471 |
| 1940 | 142 | 401 | 8 | 2 | 553 |
| 1941 | 157 | 494 | 9 | 2 | 662 |
| 1942 | 173 | 623 | 11 | 2 | 809 |
| 1943[b] | 185 | 763 | 14 | 1 | 963 |
| 1944 | 196 | 905 | 19 | 1 | 1121 |
| 1945 | 205 | 1059 | 16 | 1 | 1281 |
| 1946 | 197 | 1106 | 16 | 1 | 1320 |
| 1947 | 189 | 1070 | 19 | 1 | 1279 |
| 1948 | 181 | 967 | 21 | 1 | 1170 |
| 1949 | 174 | 989 | 24 | — | 1187 |
| 1950 | 174 | 997 | 26 | — | 1197 |
| 1951 | 178 | 1050 | 30 | — | 1258 |
| 1952 | 180 | 1121 | 34 | — | 1335 |
| 1953 | 185 | 1180 | 38 | — | 1403 |
| 1954 | 188 | 1253 | 43 | — | 1484 |
| 1955 | 194 | 1362 | 48 | — | 1604 |
| 1956 | 198 | 1439 | 53 | — | 1690 |
| 1957 | 200 | 1393 | 80 | — | 1673 |
| 1958 | 202 | 1314 | 104 | — | 1620 |
| 1959 | 205 | 1266 | 133 | — | 1604 |
| 1960 | 206 | 1199 | 169 | — | 1574 |

*Notes :*
[a] Including notes held by the Bank of England on behalf of customers, e.g. for banks of issue in Scotland and Northern Ireland as cover for their excess note issues.
[b] Issued denominations of £10 and above withdrawn, leaving £5 note as highest available denomination.

# 5

## THE PRINTING WORKS*

In 1783 a Special Committee was appointed by the Governors to 'inspect and enquire into the mode and execution of the business as now carried on in the different departments of the Bank'. In its report the Committee expressed disapproval of the arrangements then in force for printing bank notes, which had indeed scarcely altered since the Bank's foundation nearly a hundred years before. The paper which since 1724 had been provided by the firm of Portals (who are still the sole supplier of bank note paper to the Bank), arrived in Threadneedle Street in massive iron-bound chests and was delivered to the custody of the Cashiers. At the beginning of each month a quantity judged sufficient for a month's work was taken by a Cashier to the printer – at the time the Committee was in session this was Mr Cole of Kirby Street, more than a mile away from the Bank and near Field Street, a notorious haunt of thieves. The engraved copper plates were also the responsibility of the Cashiers, one of whom took them each morning to Kirby Street accompanied by a clerk who remained at the printer's premises for the rest of the day to observe the printing process and count the sheets as they came off the presses. In the evening he returned to the Bank with the plates, and the printed sheets were left in the sole custody of the printer until ten reams, or four or five days' work, were complete when they were delivered to the Bank. Not surprisingly the Committee recommended 'the notes to be printed within this House', and this recommendation was approved. It was not until 1791, however, that Cole actually moved his business into the Bank

---

* The technical work of the Printing Works is well documented in two published histories and an internal one, which are specified in the notes to this chapter. The following pages therefore provide only a summary of the technical achievements and concentrate on the managerial aspects.

where he operated independently and controlled his own staff; one of the Chief Cashier's clerks continued the previous routine of supervising the plates, paper and printing processes.

This arrangement lasted until 1803 when the Bank decided that its business should no longer be dependent on the work of a private firm and the printer of that date, Garnet Terry, was appointed Engraver and Printer to the Bank, although he retained the freedom to undertake outside work for another five years. His Office gradually assumed responsibility for a large amount of miscellaneous printing work for the Bank itself, including much that related to the administration of the National Debt, and in 1861 undertook the production of currency notes for the government of India. In 1880 Gladstone introduced postal orders, and these too were produced for the Post Office by the Bank, as were pension orders after the passing of the Old Age Pension Act in 1908.

The work of what had in 1878 become the Printing and Store-Keeper's Office was substantially increased during the First World War. The Currency and Bank Notes Act of 6 August 1914, as well as authorising the issue of £1 and 10s. notes as described in the previous chapter, made postal orders legal tender for a short period until the government had accumulated a sufficient stock of Currency notes, which led to a heavy workload. Later the Chief Cashier was asked to provide the Post Office with postal drafts for paying separation allowances to dependants of men in the services. A vast increase in printing also accrued from loan issue business, especially in the early months of the war, and pressure on the Office throughout the war years was such that, despite the understandable disappointment caused to the Bank by the Treasury's decision to have the £1 and 10s. notes printed elsewhere, the additional burden of their issue would have been considerable.[1]

Since 1808 the printers had been accommodated in quarters designed for them by Sir John Soane* in the north-west of the Threadneedle Street building, expanding when occasion allowed into neighbouring offices; in August 1915 the Bank leased two buildings in Tabernacle Street which provided an additional 33,000 square feet of space into which the Dividend Book, Warrant and Envelope printing was moved. Even with this extra room the printing operations were still hampered by lack of space and the additional work brought about by the war meant that 'envious eyes from all sides' were cast upon the Office territory. It became clear that a move would have to be made out of Threadneedle Street, and in October 1915 the Bank learnt that the Governors of St

---

* Soane, Sir John, 1753–1837. Architect and founder of the Soane Museum. Appointed Architect to the Bank in 1788, he worked on its rebuilding from then until 1828.

Plate 5.1    St Luke's Hospital for Lunatics, designed in 1782 by George Dance Jr R.A. From an 1831 engraving

Luke's Hospital in Old Street were prepared to sell. St Luke's was a former lunatic asylum, designed in 1782 by George Dance Jr.* In October 1916 the Bank concluded negotiations with the freeholders, St Bartholomew's Hospital, and commissioned the architect F.W. Troup† to convert the huge building, with its unbroken frontage of nearly 500 feet of English clamp brick, to the requirements of a modern Printing Works. The work of conversion, and the history of the Peerless Pool Estate on which the Hospital was built, are described by Herbert de Fraine in his book *The St Luke's Printing Works of the Bank of England*. By August 1920 the reconstruction was complete, three large machinery halls having been built on the northern side of the Hospital, and the new Printing Works was in operation.[2]

For the first time in its history the Bank now had a large staff working at a distance from Head Office, which was separated from St Luke's by exactly one mile, and this raised immediate questions as to how the Printing Works should be administered. Prior to the move the two Offices concerned were the Printing and Store-Keeper's Office and the Cashier's Store, both in the Cashier's Department. Two Directors,

* Dance, George, Junior, 1741–1825. Architect, pupil of Sir J. Soane.
† Troup, Francis William, 1859–1941. Architect. Did much work for Bank of England; other works include University Press, Cambridge, and Blackfriars House, EC4.

Henry Alexander Trotter and Cecil Lubbock,* reported to the Governor in June 1919 that those two Offices (and the Refinery)† should remain under the control of the Chief Cashier after the move, but that to relieve him of detailed work it might be best for all three Offices to be supervised on his behalf by a single official. This recommendation was given effect by the appointment of Herbert King, a Principal in the Cashier's Department, to be Supervisor at St Luke's.

The Governor informed the Committee of Treasury that he 'proposed to utilise to the fullest extent the services of the Supervisor', so that St Luke's would become semi-independent, although still under the control of the Chief Cashier. King, in his new position, was responsible for all purchases and sales, 'including negotiations with Portals for the supply of paper', and would act in close co-operation with de Fraine, at that time Principal of the Printing and Store-Keeper's Office. The Chief Cashier would be consulted 'on all important and difficult questions'.[3]

Evidently this arrangement did not prove entirely satisfactory, because in 1921 a Special Committee was appointed to 'report and advise on the finance, methods and administration of St Luke's'. It recommended that the Printing Works should form a separate Department under the immediate control of the Governors, who would be assisted in its management by a Standing Committee of the Court to be known as the Committee on St Luke's. The officials of St Luke's were in turn responsible to this Committee, so that overall control of the Bank's printing operations was removed from the control of the Chief Cashier; a General Manager, or Supervisor, together with a Deputy or Assistant, were to be appointed who would be responsible for St Luke's as a whole. These positions were filled by King and de Fraine as Principal Supervisor and Second Supervisor respectively. Among the Directors nominated to serve on the new Committee was Arthur Whitworth,‡ who had also been a member of the 1921 investigative Committee: in 1925 Whitworth became Chairman of the Committee on St Luke's, a position which he held until his retirement in 1946.[4]

---

* Trotter, H.A., 1869–1949. Director, Bank of England, 1909–20; 1923–6; 1927–34; Deputy Governor, 1920–3 and 1926–7. Lubbock, C., 1872–1956. Director, Bank of England, 1909–23; 1925–7; 1929–42; Deputy Governor, 1923–5 and 1927–9.

† In 1919 the Bank decided to refine gold in order to 'remove the long standing complaint of the Gold Producers about the refining charges in this country'; a Refinery was built by Troup on the Old Street site while he was converting the hospital buildings. Very small amounts of gold were refined there between 1920 and 1924, when S. Africa opened a refinery in Pretoria. After this the Refinery ceased to operate and the building housed the In-Teller's Office (qv).

‡ Whitworth, Arthur, see p. 146n.

Once St Luke's had become operative work proceeded smoothly in the new premises. In 1922 the Committee decided the 'outside' printing work was to be confined to notes and other security documents for government departments, 'Colonial or other Governments within the Empire' and central banks, and there was to be 'no active canvassing' for work.[5] Although the postal order contract was lost when it came up for renewal in 1923, because the Bank was unable to match the terms offered by commercial printers, space was soon at a premium once more. In 1926 another machinery hall was built in what remained of the old hospital garden, together with a strong room and a large paper store, and additional floors were built over the central machinery hall.[6] The extra 20,000 square feet thus obtained would all be needed as soon as the Bank was called upon to produce £1 and 10s. notes, as the Cunliffe Committee had recommended in 1918. Before the amalgamation of the note issue took place in 1928, as described in the previous chapter, there was much discussion in the Printing Works as to the production methods to be used for the new notes. Bank of England notes had always been plate printed: this involves engraving the design in recess on a metal plate, which when in use is inked, cleaned and polished, the ink remaining only in the incised lines. The paper, previously damped, is brought into contact with the plate under heavy pressure, forced into the incision and so receives the inked impression of the design. The Printing Works was familiar with other methods, chiefly letterpress or surface printing, achieved by means of type or blocks in relief of which the surface only is inked, the impression being produced by contact with the paper under a firm but comparatively light pressure. Offset-lithography was also used, among other tasks for printing the smaller denominations of the Indian currency notes; this involves first printing on to a blanket of rubber or similar material which then sets off the print on paper. Neither was considered suitable for the 1928 issue, and the 1914 design for the £1, a miniature of the £5, was soon abandoned in favour of the designs described earlier. A decision on the paper was also needed. It was thought at first that the new notes should be printed on the same hand-made rag paper as the Bank's high sum notes, but it became evident that this could not possibly be produced in adequate quantity, and Portals' mould-made paper, with a portrait watermark of Britannia, was used instead.

Although it was decided to retain plate printing for the £1 and 10s. notes, this was carried out in conjunction with a considerable amount of machine engraving – the first time that such work had embellished a Bank of England note and used primarily as an anti-counterfeiting device. Production went ahead well, aided by the fact that enormous care

Plate 5.2    St Luke's Printing Works in Old Street, 1925

had been taken in planning St Luke's to avoid any build up of silica-grit, a by-product of the printing process responsible for the heavy incidence of a chest infection, often fatal, known as 'printers' phthisis'. The installation in the new premises of a vacuum-cleaning plant with pipes carried to every floor helped to lower the rate of the disease to a significant extent among the St Luke's workers.[7]

The years between the opening of St Luke's and the outbreak of the Second World War were marked by a series of remarkable improvements and refinements to the various printing methods in use there, which were invented by Bank of England staff at the works. Many of these came from the fertile brain of S.B. Chamberlain, who was appointed to the new post of General Works Manager on the retirement of H.G. de Fraine as Principal Supervisor in 1931. Another new post created at the same time was that of Secretary & Accountant. These two officials were made individually responsible to the Governors and were to be under the immediate control of the Committee on St Luke's.[8] This arrangement was almost certainly made with the intention of freeing Chamberlain from overall responsibility for the Printing Works, to allow the fullest use of his technical brilliance.

Chamberlain's most notable invention was that of incorporating a metallic thread into bank note paper; he patented this idea in 1934. The thread was made of a 'sandwich' of Cellophane and aluminium (experiments were also made with gold and silver metals) and was supplied by the firm of Nathaniel Lloyd and Co. It was first tried out publicly in notes printed by the Bank for the South African Reserve Bank and issued in that country in January 1939, where they were judged a success in circulation – the main benefit being a safeguard against counterfeiting, although Chamberlain's original idea was that the device would be useful in mechanical note-counting machines, still in their infancy at that date. Lord Portal* was one of the most enthusiastic advocates of the thread, and considered it 'as great an advance on the watermark as the watermark was on plain paper'.[9]

A further invention of Chamberlain's was a device to make the cutting of paper a less dangerous process: this was a safety guard designed for the fleet of elderly guillotines in use at St Luke's, which made it impossible for the machine to function until the guard was down and the operator's hands safely outside it.[10] Other developments initiated in the Printing Works helped to reduce the production costs of the £1 and 10s. notes, which fell by over 40 per cent in the first ten years of issue. They included the substitution of chromium-faced nickel plates, which lasted much longer, for the copper or steel plates used previously; a device which saved ink cleaned from the recessed plates, resulting in a reduction in ink consumption of nearly two-thirds; and a method of eliminating a trimming process which had been needed to avoid distortion of the damped paper.[11]

The steadily increasing output of bank notes and dividend warrants made great demands on the available space at the Printing Works, but the position was remedied in 1934 when the Bank decided that it no longer wanted warrants individually printed with the name of the stockholder and particulars of his holding. The new warrants were blank, with the names and figures entered later by the clerical staff of the Dividend Preparation Office on office machinery,† thus obviating the necessity to keep the details of each account set up in metal type. Since there were several tons of these Linotype slugs, which took up a floor space of about 36,000 square feet, much useful room for bank note printing was provided when they were discarded along with the relevant machines.[12]

Two other landmarks in the pre-war days at St Luke's are noteworthy. One which was never forgotten by any of those concerned was the gigantic operation of converting £2,000 m. of 5% War Loan to $3\frac{1}{2}\%$

---

* Portal, 1st Viscount (1945) of Laverstoke; Baron (1935), Wyndham Raymond Portal, PC, 3rd Bt. (1901), GCMG, DSO, MVO, 1885–1949. Managing Director, Portals Ltd, 1920; Chairman and Managing Director, 1931–49.     † See chapter 2, p. 51.

War Loan in the summer of 1932. This involved the printing of 15 m. documents and their despatch in 3 m. envelopes within a period of twenty-four hours, a task which was successfully achieved with one and a half hours to spare. A description of how it was carried out – the type-setting, proof-pulling and preparation of the lithographic plates having been done in absolute secrecy some months in advance – is given by A.D. Mackenzie in *The Later Years of St Luke's Printing Works*. Mackenzie also refers to the 'shock' received by the Printing Works when, again in 1932, it was 'suddenly thrust into the retail bookselling trade' by the decision of the Bank to sell to the public its monthly *Bank of England Statistical Summary*,* which had been printed for private circulation since 1927. Quite apart from the fact that circulation immediately jumped from 150 copies per month to 2,000, this new retail venture led St Luke's into the unfamiliar territory of trade discounts, often fiercely demanded by booksellers and refused with equal tenacity by the printers on the reasonable grounds that a nominal sum of only one shilling was charged for an elegantly produced quarto of some ten to twelve pages.[13]

In June 1938 the Committee on St Luke's discussed a secret memorandum written by the General Works Manager, Chamberlain, which outlined various possible steps for safeguarding bank note production 'in the event of an emergency'. The erection of a shadow factory at Overton, first suggested by Lord Portal a few weeks earlier, was agreed to be of prime importance and Portal undertook to advise the Committee as soon as possible on the subjects of a suitable site near Overton Mills, and of cost.[14] Two factories were ultimately built at Overton as described in chapter 1, one for printing and one for the use of the Dividend Preparation Office: both were ready by June 1939.

The decision to substitute offset-lithography for the letterpress and plate printing of the notes – thus enabling the whole of the front of the note except the numbering to be printed in one operation – greatly simplified note production during the war and allowed for major economies both in numbers of staff and in space (plate printing requires room for much heavy machinery as well as far more time spent both before and after printing).

On 3 September some of the staff who had been selected beforehand were despatched to Overton where the production of bank notes and the printing of dividend books and warrants for the mechanised stocks began almost immediately. Because of the special machinery and the enormous weight of type needed for the warrants for the few remaining unmecha-

---

* See chapter 9, pp. 315–17.

nised stocks, these had to be printed at St Luke's as before until the last warrants in the old style had been produced, by the end of 1939. Bank note production ceased temporarily at St Luke's, which concentrated on essential printing for the Bank including the millions of forms urgently required by the burgeoning Exchange Control. The notes printed at Overton (at first on six second-hand lithographic offset machines bought from Co-operative Societies in Glasgow and Manchester, supplemented by four other machines purchased later in the war) were brought up to the Bank daily by an armed escort in a car. When the expected early raids on London did not materialise, note printing began again at St Luke's; between the two locations production was soon back to near pre-war levels. But staff had nearly halved from the 1,350 at St Luke's in 1939 to 700 in London and Hampshire by the end of the following year.[15]

Naturally bank note production had priority status when paper began first to be in short supply and then rationed on the basis of a percentage of pre-war consumption. None the less continuing anxiety was felt on the subject by both Portals and the Bank, and in the summer of 1940, when the threat of invasion was at its height, Portals conceived a plan to secure the manufacture of security paper not only for Bank of England notes but also to safeguard their considerable Indian business. Two paper-making machines from Overton Mill were dismantled and taken to Canada under the personal supervision of Lord Portal; however the expense and difficulty of finding suitable accommodation for them there proved too great and they eventually returned to Hampshire where they were used in the production of paper for, among other things, the 'silver' notes for 5s. and 2s. 6d.

Copies of master plates and various irreplaceable documents were stored in Threadneedle Street and at Leeds Branch, and as a further precaution against the complete failure of both St Luke's and Overton an arrangement was made with the lithographers John Waddington Ltd. A strong room which held over 6,000 reams of bank note paper was built at Waddington's works and guarded for twenty-four hours a day by a locally recruited force. In fact production was never interrupted for more than a few days at a time by damage to St Luke's and, owing to the efforts of banks and public to keep notes in circulation as long as possible, no serious shortage of notes developed at any time during the war. Nor were any stores of bank notes, either in London or the provinces, damaged by air raids.[16] The major difficulty faced by the Printing Works during the war years was provided by the quality, rather than the quantity, of the available labour. The Ministry of Labour granted priority to the Bank when petitioned at intervals by the General Works Manager, but many of the women who arrived proved incapable of the work and not a few found it so distasteful that they gave it up after a short period – occasionally only a morning. In February 1945 the Bank even briefly contemplated importing labour from France and Belgium, and the St Luke's managers were further exasperated by the arrival a few weeks later of a girl unable to read or write; however after the end of the war in Europe in May, when men began to return from the Forces, the labour position slowly improved. Even so the shortage of women, and the refusal of many of them to do any overtime, continued to cause problems and delayed, for example, the issue of the threaded £5* note for several months.[17]

The staff of the Printing Works who had been at Overton during the war were the last to leave Hampshire, finally quitting the shadow factories (which were bought by Portals) in October 1945. Work was now fully resumed at St Luke's, but plate printing of the £1 and 10s. notes did not begin again until 1948 and was preceded in that year by the issue of unthreaded notes to use up a stock of pre-war paper. In August 1948 Chamberlain retired and was succeeded as Works Manager† by his Deputy, J.R. Dudin: as described in the previous chapter, the demand for notes was now beginning its steep upward climb, and the strains on St Luke's, both physical and managerial, were in turn beginning to show.

In January 1949 Sir George Abell was given some wide powers over St Luke's, whose Committee was at this date under the Chairmanship of the Deputy Governor, Sir Dallas Bernard. Abell was authorised to 'represent the Chairman fully in his relations with the Officials of the Printing Works and, on his behalf, to maintain regular supervision over the running of the Works generally'. The Officials (managers) of St Luke's were told to 'look to Sir George Abell' for their instructions, and Abell was simultaneously appointed by Bernard to chair a special Committee to consider improvements in the security measures at the Works. This was necessary because of a recent spate of small but nevertheless serious thefts of notes and bank note paper.[18]

Abell did not at all like what he found as a result of his investigations. Before the Special Committee on Security had time to present its report, he addressed a confidential memorandum to the Committee on St Luke's in which he stated uncompromisingly that the Printing Works was 'facing a crisis'. Production was running at 20 m. notes a week, and the maximum output from Old Street was estimated to be 30 m., but the

---

* See chapter 4, p. 135
† The title of General Works Manager had been altered to that of Works Manager in 1946, as part of a reorganisation prior to the introduction of the 1947 Classification Scheme – see chapter 10, p. 335.

output required was between 35 m. and 36 m. a week. Not only had there been the serious outbreak of thefts, but defective notes had also got into circulation, and 'paper, working space, staff' all presented problems in turn; the factory was seriously strained beyond its capacity. Abell felt that it was necessary to move out of the Old Street building and, more immediately, that the entire management of the Printing Works must be reorganised.

There were many anomalies in the current situation, which Abell recognised as having its origins in the dispositions made in 1931: he found the management structure quite inadequate to the demands of a modern printing organisation. The Bank's requirement for dual control was met by the Works Manager on one side, and the Secretary and Accountant on the other; both were responsible to the Luke's Committee, but only came together in that Committee, and in effect there was no one in overall charge at St Luke's. The division of work between the two sides of the control was illogical, and Abell was especially critical of the fact that the Printing Department, whose work was becoming 'daily more exacting', had also to deal with the recruitment of staff. This meant that the Overseers, who were technical printing experts, spent a large part of their time on staff matters; recruiting, training and welfare would all improve under proper leadership. Abell's scheme of reorganisation envisaged the creation of a post of General Works Manager reporting directly to the Committee on St Luke's, with authority throughout the Printing Works and over both sides of the dual control. Under him there would be a Printing Department, Personnel Department, Secretary and Accountant and a Security Paper Store. The present Works Manager (who was already past normal retirement age) should be retired on generous terms and Abell suggested the appointment of D.W. Tilley, Principal of the Dividend Preparation Office, as General Works Manager. The new organisation would leave him free of the detail of the Printing Department and able to devote himself to overall supervision and planning.[19] Abell's radical re-structuring needed the sanction of both Staff Committee and Court, which it duly received.

An immediate reaction was required to the findings of the Security Committee, who had the benefit of advice from Superintendent Hatherill of Scotland Yard on the subject of external security. The Committee's many recommendations, all of which were implemented, included the appointment of eleven more inspectors and extra night staff, as well as the institution of a range of much more rigorous internal and external security precautions and a considerable tightening and extension of the rights of search.[20] A report on staff conditions was also commissioned from the Industrial Welfare Society. Since the middle of 1948 A.C. Legg, an Auxiliary Clerk in the Security Paper Office, had been devoting all his time to reviving the Britannia Athletic Association, the St Luke's sports club which had lapsed as a result of the war. The Works magazine, *The Britannia Quarterly*, was also published again in 1949 after a ten year absence. The report of the Industrial Welfare Society, while recognising these efforts, made various more far-reaching recommendations as to the introduction of incentive and joint consultation schemes and other welfare matters, but it was decided to delay any decision on these points until the new General Manager – a title which was ultimately preferred to General Works Manager – had had time to settle down and evolve his own ideas.[21]

Tilley took up his new position in August 1949. A new post of Staff Manager was created and filled by W.G. Cuttle, an Assistant to the Chief Accountant. It had been accepted by this date that the Printing Works must be moved out of Old Street; while detailed consideration was given to this, Abell queried whether the Bank should continue to do any commercial printing after the move, or perhaps confine itself to printing notes alone, or notes and 'security paper' of various kinds. Another Committee was set up to investigate this, and began its work by asking all the principal Bank Offices how they would be affected by any change. As well as being the channel by which much of the ordinary stationery used within the Bank was obtained from outside commercial firms, the Printing Works itself carried out many special orders for the Bank, including Minute Books for Court and the Committee of Treasury and other Committees, Blue Books,* lists of Directors and the reports of special Committees. Speed and secrecy were often essential. Enormous quantities of forms, including the millions required by the Exchange Control, were also produced at St Luke's, together with confidential documents such as prospectuses, and routine, non-confidential work, some of it for outside customers.

After an exhaustive investigation the Committee came to the conclusion that the removal of any of the printing operations would 'upset the balance both as regards cost and efficiency of service'. It had been much impressed by the arguments, forcibly advanced to the Chairman, that St Luke's was only able to respond to abnormal demands from Head Office for the completion of special tasks – whether bank notes, other security printing or important and confidential commercial printing – because of its ability to maintain an adequate supply of floating staff. Tilley and his Deputy P.J. Reeves said that if any commercial work was

* The Bank's books of account – see chapter 6, p. 197.

removed they would have either to maintain their present force of printers which then could not be employed fully during normal working, or reduce the printing force and leave St Luke's vulnerable when called upon to perform additional or special work. It was also made quite clear to the Committee that 'once having got rid of printers, it would be absolutely impossible to get them back again, owing to the great demand in the trade for skilled workmen and the fact that we cannot compete with wage rates offered by a large number of outside firms, notably the Press'.* Swayed by these arguments and by the evidence of the enormous variety of work done for the Bank by the Printing Works, the Committee came down in favour of the status quo.[22]

Meanwhile Abell and the St Luke's Committee had been fully occupied with the preliminary decisions over the move. In July 1949 Abell consulted the President of the Royal Institute of British Architects, Michael Waterhouse,† about suitable architects for a new building: the Institute's suggestion of a competition was rejected by the Bank and eventually the firm of Easton and Robertson was chosen from a short list of five. Howard (later Sir Howard) Robertson,‡ one of the senior partners, was to have overall responsibility for the design of the new building.[23] The choice of site proved more difficult. A survey revealed that 64 per cent of present Printing Works staff lived within the north-east quadrant of London, and surveyors George Head and Co. began to evaluate possible sites including several of the New Towns.[24] In October Abell detailed for the Governors the full catalogue of St Luke's physical inadequacies for its task: overcrowded machinery halls, strong rooms and canteen, and the difficulties of maintenance from the points of view of both efficiency and security. A move, he said, would give increased capacity, better working conditions and greater security for less expenditure, probably leading ultimately to lower costs of production. The bad conditions in Old Street were also adversely affecting recruitment.[25]

The post-war demand for industrial land meant that few sites of adequate size were available, and the final choice lay between two LCC estates in Essex, Harold Wood and Debden. In August 1950 it was agreed to proceed with plans to build at Debden, which was only fifteen

---

* The higher wages obtainable elsewhere were balanced in many cases, and particularly as far as the senior technical staff of the Printing Works were concerned, by the favourable pensions offered by the Bank.
† Waterhouse, Michael Thornton, CBE, MC, RIBA, 1888–1968. Architect. President of RIBA, 1948–50.
‡ Robertson, Sir Howard Morley, Kt. (1954), MC, RIBA, 1888–1963. Architect. President of RIBA, 1952–4. Works include New Hall for the Royal Horticultural Society, London, and Shell Centre, South Bank, London.

miles distant from St Luke's and possessed the great advantage of being on the Central Line of the underground.[26] An immediate necessity was for an Industrial Development Certificate (IDC) from the Board of Trade, for which the Treasury agreed to support the Bank's application. The Debden site was of 12.6 acres; the normal LCC lease was for eighty years but it agreed to extend this to ninety-nine years when the Bank pleaded the 'permanent nature of the strong rooms'. The Bank was anxious to obtain an even longer lease, one reason being that the high cost of a short one, amortised over a short period, would be reflected in the costs of the note issue; Bernard informed Sir Thomas Sheepshanks,* Permanent Secretary to the Ministry of Town and Country Planning, that 'even to contemplate a second move after 99 years is abhorrent to us' and the lease was finally re-negotiated to 200 years on condition that the Bank paid £125 per acre per annum instead of the £100 originally asked.[27]

The IDC proved very difficult to obtain and it was only after the Bank, at the suggestion of the Treasury, revised the original estimate of building costs downwards by some £60,000, which was equivalent to 5 per cent of the total, that Board of Trade approval was finally granted.[28] Meanwhile it had been decided to sell the Printing Works Sports Ground at Walthamstow (which had been briefly considered as a possible site for the new works) because of the expense of its upkeep (£1,300 p.a.) coupled with decreasing usage since the end of the war – in 1949 and early 1950 the greatest attendance on any one day was between forty and fifty people, only a few of whom were present members of St Luke's staff.[29] Eight and a half acres adjoining the Debden site were leased for a new sports ground which, it was hoped, would be more fully used.

Early in 1951 it was decided that one person should devote himself entirely to the affairs of the new factory, and V.T. Kalmar, the Deputy Works Manager, was relieved of his current duties and took over the complex business of overseeing the progress of Debden.[30] Estimated costs began to creep upwards once more, and in January 1952 the Committee was much disappointed when told by the architect that the building could not be completed before the last quarter of 1955, or more likely early 1956.[31] Pressed as he was at this period by the Treasury to make all possible economies, Governor Cobbold expressed considerable disquiet over the increases in both costs and time scale, and asked for a new and stringent re-examination of the necessity for rebuilding. Abell, himself very disturbed by the 'hideous increase' in costs, consulted Lord

* Sheepshanks, Sir Thomas Herbert, KCB, KBE, 1895–1964. Permanent Secretary, Ministry of Town and Country Planning, 1946–51.

Braintree,* who had been appointed to the Chairmanship of St Luke's Committee in May 1950, and who played a major role in planning Debden. Braintree replied at length, saying that he felt the added expenditure was not abnormal 'having regard to the unstable nature of building estimates at the present time and the many considerations which have arisen since the architects and our people have got to closer quarters with their problem'. He thought that the real crux of the matter lay in the starting date:

> At the present time the architects take the line that not a brick can be laid until all their plans are completed, and that makes our starting date fifteen months ahead. With a contractor appointed, who is interested in the time factor, it should be possible for him to make a plan with the architects which will allow a much more immediate start, and from then on we should have a driving force on the job which, at the present time, is obviously lacking. It must be remembered that if we were a commercial institution our main consideration in embarking on an enterprise of this kind would be that our Capital should be got to work at the earliest possible moment.
>
> I have already said that I appreciate the fact that the Bank must be an example in the matter of national economy, and that the Governor is placed in a false position when the Bank preaches economy and at the same time embarks on a large Capital undertaking. I am quite certain, however, that many enterprises are now on the stocks, and will be allowed to proceed, which are not nearly as justified as the vital requirement of keeping pace with the note issue ...[32]

After reading all the papers on the subject submitted to him by Abell, Cobbold minuted: 'I agree that the case is convincing and the scheme should go ahead.'[33] Braintree's advice was followed and contractors were almost immediately invited to tender, but various delays still ensued and it was not until January 1953 that Sir Robert McAlpine & Sons Ltd were appointed from a short list of six.[34] At this date the architects estimated the total cost of £2·16 m. for completion in thirty months from 1 June 1953, and work on the site duly began on that date.

The hard pressed St Luke's continued to operate at full stretch to cope with the increasing demand for bank notes. The day to day pressures were not allowed to obscure the need for long-term research and development work in the note printing field, in which the Bank had always been prominent, and several important projects were furthered during this period. One of particular concern was the possibility of 'web' printing notes from continuous reels of paper instead of by the

---

* Braintree, 1st Baron (1948), Valentine George Crittall; Kt. (1930); JP, 1884–1961. Chairman, Crittall Manufacturing Company Ltd. Director, Bank of England, 1948–55.

conventional method using separate sheets: the firm of Chambon Ltd, which printed petrol coupons for the government and had supplied the machinery for web printing old age pension orders and dividend warrants at St Luke's, was at its own expense carrying out research into the special problems posed by notes to this process as early as 1949. From 1954 onwards the Bank paid the firm an annual retaining fee.[35] Chamberlain kept in touch with this research and continued to do so after his retirement on a consultancy basis. Other developments at St Luke's included a machine to take finished sheets from the plate printing presses, previously done by hand, and a method of dispensing with the process of interleaving the sheets during printing.[36]

In 1950 Abell visited Sweden to see some new note-counting machines which had been patented there, and on his return it was decided to ask the inventor, Axel Rosswall, who had worked for many years for Sveriges Riksbank, if he would consider coming to St Luke's for a short period. This he did in April 1951, and P.R. Price, an engineer who had worked with Sir Frank Whittle on the development of the jet engine, was appointed as his assistant with a view to becoming Research Engineer at the Printing Works thereafter.[37] Rosswall stayed with the Bank for just over a year, the bulk of his time being spent in training Price in the techniques of bank note production and handling; together the two men visited English bank note machinery manufacturers and then made a tour of similar factories in eight European countries. Two note-counting machines invented by Rosswall were installed in St Luke's before his departure, six more were ordered, and two overseas firms – Winkler & Fallert of Berne and Goebel of Darmstadt – had begun to experiment with web printing of bank notes, their tests being made without charge and without prejudice to the Chambon experiments. By the time Rosswall left, Price was thoroughly conversant with all the aspects of web printing notes and was confident that this could be achieved within five years.

The report made by Price in July 1952 after his European visit emphasised that, although the output per head of the staff of St Luke's was better than that of any of the factories he and Rosswall had visited, the Printing Works was not as well staffed or equipped for research as most of them. He proposed the formation of a research section, headed by a technical manager and staffed by a chemist, physical chemist and project engineer each with his own small laboratory and assistants. This was agreed in August 1952 and the Research Section, headed by Price as Research Manager, was instituted that year and its establishment completed by the summer of the following year.[38] (It was within this

Section, by then considerably enlarged, that the Bank Note Design Section was set up in 1956. This initially consisted of D.V. Wicks, who had been assistant to Robert Austin, and H.N. Eccleston.)*[39]

Since his initial investigation into the affairs of St Luke's Abell had been convinced of the need for some sort of joint consultative machinery. Fears were expressed over the possibility of a closed shop, working to rule or the institution of restrictive practices, but Abell was sure that the Bank 'could rely on the goodwill and loyalty of the staff'.[40] In the summer of 1952 a Joint Advisory Committee was set up, with members appointed in equal numbers by management and representatives of the mechanic staff. Its aims were to 'increase efficiency and promote the well-being of those employed at St Luke's' and it was specifically constituted to avoid 'the normal concerns of the trades unions'.[41]

While Debden was still under construction a further managerial crisis arose in the closing months of 1954, which had far-reaching consequences on the way the Printing Works was organised. The crisis was sparked off by a serious loss, in the region of £30,000, which had its origins in the previous year. During 1953 preparations were made at St Luke's, as described in the previous chapter, for the production in early 1954 of the new pictorial £5 note designed by Stephen Gooden. In November 1953, at the request of the Bank, St Luke's submitted a production programme which estimated that deliveries would begin at the rate of at least 2 million per week by 1 April 1954.

Because of the urgency felt by the Bank to get the new note into circulation as quickly as possible, the production programme was telescoped to an extent which ultimately proved disastrous. It was assumed, quite wrongly as it turned out, that there would be few serious difficulties in changing over from hand-produced to machine-produced £5 notes and accordingly the programme allowed for only a short interval between the machine proof stage and the beginning of production in quantity. The first machine proofs, however, were unsatisfactory: in particular there were difficulties with the register between the plate printed design and the litho background, and alternative background designs had to be provided. Meanwhile, before the scale of the problem was fully appreciated, enough paper had been ordered from Portals to build up the customary three months' stock necessary to ensure adherence to the original programme.

Many other changes to the note, including a reduction of the size of sheet and alterations to the watermark, eventually became necessary and

---

* Eccleston subsequently designed the fine Series D 'portrait' notes, the first of which was issued in 1970.

the result was that a loss of some £30,000 was incurred on the unusable paper. The Governor was seriously displeased by the whole affair and, after asking for a full report setting out 'exactly how these troubles occurred', he noted that 'two big questions' were raised in his mind: whether St Luke's was properly equipped to produce new notes in the most efficient and economical way, and whether, particularly in view of the impending move out of London, the respective responsibilities of St Luke's Committee and of the Governors were sufficiently clear and calculated to ensure maximum efficiency.

As far as the actual loss was concerned, the General Manager (to whom the problems had not been reported until rather late in the day) accepted full responsibility; it was clear that there had been a technical error of judgement on the part of people who had no experience of plate printing both sides of a note. As Abell told Mynors, the Deputy Governor, they only discovered by experience 'how risky it was to assume that certain of their difficulties could be overcome'. But a wholesale review of the organisation of the Printing Works was set in motion as a result of the Governor's stern enquiry, and once more the industrial expertise of Lord Braintree was sought in a moment of crisis. In reply to an appeal by Mynors he wrote on 11 October 1954:

> The functions of the Committee on St Luke's can be compared with the Boards of a great many undertakings whose part-time Directors can have little inside knowledge of the workings of the business.
> More rational Boards which include full-time Directors each in charge of such main activities as manufacture, distribution, finance, supply and technical development cannot be appointed from the Court of the Bank of England.
> The question arises, does the Committee perform a useful function and/or can the function be modified with advantage... If it is thought that the Committee should exercise a more active control on the activities of St Luke's, I would suggest the formation of a Board of Management to consist of the Executive Heads of Departments or, at least, of responsible individuals who are now in charge of the main functions of the undertaking. This Board should meet regularly, I think once a week, under the Chairmanship of the General Manager. The scope of their activities would emanate from the meetings of the Committee on St Luke's, and they would produce informative reports as a result of their weekly meetings which would be made available, preferably before the Committee meetings, so that they can be studied...

Lord Braintree concluded by noting with approval what had been done to 'rationalise the undertaking' during the time that he had been associated with St Luke's, and that the improvements (which included the appointment of a General Manager, the introduction of technicians and the perfection of counting machines) originated not with himself or the Committee but were largely effected by Abell acting on behalf of the Governor. If a Committee were to remain in charge, reports from a board of management such as he had suggested 'would at least give them some idea what is going on'; and he thought that those appointed should have an industrial rather than a banking background and should remain on the Committee rather than passing on to other activities after a short stay.[42]

The incident of wasted paper had served as a painful illustration of how inadequate, in some respects, the channels of communication were between Works, Committee and Governors, and indeed on some occasions between shop floor and management within the Works. Although no such management board as that envisaged by Braintree was instituted, there was a general revision of the formal Rules and Regulations by which St Luke's was governed, with clearer demarcation of the responsibilities of the General Manager, the Committee and of the Director specifically concerned with the Printing Works – at that time Sir George Abell. Further actions taken to tighten up the administration of the works included the appointment of Kalmar as Works Manager jointly with P.J. Reeves, to take over from the latter on his retirement in March 1955. Immediately on appointment Kalmar was put in charge of all work on the new £5 note. In addition a Technical Committee was set up with a basic membership of the General Manager, Works Manager and Research Manager. This Committee considered all important technical matters including the design and printing of new notes.[43]

Abell and Tilley, who were largely responsible for formulating and implementing these changes, were both aware of one fundamental gap at St Luke's: that there was no-one on the production side with a formal engineering training. Mynors addressed himself to the subject with his habitual clarity of thought and expression:

> I do not think we should aim to man works management with engineers, or with printers from elsewhere. With efficiency in production must go security and the Bank's standard of behaviour, particularly as employer. There must be a latent clash between efficiency and security: to exaggerate, the worst that could happen would be production manned by engineers and security by clerks, regarding each other respectively as slave-driving commercial types and narks.
>
> Engineering training has now been introduced through the research section, and also a plant engineer: from this source we may well draw a future works manager. As the production side and the research side

become better integrated, we shall need to consider whether at some stage we look for another recruit of this type: we shall not get what we need ready-made.

... On *relations with the Bank*, the original idea (February 1922)[44] was that St Luke's should be 'a separate Department under the immediate control of the Governors, assisted by a Standing Committee of Directors'. This is right, and the analogy of a Chairman and Board of Directors (Deputy Governor, December 1925)* is wrong: so is the more recent suggestion that to some extent Sir George Abell exercises authority on behalf of the Chairman. What needs the approval of the Court is obviously put in the first instance to the Committee: and the Governors are well advised to get the agreement of the Committee to important executive decisions, such as arise in the building of Debden. But the Committee should not be regarded as a responsible body.

Nevertheless they can be very useful: but only if they are better informed. I think we must be prepared to trust them, for example, with knowledge of a new note at an earlier stage, if we wish them to take a real interest. When this entails going out to Debden from time to time, the Committee can justly expect to know more of what is going on: and a good, keen Committee is important.

The exceptional quality of the present Chairman may have led to a somewhat distorted idea of the duties of his office: but we cannot guarantee the succession. We should try always to have someone with relevant industrial experience, and keep him in office; and use him as father confessor to the Governors, particularly the Executive Director concerned.[45]

A few months after Mynors had written this, when the necessary administrative changes had been effected, Lord Braintree retired from the Court of Directors and in March 1955 was replaced as Chairman of the Committee on St Luke's by Sir Harry (later Baron) Pilkington,† another experienced industrialist who was chairman of the firm of glass manufacturers in Lancashire. In a note to Pilkington explaining the background to the recent reappraisal of the role of the Committee, Mynors put his finger on one of the keys to the continuing debate over its functions: 'the Governors cannot relish being responsible for a large industrial enterprise and therefore they attach the greatest importance to the help of the Committee...'[46]

By this date, in the summer of 1955, the shell of the new works was

* Sir Alan Garrett Anderson, GBE, Deputy Governor, 1925–6, had said that the Committee on St Luke's was supposed to act as Chairman and Board of Directors of the Printing Works.[44]
† Pilkington, Baron (1968) of St Helen's, Harry (William Henry) Pilkington, Kt. (1953), 1905–83. Chairman of Pilkington Bros., 1949–73. Director, Bank of England, 1955–72.

complete and the sub-contractors were busy on the interior; the site was extended by the Bank's purchase of an adjacent bookbinding factory and strip of land belonging to Messrs Collins, which had the advantage of straightening up the boundaries and making the whole more secure.[47] The Collins factory was subsequently used to store materials for making plate printing inks, which the Printing Works successfully manufactured for its own use from 1954 onwards.

It was determined from the first that the new building should have a pleasant aspect and provide an agreeable place to work: naturally security was vital but the Bank had no wish to re-create the fortress-like exterior of St Luke's with its 15 foot walls, windows protected with steel bars and wire mesh, and electrically operated doors guarded by police. The Debden site itself presented some difficulties, sloping south and east away from the River Roding, and the requirements made of the architect were formidable. All production was to be kept as far as possible on one level, and provision had thus to be made for a vast area to accommodate all the printing machinery as well as rooms for plate printing and the expanding laboratory research premises. The non-security printing operations called for space for compositors, Linotype operators, book-binders and the many others who made up the twenty-five trades represented in the Works. Boiler houses, engineers' and electricians' shops and stores, cloakroom accommodation and rooms for eating and recreation for a staff of some 1,500 were also needed, plus a good deal of office space.

The concept of Sir Howard Robertson to fulfil these requirements was strikingly original. The main production hall, 800 feet long by 125 feet wide (roughly the size of two football pitches) and 40 feet high, has floor space quite uninterrupted by any central roof support, so that its entire area can be used. Its roof is half-oval in section, supported by twenty-two pre-cast concrete arches strung together on steel cables, with five tiers of vertical windows set into the curve to give a generous amount of natural light. Alongside the main hall is a second, of similar construction but smaller; all working and machinery areas have wood-block floors to cut down both dust and noise. The administrative block, providing man-agement quarters of 'subdued luxury' running parallel with the main hall, is faced with brown Buckinghamshire brick and consists of two multi-storey wings divided by a central service tower at whose foot are the main entrance doors. Staff come into the building at the west end, while bank note paper enters at the east with each stage in its production taking it westwards – litho and plate printing, numbering and checking all done in a continuous stream: the time spent in actually moving paper

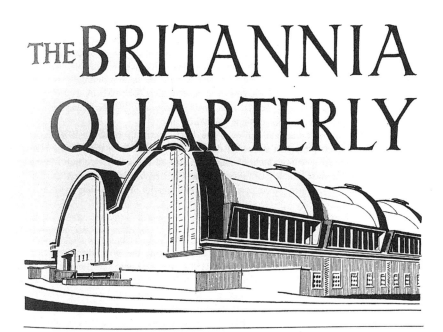

Plate 5.3   The Bank of England Printing Works at Debden. (A drawing from the August 1956 issue of the Printing Works magazine, *The Britannia Quarterly*)

about was cut by 50 per cent by the move from Old Street. Canteen and indoor recreation facilities are housed in a separate building connected to the main factory by a covered way, and include a reading room, a library and a stage (a great improvement on the modest but much-used platform at St Luke's).[48] A sports ground with football, hockey and cricket pitches and hard tennis courts was laid down outside, and a landscape artist, Mary Braendle, planted the grounds with trees and flowering shrubs.

The Bank took over the building on 20 February 1956. A party to celebrate its completion was held in Threadneedle Street on 3 May and the move, with scarcely any interruption to production, was virtually complete by 7 June.* 'Compared to St Luke's, it seemed a paradise, with the outlook on open country', remarked Arthur Whitworth after a visit to Debden in July 1956, although he also noted that 'the grim and grimy St Luke's served its purpose'.[49] Naturally there were some initial

---

* The Committee on St Luke's was re-named the Debden Committee with effect from 1 June 1956.

troubles, the turbine boiler proving particularly temperamental in the early months; less serious, but extremely time-consuming, were the problems caused by the sports ground. The surface was so poorly laid that the Bank, after considerable discussion with the contractors, eventually consulted the National Playing Fields Association, at whose intervention the contractors agreed to bear half the expense of re-turfing.[50] The total cost of Debden, including building, machinery and fees, was just under £3·5 m. This figure struck one member of the Court, Laurence Cadbury,* as 'extremely expensive', and he also mentioned to Abell his disquiet over the 'very high ratio of buildings to plant' (approximately 2·5:1) compared with his own factory where the value of 'Land and Buildings' was almost exactly equal to that of 'Plant and Machinery'.[51] In reply Abell pointed out the unusual needs of the Printing Works with its thousands of square feet of very expensive strong rooms and other security features such as space for an inspection gallery all round the printing halls. He added:

> One result of designing the building for our particular purpose was that we were able to cut down our security staff to such an extent as to make the cost of production, at our present level of output, cheaper per thousand notes than the cost of production at St Luke's. Thus, although our investment on the building was high we are getting a return which justifies the investment and reduces our dependence on the labour market.[52]

The lay-out of Debden had indeed made it possible for the Bank to effect an immediate saving of some £60,000 a year on the wages of security staff, and the increased capacity of the new works allowed weekly deliveries of £1 and 10s. notes to reach 25 m. within the first year of occupation, 3 m. more than the weekly output achieved in the final months at St Luke's. These two factors meant that Debden production costs compared satisfactorily with those at Old Street despite a rise in paper prices and trade union wage increases which were negotiated in the spring of 1956.[53] The move to Debden also meant, as Abell pointed out to Cadbury, a significant easing of the Bank's printing staff problems; and it was ultimately decisive in providing a solution to a pressing labour shortage in another area of the Bank.

Price's report of July 1952, mentioned earlier, included much information on the developments in mechanical handling and destruction of notes which, he pointed out, would involve the design of special purpose machinery: 'the specification and supervision of this could be

---

* Cadbury, Laurence John, OBE, 1889–1982. Managing Director of Cadbury Bros. and associated companies, 1919–59; Chairman, Cadbury Bros., 1944–9 and J.S. Fry & Sons, 1952–9. Director, Bank of England, 1936–61.

handled by the proposed technical Organisation at St Luke's. Handling and destruction then becomes a factory job rather than an office job and would be best sited at Debden'.[54]

This was a plain statement of something of which the truth had tacitly been acknowledged within the Bank for some time past. The dislike felt by young women office workers for the repetitive and uninteresting job of checking and counting used notes before destruction was a grave handicap to recruitment, yet the Bank had always steadfastly refused to entertain the idea of a 'second class staff' specially engaged for this purpose, less well educated than those who measured up to the normal standards for entry. In spite of the relief afforded by the introduction of the Bankers' re-issue system,* shortage of staff in the Issue Office and at the Branches made it increasingly difficult, and eventually impossible, for all the notes paid in to be examined, and a percentage examination had perforce to be accepted. The removal of the whole process to Debden and its increased mechanisation, thus downgrading it from an office to an industrial process, would obviously relieve many of these difficulties. But feathers in the Issue Office were seriously ruffled at the first hint of the loss of one of its spheres of activity, however burdensome this might be in practice.

The Old Lady, as de Fraine noted in another context, 'likes to look carefully before she leaps'; at the end of 1954, and despite the unhappiness of the Office Principals, the Chief Cashier, P.S. Beale, gave serious thought to the possibility of 'doing the work away from the Issue Office – possibly at Debden'.[55] He suggested that T. Neylan, the Principal of the Bank Note Office, should investigate and report on this; Governor Cobbold noted that he would welcome such a step and that the 'terms of reference to the investigation should be positive, i.e. that they should aim at considering ways and means of moving on these lines if a policy decision in that direction should be taken'.[56]

Neylan and his fellow Committee members came down uncompromisingly in favour of removing the work to a new building designed for the processes of inspection, checking and destruction by burning. The building should be erected adjacent to the Printing Works at Debden, and use should be made of whole-time non-clerical labour and the highest degree of automation possible, including the recent developments in automatic note-counting machines.[57]

This report was made in February 1955. The Governors approved the move 'in principle' (with the proviso that it should not take place until the experience of the Printing Works there showed that the labour

* See chapter 4, p. 145.

market in Debden was satisfactory).[58] In the following October a further
Committee was set up under the Chairmanship of H.L. Chadder (who
had just been appointed to the new post of Assistant General Manager,*
having previously been Assistant Chief of Establishments) to study
Neylan's conclusions and prepare a comprehensive plan for implementing them: in February 1956 it made a series of detailed reports
including specific recommendations on note handling methods, accounting procedure, security, destruction and the type of building
required for the work. At last, in May 1956, the decision was made by the
Committee of Treasury 'to recommend to the Court of Directors that a
building be planned at Debden to which the work connected with the
examination and destruction of paid Bank Notes may be transferred'.[59]

Matters now proceeded more swiftly, and preliminary discussions
with the Debden architects, Easton and Robertson, began within a week.
Later in the year, while the multitude of practical questions as to types of
machinery and incinerators were under constant discussion, it was
decided to commission Personnel Administration Ltd (PA) to report on
note examination and checking work in the Issue and Bank Note Offices.
The firm's preliminary findings were embodied in a brief, six-page
document which by calling into question the statistical reliability of
current examination and counting procedures offended all those directly
concerned.[60] The second stage of the assignment, however, which
consisted of a 'Method Study' in Threadneedle Street followed by work
at a specially instituted training centre at Debden, was more fruitful. The
local recruitment of examiners began; the newly installed De la Rue and
Vacuumatic counting machines (the latter developed by Portals who had
acquired the patent from Sweden) were used and evaluated. It was
planned to continue the use of the training centre as a proving ground for
new equipment, while the examiners trained there would provide a
nucleus of instructresses for the future. Meanwhile PA embarked on an
investigation into the handling and examination of new notes.[61]

The Paid Note Building, as it was finally called, was constructed in the
south-west corner of the Debden site. Sir Robert McAlpine & Sons were
again chosen as the main contractors and began work in January 1959 on
the especially deep excavations which proved necessary because of the
gradient of the ground. (The former Collins factory had to be demolished
to make room for the new building and McAlpines also built a storehouse
at the north-east corner of the Printing Works for the ink making

---

* This post, which carried staff responsibilities, was of particular importance because of
the imminence of the move to Debden. Chadder took over as General Manager of the
Printing Works in March 1959.

materials which had been housed in it.)[62] The Paid Note Building has three floors, the lowest housing the incinerators, strong rooms, workshops and plant, with administrative offices and further workshops and plant in the middle and the examination areas on the top storey. The exterior echoes some of the architectural features of the Printing Works, such as the design of the lensed windows and the use of Buckinghamshire multi-facing bricks on the reinforced concrete frame. A tile mural by Dorothy Annan decorates the front hall. The building is highly mechanised: conveyors of three types were designed largely to dispense with the need for manual handling of the work, and the eight furnaces in the incinerator room received packets of used notes fed into them under remote control. As each was filled to capacity it was fired automatically, the resulting ash being sucked away into a storage hopper: much of the heat provided by the burning notes was used in waste heat boilers attached to the furnaces, to provide hot water.[63] The final cost of the Paid Note Building, which was handed over to the Bank by the contractors in January 1961, was £1.5 m. The reduction in the numbers of examiners and supervisors needed in the new building produced immediate savings in the region of £180,000 a year, and much valuable space was released in Threadneedle Street.[64]

During the period of its construction a gradually increasing amount of the work in connection with paid notes was transferred to Debden. As briefly mentioned in the previous chapter, this involved reconsideration of the responsibility for the work, previously vested in the Chief Cashier and the Secretary who formed the two sides of the necessary dual control. As all the staff at the Printing Works were under the control of the General Manager, considerable discussion ensued as to how matters should best be arranged under the new system. A first step was the establishment at Debden of a special office, the Paid Note Office, in January 1958, but it was not until nearly three years later than an acceptable formula was achieved for the reallocation of responsibility for all aspects of paid notes between the Cashier's Department, the Secretary's Department and the Printing Works.[65]

The sale of St Luke's did not prove straightforward. As early as 1951, when negotiations for the Debden lease were taking place, the General Manager of the Printing Works was asked by the London County Council to bear in mind that they might be interested in buying the Old Street site when it became available. The staff of the Dividend Preparation Office remained at Old Street until they were able to move into New Change in March 1958; the LCC, approached in the summer of 1957, eventually decided against purchase, and the Bank accepted an offer from a property developer which fell through because he was unable to come to terms with the LCC as to the use to which the site could be put. Several other would-be purchasers also withdrew for various reasons, and it was not until November 1958 that the Bank accepted an offer of £900,000 for the freehold from a subsidiary of Oddenino's Property & Investment Co. This sale was completed in February 1960. Two years later the LCC, amid much public criticism, bought the site from Oddenino's for £1.5 m. with a view to establishing an annexe to Covent Garden Market there; eventually it was sold again, to Great Portland Estates, and redeveloped during the 1960s with a mixture of commercial and office buildings and LCC housing.[66]

# 6

---

## THE BANKING DEPARTMENT* AND THE
## PROFITABILITY OF THE BANK

The first published Bank Return was issued monthly under the provisions of the Bank of England Act of 1833 and consisted of averages of weekly figures for the preceding three months, four items only being shown: Circulation, Deposits, Securities and Bullion. Eleven years later a Schedule to the Bank Charter Act of 1844 prescribed the form which, with slight modifications, has lasted until the present day. The Return is divided into two parts, one dealing with the Issue Department and one with the Banking Department; the separation is for the purposes of accountancy only and there is not and never has been any corresponding physical separation within the organisation of the Bank.†

For well over a century, until the publication of annual accounts in line with Companies' Acts requirements and current accounting practice began in 1971, the Return was the only form of account published regularly by the Bank, although a certain amount of information about its financial position was made available at various times to Parliamentary Select Committees.[1] Under the terms of the 1844 Act the Return is produced weekly, giving figures at first for the close of business on a Saturday until 4 November 1857, after which Wednesday's figures were used – the reason for the change being, it is thought, that earlier information was called for at a particularly crucial moment during the worldwide financial crisis of that year.[2] As well as the statutory publication in *The London Gazette*, copies of the Return are produced internally by the Bank. One is displayed in the front hall at Threadneedle

---

* The Banking Department which is the subject of this chapter must not be confused with the present day Banking Department, which was created from the former Cashier's Department in the 1980 reorganisation.

† For analysis of the Bank Charter Act and the separation of Departments, see Clapham II, pp. 172–89.

Street, and others are put in a box on the Chief Cashier's Office counter for collection on Thursdays by messengers from banks and offices all over the City. (They were printed for many years on a small 'Cropper' hand press maintained in Head Office specifically for this work, but latterly have been typed.)[3]

The Return is not an easy document to interpret, even for bankers. Walter Leaf,* when chairman of the Westminster Bank, described a conversation with Governor Cunliffe which had taken place during the First World War: 'I was discussing the Bank Return with the Governor of the Bank ... and mentioned that there was only one line of it which I thought I understood; and that was the line "Gold Coin and Bullion". The Governor, with a twinkle in his eye, replied "Mr Leaf, I do not think you understand even that".' Various guides through its tortuous paths have been written, but for an appreciation of its relationship with the Bank's internal financial position a full grasp of the Return is unnecessary.[4]

The separation of the accounts of the Issue Department, as laid down by the 1844 Act, from those of all the other functions of the Bank – which together comprised the Banking Department – was accompanied by a legal requirement for all the profits of the Issue Department to be paid directly to HM Treasury, as they have been ever since. Thus all profits accruing from one of the Bank's major responsibilities and functions, the issue of the country's bank notes, are handed over to the government. In this respect (and indeed in the fact that the government owns the country's gold and foreign exchange reserves) the Bank of England differs from virtually all other central banks, including those established under its own auspices, who include in their overall profit and loss accounting the results of their currency issue and foreign exchange market activities.

The profits of the Issue Department consist of interest received on the portfolio of investments held as backing for the Fiduciary Issue,† together with capital profits arising from portfolio changes, less the costs of buying (at cost from the Printing Works), storing and distributing new notes and collecting and destroying used ones. The portfolio is used solely for market management purposes and trading profit is entirely dependent on and subordinate to market management policy. The portfolio is revalued quarterly – for many years it was done weekly – at market prices and securities are then acquired or disposed of as necessary to adjust the value of the portfolio to the total of the Fiduciary Issue. Profits are usually paid to the Treasury whenever necessary during each

---

* Leaf, Walter, Litt. D., D. Litt., 1852–1927. Chairman, Westminster Bank, 1918–27.
† The Fiduciary Issue comprises the notes backed by securities.

half year to avoid an excessive balance being held in the Banking Department's accounts.

Banking Department profits, in contrast, have always been for the Bank to dispose of as it wishes. They comprise the excess of investment income and charges for services over running expenses and amortised capital expenditure. Investment income, which includes capital profit on security transactions, is derived from the investment of capital, reserves and deposits. The basis of charges for services, discussed in detail below, varies from full recovery of assessed costs, as for the note issue and, at times, for the Exchange Equalisation Account, to scales of charges – e.g. for management of British government stocks – or ad hoc fees for various tasks and services.

The level of profitability of the Banking Department varies quite markedly from year to year. It depends largely on fluctuations in customers' deposits (mainly bankers' accounts, some government and a very few private customers, whose accounts with the Bank have to be kept at a stipulated minimum level, and which do not normally earn interest) and in the level of interest rates. Annual variations also occur as a result of capital profits from the sale of other assets, themselves often previously written down out of profits. From the passing of the Act of 1844 until 1971, expenditure on premises and equipment was written off each half year, the value of these items being written down in the balance sheet to £100 each. Securities with limited realisability and potential bad debts were also written down to a value of £100 each – out of current profits – as soon as was practicable.

Unlike those of most other central banks, the profits of the Banking Department are taxable, so that changes in tax structure and rates naturally produce variations in post-tax profits.

The financial accounts of the Banking Department, like those of any business or trading organisation, record the Bank's current income and expenditure, together with its assets and liabilities. (Balances held by banking customers are of course a liability.) The actual working of the accounts, before the 1971 changeover, presents many difficulties to the uninitiated; although naturally conducted with scrupulous accuracy and on an extremely conservative basis they were, as the Deputy Chief Accountant C.M. Wise recognised in a memorandum written in 1934 'probably unique in the United Kingdom in that it would not be incorrect to assert that the accounts are worked entirely on a Balance Sheet, the "Rest", i.e. undistributed profits, being, in fact, a Deposit Liability due to Proprietors of Bank Stock'.[5]

The word 'Rest' is a piece of banking terminology whose use has come to be particularly associated with the Bank. It has been employed by the Banking Department since 1845 as a label for the balance of the Profit and Loss Account, including the dividend payable, carried forward at the end of each accounting period. (The account itself was originally established in 1722 to provide a reserve fund – up to that time the Bank had divided all the profits among the Proprietors, which caused 'great inconvenience'. From 1722 to 1845 balances in Profit and Loss at the end of the financial year were described in the final accounts as 'Balance of Gains Resting' or 'Net Gains Resting'.) It was the convention – although not invariably followed before 1946 – that after payment of the half-yearly dividend to stockholders (or, after nationalisation, after the payment in lieu of dividend to the Treasury) the balance on Rest should show a small increase over that of the preceding accounting period. This convention, together with the amount required for the dividend, determined the amount of profit available for allocation to Reserves.[6]

In addition to the General Ledger and its associated books and records maintained in the Accounts Office there were a number of subsidiary accounting systems kept for example by the Establishment Department which included those of the Maintenance Superintendent and the Chief Engineer, all of which were reflected in the General Ledger. For operational purposes the Chief Cashier's Office maintained a set of accounts which duplicated the General Ledger in a simplified format. All these systems, including the General Ledger, were handwritten and continued to be so until the change to a more conventional method of accounting.

The accounts were prepared on a six monthly basis, at the end of August and at the end of February, the latter date being the official end of the Bank's financial year, as it still is. The reason for the choice of this particular date can be traced back to an Order of Court dated 2 February 1695: 'Ordered – Books to be ballanced – That the Accountants make up the Books to a Ballance to the last of February instant inclusive. And being called in they were acquainted therewith.' Six weeks before the adoption of this Order, sixteen By-Laws had been passed by a General Court of the Bank on 18 December 1694. One of these laid down that a General Court should be held in March and September each year 'for the considering of the Generall State and Condition of this Corporation and for the making of dividends ...'. In order for Court to be able to do this, they would have had to be provided with up-to-date figures and it would therefore be necessary to balance the books as near as possible to the date of the General Court. The final day of the preceding month was obviously a convenient date for this purpose. Originally dividends on Bank Stock seem to have been declared for half years ending 25 March and 29 September. After the adoption of the Gregorian calendar in 1752, these dates became 5 April and 10 October; and, in 1869, 10 October was altered to 5 October to conform with a similar change made at that time in the date of dividends on Public Funds.[7]

To preserve the confidentiality of the accounts, only a very limited number of sets were prepared for submission to the Committee of Treasury and to Court. The permanent record, entirely handwritten, was enshrined in a ledger entitled 'Stock Estimates &c' and known colloquially, from the colour of its cover, as the Red Book.[8] Other copies combining specially printed text with manuscript figures were known as the Blue Books. After submission to Court, where one Blue Book was shared between two Directors (who were 'not expected, nor indeed always encouraged to familiarise themselves with the details of the accounts'),[9] a few copies were retained for future use by the Governor and a small number of senior officials; the remainder were destroyed. The Auditor of the Bank checked and certified that the balances shown in the General Ledgers had been properly carried into the Red Book and both of these sets of accounts were signed by two Directors.*

It is from the profits of the Banking Department that the dividends are paid – before nationalisation of the Bank in 1946 to the Proprietors or holders of Bank Stock and afterwards to the government. In theory the dividend could vary, just like that paid by any other company, but in practice it did so very little and for the twenty-three years prior to nationalisation remained at a steady 6 per cent per half year. The aims of the Banking Department were to produce an income sufficient to meet all operating expenses; to meet capital expenditure on buildings and equipment, and provide for future capital expenditure; to meet the dividend payment to stockholders; and to create adequate reserves. Provision of service to government and the public was considered far more important than raising the dividend: as Governor Norman stated in 1939 'our Proprietors have come to realise that service, and not a larger dividend, is the first consideration ...'.[10]

Professor Sayers has described the Bank's struggle for income between the years 1890 and 1914.[11] By the latter date, its internal reserves were limited to little more than the £3 m. standing in Rest, plus a certain sum for the buildings and equipment. But from 1914 to 1927 the 'free reserves' – i.e. funds available for any purpose necessary – increased, largely as a result of the interest received on credits advanced to the Bank

---

* The accounts were also audited by Deloittes after they became the Bank's external auditors in 1919 – see below, p. 200.

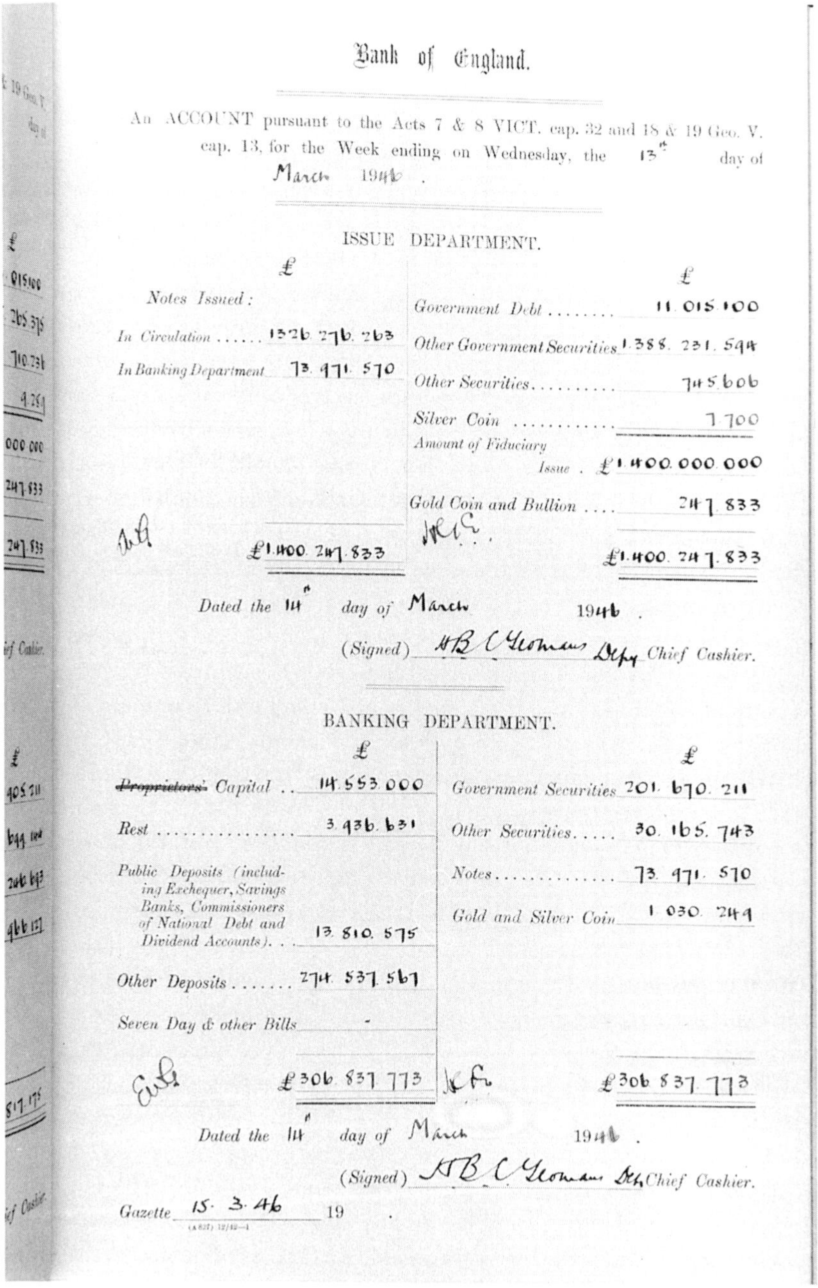

Bank of England.

An ACCOUNT pursuant to the Acts 7 & 8 VICT. cap. 32 and 18 & 19 Geo. V. cap. 13, for the Week ending on Wednesday, the 13th day of March 1946.

ISSUE DEPARTMENT.

| £ | | £ | |
|---|---|---|---|
| *Notes Issued:* | | *Government Debt* | 11.015.100 |
| *In Circulation* | 1326.276.263 | *Other Government Securities* | 1.388.231.594 |
| *In Banking Department* | 73.971.570 | *Other Securities* | 745.606 |
| | | *Silver Coin* | 7.700 |
| | | *Amount of Fiduciary Issue* | £1.400.000.000 |
| | | *Gold Coin and Bullion* | 247.833 |
| | £1.400.247.833 | | £1.400.247.833 |

*Dated the* 14th *day of* March 1946.

*(Signed)* H.B.C. Yeomans Dep.y *Chief Cashier.*

BANKING DEPARTMENT.

| £ | | £ | |
|---|---|---|---|
| ~~Proprietors'~~ *Capital* | 14.553.000 | *Government Securities* | 201.670.211 |
| *Rest* | 3.436.631 | *Other Securities* | 30.165.743 |
| *Public Deposits (including Exchequer, Savings Banks, Commissioners of National Debt and Dividend Accounts)* | 13.810.575 | *Notes* | 73.971.570 |
| *Other Deposits* | 274.537.567 | *Gold and Silver Coin* | 1.030.249 |
| *Seven Day & other Bills* | - | | |
| | £306.837.773 | | £306.837.773 |

*Dated the* 14th *day of* March 1946.

*(Signed)* H.B.C. Yeomans Dep.y *Chief Cashier.*

*Gazette* 15.3.46 19 .

Plate 6.1 The Bank Return for the week ending 13 March 1946, after the nationalisation of the Bank. The formula remains unchanged, but 'Proprietors' Capital' has been amended in ink to read 'Capital' of France, and by 1927 stood at about £23 m. By 1945 they amounted to nearly £50 m. (excluding the Rest) if the reserves held in the accounts known as 'Contingencies', 'Stock Frauds' and 'Central Banking' were considered as free. This increase of £27 m. since 1927 was partly due to profitable sales of long-dated and other securities, partly to amounts earmarked for contingencies not being required and the remainder from surplus general income. Apart from the building up of free reserves large amounts had of course been used since 1914 for capital purposes, e.g. rebuilding (that of the Threadneedle Street premises had cost over £5 m.), establishing the various Pension Funds and writing off losses on Securities and Advances. In addition to the growth of the reserves themselves, the market value of the securities had risen over the same period by between £10 m. and £12 m. over their cost.[12]

The extent of these reserves was a jealously guarded secret known to none outside the Bank and to few within it: they were concealed within the complexities of the Bank Return under the heading of Other Accounts, although anybody seriously interested in the subject might have made an informed guess.[13] The confidentiality of all banks' accounts was total, largely on the grounds that disclosure might prejudice their confidential relationship with their customers; to the weight of this argument the Bank was able to adduce a somewhat nebulous claim that the reserves of a central bank should be kept secret in the national interest. It was argued that hidden reserves enabled the Bank to 'do good by stealth', secretly helping banks or other institutions whose failure might have wide repercussions: if reserves were published regularly, a sudden reduction in the figure could allow people to deduce what had been done.

In addition to the Bank's own arcane accounting system, accounts were also prepared along more orthodox lines for submission to the Committee of Treasury.[14] Similarly, although no profit and loss account was ever published, it was drawn up every half year. In 1919, disturbed by a sharp rise in costs (largely attributable to increasing staff numbers) and anxious to institute an up-to-date method of determining the costs of work carried out on behalf of the government, the Bank took the unprecedented step of calling on the help of professional accountants. The suggestion originated with the Treasury in May of that year, during a lengthy correspondence in the wake of the enquiry* into the whole question of the Bank's profits during the war. This had been settled by the Bank paying almost £1.9 m. to the Treasury in March 1919 (in

---

* This topic was examined by a Parliamentary Sub-Committee of the Select Committee on Expenditure and by an internal Special Committee on the Bank's profits. See also Sayers Vol. 1, pp. 80–1.

addition to previous payments of Excess Profits Tax and Income Tax), but the Treasury by this date was anxious that the Bank should reduce the fees for management charges: hence the suggestion of outside accountants, as it had become apparent to both parties that the current costing methods were far from satisfactory. The Governor, Sir Brien Cokayne (later Lord Cullen),* resisted the idea at first, but soon capitulated. The firm chosen was Deloitte, Plender, Griffiths & Co., well known and respected in the City, whose senior partner was Sir William (later Lord) Plender,† three times President of the Institute of Chartered Accountants. Deloittes (now Coopers & Lybrand, Deloittes) have remained the Bank's accountants from that date onwards, although their position as such was for many years not officially acknowledged. The system of Cost Accounts which they introduced early in 1920 is still in operation, and little altered.[15]

In April 1933, when Britain was in the grip of recession, Court appointed a Special Committee to look into the whole range of the Bank's expenditure. It was required to examine all capital and current expenditure and consider 'any methods which may make for the more economical performance of any of the internal activities of the Bank'.[16] The four-strong Committee, under the chairmanship of the Hon. Alexander Shaw (later Lord Craigmyle),‡ made some fairly sharp criticisms in both its intermediate and final reports, dated April and December 1934. The most far-reaching of these concerned salary scales (that of 1926 being still in force) of which the Committee observed:

> we were struck that no salary reductions whatsoever have been made and that the salaries of the ordinary Staff are more in excess of those paid for similar work elsewhere than was the case before the war.
> It appears to us that this position would not be readily tenable in the face of public criticism. It does not seem to us to be possible to maintain indefinitely in a national institution a scale of salaries which remains entirely unaffected by the general fate of the whole population. On the contrary we believe it to be in the interests of the Bank that some account should be taken of conditions which have been widely and severely felt...

The Committee also said that there was too much Governor's leave – even probationers got eighteen days – and cuts were recommended to

* Cullen 1st Baron (1920) of Ashbourne, Brien Cokayne, KBE, 1864–1932. Director, Bank of England, 1902–15; 1920–32; Deputy Governor, 1915–18; Governor, 1918–20.
† Plender, 1st Baron (1931) of Sundridge, William Plender Bt. (1923), GBE, Kt. (1911), 1861–1946. Senior Partner of Deloittes from 1904.
‡ Craigmyle, 2nd Baron (1929) of Craigmyle; Alexander Shaw (1883–1944). Director, Bank of England, 1923–43.

make a saving of some 6,000 working days a year, equivalent to the employment of twenty-one clerks. Under the current system of promotion, clerks progressed to a higher class almost automatically, rather than as 'a recognition of special responsibility or merit', and the Committee foresaw that if this continued it would lead to the Bank in future paying high salaries for 'merely clerical and routine work involving no special responsibility'. The relatively high cost of administering the Branches was also noted, for their functions by this date were 'tending more and more to become limited to those of currency centres and collectors of revenue': however the Committee conceded that they must maintain 'the dignity and prestige of the Bank in the Provinces'. The High Sum Bank Note Register* was felt to be an extravagance: 'the Bank's system of recording particulars of the payment of every individual Note of £5 and upwards in a Register is unique amongst the principal Banks of Issue', and savings of around £4,000 a year could be made if it were abolished. Another area where economies were possible was in the materials supplied to the Bank, such as furniture, equipment and stationery (the cost of the latter was over £30,000 annually). 'As the Bank is the best customer with which a firm can deal, it is felt that there should be some competition for the supply of materials...'. Capital expenditure was limited at this date to the rebuilding of the Bank, and the Committee made several suggestions for economies in the work, largely by the use of less extravagant finishes.[17]

Some, though by no means all, of the recommendations made by the Committee were accepted by Court: the question of a reduction in salary, which was tempered by the Committee's express wish to 'cause the minimum of dislocation to existing scales', was dealt with merely by the abolition of 'risk money'† over a four year period. Leave entitlements were reduced, although only for new entrants to the Male Staff and for permanent Women Staff, and all the alterations to the rebuilding schedules were agreed. The High Sum Bank Note Register, however, was retained. There was a general acceptance of the precepts of economy in all areas, with particular emphasis on the increasing use of mechanisation wherever feasible, and the possibility of dispensing with some of the chief administrative officials at the Branches was to be 'borne in mind'.

Something which the Committee considered and rejected was the idea of instituting an annual budget. Expenditure other than on wages and

---

* See chapter 4, p. 136.
† A small proportion, usually between £15 and £50, of the salary of the permanent staff was 'at risk' and subject to review on 1 March annually.

salaries (which themselves accounted for some 80 per cent of the Bank's total costs) was almost all carried out by the newly created Establishment Department* – before that it had been in the domain of the Secretary – and required the sanction of a Governor or, on rare occasions, of the Committee of Treasury.[18] In some areas of spending the Chief of Establishments was granted discretion up to a certain limit, in other cases not; but there was no attempt to impose any formal guidelines for the coming year or years. The lack of budgetary control was one of the underlying causes of a widespread policy of overstaffing: it was accepted that the Bank had to be ready to meet any sudden rise in work levels, and this led directly to an excessive number of underemployed staff, particularly Principals and Superintendents. But the Committee was not specifically concerned with staff levels, and felt that such a thing as a budget was not feasible: 'Probably no useful purpose would be served by attempting to draw up a budget for the Bank in view of the fact that income is largely dependent on Bank Rate, which cannot be forecast, and even expenditure may be subject to sudden fluctuations from unforeseen circumstances.'

The Committee was, however, determined that there should be some form of permanent supervision of the Bank's expenditure which would mesh in with the changes then taking place as a result of the Peacock Committee* on Organisation, in particular the creation of Executive Directors and of the Establishment Department. After considering various methods by which this might be achieved it recommended that a committee should be appointed consisting of the Executive Directors and one other, who would meet periodically, consider reports from each Department, and report to the Committee of Treasury 'as to economies that had been effected since the last Meeting and as to any schemes for future economies that are being proposed'. To this suggestion Court was agreeable, and a new Standing Committee of the Bank was formed in April 1934, known as the Committee on Permanent Control of Expenditure. Its first members were the Executive Directors Clegg, Holland-Martin and Catterns, under the chairmanship of Shaw: at the end of the year Shaw was succeeded as chairman by Lord Hyndley.†[19]

Heads of Department were instructed to report half-yearly to the Expenditure Committee, one of whose early responsibilities became the surveillance of costing, now being carried out according to the system instituted by Deloittes. Before 1923 the work of costing had been

---

* See chapter 10, p. 325.

† Hyndley, 1st Viscount (1948) of Meads, John Scott Hindley, Baron (1931), Bt. (1927), GBE, 1883–1963. Managing Director of Powell Duffryn Ltd, 1931–46, Chairman, Stephenson Clarke Ltd, 1938–46. Director, Bank of England, 1931–45.

executed partly under the supervision of the Chief Accountant, partly under that of the Chief Cashier. In January of that year Court had decreed that the work should in future be done by the Audit Department. As a result of the reorganisation of the Secretary's Department in May 1934, the Costing Section had been attached to that Department, which led the Audit Committee to recommend that the work of the Section should 'more properly' be submitted to another Committee.[20] The Expenditure Committee was the obvious solution, and this was soon adopted.

The new Committee's approach was essentially that of taking an overview. Staffing levels, which gave rise to salaries, wages, overtime, pensions and other staff costs, were outside its provenance, as were salary and wage scales. At its meetings – at first twice, later three times per year – it received a considerable number of reports in addition to those of the Heads of Department which had originally been suggested. There was a detailed analysis of the Bank's expenditure at Head Office and the Branches for the period, together with comparative statements for previous half-years. The Costing Section of the Secretary's Office submitted a report, and the Superintendent of Costing presented the results of his scrutiny of the Bank's expenditure. The accounts of the Works Department for the half-year preceding the meeting were also laid before the Committee.

The report of the Costing Section consisted mainly of a summary of the Cost Accounts, analysing costs and revenue by function, e.g. note issue, deposit banking, the Exchange Equalisation Account and Stocks Management. In this pre-war period, full costs of the EEA were recovered on exactly the same basis as for the note issue. For British government stocks, the aim in the decade preceding the war was to produce a profit of between 10 and 12 per cent on costs: this was achieved by the scale of charges then in force.* There was a separate scale for issues, conversions and redemptions but because costs of these operations varied considerably with their size and nature, ad hoc as opposed to scale charges were frequently made.

The Bank also provided registrar services for some Dominion and Colonial governments, British local authorities and public boards; here again many of the charges were on an ad hoc basis although scale charges were also established, particularly for management.

The Bank's customers – government, commercial banks, other central banks and the dwindling band of private customers – were not charged

---

* £325 per million for the first £750 m. of stock managed, £100 per million thereafter, £100 per million for Bearer Bonds.

for the provision of banking services but were required to keep individually agreed minimum balances on their accounts. The costs and income of these were reviewed at intervals to assess profitability: minimum balances were increased when necessary.

The investment policy required to achieve the aims of the Banking Department as described above, while maintaining the degree of liquidity considered desirable for a central bank, was reviewed regularly. Early in 1933 it was decided that as many investments as possible should be in readily realisable form, the majority being British Government Securities of which about 75 per cent should be dated and the remainder irredeemable. At the time the decision was taken the percentage of redeemable stocks was only 6 per cent, but within six months this proportion had been raised to 60 per cent. The holdings were switched frequently in pursuance of this policy between 1933 and 1937, by which time the redeemable proportion had reached 73 per cent. As further changes would have incurred a large tax liability, no more action was taken for the time being. The book value of each holding of irredeemable stock had been written down to £100.[21]

By the middle of 1936 the Bank was seriously troubled about the high level of its profits which, after payment of the half-yearly dividend at 6 per cent and of the annual contribution to the Superannuation Fund, were running at a level of between £250,000 and £300,000 a year. A careful examination of various methods of 'dealing with this position' ensued, and suggestions were put to the Committee of Treasury. The first of these was to raise the dividend, where an increase of 1 per cent half yearly would have involved a net additional payment of £222,000 per annum (Income Tax was currently 4s. 9d. in the pound). The Committee of Treasury, however, thought that 'any increase at the present time would be impolitic'. Another possibility was to reduce the charges for Stock Management, but here again it was felt that the time was not ripe for change: the newly mechanised methods of transfer and dividend payment were still being evaluated, questions of the maintenance of machinery and any spare space in the Printing Works had not yet been fully considered and the Committee of Treasury decided that the whole position should be viewed in perspective before any concrete proposals were put forward.

An ex gratia payment to the government was considered to be unsuitable, and the suggestion of a purchase of gold from the Exchange Equalisation Account (a non-interest bearing investment) at current prices failed to find favour with the Treasury. But the Bank still felt uneasy about continuing its policy of placing any surplus to the various

reserve accounts, especially since the possibility of 'an enforced examination of the Bank's accounts in the future must be faced with a resulting
criticism that money has been accumulated at the expense of the
government and of industry'.[22] On the other hand, it could take comfort
in an exchange during the hearing of evidence of the Macmillan
Committee* a few years earlier:

> *Chairman*: Suppose that the suggestion of a fixed dividend were adopted
> and that the State received the profits of the note issue on some new
> principle such as Mr. Keynes has suggested, what would happen to the
> balance of the profits; would they all go to the reserve, or are they to be
> shared by the State and the Bank on some basis?
>
> *Sir Ernest Harvey*:† Well, I should be afraid of a system under which,
> having paid $X$ per cent on Bank Stock, and having paid to the Treasury the
> profits of the issue, the balance of profits had to be divided in a fixed
> proportion. A Central Bank should be free to maintain its position which
> will permit it to shape its policy without the need to pay regard to mere
> profit making.
>
> *Mr Keynes*: I did not intend to suggest any change on that point. My idea
> was that at present dividends are in effect fixed, and therefore the surplus
> goes to reserve. It seems to me very desirable that the Bank of England
> should control very large reserves, and that the building up of those
> reserves is not a thing that one should object to. I think that system has
> been adopted in many countries, and I see nothing against it.'[23]

In the event no action was taken in 1936, and a year later, when the
question surfaced once more, profits had risen again – they were in the
region of £800,000 for the year – while 'free' reserves amounted to about
£30 m. with securities undervalued to the extent of some £16 m. A
memorandum from E.M. Stapley, the Secretary, proposed that Deloittes
should be requested to 'consider the position thus created and report as
to future policy'. Governor Norman decided, in agreement with the
Committee of Treasury, to consult Lord Plender personally, and did so
on 22 June. Plender reviewed the Bank's entire reserve and investment
policy, embodying his views in a letter to Norman a week later. In his
opinion recent and current policies were justified, and he, like the Bank,
thought that an increase in the dividend would be 'inadvisable', nor did

* The Treasury Committee on Finance and Industry, 1929, was under the chairmanship
of Baron Macmillan of Aberfeldy (1930), Hugh Pattison Macmillan, PC, GCVO, KC,
1873–1952
† Harvey, Sir Ernest Musgrave, 1st Bt. (1933), KBE, 1867–1955. Entered Bank of
England, 1885; Chief Cashier 1918–25; Comptroller, 1925–8; Deputy Governor,
1929–36.

he favour making a voluntary gift to the government. He could see no reason why management charges should be reduced 'unless appreciable savings in costs are effected by reason of the recent installation of a mechanised system'.

Regarding the allocation of the surplus, Plender doubted whether it would be advisable to 'depart from precedent' by increasing the Rest rather than the inner reserves: 'I do not think there is much to choose between increasing the inner reserve included in "Other Deposits" or the Investment Reserve', but was inclined to favour the latter. On the delicate subject of the disclosure of reserves Plender added this:

> The point may at some time be raised that there is no indication in the Bank Return as to the existence of inner reserves. The answer, I suggest, is that it should be obvious that there must be such reserves, since the Rest has remained practically unchanged for a great number of years, and it can hardly be imagined that the Bank's profits have only just been sufficient to pay the dividend of 12% year after year. Moreover, at the half-yearly General Court it is your practice to announce the figure of profit 'after making provision for all contingencies' and your remarks are freely quoted in the newspapers.[24]

'We are happy to have your approval of what has been done in the past and of the position as it stands today', replied the Governor; adding 'your letter will be valuable evidence for the defence if there should be an attack on the Bank one of these days'.[25] A further enquiry along similar lines made of Deloittes by the Secretary in February 1939 spelt out quite plainly just what type of attack it was that the Bank envisaged: 'In considering these questions, it must be borne in mind that the Institution in question might possibly be nationalised in one form or another at some future date.'[26]

The outbreak of war necessitated fresh appraisals of the liquidity position of the Banking Department and of its investment policies.[27] By the time they took place, in October 1939 and February 1940, further preoccupations had arisen for those concerned with the accounts of the Bank. Chief among them was the question of Exchange Control. Initially the full costs of administration of the Defence (Finance) Regulations, which governed the operation of Exchange Control, combined with the costs of the EEA, were recovered from the government. But, because the Cost Accounting system provided for the distribution of all costs among all activities, the effect of introducing this new and substantial responsibility – without any proportionate increase in the Bank's overhead costs – was to reduce the overhead charge for all other activities. This in turn reduced their costs and, in some cases, increased their profitability. To negate this undesirable state of affairs the Bank decided in 1941 that, although the costing system would calculate the full costs of Exchange Control, some costs would not be charged; this system was applied retrospectively for 1940 and continued until the changes in 1952/3 described below.[28]

The enormous amount of extra work occasioned by Exchange Control in the early months of the war meant that many thousands of hours of overtime were worked, and the upheaval brought about by the move of the Accountant's Department to Hampshire ensured that there, too, staff worked inordinately long hours during the first year at the locations.* The Expenditure Committee became concerned about the level of extra work and its cost to the Bank, which was considerable: in the half year to 29 February 1940 money paid for overtime and in gratuities in lieu of overtime amounted to more than £62,000, equivalent to 10 per cent of the cost of salaries and wages for the same period. The expansion of Exchange Control also caused a sharp rise in numbers, and hence in salaries, and a further expense was the cost of running the emergency locations, which by the summer of 1941 had stabilised at approximately £100,000 per year. The first full year of the war saw the Bank's expenditure rise by nearly £1 m. over the last full year of peace, although costs did fall as the war progressed, helped by the fact that maintenance was kept at a minimum.[29]

By 1942 Stock Management costs were falling because of simplified working procedures, the benefits of mechanisation and a general lower level of activity than that experienced pre-war. The profit margin on Stock Management began to rise correspondingly, and the Bank felt renewed apprehension that this might lead to criticism on the grounds that it was profiting at the expense of the public. A new reduced scale for management charges† was therefore proposed to the Treasury, who accepted it: this remained in force until 1971.[30]

As the result of the General Election of July 1945 there came to power a Labour government one of whose main policies was nationalisation of much of British industry. As a preliminary to bringing into public ownership the railways, gas and electricity supply and steel, a first priority was to nationalise the Bank – just as the Bank had feared before the outbreak of war.

The 1945 Bank of England Bill (which received Royal Assent in February 1946) was not in fact the first time that such an action had been attempted. In March 1926 the Labour Party had tried unsuccessfully,

---

* See chapter 1, p. 10.
† £325 per million for the first £750 m. of stock managed, £150 per million for the next £5,250 m., £50 per million thereafter.

through the medium of private members' Bills, to bring in legislation on a variety of matters in which it was interested. James Maxton,* the member for the Bridgeton Division of Glasgow, sponsored a Bill 'To provide for the national acquisition and control of the Bank of England'. Three Commissioners were to be appointed to determine the purchase price of Bank Stock, presumably by examination of the reserves; the Bank would be under the direction of a Bank Council one of whose duties was the keeping of 'full and faithful accounts' to be laid annually before Parliament. Surplus profits – after due provision for outgoings, losses and liabilities for the year – were to be applied to the establishment of a sinking fund and a depreciation fund 'in respect of capital expended'. The Bill was objected to, however, on the grounds of conflict with the Standing Orders of the House in that it affected private interests. A Select Committee looked into the matter and decided that the Orders could not be laid aside, so the Bill got no further than its first reading.[31]

The 1945 Bill was much less radical than Maxton's, especially on the matters of disclosure of reserves and accountability. There was no question of any Commissioners being appointed to determine the 'value' of the Bank: it was simply proposed that the government should create an issue of stock at 3 per cent per annum and offer each of the current Proprietors of Bank Stock £400 of the new issue for every £100 of the old, making the total purchase price £58,212,000. The figure was subject to a certain amount of criticism as the Bill made its passage through the Commons, largely on the grounds that, while the compensation terms ensured the continuance of past income, they gave the Proprietors no credit for the 'equity' of the Bank's business – i.e. the extensive reserves which the Bank was understood to have built up by withholding much of its profit from distribution. All sorts of figures for these were bandied about and they were frequently rumoured to be as much as £100 m., which was of course almost twice the true amount. The Governor told Court in November that he thought it possible that the Bank might be 'compelled' to disclose the volume of reserves but that he would resist doing so 'as being against national interests'.[32] The exact figures became a subject of intense debate both in the Commons and at the Committee stage, with many questions along the lines of that put by Sir J. Stanley Holmes† during the Second Reading of the Bill: 'Would the Minister be good enough to answer the question which I asked him earlier this evening? What is the amount of the Reserve Fund of the Bank of

---

* Maxton, James, 1885–1946. MP (Lab.), Bridgeton Division of Glasgow, 1922–6.
† Holmes, Sir J. Stanley, 1878–1954. MP (Lib. Nat. and Con.), Harwich, 1935–53.

NOT THIS TIME!

Citizen Attlee (to the Old Lady of Threadneedle Street): "Cab, lady?"

[Tumbril, lady?]

Plate 6.2   Pen and ink drawing by Bernard Partridge, *Punch*, 20 November 1935. Citizen Attlee is saying to the Old Lady of Threadneedle Street: 'Cab, lady?'. The 'cab' is in fact a tumbril with a banner proclaiming 'Nationalisation of Banks'. There is a signpost – 'To the Guillotine'. In a speech made at Accrington on 13 October 1935, Clement Attlee, the leader of the Labour Party, said: 'If the Labour Party resumed power the first thing they would invade would be the "Temple of the Golden Calf" in Threadneedle Street – the Bank of England.' In the period between the speech and the publication of the cartoon a general election had been held at which the National Government, dominated by the Conservatives, had been returned with a large majority.

England?' To this he received a dusty answer from Glenvil Hall,* Financial Secretary to the Treasury:

> The answer to that question is quite irrelevant. The price to be paid, as my Right Honourable Friend the Chancellor of the Exchequer has said, and as I have now tried to amplify and repeat, has been based on the market price

* Hall, Rt Hon. William Glenvil, PC (1947), 1887–1962. MP. (Lab.), Colne Valley Div. of Yorkshire, from 1939; Financial Secretary to the Treasury, 1945–50.

of the present stock...what the reserves amount to is quite irrelevant to this matter. For one thing the Bank of England is a private institution and publishes no balance sheet.[33]

At the Committee stage, Governor Catto was asked a similar question, although put hypothetically, by Sir Cyril Radcliffe KC,* one of the two Counsel acting for the promoters of the Bill:

> Lord Catto, if you were asked by somebody questions to this effect: It does not seem to us that we can value the stock which is being offered for exchange to the stockholders without full discovery of what is called the Bank's secret reserves, or inner reserves, rather, what answer would you give to the wisdom of such a question?

Catto had already had to deal with such awkward questions on his home ground: a month earlier, in October 1945, he had given the Court confidential advance notice of the provisions of the Bill and had subsequently been strongly pressed by Lord Kindersley† who was aggrieved that 'no information had been given to Proprietors as to the value of the assets which they were asked to surrender. He felt that they had a moral right to know the position.'[34] Then, as now, the Governor reiterated his belief that the terms were 'fair and reasonable'; to the Committee he was more explicit, saying that the suggestion

> that it is necessary to disclose the whole of the inner reserves of the Bank is I think most unfair and most unreasonable...I know of no case where a Bank, when there has been an amalgamation or a purchase, has disclosed to the public the inner reserves of either institution. Inner reserves are essential to the strength and prestige of any great institution such as the Bank of England...I assure you...they are in no sense larger than is necessary for the proper conduct and prestige and confidence of the institution all over the world.[35]

And despite repeated questions – some of them distinctly hostile – to the Chancellor of the Exchequer‡ in the Commons, there was no disclosure of the reserves.

Less interest was shown in the subject of the publication of any sort of Annual Report or accounts, of which the Bill made no mention. On one of the few occasions that Dalton was asked about this in the House of Commons, he asserted that it would be premature to discuss the matter before the Bill had gone through. When it had done so, he would

---

* Radcliffe, 1st Viscount (1962), John Cyril Radcliffe, PC, GBE, FBA, Baron (1949), 1899–1977. Chairman, Committee of Inquiry into the Monetary and Credit System, 1957–9.
† Kindersley, 1st Baron (1941) of West Hoathly, Robert Molesworth Kindersley, GBE, 1871–1954. Director, Bank of England, 1914–46.
‡ Dalton, Baron (1960) of Forest and Frith, Co. Palatine of Durham, Edward Hugh John Neale Dalton, PC, MA, 1887–1962. Chancellor of the Exchequer, 1945–7.

discuss with the Governor of the Bank of England what would be the most useful form for the laying of an annual Report which could, of course, be discussed in the House, on the operations of the Bank, and what would be the most convenient form that that should take. My approach to that would be that we desire to give the maximum of information about the operation of the Bank under the new conditions which will be consistent with the public interest and the reasonable requirements of discretion, and even of secrecy, on which point I would be disposed to be guided very much on what the Governor himself and the Bank thought. Subject to that, we would be prepared to lay a report in Parliament, but its exact form I would not like to indicate at this stage.[36]

This left the Bank with plenty of room for manoeuvre, but meanwhile there was a more pressing subject for internal debate: the annual payment to be made to the Exchequer in lieu of dividend. The Bank was anxious from the start that it should be made clear in the wording of the Bill that the intention was for the half-yearly payments to be made out of accruing profits and not by drawing upon reserves: in a conversation with the Chancellor in September 1945 the Governor pointed out that the country was purchasing the Bank for approximately £58 m. and that he felt a responsibility to ensure as far as he could 'that the value of the asset should be maintained'. If the reserves were drawn upon, then the assets might gradually be reduced to less than the amount to be paid. The Chancellor agreed that this was an important point and said that he could see no objection if a satisfactory wording could be worked out between the Treasury and the Bank. The Bank pressed hard for the inclusion of the words 'out of profit' in the clause relating to the payment in lieu of dividend, but were eventually defeated by the opinion in the Treasury that 'it might do more harm than good ... as it would probably require definition and might raise questions in debate'. The Treasury also felt that if in any particular half year Bank profits were to fall short of the stated amount it would be reasonable that the full figure should nevertheless be paid.[37]

In the Bill presented to Parliament and approved by them, the relative clause read:

> 1. (4) After the appointed day, no dividends on Bank stock shall be declared but in lieu of any such dividends the Bank shall pay to the Treasury, on every fifth day of April and of October, the sum of eight hundred and seventy-three thousand, one hundred and eighty pounds, or such less or greater sum as may from time to time be agreed upon between the Treasury and the Bank.

This sum represented a half year's interest at the rate of 3 per cent per annum on the amount of government stock which was issued, and equalled the gross sum of the annual dividends that the Bank had paid in the previous twenty-three years to the holders of its stock. Lord Catto, in his evidence to the Select Committee, emphasised the distinction between the two: 'The dividend on the new stock that will be issued in exchange for the stock of the Bank has no connection with what the Bank may pay over to the Government.'[38]

In the Commons the main criticism of the Conservative opposition to the half-yearly payment centred on a dislike of the provision that it might be increased by agreement between the Treasury and the Bank. A typical comment was that made by Sir John Mellor,* who felt that it was 'quite unjustifiable that the Treasury should desire now in the terms of this Bill to have a right to extract more from the Bank than the Bank would have paid to stockholders if it had continued under private enterprise'. To this and similar comments the Chancellor replied that the Treasury wanted to ensure flexibility:

> We are legislating for the long future. I do not known when it will again be necessary to pass a Bill relating to the Bank of England; it may be a very long time. We think this will operate very well and beneficially to the national interest and it will be just as well to keep a variation one way or another so that if it seems in the national interest, both to the Treasury and to the Bank of England either to raise or lower the amount, it can be done. I think it is a wise precaution to put in this degree of flexibility, but I hasten to add that I have no present intention of suggesting a variation. I have no reason to think that the Bank of England has any reason to suggest a variation but if it seemed to both the parties reasonable to alter it, it would be a pity if they were prevented from doing so by rigidity in the Statute.[39]

In the House of Lords, Lord Balfour of Inchrye† attempted to have the clause amended so that no greater sum than £873,180 could be paid without prior notification to Parliament; but the amendment was withdrawn when it was made clear that any increase in the half-yearly payment would be evident from the Public Accounts and would be discussed by the Public Accounts Committee.

With these major aspects of nationalisation safely decided in a manner which was satisfactory to both the Treasury and the Bank, attention within the latter could be given to the question of the Annual Report, the first of which would cover the year to the end of February 1947. Governor Catto intimated in March 1946 that he wanted consideration to be given to the drafting of a Report 'of a very informative character',

---

\* Mellor, Sir John, 2nd Bt. (1924), 1893–1986. MP (Con.), Tamworth, 1935–45, Sutton Coldfield, 1945–55.

† Balfour of Inchrye, 1st Baron (1945) of Shefford, Harold Harington Balfour, PC, MC and Bar, 1897–.

Plate 6.3   The Court, 1946, just before nationalisation. Governor Catto is at the head of the table with the Deputy Governor, C.F. Cobbold, on his left. The Secretary, W.H. Nevill, is standing on the left.

adding that this description did not necessarily cover the Bank's own financial position. He suggested something on the lines of the Report of the Bank for International Settlements although shorter and not of world-wide scope.[40] Heads of Departments were asked by the Secretary to keep a brief diary of the principal events which might be included, such as payments agreements, government stock issues and matters affecting the note issue. The Bank's first intention was that the Report should not be a Stationery Office publication, but that it should be printed at St Luke's and available free of charge to all bona fide applicants. The Chancellor of the Exchequer however, although sympathetic, was insistent that it must be published as a Command Paper as well, and despite strong pressure from Catto the Treasury views prevailed.

Whatever the Governor's original intentions may have been as to the fullness of information to be contained in the Reports, they emerged as singularly bland documents giving little information unavailable elsewhere. At first the Bank was nervous that a Profit and Loss Account might be insisted on, but the Treasury made no moves in that direction and such accounts were not included, the Bank opting instead to publish a Bank Return for the last weekday in February. A few questions were asked in Parliament on this topic, but were deflected by the Chancellor, who affirmed that the Bank's internal accounts were its own affair with which nobody else need be concerned.[41] The unsatisfactory nature of the Report was recognised within the Bank but the general consensus of opinion followed Mynors' view that further information could not readily be given 'without impinging on Government policy or disclosing the domestic affairs of the Bank in a way which might well lead to pressure for yet more domestic detail'. The Chief Cashier, P.S. Beale, remarked in May 1953 that: 'The Report is as dull and free from controversy as usual – rightly in my view.'[42]

From its first publication outsiders were far from complimentary and the Report was compared unfavourably with those of other central banks which gave much more detailed information, the Bank of Canada's report in particular being held up as a model which the Bank of England might well emulate. Professor Sayers, in a lecture entitled *Central Banking in Britain Today* which he delivered to the Institute of Bankers in February 1953, had this to say:

> The Bank of England issues a weekly statement of accounts, cast in a form dictated by a theory abandoned eighty years or more ago, and meaning scarcely anything. As a nationalised industry it publishes an annual report in which it gives us a few new facts, some of interest but most of them only curiosities, and pads this out with a few pages of facts already published elsewhere. I do not want to be thought too critical of this; I recognise that there are quite exceptional difficulties which go some way to justifying the Bank of England in producing the dullest central bank report in the world.[43]

It was presumably this informed comment that led Governor Cobbold, at the end of 1953, to ask Sayers for his ideas on further material which might be included. Sayers replied with a long list of suggestions, including a full analysis of the National Debt with the total for Public Departments and an analysis by maturity dates; further figures on assets and deposits of the Clearing Banks; more detail and explanation of the classification used in the Bank Return, including an analysis of the various accounts; summaries of balance sheets of Discount and Accepting Houses; an explanation of the technique of the issue of Treasury Bills; considerably more detail on the Balance of Payments including the origins of gold purchases; and a 'running commentary' on the economic and financial scene.[44] Few of these suggestions were implemented in the years immediately following Sayers' letter, but for the first time in 1958 the Report opened with a brief commentary on the monetary situation in the year under review. In 1960, following the recommendations of the Radcliffe Committee, the Bank did give considerably more statistical detail in the Report, and this was supplemented by the publication of *The Bank of England Quarterly Bulletin* which first appeared at the end of that year.

The Bank's own finances, however, remained carefully veiled from outside eyes. The case for non-disclosure was strengthened by the passing of the 1948 Companies' Act, which codified the Companies' Acts of 1927 and 1947. The Board of Trade had powers to exempt bodies from the provisions which concerned annual returns, accounts and audits, and did so in the case of the Bank of England; other banks, too, were generally exempted from the full requirements by virtue of Schedule 8, Part III of the Act, which allowed them among other things to maintain undisclosed reserves. In spite of this the Bank did from time to time consult Deloittes as to how the various Suspense Accounts should be grouped if it ever became necessary to conform to the requirements made of other institutions and companies by the 1948 Act.[45]

With the return to peacetime conditions the expenses of the Bank began a steady climb. By 1947 the costs of maintenance (including special payments made to the staff of the Works Department as a measure of compensation for the delay in introducing new wage and salary schemes) overheads and capital expenditure had all risen appreciably. Total expenditure for the year ending 31 August 1947 was £4·6 m., over £900,000 more than that for the previous year.[46] At the end of 1947 the Governors instructed the Expenditure Committee and the Secretary to reconsider the methods by which domestic expenditure was sanctioned, still at this date virtually unchanged from the pre-war system outlined above. They came to the conclusion that the institution of some form of budget was unavoidable.

Under the new system, agreed by Court in January 1948,[47] estimates of domestic expenditure classified under appropriate heads to be incurred by the Chief of Establishments each half year were to be prepared by him (with a 5 per cent allowance for contingencies) and submitted to the Expenditure Committee. If approved by the Committee, they would be submitted in turn to the Committee of Treasury for adoption, following which expenditure within the budget limits for the purposes specified could be incurred by the Chief of Establishments without further sanction. Money would be advanced to him from the General Ledger as required, and he would account for expenditure monthly – or, in the case of the Works Department, half yearly. Expenditure in excess of the limits, or unforeseeable capital expenditure, required specific sanction from the Governors as before: supplementary estimates would be prepared if necessary. By this method, noted E.N. Dalton, Chief of Establishments, it was hoped to overcome 'many of the difficulties of the present time by planning in advance'.[48]

Even with this more orderly approach, the Expenditure Committee experienced many problems. The expenditure covered by the budget was only a fraction of the Bank's total outgoings, some 75 to 80 per cent of which was incurred by staff costs with which the budget was not concerned. Dallas Bernard, when first appointed as a member of the Committee in June 1948, was pained by what he perceived as its innate contradictions, particularly the fact that the Director in charge of Domestic Organisation was a member. 'If the purpose of the Committee is to report to the Committee of Treasury, the DICDO cannot act as a spearhead of the Committee.' Bernard also thought that the budget arrangements had not tightened up the control over expenditure 'but rather the reverse' and that the 5 per cent margin for contingencies was too large.[49] Many of the expenses of this period were however of a non-recurring nature, such as the complete furnishing of Regent Arcade House* and new mechanisation in various offices in Threadneedle Street; a scheme of cleaning and decorating was initiated in July 1948, involving work by outside contractors to make good the unavoidable neglect during the war years.[50]

In October 1948 the post of Supervisor of Expenditure† was created, its first incumbent being F.E. Weston, Assistant to the Chief of Establishments. It was an extra-Departmental appointment: the Supervisor had 'no other duties than to examine expenditure throughout the Bank and consider ways and means of economising'. Wages and salaries were outside his province, but he was to consider staffing levels.[51] Seven months later, in March 1949, one of the first acts of Cobbold on taking up office as Governor was the institution of a new Committee to scrutinise expenditure at the highest level. This was the Blue Book Committee, consisting of the Deputy Governor, Sir Kenneth Peppiatt and the Secretary.[52] It was in existence for ten years, with three main areas of responsibility: examination of the half yearly accounts and approval of the draft of the statement for the Committee of Treasury and Court; examination of the estimates for the succeeding periods, making any recommendations considered necessary; and examining, annually or more often, the Stock Management charge and other estimates or charges for work done on account of the government. In practice the Blue Book Committee had the additional responsibility for making proposals for the allocation of the half-yearly surplus.

The increasing emphasis laid by the Bank in this early post-nationalisation period on economy and, by implication, efficiency,

---

* See chapter 2, p. 63.

† The post of Supervisor of Expenditure was amalgamated with that of the Inspector of Offices and Branches in 1952.

certainly stemmed in part from a realisation that as a nationalised body the question of its accountability must surface sooner or later. Mynors had followed the debate on Public Accountability in the House of Commons on 3 March 1948, reporting later to the Governor that the discussion had not been 'very much relevant to the Bank' but that, if there should be a general drive to submit all nationalised bodies to the scrutiny of the Auditor-General and the Public Accounts Committee, the Bank could probably not be exempted unless by its statutory position. 'If this failed, no excellence of their own [i.e. the Bank's] "private" arrangements would preserve them from being included in the scrutiny.'[53] No such scrutiny was imposed, but the Bank was not to be wholly excluded from general considerations of public expenditure.

Throughout 1949 the government made repeated efforts to reduce spending by its own departments, and the Treasury approached the Bank on the subject with specific reference to Exchange Control, whose costs were a direct charge upon them. The Bank was able to reply citing the continuous internal review of Exchange Control expenditure, and concluding that unless there was a change in government policy the tendency was likely to be an increase in staff rather than any reduction. This the Treasury accepted. In October, the Prime Minister Clement Attlee\* and Chancellor Stafford Cripps† again stated that national expenditure must be cut, and appealed to people throughout the country not to incur any further outlay on buildings and repair work unless absolutely necessary.

A month after this appeal Sir Edward Bridges wrote to the Deputy Governor telling him that the Chancellor wished the Bank 'to inform him of any further measures adopted as part of the process of securing economies in administrative costs'. Bernard replied that the Governor, the previous week, had called for a reduction in expenditure which would fall principally on premises, and that the allotment in the next half-year's budget would be cut by about 30 per cent. (This, as the chairman of the Expenditure Committee, Sir Patrick Ashley Cooper,‡ pointed out, in practice amounted to less than 1·3 per cent of the Bank's total expenditure, by now nearly £6 m. annually.) The cuts were duly made, principally in non-recurring items of building and equipment, and much internal re-decoration and improvement was deferred; work on some of the Branches was cancelled and closer estimating was demanded by the

---

\* Attlee, 1st Earl (1955), Viscount Prestwood (1955); Clement Richard Attlee, PC, OM, CH, FRS, 1883–1967. Prime Minister and First Lord of the Treasury, 1945–51.

† Cripps, Rt Hon. Sir (Richard) Stafford, PC, CH, Kt., FRS, QC, 1889–1952. Chancellor of the Exchequer, 1947–50.

‡ Cooper, Sir Patrick Ashley, Kt. (1944), 1887–1961. Governor, Hudson's Bay Company, 1931–52. Director, Bank of England, 1932–55.

Committee who thought that over-estimating was all too frequent. It was recognised that any reduction in staff costs, currently in the region of £4·25 m. a year, was a highly sensitive area, but the Committee advocated 'the utmost vigilance' in this respect. The position was very frankly and fully described by the Deputy Governor in February 1950 when he addressed a meeting of Heads of Department and Principals, asking them to consider all possible ways of economising. It was essential, he said, that the Bank should be able to satisfy any queries as to its efficiency: otherwise, whichever party was returned in the forthcoming General Election, it might be faced with a committee of enquiry into its affairs which would be 'a grave threat to our independence'.[54]

The decade of the 1950s was a period of considerable capital expenditure, including the costs of building New Change, the Printing Works and the Paid Note Office at Debden, and major rebuilding schemes in some of the Branches as well as various works in London. Mechanisation increased, and the sums spent on foreign travel, chiefly by the Overseas Department, rose sharply. Staff costs continued to account for about four-fifths of total expenditure, but by 1956 the decreasing work in Exchange Control allowed smaller numbers to be employed there, and further reductions were achieved by the discharge of most of the Supplementary Staff* and early pension offers to various other categories of staff. By 1960 the Bank's total expenditure was just below £8 m. a year.[55]

Genuine anxiety about rising costs on the one hand did not preclude close attention to the potential embarrassment of large profits on the other: an almost schizophrenic state of affairs which was compounded by continuing nervousness over outside interference. In March 1950 Sir Wilfrid Eady raised the question of the half-yearly payment to the Treasury. He told Governor Cobbold that he 'wondered whether there ought not to be some procedure by which the Treasury and the Bank discussed the amount before the end of each half-year, particularly in view of the heavy payments made by the Treasury to the Bank for various services'. Cobbold's response was unequivocal:

> I said that I was entirely opposed to raising this matter. I did not see how any such discussions could take place without going into the accounts as a whole. It had been clearly understood when the Act was drafted, and the intention is reflected in the drafting, that the Bank's policy and practice in these matters should be their own responsibility. I should certainly not be prepared to have any informal discussions with the Treasury on the subject. It was always open to the Treasury or the Bank to suggest a different figure but that would have to be done in the most formal way

* The Supplementary Staff was largely composed of staff recruited on a non-permanent basis during the Second World War for work in Exchange Control.

between the Court and the Lords Commissioners and I much hoped that it would not arise.

I said that I was prepared to tell him, as we had stated to the Treasury on other occasions, that we looked carefully at the charges made to the Treasury over the whole field and that it would never occur to us to overcharge the Treasury in order to swell our undisclosed reserves. Again, as we had often told the Treasury, we looked in quite different directions for our main earning capacity.[56]

Far from overcharging the Treasury, the Bank had been carrying out work for the government at a loss since 1941/2, and in the year to the end of February 1950 undercharged it by £221,000 for services provided.[57] By this date the Bank had assumed the management of the stocks issued in compensation for the nationalisation of the railways and the gas and electricity supply undertakings and would shortly do the same for iron and steel. Initially many of the charges for these services were on an ad hoc basis, with scale charges instituted later: on a full costs basis much of the work was 'unprofitable'.

The question of the charge for Exchange Control now surfaced once more. The Bank was very conscious that it administered the Control as agents of the Treasury: as the charge was much the largest item on the Treasury's own vote it allowed potential interference with what were firmly regarded as the private affairs of the Bank. A management charge, as opposed to the cost recovery basis which had been in force since 1941, was thought preferable to avoid any such erosion of the Bank's jealously guarded independence. Another drawback to the current method was that it involved a higher charge to the Treasury every time there was an increase in staff salaries.

In 1951 the Governor decided to initiate discussions with the Treasury on a changeover to an annual fee, with provision for raising it if costs should increase 'unreasonably'. Investigations were begun into working out a basis which would enable the Bank to make a lower annual charge than it was currently imposing, even though this might result in some loss – as in the case of Stock Management. An unsatisfactory attempt had been made three years before to establish a formula based on units of work; the position was no easier now, because it was impossible for anyone to foresee whether Exchange Control would be contracted or, much more likely, expanded. The only safe assumption was, as the Chief Cashier pointed out, that over the next two or three years the same numbers of staff, or approximately the same distribution of salary grades, would continue to be employed.

Dialogue with the Treasury on the subject continued during the first part of 1952, during which it was learnt that the Treasury had given an undertaking to the Public Accounts Committee to supply a detailed analysis of Exchange Control costs: not unreasonably, the Auditor-General had expressed disquiet over the fact that the very large figure for Exchange Control was passed by him without scrutiny or government Auditor's report. Although the Bank had successfully resisted an earlier attempt to publish a much less comprehensive analysis, this time a breakdown of costs was rather grudgingly supplied. Finally, early in 1953, a formula acceptable to both parties was agreed: the Treasury accepted the Bank's suggestion that the fee should be, initially, £1·3 m. per fiscal year, starting in 1952/3 and subject to annual review. This figure represented a substantial reduction from recent charges which had averaged well over £1·5 m. for the past three years.[58]

Allied to the question of Exchange Control costs was that of charges for the EEA. In 1946 it was agreed that separate, full cost recovery should be resumed on the pre-war basis, but after the new arrangements for Exchange Control the Treasury suggested a fixed fee should also be adopted for the EEA. The Bank argued that the activity was more akin to that of the note issue; the Treasury did not agree with this but the point was not pursued. Some years later the Treasury queried the costs and details were provided, the full cost recovery system remaining in place until 1966 after which the Bank ceased to make any charge 'in view of prevailing high money rates'.[59]

Any dent in the Bank's profits made by the change to a fixed fee for Exchange Control was hardly noticeable because a significant development affecting its overall profitability had taken place at the end of 1951. Within a few days of taking office members of the new Conservative administration under Winston Churchill were elaborating on the actions they proposed to take to combat the economic situation of the country, which they viewed with 'grave concern'. On 7 November the Chancellor, R.A. (later Lord) Butler,* announced a package of measures to curb inflation which needed, he said, the support of a monetary policy more direct in its effect than the system of guidance to the banks which had been employed since the war. An immediate increase in Bank Rate from 2 to 2½ per cent was imposed, and flexibility was to be restored to the short-term market.[60]

Bank Rate had been steady at 2 per cent since June 1932, except for a brief period from August to October 1939. This return to a more orthodox method of monetary control, and to dearer money (prompting the murmur in the Stock Exchange 'the headmaster is back'), naturally boosted the income of the Bank. In September 1952 the Governor told

---

* Butler, Baron (1965) of Saffron Walden, Richard Austen Butler, KG, PC, CH, MA, 1902–82. Chancellor of the Exchequer, 1951–5.

Court that the profits of the Banking Department for the previous half year had been over £1·5 m., compared with £685,000 a year earlier.

> The rise is a consequence of the alteration in monetary policy introduced last November. On the other hand, the fall in the price of securities, which is partly connected with the new monetary policy, has reduced the value of our British Government securities by more than £6 m. An increase from our previous level of profits is welcome, and indeed necessary, in view of the growth in our running costs, particularly salaries and pensions, and also to enable us to make provision for the large capital expenditure we shall have to meet on new premises for the Printing Works and Accountant's Department particularly.[61]

Profit figures throughout the rest of the 1950s and 1960s remained mostly on an upwards trend with variations largely reflecting changes in Bank Rate and the consequent effect on short-term interest rates. Substantial sums received by the Bank included the proceeds from the sale of the former Printing Works, St Luke's, and of the offices at Finsbury Circus vacated by the Accountant's Department.*

Appendix A. *Banking Department profits and reserves 1940–1960*

1 *Profits* (after tax but before payment of dividends and any writing down of securities)

| Year to end Feb. | £000s | |
|---|---|---|
| 1940 | 4,214 | £1,500 profit on sale of British government securities. Rate of Income Tax increased, so net dividend reduced in Feb. $\frac{1}{2}$ year. |
| 1941 | 2,433 | Full year of reduced net dividend. |
| 1942 | 1,964 | Further increase in Income Tax. |
| 1943 | 2,069 | |
| 1944 | 2,332 | |
| 1945 | 2,112 | |
| 1946 | 3,574 | Income Tax adjustments following nationalisation. Feb. $\frac{1}{2}$ year dividend paid gross. |
| 1947 | 4,508 | Abnormal profits from sales and redemption of BGS (mainly Local Loans Stock). Repayments of debts previously written down. Full year of dividend payment gross. |
| 1948 | 2,916 | Capital profit on sale of securities. Repayment of debts previously written down. |

* See appendix A.

## Appendix A. (*cont.*)

| Year to end Feb. | £000s | |
|---|---|---|
| 1949 | 3,061 | Capital profit on sale of securities. Repayment of debts previously written down. |
| 1950 | 2,812 | |
| 1951 | 3,396 | £1·3 m. compensation received o/a Lancs Steel Corp. shares held by Securities Management Trust for Bank. |
| 1952 | 3,228 | Bank Rate increased from 2% to 2½%, Nov. 8 1951. |
| 1953 | 3,768 | Full year effect of further increase in Bank Rate. |
| 1954 | 4,329 | |
| 1955 | 3,868 | |
| 1956 | 4,969 | |
| 1957 | 6,285 | |
| 1958 | 5,750 | Variations mainly reflecting changes in Bank Rate. |
| 1959 | 5,229 | |
| 1960 | 5,906 | Sale of St Luke's, Old St, £900,000. |
| 1961 | 6,692 | Sale of 18 Finsbury Circus, £561,000. |

*Sources :* ADM 19/12–13 Stock Estimates etc. Book (Profit and Loss Account).
ADM 6/92–7 Half-yearly Accounts.
ADM 6/89–90 Bank's Accounts – General.
Table compiled by D.L. Best.

## 2 *Reserves*

| Years to end Feb. | | Years to end Feb. | |
|---|---|---|---|
| 1940 | 41,858,622 | 1951 | 59,946,910 |
| 1941 | 42,271,154 | 1952 | 60,556,857 |
| 1942 | 41,543,050 | 1953 | 61,995,158 |
| 1943 | 42,161,267 | 1954 | 63,776,248 |
| 1944 | 53,261,247* | 1955 | 64,175,237 |
| 1945 | 54,015,894 | 1956 | 65,278,301 |
| 1946 | 55,966,221 | 1957 | 68,289,382 |
| 1947 | 56,177,891 | 1958 | 70,418,214 |
| 1948 | 56,765,086 | 1959 | 72,529,585 |
| 1949 | 57,424,048 | 1960 | 74,999,600 |
| 1950 | 57,684,798 | 1961 | 78,168,491 |

* *Note :* Book cost of holdings of £10 m. 3½% Conversion Stock (1961 or after) and £5 m. Local Loans Stock (1912 or after), written up from £100 each to

'average cost' (total approx. £9·5 m.). Other BGS were also put on an 'average cost' basis.

Figures comprise: Suspense Accounts
Security reserve accounts
Rest – end year balance less dividend due on following April 5
*Less* Provision for taxation
Table compiled by Financial Accounting Office, FRPD (D.J. Gould and M.J. Wallace).

Appendix B. *Receipts for major activities 1946–1961*

| Year to end Feb. | BGS management | Other Stocks management | Note issue | Exchange Control | £000s EEA |
|---|---|---|---|---|---|
| 1946 | 1,334·7 | 170·8 | 330·1 | 781·1 | |
| 1947 | 1,391·9 | 174·6 | 455·6 | 956·4 | |
| 1948 | 1,401·6 | 162·8 | 502·0 | 1,107·5 | 140·9 |
| 1949 | 1,387·7 | 272·3 | 559·5 | 1,260·3 | 132·6 |
| 1950 | 1,387·0 | 421·8 | 561·5 | 1,286·2 | 135·0 |
| 1951 | 1,383·5 | 598·6 | 600·6 | 1,401·1 | 140·8 |
| 1952 | 1,394·9 | 564·0 | 605·4 | 1,364·6 | 177·8 |
| 1953 | 1,443·1 | 596·5 | 752·6 | 1,374·6 | 174·8 |
| 1954 | 1,455·4 | 625·7 | 741·5 | 1,300·0 | 156·8 |
| 1955 | 1,482·4 | 686·6 | 769·7 | 1,268·7 | 159·9 |
| 1956 | 1,487·3 | 653·6 | 879·5 | 1,193·7 | 178·2 |
| 1957 | 1,507·8 | 643·0 | 921·4 | 1,016·7 | 201·7 |
| 1958 | 1,525·7 | 640·2 | 889·0 | 929·2 | 198·2 |
| 1959 | 1,524·6 | 652·0 | 961·9 | 900·0 | 234·4 |
| 1960 | 1,500·2 | 638·1 | 1,048·0 | 837·0 | 201·7 |
| 1961 | 1,496·7 | 609·5 | 1,047·2 | 687·5 | 234·2 |

*Notes : British Government stocks management*
Receipts were based on a scale of charges related to the nominal value of stock managed. The scale which operated during this period was introduced in 1942 and remained in operation until 1971. Variations in the amount received reflect variations in the nominal value of stock managed.
*Other stocks management*
Receipts were normally based on a half-yearly charge per stockholding managed. The increase in receipts from 1949 onwards reflects the assumption of management responsibility for nationalised industry stocks.
*Source :* ADM 6/92–7 Half-yearly Accounts.
Table compiled by D.L. Best.

# 7

## THE CASHIER'S DEPARTMENT

The office of First or Chief Cashier was one of the original appointments on the foundation of the Bank of England in 1694: the Chief Cashier was at that time *primus inter pares* of the senior officials of the Bank and continued to be so until the rearrangement of responsibilities introduced by Governor Richardson nearly 300 years later in 1980. At that date the Bank's market responsibilities were transferred to newly formed Divisions and the remainder of the Cashier's Department became the Banking Department. This chapter describes the organisation and activities of the Cashier's Department in the years during and after the Second World War. The principal operational Department of the Bank, it undertook a full range of banking services for the Bank's customers, including discounts and advances, handled the Bank's day-to-day operations in the gilt-edged, money and foreign exchange markets* and was responsible for the management of the note issue. It also acted as an issuing house on behalf of the government and of various other customers. In 1939 the Chief Cashier assumed responsibility for Exchange Control, which he retained until 1972 when it became a separate Department; its organisation is described in chapter 3. The Department's responsibilities for the note issue and for Branch banking, carried out via the Issue and Branch Banks Offices respectively, have also been fully covered in the relevant chapters and these Offices are not included here.

There were three Chief Cashiers in the period under discussion. K.O. (later Sir Kenneth) Peppiatt† was in office from 1934 until 1949, when he

---

* The Bank's foreign exchange market operations were (and still are) for the account of the Treasury's Exchange Equalisation Account.
† Peppiatt, Sir Kenneth Oswald, KBE (1941) MC, 1893–1983. Entered Bank, 1911; Principal of Discount Office, 1928–34; Chief Cashier, 1934–9; Executive Director, 1949–57.

Plate 7.1   Sir K.O. Peppiatt in 1943. Peppiatt was Chief Cashier from 1934 to 1949

became Home Finance Director and was succeeded by Percy Beale.* Beale retired from the Bank in January 1955 and went to India as the first managing director of the Industrial Credit and Investment Corporation of India. Leslie (later Lord) O'Brien† was Chief Cashier for the next seven years until he succeeded Sir Cyril Hawker as Home Finance Director at the beginning of March 1962.

The Chief Cashier himself managed the gilt-edged market, and advised the Governors and Executive Directors on the planning and execution of domestic monetary policy. Under him were two and later four Deputy Chief Cashiers with individual responsibilities for assistance with the gilt-edged market and the implementation of credit control policies; the management of the money market and customer services;

---

\* Beale, Percival Spencer, 1906–81. Entered Bank, 1924; Chief Cashier, 1949–January 1955. General Manager, Industrial Credit and Investment Corporation of India, 1955–8.

† See note, p. 102.

the staffing and administration of the Department and matters relating to bank notes; and gold and foreign exchange operations. Also assisting the Chief Cashier, but with direct access to the Governors, was the Principal of the Discount Office. A further layer of responsibility was formed by the Assistant Chief Cashiers and Assistants to the Chief Cashier. Each of the eleven Offices of the Department dealt with a specialised aspect of the work and was under the administrative control of a Principal answering, save for the Discount Office, directly to the Deputy Chief Cashier concerned with the particular operation of his Office. Total staff numbers during this period were between 1,100 and 1,200.[1]

The Chief Cashier's Office (CCO) was the hub of the Department, and naturally ranked as one of the Special Offices of the Bank whose staff received additional salary in recognition of the importance of their tasks and the demands made on them for a particularly high standard of work.* The CCO consisted of a General Office sub-divided into a number of 'Posts' each undertaking a different activity, separate Sections concerned with filing and typing, a Cable Section (which worked for the whole Bank) and Rooms 1 and 2. The Posts, the majority of which were staffed by between two and four clerks, worked closely with those Offices of the Department whose work complemented or overlapped theirs.

The daily stock market operations for the National Debt Commissioners were carried out by the Commissioners for the Reduction of the National Debt (CRND) Post, which also executed transfers of stock and work in connection with Customers' Money transactions and Sinking Fund management. The National Debt Commission, composed of six Commissioners whose business was conducted by a Comptroller-General, had executed a Power of Attorney in favour of the Chief Cashier and Deputy Chief Cashier whereby the latter, jointly and severally, had power to transfer, accept and execute all transfers of stock on behalf of the Commissioners provided that the orders were signed by the Comptroller-General or his Assistant. When the contract notes were received by Mullens and Co., the Government Brokers, they were passed to the CRND Post and checked by its staff. After the transfers were executed, the post prepared the appropriate cash vouchers through the Drawing Office and set in motion the machinery for effecting the transfers of stock in the Accountant's Department.[2]

There was little change in the nature of the work of the CRND Post during these years, but its volume fluctuated considerably as did the

---

* 'Special Office money' was abolished under the 1947 Salary Reclassification Scheme. See chapter 10, p. 335.

average daily amount of Customers' Money Employed* which reached a high point for the period of £76m. in the early months of 1954: by 1960 this figure had fallen to around £39m. Many of the Sinking Funds had by then been wound up and their assets distributed.[3]

The Correspondence Post handled most of the non-routine Departmental correspondence, and undertook a considerable amount of work in connection with investments on behalf of customers, including Treasury Bill transactions. The Bank was (and still is) continually in receipt of letters from claimants believing, almost always mistakenly, that it was holding money to which they were entitled, deposited in the distant past: all such claims had to be investigated although many were plainly from lunatics, some of whom, including one self-styled Archduke, became all too familiar correspondents over the years. Requests for advances, enquiries regarding the estates of deceased persons and applications to open accounts at the Bank were also regularly received and dealt with by 'helpful but non-committal replies'. No reply has survived to a letter received during 1952 which 'purported to enclose the formula for the "H" bomb (with ingredients)'.[4]

The Counter Post was so-called as it was situated beside the counter and the junior clerk on it answered calls there, finding the appropriate person to deal with any visitors. Its work was mainly concerned with procedures for raising, administering and redeeming stocks, embracing questions of policy and all matters which the Dividend Pay and Loans Office (concerned solely with the mechanics of operation) and the Accountant's Department (whose functions were limited to those of a Registrar) did not undertake. The Post provided the link between the issuing body and the Bank, and all correspondence passed through its hands. Colonial borrowing was resumed in 1947 with a new Southern Rhodesian loan of £32m., and the following year the Post was much occupied with the issue of British Transport and Electricity Stocks in compensation to the stockholders of the nationalised undertakings. The Post was subsequently involved in the general question of the Bank's remuneration for the management of the stocks of the nationalised industries, and the agreement of a permanent scale of charges.

A considerable amount of work accrued to this Post after the war in connection with Bearer Bonds (for British government securities)

---

\* A system whereby certain customers (chiefly central banks) were invited to allow the employment of surplus funds, under the Bank's guarantee and at a variable rate of interest determined by the Bank. The total so employed was matched by transfers to or from the Bank's portfolios of Treasury Bills and Commercial Bills. The arrangements effectively gave customers interest-bearing accounts, but until 1970 they were off the Bank's balance sheet.

believed to have been misappropriated by the enemy, which caused much correspondence over the difficult legalities involved. The bulk of the notifications were from Dutch sources. In July 1950 the Treasury issued a directive which stated that payment of capital and interest was to be refused unless the presenters of Bonds and/or coupons of disputed ownership could furnish a declaration that the Bonds were 'deposited'* securities, which clarified the position to some extent but involved more correspondence with the Treasury and the presenters. A further responsibility of the Counter Post concerned the payment of notes no longer of legal tender and of mutilated or lost High Sum Notes[5] – similar work in respect of £1 and 10s. notes was undertaken by the Issue Office, as described in chapter 4.

Work in connection with German debt settlement was a major preoccupation of the Loans Post, which was staffed by one of the Clerks on the Counter. The London Agreement on German External Debts (for which Sir Otto Niemeyer was largely responsible) was signed in February 1953, when consensus had been reached as to the broad lines of the exchange of securities, and an extra clerk was added to the Post to help in the work of preparing the text of bonds, checking proofs and other details all of which involved consultation with the Committee of British Long Term and Medium Term Creditors of Germany, the Stock Exchange, Freshfields, Loans Office and the Exchange Control. Quite tough negotiations took place between the Bank, the BIS and the German Federal Debt Administration over the terms of purchase and surrender of the bonds. Clearing up outstanding pre-war items was also necessary, such as release by the Custodian of Enemy Property of Konversionskasse Bonds bought on account of the Sinking Fund for cancellation and shipment to Germany. Other bonds with which the Post was concerned included those of the Dawes and Young Loans.†

More straightforward banking experience was provided by the Advances Post, which handled loans to customers on security, confidential special advances, securities held in the name of Governor & Company nominees, Treasury deposit receipt work and loans to the market – the last activity having virtually disappeared during the war. The Post also dealt with occasional advances to members of Bank staff against the security of a Bank Provident Society deposit account, but this practice was replaced in 1952 by a different arrangement (not involving

---

* That is, deposited with an Authorised Depositary; see p. 85.
† Loans made as a result of the American Dawes and Young Plans (1924 and 1929 respectively) for German reparations after the First World War. The Young Plan was responsible for the setting up of the BIS.

advances) available to BPS depositors. Changes in senior Bank appointments necessitated corresponding changes in Powers of Attorney; securities held in the names of the Bank's nominees, other than those registered in the name of the Governor & Company, had to be transferred into new names and before that could take place new Powers of Attorney had to be prepared by the Post. The Post handled the security activities of the Bank Provident Society, and dividend management on stocks held – a large proportion of the latter work was occasioned by substantial nominee holdings for a Middle Eastern customer. The difficulties of overseas central banks in obtaining tax exemption on their securities holdings were a further preoccupation of the Advances Post, and partly as a result of its work the 1957 Finance Act incorporated legislation to make certain of the Banks, including the National Bank of Libya and the Bank of Rhodesia and Nyasaland, eligible for such exemption. This, it was hoped, would encourage them to hold greater sterling reserves.[6]

At the end of the war there were between eighty and ninety accounts in the names of central banks with the Bank of England, whose overall conduct was the responsibility of the Central Banks Post of the CCO. This was one of the largest posts, staffed by about ten clerks. The Inspector of Offices and Branches noted in his 1945 Report on the Office that there were 'widely differing methods of dealing with the Central Bank Accounts', arising from the fact that negotiations for opening the accounts or for setting up new monetary agreements were conducted by the Overseas and Foreign Office 'and the political aspects rather submerge the mechanics of the operation'.[7] The result was that the staff of the Post had frequently to create a procedure to meet an individual case, rather than fitting the case in a well-defined framework. The early post-war years were marked by an increase in sterling in the hands of central banks; by the end of 1946 banking relations had been resumed with all pre-war customers except Germany, Japan and the Russian-occupied Baltic States. Two years later there were 140 central bank accounts, and the number continued to grow: together with the Drawing Office, the Post began to aim at complete uniformity of practice in their operation, and their routine banking operations were gradually diverted to commercial banks in London.

In 1949 the post was retitled the Central Banks Section. The technical work of the Section, which included the purchase and sale of Treasury Bills on behalf of central bank customers, increased throughout the period. There was a marked rise in the level of activity on these accounts towards the end of the 1950s, especially when in mid 1957 the pressure on sterling, following the partial devaluation of the French franc, led to considerable increases in the funds accruing to various European central banks. The Section was also responsible for providing for the use of the BIS, as Agent, figures which were needed as a basis for multilateral clearing operations under the intra-European payments agreements of 1948–50. From 1950 to December 1958 similar figures were reported to the BIS, now acting as Agent of the newly created European Payments Union.[8]

The work of the Governor & Company Post was concerned with the securities held for the Banking Department in the name of the Governor & Co., and with Treasury Bills bought, sold or matured for Governor & Co. It also dealt with Treasury Bills transferred from or to Customer's Money accounts. A further task was the management of housing loans made to the staff of the Bank: a new scheme replacing the pre-war 'loan against mortgage' arrangement was introduced in 1945, and made total advances in the region of £150,000 per year in the first few years of operation. The popularity of the new scheme, details of which are given in chapter 10, is evidenced by the fact that in 1960 the balance outstanding was £4.7m.[9]

The securities held by Issue Department in the form of bills and stock were managed by the Issue Post, the volume of whose work was naturally much affected by the changes in the fiduciary issue as described in chapter 4. Issue and Governor & Co. were each normally staffed by one clerk, who together formed a separate team and helped each other out when necessary.

At the apex of the Chief Cashier's Office were the two small sections – usually staffed by three or four clerks – known as Rooms 1 and 2, whose occupants worked directly for the Chief Cashier and who were under careful scrutiny from him and his Deputies and Assistants in order to assess their suitability for the higher echelons of the Bank. It was usual to be appointed to Room 1 first: here the movements in the Bank's figures, confidential and otherwise, were recorded daily before presentation and explanation to the Chief Cashier, and embodied weekly in the Bank Return. Men in Room 1 (it was not until 1959 that a woman, Mrs P.M. Gross, first 'did the Books' here, and several more years passed before another woman did so) had to be able to 'clerk and figure accurately under more than normal pressure', and needed a sufficient knowledge of money and banking to understand the meaning of the credit base and hence something of the use to which the Chief Cashier put the figures in the construction of home finance policy. When a clerk had successfully survived the ordeal of first doing and presenting the Books on his own, his photograph was taken for inclusion in a vellum-covered ledger, begun in the early years of the twentieth century, whose important looking exterior contrasts nicely with the increasingly casual pose of the sitters and various quips pencilled in by subsequent occupants of the Room.

The work of Room 2 demanded not only accuracy, as demonstrated by a successful spell in Room 1, but the ability to 'devil' thoroughly and intelligently and to write an articulate memorandum on often highly complex (and confidential) issues. Much of the work was passed on by the Chief Cashier to the Governors or the Treasury. Positions in both Rooms were naturally highly prized by the more ambitious, and numbers were kept low in order to maintain pressure: in 1959 a general criterion for selection was 'how we can see a man meriting promotion to Assistant Principal at the end of a fifteen to eighteen month spell in the rooms'.[10]

Special work undertaken by Room 1 included the production of the Bank's first Annual Report, for the year ended 1947. The effect of 'Marshall Aid accounting' on the Bank Return and the Books was also dealt with by Room 1: the Americans' desire for the relative account to appear in the Books of the Bank resulted in the opening of the 'HM Treasury Special Account' which had to be included in the Bank Return figure of Public Deposits. A complementary security item (Treasury Notes – Non-Interest Bearing) was then included in the Banking Department Government Securities. In 1957 some of the preparatory work for the Radcliffe Committee hearings was carried out here. The work of Room 2 was extremely varied and included research into legal matters which might affect the Bank, preliminary work for Bretton Woods and for nationalisation Bills, and supervision of various funds of which the Governor was a Trustee, such as the King George VI National Memorial Fund* and the St Paul's Cathedral Trust Fund. Room 2 was also much concerned with work on the ill-fated £2 note,† the introduction of Premium Bonds (first suggested within the CCO), and with the feasibility of opening new Branches of the Bank (as mentioned in chapter 8). Questions from the Treasury, too, were frequently received and answers prepared for the Chief Cashier.[11]

The multiplicity and variety of all this work in the Chief Cashier's Office required a large body of typists (both routine and confidential), filists and cablists – the latter responsible for the maintenance of the secret codes in which the Bank corresponded with its central bank customers.

---

* The primary object of this fund was to raise money for a statue of the late King, who died in 1952. The statue was sculpted by W. McMillan and erected in Carlton Gardens, London, in 1955.

† See chapter 4, p. 157.

It was the Cashier's Department which was responsible, as mentioned earlier, for the day-to-day operations performed in the Bank's name in the gilt-edged, money and foreign exchange markets. The main object of these activities was, as it has remained, to finance the government's long- and short-term borrowing requirements, to prevent undue fluctuation in the international value of sterling and to conserve and safeguard the country's gold and foreign exchange reserves. The Offices within the Department primarily concerned with carrying out these functions were (apart from the CCO) the Dealing and Accounts Office and, to a lesser extent, the Discount Office.

The role of the Discount Office was to maintain day-to-day contact between the Bank and the money market and with the City's financial community as a whole, and to keep the Governors and the Chief Cashier informed of events, personalities and developments of interest to the Bank. It was also the most important of the various channels by which guidance was given to the commercial banks about the detailed implementation of credit restrictions. The Office acted as 'lender of last resort' when the discount houses found themselves short of cash and the Bank was unwilling to relieve the shortage by means of the purchase of Treasury, commercial or local authority Bills.* A further function was the seeking of bankers' references on behalf of customers of the Bank; it also provided references in answer to enquiries about banks with accounts in the Drawing Office.

In the years immediately following the end of the Second World War, the work of the Discount Office increased in volume as the value of commercial bills purchased for both Banking and Issue Departments rose as did the number of Treasury Bills discounted for customers. Discount of commercial bills, which did not occur post-war until 1948, also began to rise after that date, although more slowly. In 1951, however, there was a sudden and unexpected shake-up in the Discount Market. On 7 November the Chancellor of the Exchequer, R.A. Butler, announced in the House of Commons the new Conservative Government's monetary policy, designed to control inflation, to make possible more direct control of the volume of credit and restore flexibility to the short-term market. It was necessary, he said, to depart from the existing arrangements under which, in practice, Bank Rate was ineffective and the Bank supplied the needs of the money market at very low rates.[12] Bank Rate was raised with effect from 8 November 1951 from 2 per cent to $2\frac{1}{2}$ per cent – the first change for nineteen years apart from a

---

* Other day-to-day operations in gilts and money were the preserve of the Deputy Chief Cashiers assisted by Assistant Chief Cashiers and Assistants to the Chief Cashier.

short-lived rise at the beginning of the war – and at the same time a special rate of 2 per cent was introduced for loans to the market against Treasury Bills. Market rates were immediately increased, and they rose again the following March when the anti-inflationary policy was reinforced by the raising of Bank Rate to 4 per cent and the lending rate to the market against Treasury Bills became $3\frac{1}{2}$ per cent. In the words of the Principal of the Discount Office 'the market quickly re-learned the techniques required by a moving rate and after a lapse of 13 years the first market advance was made on 19 November 1951'.[13]

On 17 September 1953 Bank Rate was reduced by $\frac{1}{2}$ per cent, and this change saw a return to the traditional manner of announcing it (on the two previous occasions it had been announced in association with fiscal measures proposed by the Chancellor). In the long-established ritual form this involved its consideration by Court as the first item on the agenda at the regular weekly meeting at 11.30 a.m. on a Thursday. The most junior of the Directors present then opened the door of the Court Room and gave the new figure – or the fact that it remained unaltered – to those waiting outside: the Chief Cashier, the Principal of the Discount Office, the Assistant Secretary of the Bank and the Principal of the Branch Banks Office. The Chief Cashier returned to his own room and gave the news to the Government Broker who proceeded to the Stock Exchange and announced it on the floor; meanwhile the Principal of the Discount Office had entrusted his Office Messenger with a notice of the figure in a closed leather frame, to be taken to the front hall of the Bank. Here, at a time carefully judged to coincide with the Government Broker's disclosure, the news was imparted to the waiting throng of messengers from banks, discount and finance houses and other City institutions.[14]

Hilton Clarke was the Principal of the Discount Office at the time of the return to this agreeable ceremony, having been appointed in April 1953 after three years as Deputy Principal. This was particularly appropriate as Clarke, in the fourteen years he headed the Office, was to make a significant contribution to the good relationship between the Bank and the City. To the job of interpreting the Bank's policy to the City and the City's thoughts and actions to the Bank he brought additionally the desire to know as much as possible about what was going on in the Square Mile; and in return to impart information about the Bank to a degree which had certainly not been achieved before. As the Bank during the 1950s became considerably more willing to communicate with the outside world – as noted, for example, in relation to exchange control – so this tendency was specifically and beneficially reinforced in the City by the attitude prevailing in the Discount Office.

Plate 7.2     Mr William Thompson, Discount Office messenger from 1933 to
1965, displaying the Bank Rate notice in the Front Hall, Threadneedle Street, in
1957

The almost continuous credit restrictions in force during the 1950s,
achieved by the manipulation of interest rates and by intensified controls
over borrowing, resulted in increased work for the Office including the
introduction of various new measures such as the 63-Day Treasury Bill
which made its first appearance in November 1955. The Office was
consequently much occupied with discussions with individual bankers
over the interpretation of the Chancellor's requests on advances and the
implications of directives given to the Capital Issues Committee; a
further result was a sharp increase in commercial bill purchases. The
number of discounts rose too (prompting in 1957 the plaintive query of
the Chief Cashier, O'Brien: 'Can nothing be done to cut down
discounts?' – which that year had risen by more than 65 per cent over the
previous year, to 778 in all). A more lenient financial climate and a falling
Bank Rate from the spring of 1958 brought about an increase in the
number of confidential enquiries to the Office on the status of hire
purchase companies and 'fringe' banks.[15]

Plate 7.3   Messengers rushing from the Bank to give news of the change in Bank Rate, 27 January 1955

The Dealing and Accounts Office was formed in 1941* and was situated within the Cashier's Department (Exchange Control) until 1957 when this grouping was abolished and together with the other four remaining Control Offices Dealing and Accounts was transferred to the Cashier's Department.† It carried out operations on behalf of the Exchange Equalisation Account (EEA) in gold, foreign exchange and foreign securities. The 1946 Finance Act widened the EEA's functions to include 'the conservation of the means of making payments abroad', and after the creation of the European Payments Union (EPU) in 1950 the EEA was the channel used for all UK transactions with the EPU and was authorised to hold European units of account for the purpose. Its role became still more active in 1951 when the London Foreign Exchange market was reopened; Authorised Dealers were then allowed to deal with

---

\* A Foreign Exchange Section had been set up in the Bank in 1926 and its scope progressively widened by the crisis of 1931 and the institution of the Exchange Equalisation Account in the following year.       † See chapter 3, p. 123.

their customers and among themselves at market rates inside the official buying and selling rates, and also to maintain open positions in foreign currency, both spot and forward, and to hold spot currency against forward commitments within limits laid down by the Bank. As well as its operative function with regard to all the Bank's dealings with the EEA, Dealing and Accounts also carried out the supervision of the banks which were authorised (by the Defence (Finance) Regulations and later by the 1947 Exchange Control Act) to deal in gold and foreign currencies, together with all questions concerning access to the forward market, the industrial use of gold and the control of dealings in gold coin.[16]

The provision of banking services to its customers was one of the main demands on the resources of the Cashier's Department. The Bank's customers include the government, overseas central banks, most domestic commercial banks and other financial institutions, members of Bank of England staff and its pensioners, and a very few private customers who have particular associations with the Bank. The custody and maintenance of their current and deposit accounts in Threadneedle Street was the responsibility of the Drawing Office,* so called from the time when current accounts were known as Drawing Accounts. One Section of the Drawing Office was in close liaison with the CCO and the departments of central government, primarily HM Treasury, the Paymaster General, the Commissioners of Inland Revenue and Customs and Excise, to establish the daily cash position of the funds on public account, which is important in the operational management of the money market. An early post-war development in the Drawing Office was the reversion to the former practice of crediting effects to the main government accounts only when cleared. During the war years under Emergency Clearing arrangements, the Bank was continually advancing money free of interest by crediting uncleared effects to these accounts. Negotiations on this rather delicate matter were satisfactorily concluded in 1947 with the result, in the words of the Office Principal, that 'the main Government accounts have now been placed on a correct accounting basis'.[17]

Many other usual banking services were provided by the Office such as payment under standing orders, supply of foreign exchange, custody of valuables other than securities, and, for some customers, the provision of advances. This Office was, therefore, the principal one within Head Office where the techniques of 'ordinary' banking were practised, and as such it provided an invaluable training ground and work for a large number of clerks: each Section (Government, Private, Bankers, Central

---

* The Drawing Office had been formed in 1933 by the amalgamation of the Public Drawing Office and the Private Drawing Office.

Banks and Box Room – which dealt with boxes held in safe custody for customers and also with standing orders and postal credits) was headed by a Superintendent and staffed by a Senior Clerk, payers, an Agreement Clerk and his Assistant, machine operators concerned with ledgers and payments, several juniors and countermen to deal with the public where required. In addition a large General Section dealt with statements, authorities and bank notes, correspondence, filing and records, dividends, indemnities, mechanisation, exchange control regulations, charges, contras, stores, Cash Waiting and Waiting for House Balance. These latter were jobs for clerks designated in turn to remain behind at the end of the day until all the books had been balanced to the last penny, when a pen or ruler was struck on a lampstand to signal the satisfactory conclusion of the day's work.

Mechanisation, by Mercedes accounting machines installed in 1934, was the very heart of the accounting system of the Drawing Office: by 1947 these machines were beginning to experience mechanical faults to an unacceptable degree and various new types were tested in conjunction with the Bank's Central Mechanisation Office. From the spring of 1954 the doughty Mercedes equipment, which had been subjected to very heavy use but had even so lasted for twice its original life expectancy of ten years, was gradually replaced by National Cash Register machines imported from the US.[18]

The Bank, as a central bank and in order to minimise competition with the commercial banks, was anxious to cut down the number of private accounts – other than those for staff – and the Office carried out regular reviews after which negotiations took place for the closure or removal, where possible, of dormant and unprofitable accounts. 'The exercise of the pruning hook by the Loans Office amongst the dividend and other internal accounts ... and the scythe of Father Time ... [in] accounts in the sole or joint name of individuals'[19] gradually reduced the numbers. The age of the remaining customers often gave rise to anxiety about their ability to operate their accounts. Doubts as to the mental capacity of one eighty-seven year old were expressed to his solicitor, who replied reassuringly that the old gentleman had been 'singing lustily in Church on the previous Sunday and still understood *The Times*'.[20]

Among the various boxes and sealed packets of which the Drawing Office held custody there were, during a two year period from 1945 to 1947, thirty-four boxes containing the Crown Jewels. These had been stored during the war under guard at Windsor Castle, and were deposited in the Bank while bomb damage to the Jewel House at the Tower of London was repaired. The Principal admitted to a 'sigh of relief' on the removal of the Regalia, 'of such embarrassing value and national significance', which was shortly afterwards returned to public display at the Tower.[21]

In 1952 the occasion was taken to open some unclaimed boxes, many of which proved to be empty, and amalgamate the contents of any possible value in a sealed parcel. One in particular was the object of some interest. It had been deposited in the Bank in 1900 by a lady living in Sydney of whom all trace had subsequently been lost, and had been specifically mentioned by Governor Cokayne in evidence before a Parliamentary Select Committee on the Dormant Bank Balances and Unclaimed Securities Bill in 1919. The box was stated to contain pictures, which Horatio Bottomley,* a member of the Committee, speculated might be 'of enormous national interest and value', although the chairman, the Rt Hon. Lord Hugh Cecil (later Lord Quickswood)† thought it was 'more probably a portrait of some interest to the family who deposited it'.[22] There was great excitement when the box was finally opened in the presence of the Office Principal and representatives of the Chief Cashier, the Historical Records Section and the Auditor. Disappointingly, it was found to contain 'three unframed paintings of animals, one of a dog, another a horse and the third a hybrid, which were obviously of no artistic value and, after this lapse of time, hardly likely to be of any sentimental value either'; nevertheless in view of the history of the box it was decided that they should not be destroyed but be retained 'under simple sealed cover'.[23]

The reduction in the number of accounts, which excluding those held by staff fell by nearly 50 per cent between 1939 (1,633 including 591 private) and 1956 (854, including 140 private) together with increased mechanisation, meant the disappearance of books of record such as cash books, passbooks, ledgers and to a large extent waste books,‡ and with them disappeared many of the opportunities for training young clerks in the rudiments of banking. In order to introduce Probationary Clerks§ to some of these disciplines it was decided in August 1954 to inaugurate a

---

* Bottomley, Horatio William, 1860–1933. Founder of *John Bull* magazine. MP (Liberal), South Hackney, 1906–12 and 1918–22, when he was expelled from the House of Commons because of conviction for fraudulent conversion.

† Quickswood, 1st Baron (1941) of Clothall, Rt Hon. Lord Hugh R.H. Gascoyne-Cecil PC, younger son of Lord Salisbury, 1869–1956. MP (Con), Greenwich, 1895–1906; Oxford University, 1910–37.

‡ Details of transactions were entered immediately in waste books before being transferred to permanent books of record.

§ Clerks spent a probationary period of up to two years (three years before the Second World War) before being taken on to the permanent staff of the Bank. See chapter 10, p. 329.

Training School on an experimental basis. The scheme was based primarily on the basic work of the Drawing Office and the Bill Office (see below) and the Principal of the former was given overriding control of a course of which drawing accounts formed the focal point.

The first syllabus consisted of nine or ten main lectures on the elements of banking and on the Bank of England as a central bank, interspersed with visits to the Drawing and Bill Offices. Talks on clearings, the working of government accounts and the Institute of Bankers plus a visit to the Institute's library, were added to give some variety and the school was converted into a working 'bank' embodying manuscript waste books, ledgers and so on, all under the surveillance of a Control Book in whose hands rested the responsibility of a final agreement by all sections leading to the production of a 'House Balance'. This included uncleared drafts (credits and debits), returned cheques in and out and finally the figures from a supposed clearing house balance. The school ran for a three week period under a 'Schoolmaster' and his assistant (the first two being Richard Bridge and A.C.J. Lagden) at the end of which the pupils were classified on a scale of 6 to 1. The experiment proved very successful and the school became a standard feature of the Department.[24]

There was little other change in the Drawing Office routine, although some respite was given by the provisions of the 1957 Cheques Act which made endorsement of cheques by the recipient unnecessary in all but a few cases, which themselves became the responsibility of the collecting bank. A major operation took place within the Office in 1959 when heavy repayments of Post War Credits were made: special arrangements were made with the Treasury and Inland Revenue, and nearly £36m. was paid during a ten week period. The number of staff accounts continued to rise, although many clerks opened accounts with the commercial banks as well, as these were readier to furnish them with personal loans and overdraft facilities; staff accounts in the Bank also became more active with the increasing use of cheques and of standing orders for hire purchase.[25]

The Bill Office worked in close co-operation with the Drawing Office, obtaining payment for items which customers paid into the Drawing Office and the Branches, and making payment for items drawn on the Bank and presented via the London Bankers' Clearing House. It also presented for payment, on the due date, bills of exchange held in safe custody for customers and for the Banking and Issue Departments. The Office was certainly busy, but there was little variety or intrinsic interest in the work and indeed the Bill Office was regarded as 'Siberia' by the more ambitious and able of the junior clerks doing a tour of duty in it: however it did offer what some appreciated as the mild pleasure of escape from the confines of Head Office on the regular 'Walks' round the City and West End to present items for payment.

During the Second World War the Section of the Bill Office which dealt with the Bank's own clearing moved to Trentham Park in Staffordshire with the Central London Clearing House, as described in chapter 1. The character of the work changed considerably: the four pre-war categories of clearings (Town, Metropolitan, Country and Out-Telling*) ceased to exist and only 'local' cheques, i.e. those drawn on a small number of banks in the heart of the City, were presented by the Bill Office through the London Clearing House. All other clearing items were sorted into banks, machined, agreed and despatched to Trentham for presentation through the Central Clearing organisation there. The decline in the volume of general clearing in London, about 20 per cent during the war years, was matched by a similar fall in Revenue Collections – of the seventeen area collections made daily pre-war, only six were visited by 1945, the rest remitting through the joint stock banks.

The Trentham organisation was closed during the summer of 1946 and the members of the Bill Office who were up there returned to London. It was decided that the pre-war arrangements for collecting government drafts could well be simplified, and, after a good deal of discussion with the clearing banks, a new system known as Amalgamated Walks was devised in the same year. Under this system, the six smaller clearing banks† and the Bank of England mutually assisted each other in collecting Walks items, i.e. items drawn on non-clearing banks and government offices in an area within easy reach of the City. The Big Five banks each collected their own Walks items.

The Amalgamated Walks area was divided into thirteen routes, each of the six banks being responsible for two; Bank of England clerks made the collections from government offices. In the morning two representatives from each bank, having previously sorted and listed Walks items presented to their bank, brought them to the Bank of England where the charges were amalgamated; each clerk was allocated all the items drawn within his particular Walk which he then took out and presented to the various drawee offices. Later in the day he collected from each drawee in his Walk a banker's payment in favour of the Bank of England for the amount of items presented, less the amount of any returns. The Bank

---

* See note p. 250.
† Coutts & Co., the District Bank, Glyn Mills & Co., Martins Bank, the National Bank and Williams Deacons Bank.

provided premises in Threadneedle Street and a Superintendent to oversee the whole operation. Each bank made its own arrangements for the collection, usually by post, of Walks items drawn outside the Amalgamated Walks area.[26]

Once this scheme was running smoothly, there was little change in the nature of the work during the 1950s, but by the end of the decade the Office was engaged, together with the Committee of London Clearing Bankers, in the preparatory work on automatic cheque processing which was to revolutionise the whole field of clearings within a few years. In 1960, the clearing banks introduced for the first time a Credit Transfer System. This was an extension of the former Traders' Credit system and included inter-bank counter credits along the lines of the cheque or debit clearing which had been in operation for many years. As with the question of automatic processing, the senior staff of the Bill Office were closely involved in the design as well as the introduction and implementation of the system – which also concerned, naturally, the Drawing Office and the Branches.[27]

A further banking facility, the maintenance of customers' securities deposited with the Bank and held in the name of the Bank's nominee company or the customer's own name, was provided by the Securities Office. This Office was responsible for implementing instructions given by customers in respect of these securities, as well as for servicing Bearer securities. The work included settlement with brokers for purchases and sales, the collection of interest and dividends, the payment of cash on allotment letters and the subsequent collection of certificates. The Office also collected, on behalf of the Inland Revenue, income tax on interest and dividends received in the Bank and denominated in currencies other than sterling. Custody of securities was carried out free of charge in all but a very small number of cases – the Bank looked to the maintenance of a balance in the Drawing Office sufficient to cover these and other costs.

The end of the war brought a considerable increase in the work of the Securities Office as extensive stock transactions took place prior to nationalisation; provisions of the 1947 Exchange Control Act also affected it, when the obligation to lodge certain types of securities with an 'Authorised Depositary' caused customers who had previously held such securities in the Drawing Office Box Room or elsewhere to lodge them in the Securities Office. Many of them consisted of obscure issues which involved much work and expense in keeping track of dividends and redemptions. Coupon work was heavy in the post-war period, and in addition to coupons detached from securities the Office received huge quantities (427,000 in 1947 alone) from the Bank of Portugal for collection and credit to its account. To the relief of the staff the Portuguese, after some prompting, made other arrangements in 1949 for the handling of its coupon business.

Throughout the 1950s the level of investment activity on the part of the Bank's institutional customers was very irregular. Events such as General Elections and rail strikes had an adverse effect: the periods of credit squeeze coupled with a heavy fall in share prices caused surplus funds to be temporarily invested in Treasury Bills. It was only after the relaxing of credit restrictions towards the end of the decade that investment in equities became an attractive proposition once more.[28]

The Treasury was a small Office which provided one side of the Department's dual control required by the Bank over all valuables,* the other side being maintained by the particular Office concerned. The Treasury was staffed by clerks bearing the title of Cashiers, who were authorised to endorse cheques on behalf of the Bank and to sign Scrip in connection with loans issued through the Bank. At the end of the Second World War there were a Senior and Second Cashier, ranking as Principal and Deputy Principal respectively, nine Cashiers and ten Sub-Cashiers. Both Cashiers and Sub-Cashiers did precisely the same work and accepted the same responsibilities (indeed the rank of Sub-Cashier was discontinued in 1965); their duties were neither complicated nor onerous, but of a highly responsible nature calling for 'ceaseless and meticulous supervision'.

Appointments to the Treasury were made almost exclusively from the staff of the Cashier's Department – an enquiry during the war as to whether men from the Accountant's Department might be appointed to it had been shelved. The positions were 'really a reward to a Clerk who otherwise would not receive advancement': those who had achieved a specified level, but were unlikely to progress further. Because they received extra salary and pension rights, such appointments were jealously sought at the end of a routine Bank career. Until the election of 15 October 1914 clerks were allowed to choose whether they should be fixed in the Cashier's or Accountant's Department, and it was frequently claimed that those opting for the 'cash side' had based their choice on the expectation of eventually becoming Treasury Cashiers should they fail to achieve other, more senior positions.

Before the end of the war it had become apparent that the supply of Cashiers from staff appointed not later than 15 October 1914 would be exhausted by 1951/2. A report by the Inspector of Offices and Branches recommended that the Treasury should become part of the CCO and

---

* Gold was held under quadruple control – see below.

be staffed by a cross-section from all Departments to include younger men. This report too had been shelved, but the position was reviewed once again in 1950. Various changes, principally in the names of the different ranks, were effected the following year, but the policy of recruitment from among the older and senior clerks of the Cashier's Department remained in force. The new arrangements continued until June 1974 when the Treasury ceased to function as a separate Office and its staff and their control duties were transferred to a new Section in the CCO known as the Control Section.[29]

The physical handling and custody of all the gold kept in the Bank for the EEA and for other customers, and the supervision of the Bank's store of gold coin, was the responsibility of the Bullion Office. Gold in the Bank was kept under quadruple control: the four arms of the control were formed by the Chief Cashier, the Treasury Cashiers, the Bullion Office and the Auditor.* The work of the Bullion Office was greatly simplified by a mechanisation scheme devised largely by the Principal, F.W.R. Laverack (later Inspector of Offices and Branches) and implemented in 1939/40. This included the use of Hollerith punched cards, raised for each bar of gold, on machines built to Bank specification by the British Tabulating Machine Co. under Hollerith patent: a considerable improvement over the former laborious methods of book-keeping. The physical movement of the metal had also been greatly eased by the introduction of transveyors which enabled a stack of gold bars weighing up to a ton to be moved by one porter.[30] Despite these improvements, the physical demands of exports and imports remained considerable. Imported gold had to be unpacked, examined and checked against weight lists, and each bar stamped with a unique serial number and letter and an impression of the Bank of England medallion.† If assaying was necessary assay cuts were made; the bars were weighed, the fine gold content of each worked out, punched cards in respect of each raised, and new weight lists produced. Exporting procedures, while still complex and requiring much supervision and control, were less demanding but involved a hefty packing operation in which the bars were normally protected by sawdust and stacked in sturdy wooden crates sealed with metal bands nailed down by special machinery. The physical work of the Office, carried out by a large team of porters specially trained and paid additional wages 'in

* This arrangement dated from 1932. In this year Directors of the Bank, who had previously controlled bullion movements jointly with the Bullion Office, relinquished their control as a result of the recommendations of the 1932 Peacock Committee on Organisation. The practice of quadruple control was interrupted in 1940 to expedite packing as described below, and reinstated in 1943.[31]

† Use of the medallion, picturing Britannia, was discontinued in May 1954.[32]

Plate 7.4    Weighing gold bars in the Bullion Office in the 1940s

recognition of the arduous nature of their work ', remained a heavy, noisy and dirty undertaking.

London's pre-eminence as the centre of the gold market dated from the nineteenth century when the city provided not only the development capital for the gold-mining industry but the refining capacity too. The refiners sold the gold direct to the Bank or to brokers. All the metal was sold to the Bank during the First World War, Rothschilds – with their financial resources – being selected to act as broker when peace was restored. A few years later the new Reserve Bank in Pretoria took over the disposal of South African production, and sold the gold in London through the agency of the Bank of England. This meant that a large proportion of the clearing of transactions in physical gold took place in London; in addition, the members of the London Gold Market controlled, as they still do, the Good Delivery list – the list of assayers and melters whose marks are acceptable as assurance of the weight and quality of gold bars. The London market was shut down at the beginning of the Second World War, but the Bullion Office was extremely busy throughout the war years. For reasons of safety almost all the gold held by the Bank was dispersed overseas in the spring of 1940, which involved a mammoth packing operation accomplished by eighty porters. To have sorted and identified every bar before packing would have prolonged the whole operation by many weeks, and in order to expedite matters an important change in the Bank's policy affecting the custody of bar gold was made at the end of May 1940: the recognition of the 'fungibility' of gold. This is a legal term meaning that an article contracted for can serve for, or be replaced by, another answering to the same definition. In other words gold would be held on a fine ounce basis rather than as specific bars, and central banks were advised that, with a very few exceptions, specific bars would no longer be held for 'set-aside' accounts.[33] Early in 1941 the Treasury asked the Bank to handle all large imports of silver bullion (most of them from the US under the Lease-Lend scheme), and to supply the requirements of the market. In 1944 there was a huge increase in gold movements due to the resumption of imports from the US and exports to India.

When the war was over the repatriation of the gold exported in 1940 began and in 1946 the Bank started to receive the accumulated stock of gold purchased and held in South Africa, Australia and other centres during the years of the war: for some time this averaged £2m. per week, and the volume was only restricted by the lack of shipping. In all, arrangements had been made by the South African Reserve Bank that £80m. of gold was to be made available for sale to the UK in each of the years 1946/7. On 1 February 1947 the number of full-sized bars in the Bank reached the 100,000 mark for the first time since the dispersal of gold in 1940.[34]

A problem causing international concern at this period was the question of the quantity of gold bullion and coin captured, found or taken over from the Germans in 1945. It comprised both the reserve rightfully held by the Germans together with various amounts looted by them in occupied countries. The Tripartite Commission for the Restitution of Monetary Gold was set up by Great Britain, the US and France in September 1946 to assess the value of the gold recovered and investigate the claims on it; after nearly two years of discussion it was finally agreed that as Britain was not a claimant, and the expense of taking the gold to America was considerable, some of it should be sent to the Bank of England for an accurate valuation before being held there for the joint account of the three governments prior to settlement by the Commission and disposal to the various claimant countries. It was also decided that the Bank should not itself be involved in the assessment of claims.

Accordingly from the middle of June 1948 until the beginning of August, two consignments were received by air from the US military authorities in Frankfurt nearly every day. The total weight of gold sent to the Bank amounted to some seventy-five tons of bars, coin and other forms of bullion. The coin presented special difficulties: lead seals and nickel and copper coins had been included in the original weight or thrown in after weighing, and one batch of eighteen bags contained 138 ounces of dirt and small pieces of cement. One particular bag contained denominations of twenty-six different currencies plus a number of coins and medals which nobody in the Bank could identify and which had to be specially examined by an expert from the British Museum. Many of the bars were melted by German mints and thus would not be acceptable on the London market;* others bore the stamps of unknown melters or fell outside the range of acceptable weights or assays. All this put a considerable strain on the resources of the Bullion Office, and involved arrangements for a series of melting, refining and repacking operations. The latter were necessary because the gold was mostly packed in old German ammunition boxes, many of them inadequately fastened and in a rotting condition. The work was not completed until the end of October, by which time the Bank had received an unwelcome intimation that its custody of the gold was unlikely to be as straightforward as it had hoped.

In July the Tripartite Commission had advised the Bank that one of the consignments would contain sixty-four bars whose title was claimed by Dollfus Mieg et Cie of Alsace, who stated that they had bought the bars in Switzerland and lodged them in a bank at Limoges from where they were looted by the Germans in 1944. The claim was currently being examined by the French government to whom it was likely that the gold would be apportioned by the Commission. The French representative on the Commission requested that the bars should be identified and segregated on receipt, in distinction to the normal Bank practice of gold being held for customers on a basis of fine ounces, with individual bars not earmarked. The Bank agreed to this; the gold duly appeared as part of a consignment on 3 August and was subsequently segregated. In September, a letter to the Bank from a firm of solicitors acting on behalf of Dollfus Mieg gave formal notice of the latter's claim on the Bank for the sixty-four bars, stating that the gold was not monetary gold and should not come within the jurisdiction of the Commission.

This claim was the forerunner of several years of complex litigation. In March 1949 the Bank sought in the High Court to have the proceedings stayed on the grounds of sovereign immunity, and was successful; however Dollfus Mieg appealed against the verdict and the case was reconsidered in the Court of Appeal the following January, when an

---

* The two German melters and assayers whose bars were acceptable on the pre-war London market were 'disqualified' in 1947 because of fears about the origin of their gold. When the London market re-opened in 1954, their bars were accepted as good delivery when bearing date stamps of 1953 onwards.

unfortunate incident occurred. L.J. (later Sir Laurence) Menzies,* an Acting Deputy Chief Cashier, swore an affidavit on behalf of the Bank testifying that the sixty-four bars in dispute had been segregated 'on behalf of the three Governments' and had at no time been intermixed with gold held on behalf of any other customer. This he testified at 2.30 p.m. on 2 February; at 4 p.m. on the same day he learnt from the hapless Principal of the Bullion Office that it had been discovered that thirteen of the original bars had in fact, by error, been delivered out at the beginning of 1949 and thirteen different bars of the same weight substituted. Precautions had been taken to make a separate stack of the bars, and a warning notice put on them that they were not to be handled or sold; a similar notice should have been attached to the Hollerith cards forming the Office record of the bars but for some reason this had not been done.

'A pretty kettle of fish' was the response of the Master of the Rolls on learning of this sorry affair: the Bank, unsurprisingly, felt more strongly. The outcome was that the House of Lords ruled that, out of the original sixty-four bars, the fifty-one still in the Bank were 'immune from suit'. Action however could proceed as to the remainder; Dollfus Mieg proceeded to claim damages from the Bank for the wrongful disposal of the bars. Had the Bank had to deliver up the substituted thirteen bars to the Commission and lost the action by Dollfus Mieg, it would have meant a loss of some £65,000 apart from costs; however the matter was settled in April 1953 by the French government who promised to pay Dollfus Mieg 60 per cent of the value of the gold on the understanding that all further claims were withdrawn.[35]

In March 1950, primarily as a result of the Dollfus Mieg case and after having taken Counsel's advice, the Bank reverted to its earlier practice of holding gold on a specific bar basis.[36]

Since the outbreak of war in September 1939 the Bank had been the sole buyer and seller of monetary gold in the United Kingdom. After the war, markets grew up or resumed in other parts of the world such as Switzerland, Beirut and Tangier (with operations settled mainly in dollars) and it was decided in 1954 to re-open the London Gold Market, with the aim of restoring London to its position as an international market in which people who were buying and selling against dollars would now be able to do so for sterling. The price was to be determined by supply and demand; but in practice, as the US stood ready to buy at a fixed price ($35 per ounce, equivalent to £12 8s., when the market re-

---

* Menzies, Sir Laurence James, Kt. (1962), 1906–83. Entered Bank of England, 1925; Asst. Chief Cashier, 1943; Deputy Chief Cashier, 1952; Adviser to Governors, 1957–8, 1962–4; Secretary of Export Credits Guarantee Dept., 1958–61.

Plate 7.5   P.S. Beale on his appointment as Chief Cashier in 1949. He held the post from 1949 to 1955

opened in March 1954) this had the effect of providing a 'floor' to the London market and to any other. Anybody was permitted to sell in the newly opened market, but the only people who could buy were those who had American, Canadian or registered sterling accounts.* Residents of the sterling area with special licence from the Bank of England were able

* Registered sterling was a new type of sterling account which was obtainable against US or Canadian dollars, or gold, by a resident outside North America and the sterling area.

to buy to the same limited extent that they had before, for industrial purposes.[37]

The re-opening of the market naturally caused a considerable increase in the daily work of the Office, and nearly 300 tons of bullion were handled in the first six months. The Bullion Office participated in the discussions over the new London Market specification, which included the acceptance of the Russian assay. Before this, Russian gold was only 'Good Delivery' on the London market if accompanied by an assay certificate from one of the recognised firms of assayers, none of which at that time were themselves Russian.

The Russian assay posed something of a problem to the Bank. There was a faint fear, as the Chief Cashier Beale explained to the Governors, lest 'the technicians concerned should put unduly high assay marks under duress. This [risk] was thought to be remote; nevertheless it was not a contingency to be ignored entirely and we would propose therefore to re-assay a minimum of 5 % of all bars bearing either of these two assays [The State Refinery and the All Union Gold Factory], at the cost of HMT'.[38] This proportionate re-assay was duly carried out. Even so the rest of the market tended to be wary of gold of Russian origin, and this for political as well as commercial reasons: for a long time the Bank would not ship Russian gold bars to the US as this might have led 'to a complete freezing of our gold held with the Federal Reserve Bank'[39] – whether the sale was on behalf of the EEA or of other customers. In January 1955 it was agreed by the Treasury and the Governors that all 8,101 Russian bars currently held for the EEA should be melted.[40] Reluctance to accept Russian bars freely continued for some years, affecting their easy disposability, but the Bank was anxious both politically and, to a lesser extent, because the bars themselves were technically of a very high quality, to do everything 'to maintain the marketability and acceptability of Russian gold bars'.

The Bank's silver operations, which had begun as noted earlier soon after the outbreak of the Second World War, virtually finished with the despatch in April 1957 of the last instalment of silver in repayment of loans made by the US to Britain under Lease-Lend agreements.* Much of this silver was in the form of Russian bars (less unacceptable to the Americans than Russian gold, but even so carefully packed in crates in

---

* Under Lease-Lend Britain had borrowed 88 million ounces (2,750 tons) of silver from the US, and had additionally guaranteed 206 million ounces of the 226 million ounces owed by India and Pakistan jointly (this latter debt was in fact discharged without any help from Britain being required). Repayment of the 88 million ounces, on an ounce for ounce basis, took place over a five year period from 1952 to 1957.[41]

such a way that its origin was not too readily apparent) and the bulk of the remainder had been recovered from the British coinage under a programme carried out by the In-Tellers' Office as described below.[42]

The character of the gold market changed dramatically in 1960. It had stayed calm since re-opening six years earlier, with gold prices remaining within a few cents of the US Treasury's buying and selling prices (respectively $34·9125 and $35·0875 per ounce). But after the Cuban missile crisis in 1960 the price of gold shot up; dealing became hectic and on each of the mornings of 20 and 21 October the Bank delivered over 1,250 bars to the market. In the afternoon of 21 October the price reached $41 per fine ounce, and this rise caused many central banks to cash in surplus dollars at the US gold 'window'. The dollar had thus effectively become convertible into gold on demand not only by central banks but also by private speculators throughout the world; to counteract this the Gold Pool was created in 1961. This was an agreement whereby the Bank would sell gold on behalf of the central banks of the US, the UK, Switzerland, Belgium, France, Germany, Italy and the Netherlands, in sufficient quantities to keep the price at $35 per ounce. The Gold Pool was abolished in March 1968.[43]

The In-Tellers' Office* was responsible for all the Bank's receipts and issue of coin. On behalf of the Royal Mint it made all arrangements for the withdrawal from circulation and examination of certain types of silver coin; it took from the Mint almost the entire output of newly minted British silver and cupro-nickel coin, and issued this to the other banks as required; and it supplied the needs of the Bank's own customers via the Drawing Office and the Branches. Pennies, halfpennies and farthings and nickel-brass threepenny pieces were issued direct from the Mint to the bankers.

In one form or another the withdrawal of silver coins had been a continuous process from 1920 onwards. At first the objective was the withdrawal of silver coins issued between the years 1816 and 1919 inclusive – they contained 0·925 pure silver and 0·075 copper, and were returned to the Mint to be melted down for the recovery of their bullion content. The sorting was carried out in the Refinery building at St Luke's Printing Works: with practice, the sorters could distinguish the 0·925 coins from the subsequent issue (1920–1946, containing 0·500 silver, 0·400 copper, 0·050 nickel and 0·050 zinc) by their colour and 'ring'.

---

* The Tellers of the Bank on its foundation in 1694 included both those who received and paid money inside the building and those who went out to collect money due on Bills and notes. The distinction between the two was made in 1726; the Out-Tellers' Office subsequently became the Bill Office.[44]

Further schemes included the withdrawal of those 'binary' coins, minted between 1923 and 1927 and containing half silver and half copper, which had developed a coppery tarnish. The sorters also picked out counterfeits, defaced, mutilated, Colonial and foreign coins, as well as silver coins dated before 1816 which had been demonetized and were not legal tender.[45] Once these had all been removed, the remainder were fed into one of a battery of counting machines. Three types of electrically operated machines, made by the International Counting Machine Co. Ltd, were used in the Office: a mixed coin counter, a separating machine which sorted half-crowns, florins, shillings and sixpences in to different containers, and a denominational counting machine, all of which filled bags with £10 worth of coins.[46] A representative of a 'rag factory' was a regular pre-war caller to the Refinery with between £4 and £5 worth of bent and battered coins left in pocket linings and thrown out by the cloth shredding machinery, which was duly sorted for him. Although there was a certain interest and even an occasional thrill in picking over the silver by hand, and some of the clerks became extremely knowledgeable numismatists, operating the machines was monotonous work allotted to Bank trainees at this date for periods of up to six months at a time.

During the war years the In-Tellers' Office was fully occupied meeting the heavy requirements for coin by the Services and 'the large body of wage earners engaged on work of National Importance'. Much work was also done counting and sorting foreign coins for Exchange Control Offices. For reasons of safety the sorting section was removed to Head Office in 1941 and located underground in the vaults; it did not return to the Refinery until March 1948. All transport of the coins, packed in heavy wooden boxes, between the Bank, the Refinery and the Mint was undertaken by the horse-drawn vans of Charlie and Ernest Wells, who had provided this service since January 1912 (and also transported gold bars). It was not until May 1944 that the Mint introduced the use of its own motor van, and Wells' horses were still used by the Bank until 1948.[47]

The withdrawal scheme was suspended during the war. The 1946 Coinage Act provided for a new scheme covering withdrawal of both types of silver in lieu of which cupro-nickel coin was issued. The immediate objective was the extraction of all silver from the coinage to meet essential industrial needs without dollar expenditure; in the longer term, silver was to be accumulated towards meeting Britain's repayment of silver borrowed from the Americans under Lease-Lend.

Work did not start until 1949, after delays caused by the need to concentrate on meeting abnormal demands for coinage of all denominations which developed during 1947 and 1948 as a result of rumours that the current issue of notes was to be withdrawn and replaced. In the next two years the withdrawal of £30m. of silver coin, containing 54m. ounces of silver, was accomplished. The scheme was suspended in the autumn of 1951 when, owing to the world shortage of nickel brought about by the Korean war, the Mint decided to conserve its meagre supplies of the metal first by reducing the production of new cupro-nickel coins and finally, at the end of 1951, by ceasing to strike any at all. The ensuing shortages were highly inconvenient to banks and customers alike; the Bank was unable to continue supplying new money to the other banks, and also had to end its earlier practice of acting as the medium for ironing out the individual surpluses and shortages which arose from time to time in certain areas or at certain banks. Receiving banks now had to find an outlet for their own surpluses, paying banks had to find a source of supply: the Bank of England, falling in the latter category, had on occasion to seek out and purchase stocks of coin held by other banks, with which to meet the demands of its customers including many government departments. In 1953 the Mint resumed the production of cupro-nickel coins, and from that date onwards itself supplied the banks with their requirements. The recovery programme began again in October 1953, and the requisite amount of silver was successfully repaid to the US a month before the due date of 28 April 1957. The silver recovery programme continued, however, in order to supply industrial needs. The availability of 'silver' coins continued to fluctuate, sometimes quite markedly, for some years, one reason being the increased use of automatic change-giving machines.[48]

The work of the Office which was not concerned with silver withdrawal continued uneventfully in the post-war years. The counting of coins from overseas for exchange control was enlivened at the end of 1947 by the discovery of packets of soap, tea, dried fruit, tinned food and other groceries packed in boxes of silver coin received from the Bank of Canada. The staff there, sympathetic to the shortages in still-rationed Britain, had kindly sent them as a gift, and further suggested that orders should be put in for any specific foodstuffs required. The first batch was distributed among the In-Tellers' staff, but such an irregular happening could not be allowed to recur. N. Redfern, a Deputy Chief Cashier, wrote to thank the Canadians but pointed out that further gifts would put the Bank in an invidious position with the Customs, as the boxes came in under open licence under the express condition of containing coins only.[49]

Another duty of In-Tellers' was to undertake for the Bank arrangements for the distribution of various special coin issues such as the commemorative crowns struck for the Festival of Britain in 1951 and the coronation of Queen Elizabeth II in 1953. A further service provided for the public was the issue on demand of coin against bank notes. But the continued existence of the Office as an independent unit became increasingly unlikely with the end of its responsibilities of silver distribution to the banks and then of the major efforts of silver withdrawal once the American loan had been repaid. In May 1956 the Inspector of Offices and Branches was asked by the Chief Cashier to examine the possibility of its work being done by 'one or more of the existing Cash Offices'; as a result of his report In-Tellers' was amalgamated in May 1957 with the Bullion Office where it formed firstly the In-Tellers' Section and then, from 1960, the Coin Section.[50]

Finally, the work of the Bank in its capacity as an issuing house was shared between the Chief Cashier's Office, as described above and the Dividend Pay and Loans Office. This as its name implies was formed by an amalgamation of two separate Offices. The Dividend Pay Office was the older of the two, dating back to 1845: its function was the payment of dividend warrants and coupons in respect of loans domiciled at the Bank (i.e. for which the Bank was Registrar and/or Paying Agent) and of coupons of some foreign issues for which the Bank was the Paying Agent. It was also responsible for payment of bearer bonds.

The work of issuing loans was originally performed by a Section of the Chief Cashier's Office, which in 1916 was moved to new premises in Lombard Street and thereafter called the Loans Office. In December 1920 the two Offices were amalgamated. A Sub-Treasury Office was created by Order of Court of 13 November 1919, in order to take over from the Chief Cashier's Office the issue and repayment of Treasury Bills and the issue of Bearer bonds in exchange for stock. It was absorbed into the Dividend Pay and Loans Office in August 1934. In that year the Office moved to Bank Buildings in Princes Street and then in April 1939 into what was visualised as its permanent home on the third floor of the newly rebuilt Threadneedle Street.[51] During the Second World War about a third of the Office and some of the machines were evacuated to Barlaston to be near the Central Clearing House at Trentham Park, but on the recommendation of the Inspector of Offices and Branches all Sections of the Office were reunited in London in March 1944, in order to make more efficient use of the available manpower.[52]

The chief work of the Office was the issue of loans which were to be domiciled in the Bank. The speedy and efficient way in which big government loans, on offer to the public for a limited time, were handled

Plate 7.6    Miss M.J. Vidler operating a Hollerith Tabulator in the Dividend Pay and Loans Office, 1941

within the Office had earned for the Bank a high reputation as an issuing house, which had been helped by a mechanisation programme successfully initiated during the 1930s. After a trial of Powers-Samas machines and the Hollerith machines manufactured by the British Tabulating Machine Co. the latter were installed in 1937 for use daily on dividend warrant work and for loan work as and when required.[53]

The traditional method of tender for Treasury Bills, which lapsed during the Second World War, was revived in 1948. The announcement was made at the Bank every Friday afternoon – with the result of that day's tender – and confirmed later in *The London Gazette*, of the amount of Treasury Bills to be offered at the tender on the next Friday for payment on any business day in the following week. Tenders, which had to be made through a London banker, discount house or broker, were made on forms provided for the purpose. On these had to be stated the amount tendered for, the price offered and the date on which Bills would be taken up and paid for. The forms were securely folded before being handed in at the Bank, and revealed on the outside the amount of the tender and the day the Bills were to be dated, but not the name of the tenderer or the price offered. They were received at the Bank up to 1 p.m.

Plate 7.7 Opening Tenders at the Weekly Treasury Bill Tender in the Parlours. This photograph was taken in 1965 but the procedure was unchanged from that described below. At the table nearest to the camera are, left to right: Deputy Chief Cashier, M.J. Thornton, Chief Cashier, J.Q. Hollom, Deputy Governor, L.K. O'Brien and Secretary to the Treasury, Sir William Armstrong. The men at the far tables are left to right: G. Essex, J. Stringer, A. Penny and A. Long

and immediately sorted by date, listed and retotalled by staff of the Dividend Pay and Loans Office, supplemented by staff from CCO.

The tenders were then opened in the presence of the Governor and of the Secretary to the Treasury, or (more frequently) their representatives, in the first floor Committee Room in the Parlours of the Bank. Each form was checked to ensure that it was correctly filled in, and then the tenders sorted by the price offered, those for different dates being kept apart. The lowest price, at which the total of Bills on offer would be taken up, was established, and a proportional allotment made if necessary. At about 1.30 p.m. a provisional announcement of the result was made, quoting the lowest price at which tenders had been accepted and approximately what proportional allotment each bid at the price would receive. The tenders were then checked in detail, the results calculated exactly and announced definitively at about 3 p.m. The final announcement stated the total numbers of tenders received, the amount allotted, the average rate of discount for Bills allotted and the amount of Bills to be offered for tender on the following Friday.[54] The calculations were made by the staff of Room 1 : the calls for speed and accuracy, and the semi-public nature of the ceremony, are a good example of the type of quite gruelling hurdles faced by the clerks working there.

During the war, apart from the issue in 1940 of 3% War Loan, the government borrowed for both medium and long terms by means of Tap Loans. With the end of the war and the resumption of public loans, the numbers of staff in this large Office – well over 100 strong – and the space needed for major loan operations made another move necessary and in September 1951 the Office moved back to Bank Buildings, which had by that date been partly rebuilt after the flying bomb damage suffered in 1944. The Loans and Treasury Bill Sections occupied the banking halls on the ground floor and the Mechanisation and Warrants Sections were on the first floor.[55]

It was not an easy Office to administer, because of the seasonal nature of the work. There were periods of great activity, especially in the aftermath of new issues which involved the receipt of call money, the exchange of Allotment Letters for Scrip, the examination of registration forms and the calculation and payment of commissions. Similarly there were monthly peaks for warrants and the issue of Tax Reserve Certificates, weekly ones for Treasury Bills, much coupon work before dividend dates and a three month run of surrender of Tax Reserve Certificates from mid December to mid March. But there were still idle periods, especially when new issues were confined to government issues which did not involve calls, and as far as possible these times were used to arrange dummy loans and lectures. Loan work in 1953/4 was heavier than it had been for thirty years because of the number of new issues (twelve, involving handling over 80,000 applications) and the registration of steel denationalisation issues. The following year the Office handled a total of 239,000 applications, which included 160,000 for the offer for sale of shares in Colvilles Ltd, a steel company. The office was also busy at this period on issue management under the terms of the German debt settlement; however, the restrictive monetary policy initiated in 1956 had a dampening effect on the UK issue market. Tax Reserve Certificates continued to gain in popularity. There was much routine work and book-keeping, and sometimes for particularly large issues staff had to be borrowed from other parts of the Bank: the offer for sale of shares in the Steel Company of Wales in March 1957, for example, necessitated 180 borrowed staff to enable the Letters of Acceptance to be posted in the early hours of the morning following the day of issue. This issue was

Plate 7.8   Leslie O'Brien in 1954, the year before he became Chief Cashier, a position in which he remained until 1962

responsible for over 9,000 hours of overtime by the normal Office staff plus another 4,000 hours by borrowed staff.[56]

In June 1958 the first mechanised drawing of Victory Bonds took place, the Bank's proposals concerning this having been accepted by the Treasury and the National Debt Office. The preparatory work, which included punching 213,000 Hollerith cards, proved a formidable task but the first draw by the new method was made 'without a hitch'; subsequently the use of cards was applied to the lengthy job of checking the proofs of the published lists of drawn bond numbers, which could then be carried out much more quickly and accurately.[57]

# 8

## THE BRANCHES*

In November 1936 the Court of the Bank discussed the report of a recent visit to the Birmingham Branch made by two Directors, Arthur Whitworth and James Weir,† which from unfavourable comment on the Birmingham premises moved to consideration of the possibility of a rebuilding scheme for all the Branches, and, more radically, questioned whether there was really any need for Country Branches at all. At this date the Bank had nine Branches, eight in the provinces and one adjacent to the Law Courts in the Strand; a second London Branch, Western Branch in Burlington Gardens, had been sold to the Royal Bank of Scotland in 1930.[1] Branch activity had been gradually eroded by the Bank's disinclination, since the First World War, to compete for local business with the clearing banks. Messrs Whitworth and Weir were not the first to comment on the costs of maintaining considerable numbers of staff in large and in many cases quite unsuitable buildings: the Economy Committee of 1933‡ had been critical of the expense of the Branches and the Directors' report crystallised misgivings which the Deputy Governor, B.G. Catterns, had felt for some time. In the following March, after discussion by the Committee of Treasury, a four-man Special Committee under the chairmanship of Roland Kitson (later Lord Airedale)§ was formed to investigate three aspects of the Branches – their 'proper protection' out of business hours and the desirability or otherwise of resident Agents and Sub-Agents (the managers of the Branches and their deputies); the accommodation necessary to perform

* See also Sayers, Vol. 3, pp. 335–7, and QB, December 1963, pp. 279–84.
† Whitworth, Arthur, see p. 146n. Weir, James George, CMG, 1887–1973. Chairman, Cierva Rotorcaft. Director, Bank of England, 1935–46.
‡ See chapter 6, p. 200.
§ Airedale, Baron, 1944, Roland Dudley Kitson, DSO, MC, 1882–1958. Director, Ford Motor Co., London Assurance Corporation. Director, Bank of England, 1923–47.

adequately the present and likely future functions of the Branches; and whether any rebuilding or alterations were necessary.

The Deputy Governor wrote to the Chairman of the Committee of London Clearing Bankers, Lord Wardington,* asking him if in his members' opinion the Branches were needed, receiving in reply a definite assurance that they served 'a most useful purpose, not only to the Joint Stock Banks, but to the public generally'; in answer to subsequent questioning the bankers affirmed that they saw no particular need for any changes in the geographical locations of the Branches, currently sited at Newcastle, Birmingham, Hull, Leeds, Liverpool, Manchester, Plymouth, Bristol and the Law Courts.

For the benefit of the Committee Catterns defined the responsibilities of the Branches as three-fold: the distribution and receipt of currency, the provision of clearing facilities for the banks, and the collection of government revenues. The Agent usually acted *ex officio* as Chairman of the local clearing. The few private accounts maintained at the Branches, other than those for the staff, were mostly held by customers with long family or commercial connections with the Bank, and discounting business by this date was virtually non-existent. It was as note distribution and reception centres that the Branches were really important, and it was on this function that the Special Committee focused its discussions. Members visited every Branch and made specific recommendations about the premises of each, as well as giving general consideration to questions of security and future accommodation. They made their report in September 1937, the main conclusion being that all the premises were too old to meet modern requirements and that the time had arrived 'for the consideration of a programme of reconstruction'. The state of the fabric of the Hull Branch, and the inconvenience of its building which dated from 1856 – the Branch had been in existence since 1829 – made it necessary in the opinion of the Committee to rebuild it as soon as possible on a new site, but before this was agreed, it was recommended that the retention of the Branch should be carefully examined as 'it would appear doubtful whether the Branch fulfils any functions which could not be done equally well by the Leeds Branch apart from the work in connection with the Public Accounts and the Hull Corporation'. All the other Branches should be rebuilt, Birmingham first followed by Manchester, Liverpool and Leeds, with Bristol, Newcastle and Plymouth left until last. The Committee put forward detailed

---

* Wardington, 1st Baron (1936) of Alnmouth, John William Beaumont Pease, 1869–1950. Chairman, Lloyds Bank, 1922–45, Bank of London and South America, 1922–48.

suggestions as to how the premises should be rebuilt, preferably, 'for reasons of economy and to save reorganisation', on new sites, most of which could be considerably smaller than those occupied by existing Branches. It was important that the plans should include Bullion Yards separated from the public roadways, for the safer loading and unloading of consignments of notes ('Treasure' in Bank parlance). The Committee had also paid attention to the subject of Bank Chambers, office buildings adjacent to the Branches and owned and sub-let by the Bank. These had originally been thought desirable in certain places so that the Bank could exercise discretion as to whom it would have as its immediate neighbours, and were currently in existence at Manchester, Birmingham, Liverpool and Hull. The Committee estimated the combined net income from these Chambers to be about £2,800 a year – a meagre return on the large amount of capital invested in the buildings. 'We consider that the Bank should not undertake the business of a landlord and we suggest that Chambers should not be included in plans for rebuilding.'

In an interim report, made the previous April, the Committee had already submitted that it was no longer necessary for Agents and Sub-Agents to live on Branch premises, except in the case of the Law Courts Branch. Further recommendations were now made that none of them should live on the premises after the Branches had been rebuilt, but should be granted by way of compensation 'such allowance as may be found appropriate': annual sums of £350 and £225 for Agents and Sub-Agents respectively were suggested. The officials should, however, be required to live 'within a reasonable limit or distance from the Branch', and detailed guide-lines were laid down for the construction of Treasuries (where notes were stored), numbers and activities of Night Watchmen, and the communication of Watchmen with the Agent and with the police. The Committee further recommended that an expansion of not less than 20 per cent in the work of note counting, and of 10 per cent in general banking work, should be allowed for in any new premises; but the whole problem of administration and rebuilding could be greatly simplified if the note counting work were more evenly distributed among the Branches. Currently Manchester was dealing with some 93·3 million paid £1 and 10s. notes annually, employing twenty-eight women to inspect and count them, while Hull, at the bottom of the league, employed four women to process 11·4 million notes annually.[2]

The Court considered this report in October 1937 and agreed that the Staff Committee should look into the question of allowances to Agents and Sub-Agents in lieu of residence at the Branch. A further Special

Committee, with the same members as the previous one, was appointed on a permanent basis, first to decide on the closure or retention of Hull Branch, then to consider how best the other recommendations should be implemented. The Committee would be responsible for the choice of 'an Architect or Architects', the style and construction of any Branch to be rebuilt, the sale of unneeded sites and the purchase of others. It would also consider the closing of existing and the establishment of new Branches, in conjunction with the Governor and Deputy Governor, through whom any approach to the clearing banks was to be effected. This new Committee was known as the Special Committee on Branch Premises and was appointed on 21 October 1937.[3]

The clearers were duly approached once more by the Deputy Governor and a series of meetings with their Chief Accountants was held in the Bank under the chairmanship of H.B.C. Yeomans, Deputy Chief Cashier. The earlier enquiries had disclosed that the practices of the banks, with regard to note collection and distribution, were far from uniform. Some used the post, some road, some rail; some distributed new notes and collected used ones via their larger branch offices, while others worked directly to and from London. Now they were asked for their views on new Branches, bearing in mind that the Bank would expect both existing and any new Branches to be of definite value to all, or at least a good number, of the banks. The Bank would need to be assured that the Branch would be 'adequately used' for the note work, and that a local clearing based on a Branch would be desirable; the Bank would welcome decentralisation, said Yeomans, provided that it genuinely met the desire of the banks.

The outcome of these discussions was that there was little consensus on the use that would be made of Branches, nor, with one exception, would the banks agree to co-operate with the Bank by making any substantial change in their methods of note distribution.[4] However, as a result of the exchanges, the Bank decided in April 1938 to close the Hull Branch 'on such date as may be found convenient', and to open a new Branch in Southampton, which it was felt would fill a greater need.[5]

The Special Committee was asked to advise the Court as early as possible on the necessary arrangements for the acquisition of a suitable site in Southampton and for the construction of Branch premises – the first to have been built by the Bank since 1865 when Leeds Branch moved into a building designed for it by the architect P.C. Hardwick.* Meanwhile the vexed question of salaries of Agents and Sub-Agents in

---

* Hardwick, Philip Charles, architect; Architect to Bank of England, 1855–83.

the provincial Branches was being ventilated as a result of the decision to recompense them finally when they gave up their living accommodation in or near Bank premises. It had been recognised for some time, at least in Threadneedle Street, that their salary scales compared favourably with those paid to (roughly) comparable jobs at Head Office: Branches were graded according to the size and importance of the cities in which they were situated, and Agents at Grade 1 Branches (Law Courts, Manchester and Liverpool) were currently receiving £2,500 per year plus either a house or £450 allowance in lieu. Agents at the other Branches were paid either £2,000 plus £450 allowance, or £1,600 plus £425. At Head Office, the Chief of Establishments received £2,750, and the Deputy Chief Cashiers £2,500.

Until 1906, Agents and Sub-Agents had not been drawn from the clerical staff of the Bank but were selected by Governors and Directors, usually from among their personal friends and connections. The men appointed were often inexperienced in banking but were 'doubtless of such personal or social distinction as assured them a welcome into the circles of local County society and business magnates in the neighbourhood of the Branch'. Many of them had private means, which, naturally, the men from the clerical staff rarely possessed. The official residences often proved more of a burden to them than an advantage, as they were old-fashioned, expensive and difficult to heat and to run without a staff of servants. In 1926 this had at last been recognised by the Bank and Agents' salaries (and, to some extent, those of Sub-Agents) were adjusted to relieve these difficulties. The report of the Economy Committee in 1934 referred to the high cost of Branch administration but the 1936 Salary Scheme made no changes in their salaries. What was at issue now was that, when the house allowances to those who vacated Branch houses were fixed, 'the extent to which the basic salaries had been inflated to meet the extra expenses entailed by living in the large and often incommodious Branch houses' had been overlooked.

The Agent certainly had an important role to fulfil in his area. He was the personal representative of the Bank, had to be an efficient 'all-rounder' rather than a specialist, and, being at a distance from London, must accept a certain measure of responsibility. He also needed a sound general knowledge and ability to understand and assimilate business, as well as banking, affairs – since 1930 Agents had been required to provide a regular bulletin of local industrial and commercial intelligence. Socially, he had to be 'acceptable to, and welcome in, the higher representative circles of local society', and here his wife had a part to play. Set against all these requirements, which in the opinion of the Agents themselves militated in favour of generous salaries, was the undeniable fact that since the end of the First World War the advance and discount work of the Branches had been eroded year by year to its current negligible level. Commercial banking was also on the decrease, and the only aspect of Branch work which was increasing was work for the government.

All these factors were carefully weighed before the new salary levels for both Agents and Sub-Agents were agreed in October 1938. The Branches were re-graded and the salaries adjusted downwards, with tax-free allowances (non-pensionable) made in lieu of a house to all except the Agent at the Law Courts Branch. The Agent at the Law Courts received £2,000 p.a. plus his house; Manchester, Liverpool and Birmingham were graded together as First Class Branches whose Agents received £1,800 annually plus a tax-free (but non-pensionable) allowance of £200. The remainder, including the doomed Hull and the future Branch at Southampton, were Grade 2 Branches with salaries for the Agents of £1,600 plus an allowance of £150. Unsurprisingly, news of the scheme was received by the Agents without enthusiasm, and they referred to it among themselves as 'The Munich Agreement'.[6]

While these delicate negotiations were taking place the Committee on Branch Premises made good progress with the modernisation and rebuilding plans. It had been decided to give priority to building the new Branch at Southampton, and that its design should be such that 'when other Branches are rebuilt they may be of similar character where possible'. Various sites were selected by the Bank's chartered surveyors, St Quintin, Son & Stanley; L.A. Gash, currently Principal of the Drawing Office but shortly to be appointed Deputy Chief of Establishments, who had served in three Branches, inspected them in company with R.C. Stevenson, Principal of the Branch Banks Office. The BBO, as it was known, was the main conduit between the Branches and the Chief Cashier, in whose Department they were placed: it handled all correspondence in both directions, was responsible (in conjunction with the Chief Cashier and the Auditor) for drawing up the enormously detailed manual of *Standing Instructions* for the conduct of banking and other Branch activities, and organised the 'Treasure journeys' for the delivery and collection of bank notes as described below. Among its records were a series of 'control' accounts giving day-to-day information on the banking position of each Branch.*

Stevenson and Gash decided that the best of the Southampton sites was in the lower part of the High Street, below the Bar Gate, which ran

---

* The Branch Banks Office had been established in 1827. It was wound up in 1975, largely because much of its work was rendered unnecessary by increasing computerisation.

up from the docks and contained the Inland Revenue Offices, the General Post Office and the offices of all the Big Five and Martins banks. Their visit was followed by that of the Premises Committee who agreed with their choice and by the end of May 1938 the Bank had undertaken to buy the freehold of Nos. 31, 32 and 33 High Street for the sum of £15,500. The Establishment Department drew up a detailed list of requirements for the new building and it was then necessary to choose an architect – not only for the new Branch but for the entire modernisation programme. This plan was preferred to the alternative of appointing a local architect at each centre, which would have involved 'making a series of agreements with different individuals all of whom would be strange to the Bank's methods and requirements'. The work of some of the more prominent of the younger architects of the day was considered and two of them, H. James and A.V. Heal, both Fellows of the Royal Institute of British Architects, were invited to draw up plans in competition. Each after visiting some of the existing Branches submitted his version to Freshfields, who passed them on to the Bank identified only by the letters A and B. The Committee, supported by the views of C.E. Dunkin, the Bank's Clerk of Works, preferred those of Heal, who in September 1938 was duly appointed 'Architect in connection with the building programme for the Provincial Branches'.[7]

Authority to proceed with the building of Southampton having been obtained from Court, planning and construction proceeded very rapidly. Demolition of the existing buildings on the site began on 31 October 1938 and was completed by the middle of the following January; the contractors, Trollope & Colls, began work on 30 January. Some early problems were encountered with water in the excavated foundations, necessarily deep because plans for the building included extensive bullion vaults. These were intended for the storage of gold, primarily from South Africa, if the expected war materialised and prevented gold shipments from being moved readily to London which was the only place of delivery in the UK acceptable to the market.

The Agents of the other Branches were invited to inspect and comment on the plans for Southampton, which was designed on four floors and a mezzanine. The sub-basement contained gold vaults measuring 23 feet by 60 feet, an area which allowed for the handling and storage of some 24,000 gold bars, and an ARP shelter with independent ventilation and arrangements for First Aid and decontamination. Above the vault in the basement was a Treasury of similar dimensions. The Banking Hall on the ground floor was finished in Ancaster stone and bronze. The Agent's room (shared as in all Branches by Agent and Sub-Agent) was also on the ground floor, with the note counting room above. The facade of the building was of Portland Stone, with carved motifs of the familiar 'Lions and Gold' and the 'Old Lady' provided by Charles Wheeler who had executed the majority of stone decorations in the rebuilt Threadneedle Street premises. Heal described the new Branch as a 'normal modern development of the Soane tradition expressing the ownership and purpose of the building as strongly as possible', and it was therefore decided not to have any title or name-plate on it; in practice this proved unsatisfactory and the words The Bank of England were subsequently carved at the entrance. An adjoining Bullion Yard, cut off from the street by an archway and wrought iron gates, avoided the troublesome and potentially dangerous practice, necessary in several of the existing Branches, of loading and unloading bank notes in the road and across the pavement.

The outbreak of war in September 1939 naturally caused some delays to the building programme. The exceptionally wet weather which prevailed for much of the winter while the Branch was under construction, and the addition of several last-minute extras such as a bullion hoist, were further hazards, but even so the work was completed nearly a month ahead of schedule and well within the total sum of £127,000 authorised by Court. Southampton Branch began business on 29 April 1940, just fifteen months after the start of building. Edward Holland-Martin,* the Staff Director, was there as the doors opened at 10 a.m., and drew the first notes issued, watched by the Agent, G.E. Carr, previously Sub-Agent at Law Courts Branch.†[8]

Hull Branch had closed two months earlier on 28 February, despite representations to the Deputy Governor from Hull Corporation by letter and in person. The Corporation feared that the prestige of the city would suffer, and also told the Deputy Governor that closure of the Branch 'might emphasise the drift of industry to the south', but Catterns was able to convince them that the Bank felt that there was really no justification for maintaining the expensive organisation in Hull, or for incurring the considerable expenditure necessary if the Branch were to be modernised or rebuilt. Staff at Hull sent a final telegram to the Branch Banks Office: 'Te morituri salutamus', and received one in reply: 'Thanks for salutation Jacta alea est mors janua vitae'.[9]

Birmingham had been recommended by the Committee as the first Branch to be rebuilt because its office accommodation was very cramped

---

* Holland-Martin, Edward, see chapter 1, p. 14n.
† Carr became Agent at Law Courts Branch in 1946.

and the external masonry of the building, which dated from 1885 and had been taken over by the Bank from the Staffordshire Joint Stock Bank in 1890, was crumbling. The Agent, at the request of the Chief of Establishments, began making discreet enquiries about suitable sites in the centre of the city in November 1937; at the same period Heal was drawing up plans for a new Birmingham Branch building. The quest for a site was unsuccessful and by the following March it had been decided to adapt Heal's plans for use on the present site between St Phillip's Place and Temple Row. A search for a new site for Manchester Branch also proved unsuccessful, and pending rebuilding and the sale of Bank Chambers the Bank's Clerk of Works drew up provisional plans for alterations to the Manchester building, to which the Branch had moved in 1847 and which had been designed for it by C.R. Cockerell,* who succeeded Sir John Soane as Architect to the Bank in 1833. Preliminary moves to terminate the tenancies of Bank Chambers at both Manchester and Birmingham were made in the early months of 1939, with a view to obtaining vacant possession by March 1940.

The provision of ARP facilities at all the Branches, including the strengthening of several of the Treasuries and the construction of air-raid shelters, had been undertaken in parallel with the arrangements made in Threadneedle Street and St Luke's, as described in chapter 1. But as late as July 1939 the Committee was still hoping to be able to proceed with the rebuilding at Manchester and Birmingham, and drew up a provisional programme which envisaged work starting at the latter in May 1940, when Southampton would be nearly complete. In Manchester, conversion of the Chambers would start in January 1940, with demolition and rebuilding of the main Branch building scheduled to begin the following September. Less than two months after the formulation of this optimistic timetable, the outbreak of war meant that it had to be suspended. The Committee continued to meet infrequently until early in 1941: after that its activities, too, were suspended.[10]

The war brought a considerable number of new tasks to the Branches. The country was divided into Civil Defence Regional Areas, as a precaution against general confusion in the case of invasion, and the Branches functioned in accordance with these divisions and later with the government's instructions, issued in July 1940, about emergency arrangements for banking and currency, payments to refugees, the

---

* Cockerell, Charles Robert, 1788–1863. Architect to the Bank, 1833–55. Professor of Architecture, Royal Academy, 1840–57. He designed the Taylorian Building in Oxford. His father, Samuel Pepys Cockerell, was a pupil of Sir Robert Taylor, Architect to the Bank 1765–88.

destruction of any bank notes that could not be removed to a place of safety, and the provision of currency for the Army and the government departments. The scheme, drawn up by the War Office and the banks, provided for mobile cashiers who could obtain currency at short notice for paying troops from specified banks throughout Britain, including the Branches. The Branches also made arrangements for alternative accommodation for notes and other valuables, usually at another bank, and in June 1940 were listed by the Ministry of Home Security as 'Key Points', which meant that the Ministry would inform Head Office at once in the event of any major damage.

The duplication of records had been discussed in the Bank as early as May 1938, and was put into operation at the beginning of the following year. From the outbreak of war Branches exchanged copies of many documents and accounting records and, although they were not required because of bomb damage, the system did bear fruit in August 1944. Three Central Clearing remittances to Bristol Branch were lost in a mail-bag robbery, and the reconstruction of the necessary information was obtained from photographic copies which had been made of the cheques.

The introduction of exchange control, as described in chapter 3, gave an important new function to the Branches, all of which with the exception of Plymouth operated their own control departments. Arrangements were made for the London exchange control staff to move to Manchester, Bristol, Leeds and Newcastle should London have to be evacuated, while Head Office was prepared to receive staff from Law Courts Branch if their premises became uninhabitable. Exchange control, too, caused the Bank to open its first Office in Scotland, again described in chapter 3. All the Branches held reserve stocks of notes, although that at Southampton – which soon became an important centre for note supply and collection, covering the area from Bognor to Lyme Regis and from Bradford-on-Avon to Bournemouth – was drastically reduced early in the war. Bomb damage to the Branches has been detailed earlier, and was only really extensive at Liverpool, most of whose roof was destroyed by fire which also affected much of the interior of the building. Southampton was especially lucky in this respect, as the opposite side of the High Street was destroyed, and the only buildings left Below Bar formed a small island of which the Branch was the centre.

Staffing problems in the provinces were no less severe than in London and a certain amount of local recruitment had to take place – before the war only women and non-clerical staff had been engaged locally, the needs of the Branches for male clerks being met from Head Office. (It was made clear to new entrants to the service of the Bank that they might be

'You're going on a
journey – it will
either be Liverpool
or Manchester'

Plate 8.1    Drawing by Basil Hone in the *Old Lady of Threadneedle Street*,
December 1952

required to work for about two years at any Branch, although in practice
vacancies could sometimes be filled by those who for domestic reasons
had a particular wish to work in one Branch or another.) In order to
ensure that the Agents were properly supported during the war, five
retired pensioners of the Bank were either appointed Sub-Agents or
authorised to sign letters and documents 'for the Agents'; other staff
from Threadneedle Street and the Branches received similar authorisation. Some of these men moved about a great deal, and one of them
served during the war at five different Branches including five separate
spells at Southampton.

A further important extension of Branch work during the war was that
connected with government accounts. About 120 new ones were opened
at the Branches, principally for the Admiralty, the Air Ministry, the
Ministry of Home Security, the Ministry of Supply, the War Office, the
War Damage Commission and the Custodian of Enemy Property. Many
of the Admiralty accounts were opened in Liverpool, where also for a
time all credit effects were cleared for the Inland Revenue Department
when it moved to Llandudno in North Wales. The Army made good use
of Manchester Branch, where it operated a large and active account
entitled 'Army Pay Office, Officers' Accounts'. The Law Courts Branch
was responsible for much of the investment of surplus funds for the
Custodian of Enemy Property, who opened twenty-two accounts there.
This activity was on the whole welcomed by the Agents, who were
inclined to deplore the lack of banking work on which their young men
could be trained, although the 'somewhat unorthodox ideas and
methods' employed in the conduct of their accounts by some of the
newer Departments caused raised eyebrows and an occasional reproof.

Women benefited from the extra workload, as more and more of them had perforce to be employed in jobs from which they had always been excluded before the war. In 1943 the Chief Cashier instituted annual reports to him from each of the Agents, and as the war progressed most of them noted with a faint but perceptible air of surprise the maintenance of the Bank's high standards of efficiency by women clerks in every aspect of Branch work, including that of cashiers, both on the counter and in a supervisory capacity, and even in supervising the local clearing.

Note counting, the habitual if unpopular preserve of women, was a continual problem because of shortage of staff. Before the war Branches each dealt with their own intake of £1 and 10s. notes and it was only occasionally, when a particular Branch fell behind with the work, that the excess was sent to be dealt with in Threadneedle Street. During the summer of 1942, when the Bank was being pressed to release staff to the services, arrangements were made for notes which could not be counted by the Branches to be sent up to London, and a 'percentage count' system was adopted, although unwillingly. At one time the percentage of notes cancelled without examination rose as high as 70·2, but this was exceptional. As a result of the 1942 arrangements, some fifty women were released, at a cost, as described in chapter 4, of considerable strain to the Issue Office in London. Notes of £5 and above, which until 1938 bore the name of the city of the issuing Branch, had always been sent back to Head Office via the Daily Letter* service between Branches and BBO. To guard against delay in postal deliveries, from September 1940 onwards these Letters were sent by railway under special arrangements: they were placed in a canvas bag, taken to the station by a messenger and conveyed by the next fast passenger train in the care of the guard and insured for £50. The bag was then collected by a Bank representative the following morning.

The gold which left Britain for the United States in 1939 and 1940 involved the use of the Liverpool, Plymouth and Southampton Branches, Liverpool having to take over extra vault accommodation for the work from a local branch of Martins Bank. (In Scotland, use was made of the Royal Bank of Scotland in Glasgow.) All three, together with Manchester and Bristol, also accepted inward shipments of gold and escorted them to London. Other, more unusual incidents occurred at the Branches from time to time, including the receipt of gold rescued from Norway by a British cruiser, which was taken over by Plymouth Branch and delivered to London by Branch staff. The Agent at Plymouth also held for a time

---

* A Branch Daily Letter consisted of a sealed packet containing advice of the day's transactions at the Branch, cancelled High Sum notes received from customers for payment at Head Office and cheques for collection.

a receipt for Belgian notes and coin with a nominal value of around £19m. brought into the port by an armed trawler and deposited in the Royal William Dock Yard because it was too bulky for storage in the Branch. It was Plymouth, too, which held all the invasion French franc notes before D-Day for the American authorities: the division and parcelling of the notes for the various detachments of troops was carried out in the Agent's room. The Navy deposited the Belgian Foreign Office records with Southampton Branch in 1940, packed in 773 boxes. Leeds Branch in June 1940 took over the dual control of a strong room in the premises of J. Waddington Ltd, in which some 6,300 reams of bank note paper was stored; and Bristol Branch held a number of duplicates of master tools for the imperial coinage, lodged there by the Royal Mint in the summer before the outbreak of war.[11]

The increase and variety of work during the war years was encouraging to the Branches, who, having as one Agent put it 'felt the east wind of the Economy Committee pretty keenly', were able to prove their usefulness as more than mere currency centres. There was still concern that opportunities for advancement and promotion were scarcer in the provinces than in Head Office, a feeling which was intensified in the spring of 1945 by the appointment in fairly rapid succession of Head Office men to three vacant Chief Clerkships.[12] But the pre-war feeling of isolation from the main current of Bank life had certainly been lessened by exchange control in particular, which called for much more contact with Head Office as well as with the local banking community, and provided welcome outlets for the abilities and initiative of some of the junior Branch staff.

The increasing mechanisation in Threadneedle Street, where a Central Mechanisation Office was set up within the Establishment Department in the summer of 1945, led naturally to a standardisation of work procedures and this was extended to the Branches the following year. The Inspector of Offices and Branches visited them all in 1946 with the object of 'standardising routine work processes and reducing the number of forms, books and ledgers'. Within a couple of years almost every component of Branch work was brought under uniform regulation, an exercise which involved the exchange of some 600 memoranda between BBO and Branches, and the volume of *Standing Instructions* was revised and expanded.[13] This was not always appreciated by the Agents, who complained variously of the 'passing of the glories of pre-war ledger-keeping now that we have...ploughed up all our training gallops', and, more seriously, of the progressive erosion of the Agents' 'discretion and scope for organization'.[14] Some compensation for this tighter control of banking and of security procedures, which were also vigorously over-hauled at each Branch at this period, could be found in the expanding horizons of Agent and Sub-Agent. Agents in particular were encouraged to take an increasing part in local affairs (subject to the avoidance of 'political controversy'), subscriptions to one or more clubs were paid for them, and expense accounts, virtually unknown elsewhere in the Bank, provided for relatively modest entertaining. The previously rather formless reports on local industry were sharpened up and extended, and the Agents paid an increasing number of visits to companies within their regions, often inviting the more prominent of their contacts to lunch parties when the Branches received their regular visits from pairs of Directors. The Principal of the BBO resumed his pre-war practice of making the round of the Branches at least annually, and the Agents came to Threadneedle Street every year for two or three days, for an exchange of views and meetings at which they were addressed by the Governors and other senior Bank officials. Chief Clerks of the Branches (whose authority was extended in 1952 by the power to sign 'for the Agent' in various specified transactions)[15] also began to visit Head Office to meet and talk together. More fearsome occasions were provided by the arrival at the Branch of a team from the Audit Department, appearing at irregular intervals and unheralded, usually just as the doors had closed to the public in the afternoon. Every book and record was closely checked, from government accounts to petty cash, and a detailed report was made to the Governor accompanied by comments on the overall book-keeping abilities of the Branch.

'Treasure journeys' gave the staff of the BBO the opportunity of visiting the Branches on excursions that many found enjoyable. South-ampton and Birmingham were the only Branches that could be visited within a day; journeys to the others involved an overnight stay in a hotel or, if preferred, with friends or relatives. BBO staff took it in turns to escort the notes which, having been drawn from the Issue Office, were packed in wooden boxes with the lids nailed down and secured with metal straps, then loaded on to railway-owned motor vans and taken under the control of a clerk and a messenger (both of whom received a special payment for the journey as well as expenses) to the appropriate station. The bullion van drew up alongside an armoured railway wagon, usually shunted into a convenient siding, and the notes were loaded under the dual control of Bank and railway staff, each of whom had a separate set of keys. An engine then pushed the wagon to the train, often to the great interest of bystanders whose curiosity as to what was in the van remained unsatisfied.

The escorts travelled either at the back of the wagon in a small built-in passenger compartment or in a reserved compartment as near as possible to the load. On arrival the whole procedure took place in reverse, the signature of Agent or Chief Clerk was obtained in receipt, and the following day the escorts returned to London with the paid notes under conditions of security equally strict. The number of journeys increased as the note issue rose, but there was little change in this routine throughout the 1950s apart from the fact that the bullion vans were equipped with radio telephones in 1957.[16]

No maintenance other than the most vital had been possible in the Branches during the war, and all except Southampton had become progressively shabbier and more dilapidated. When the Special Committee on Branch Premises began to meet regularly again in June 1945 one of its first concerns was to review the order of priority for rebuilding, agreeing unanimously to put Liverpool at the top of the new list because of the serious damage it had suffered. Plymouth should come next, followed by Bristol and Birmingham, and the Committee felt that Manchester, Leeds and Newcastle could be left until the other Branches had been rebuilt.[17] There was also the question of building licences, which, because of the shortage of materials, were difficult to obtain except for the most essential work; and it was recognised that whatever plans the Bank made would have to take account of the rebuilding and development programme of the various cities concerned.

At the end of 1947 the Committee was, by Order of Court, re-styled 'Special Committee on Bank Premises':[18] a change of name merely reflecting the range of its interests which even before the war had included almost all the Bank's properties in London and elsewhere. In May 1948 Bernard, the Committee's Chairman, visited Plymouth Branch to consider the necessary rebuilding. There was a good deal of uncertainty about the Corporation's intentions for the area in which the Branch was situated – demolition was likely within five to ten years and there was a distinct possibility that the building might be purchased compulsorily during that period. In Bernard's opinion the best solution would be to close the Branch altogether. The Chief Cashier, Peppiatt, agreed. Plymouth was currently incurring an annual loss of between £18,000 and £20,000, was little used for shipping or storage of gold and because it was in a lightly populated area the loss of its trade reports would be 'of little significance'. Exchange control had never been carried out there, and the whole of the west country was quite adequately served in this respect by Bristol, nor was there any local clearing. Only two of the commercial banks made significant use of Plymouth as a currency centre, and Peppiatt considered that their requirements could equally well be met by Bristol.

On 9 June the Governor told the Committee of Treasury that the decision to close Plymouth Branch had been taken. Arrangements for its demise proceeded with almost equal rapidity, and the news was made public on 7 August. Preparations were made for the transfer of accounts, the few private ones and those of government departments, the latter headed by that of the Naval Dockyard. The Branch ceased to act as a currency centre from 29 January 1949 and finally closed its doors on the evening of 15 February after an existence of just under 115 years. The premises were shortly afterwards acquired under a compulsory purchase order by Plymouth Corporation, who paid the Bank the sum of £44,600 in compensation.[19]

In July 1949 the Chief of Establishments informed the Governors that he doubted the wisdom of adhering to the pre-war plan to rebuild all the country Branches – internal modernisation should be carried out at Manchester, Liverpool, Leeds and Newcastle and this would be less expensive and troublesome than rebuilding. Birmingham, however, he felt would be 'a source of trouble' until it was completely rebuilt, because of the softness of the stone and the fact that, despite the considerable amount of money which had been spent on it, the premises were probably the most inconveniently planned of all the Branches.[20] In January 1950 the Deputy Governor decided that, because of the unlikelihood of obtaining the necessary licences and the restrictions on capital investment, there could be 'no question of rebuilding any of the Branches in the near future', and the Agents were told of this decision in March at their annual meeting at Head Office.[21]

It was thus in the wartime spirit of 'make do and mend' that the Committee had to approach the Branches during the greater part of the 1950s. The chief problem encountered at almost all of them was the increase in the note issue, which put a strain on note counting and Treasury storage space alike. The position was complicated by action under the post-war Town and Country Planning Acts; Bristol, built by Cockerell in 1847, was scheduled as an Ancient Monument in 1949 which meant that any modernisation schemes would have to be approved by the Ministry of Works.[22] Manchester was scheduled by the Ministry of Housing and Local Government as a building 'of special architectural interest' in March 1952.[23] The effect of this latter order was to place the Bank under the obligation to give at least two months' notice to the local planning authorities of any major structural alterations which were contemplated. To the Directors Sir John Hanbury-Williams and Basil (later Lord) Sanderson,* visiting the Branch shortly afterwards, it seemed 'that any opportunity for rebuilding which did indeed exist has disappeared for a long period' and that the recommendation of 'some good architect should be obtained as to how the interior of the existing building might be improved'.[24]

In consequence of this report, and following the request by the Chief Cashier at the Branch for greatly increased Treasury accommodation, plans were drawn up by Victor Heal for an overall modernisation of the interior of Manchester Branch. The necessary works were on a scale which would make the building uninhabitable while they were being carried out, and a survey of the city was made in 1953 which failed to locate any suitable alternative accommodation for the Branch. The following year it was decided that Bank Chambers – which had never been fully vacated pre-war, and were now again completely occupied – should be adapted to serve this purpose. The tenants were given notice and the building was empty by May 1955; however, both the Branch's Exchange Control Section and the bankers' Clearing House had been housed in the Chambers and although the Bank felt under no obligation to provide premises for the latter it was necessary to find somewhere for Exchange Control to move. With some difficulty, a five year lease was arranged on a building in Pall Mall.

Heal envisaged the work in four stages. Firstly the Chambers were to be adapted to house the banking activities of the Branch during the modernisation, and a Treasury and Sub-Treasury constructed under the building. The main premises would then be modernised, followed by the adaptation of part of the basement to link up with the new Treasury. Finally, Chambers would be restored 'to a form suitable for letting to tenants'. Heal estimated that Phase One would take about a year, Phase Two a further two, and work would be completed in three, at a total cost of approximately £300,000. However, the financial crisis of the autumn of 1955, and the Chancellor's request for a halt to capital expenditure, led Governor Cobbold to express to Sir George Abell† his wish that a new Treasury only should be provided (at an estimated cost of around £30,000); this was approved by Court on 22 September 1955, and costing work was put in hand. The credit squeeze at the beginning of the following year put an end even to the limited work on the new Treasury,

---

* Hanbury-Williams, Sir John – see chapter 1, p. 35.
   Sanderson 1st Baron (1960) of Ayot, Basil Sanderson, MC, 1894–1971. Chairman, Shaw Savill & Albion Co. Ltd, 1947–63. Director, Bank of England, 1943–65.
† Abell, Sir George, see chapter 1, p. 66.

but the Agent was requested to keep the Bank advised on the possibility of 'abnormal risks, both as to security and to the provision of normal facilities to bankers and public'.

Inflation and the rapid rise in the note circulation during 1956 were greater than the Bank expected or feared, and by the autumn the lack of space in Manchester's Treasury was causing considerable apprehension to both the Agent and the Committee. The Chief Cashier, O'Brien, visited Manchester to see the situation for himself and as the economic position was slightly improved the Governor decided in November that the first phase of the reconstruction programme might go ahead.[25]

Early in 1957 Heal ascertained from the Ministry of Housing and Local Government that objections to any alterations, however drastic, of the interior of the existing building were unlikely, provided that the facade was maintained. There were some reservations in the Bank about this, because it was realised that the Minister might ultimately consult the Royal Fine Art Commission, whose 'dominant member so far as 19th century architecture is concerned', Professor Albert Richardson,* might well himself object to any alterations. But by this date the uncertainty over the future of note counting at the Branches had largely replaced economic considerations as the major obstacle in the path of rebuilding plans. The Neylan Committee of 1955 assumed that no change in the system of paying notes at Branches was contemplated; the Chadder Committee of the following year accepted that, as long as recruitment at Branches was satisfactory, Branch examination of Low Sum notes would continue and checking only would be done at Debden.† Therefore every Branch would need a certain number of women to deal with High Sum notes and also to examine and cancel Low Sum notes. It was not until 1959 that the uncertainty over the role of the Paid Note Building at Debden was resolved and the decision that it should undertake the bulk of Low Sum note examination cleared away the tangle of difficulties over the size of Treasuries and Note Rooms which would be needed in any rebuilt Branch.

Manchester's new Treasury was complete by November 1957, but conditions in the note counting room became more and more congested. The total number of notes paid in there during the first half of the year was 90 million, compared with 81 million in the first half of 1956, yet the increasing number of notes had to be dealt with by fewer staff because of the lack of working space. In September 1957 O'Brien informed Abell and the Governors of his anxiety that the situation should be remedied by

---

* Richardson, Professor Albert, see chapter 2, p. 72n.    † See chapter 5, p. 189.

the note room being extended into Bank Chambers over the new Treasury: this work was put in hand early the following year.*[26]

In Birmingham, where post-war difficulties also ruled out the total rebuilding that had been envisaged by the pre-war Committee, a certain amount of re-decoration was carried out during 1949, but a visit from the Directors Basil Sanderson and Lord Braintree† in June 1950 was followed by a report highly critical of the 'large, antiquated, rambling and ill-equipped building, which was never designed for the purpose it now has to fulfil' and which only housed a small staff of some sixty all told. The Directors urged that immediate consideration should be given to modernisation of the Treasury; a further search for a new site was carried out, but without any more success than that made in 1938.

In January 1954 Abell decided that the 1937 appointment of Heal as architect for the complete Branch rebuilding programme was 'out of date', and that, although he should be retained to plan for Liverpool and Manchester, Court should rescind the appointment in view of his age, and the Birmingham project should be used to 'select and try out a possible successor to Heal'. The appointment was duly rescinded, with Heal's agreement, in April 1954; at this period he was still deeply involved with the building of New Change.[27] However it was his plans which were used for the reconstruction of the Birmingham Treasury and Sub-Treasury during 1955. Four years later, again following adverse comments by visiting Directors, serious consideration was given to pulling down Bank Chambers in order to facilitate the construction of an expanded and improved Bullion Yard; eventually it was decided to leave the Chambers standing, but the entrance to the Yard was widened in 1961 to give improved convenience and security.‡

The premises of Liverpool Branch posed considerably greater problems. In 1949, when the temporary roof of corrugated iron was still in place and no licences for the necessary steel and manpower to repair the bomb damage were obtainable, the Bank discussed the question of rebuilding on the same site with the city planning authorities. It was made clear that the Corporation would view 'with very great regret' the demolition of the Cockerell building in Castle Street, and would much prefer the Bank to carry out internal modernisation. Bank Chambers (also designed by Cockerell) could however come down at once. In August 1952 the Branch, which had been one of the first buildings to be

---

* Manchester Branch was later rebuilt on a new site; the building was open for business in January 1971.     † Braintree, Lord, see chapter 5, p. 180n.

‡ Birmingham Branch was later rebuilt on the same site; the building was open for business in November 1970.

Plate 8.2   Liverpool Branch in Castle Street, designed by Charles Cockerell in 1849 and occupied by the Bank until 1986

surveyed for the government under the auspices of the National Buildings Record Survey, was scheduled as a building of special architectural or historic importance under the provisions of the Town and Country Planning Act, 1947.[28]

It was not until the autumn of the same year that the licences were forthcoming for a permanent roof, and even then the Bank was unable to get permission to restore the third floor, which had also been badly damaged by fire, because it could not claim a need for the floor for a specific purpose. One of Heal's assistants visited the Branch in 1953 – during which, as it was Coronation year, the paintwork was washed down – and made some preliminary plans for modernisation, but no work had been started by the time a new Agent, D.D.W. Wynn-Williams, took over in the summer of 1954. His 'first shock of discovery' of what he called 'this filthy hole' prompted an urgent request to the Establishment Department for an improved entrance for Treasure, perhaps using hoist equipment, and a larger, better lit and properly laid out Note Room. The Branch's 'rather dismal note counting record' might, he felt, be partly accounted for by the poor lighting.[29]

It was while these plans were under discussion that Professor Richardson made clear his views on Cockerell's works when he visited Threadneedle Street to discuss with the internal Fine Arts Committee some proposed alterations to the Court Room.* Among the various reference books he brought with him was his own *Monumental Architecture*, whose frontispiece showed the Castle Street elevation of Liverpool Branch. Geoffrey Noakes, Assistant Chief of Establishments, mentioned the Branch plans to Richardson and asked the architect his views on the building: 'Cockerell at his very best' was Richardson's uncompromising reply, and he went on to say that should the Bank demolish the building and erect a modern one in its place: 'You would deserve to have the wrath of God called down on you for it would be vandalism of the very worst kind.' It was quite obvious, remarked Noakes, 'that if any attempt were made to obtain permission to demolish the existing Liverpool Branch, we should in all probability be up against not only the City fathers and the Ministry of Housing and Local Government but also the Royal Fine Art Commission, with all the publicity that would entail.'[30]

As a preliminary measure it was decided to instal a conveyor to assist the loading and unloading of Treasure: the work was approved in October 1954 but its implementation was fraught with a series of delays and difficulties which included the discovery, when the conveyor was first delivered, that it was 12 inches wider than expected and would not go through the door. It was not until almost eighteen months after its arrival at the Branch that it was working satisfactorily. Once this had been achieved it was decided to proceed with the extension of the Treasury and Sub-Treasury, which was completed without incident by April 1957. There remained the problems associated with loading and unloading the Treasure across the busy pavement of Union Court, which, at a period of increasing numbers of armed robberies, left much to be desired from the point of view of security. There was no Bullion Yard at Liverpool Branch, and the Agent put forward a scheme which involved demolition of the Chambers to provide space for one.

The principal objection to this was that, under previous plans, Chambers would be used to house the activities of the Branch during a complete rebuilding. By 1957 it was clear that it could well be ten years or more before this could be achieved, and George Head & Co., of Baker Street, were asked to examine and advise on the new idea.

Their views were favourable, but – since complete rebuilding was still envisaged as beginning in about 1962, after Manchester had been rebuilt – Abell realised that any final decision on the point must commit the future architect who, with no Bank Chambers, might find it impossible to provide space for the operation of the Branch during rebuilding. By

* See chapter 10, p. 369.

this date Heal was seventy-three years old, and his New Change building was nearing completion. Although Heal remained physically and mentally strong, Abell felt it undesirable to give him this new work and one of his younger partners, P.S. Russell ARIBA, was engaged for the task in August 1957. The tenants of the Chambers, who included the local office of the Institute of Bankers and a number of professional men such as barristers and solicitors, were duly given notice in early 1958; demolition began in April the following year. The construction of the Yard was held up for a short period by a national shortage of bricks, but was completed by January 1960.

Russell's plan for the Branch was in three phases, of which the Bullion Yard formed the first. As the economic climate was now more favourable (both nationally and domestically) the remainder of the work was able to proceed at once: it included the extension of the Treasury, reinstatement of the bomb-damaged third floor to include a flat for use as 'emergency quarters' by the Agents, and considerable replanning of rooms on the second and first floors plus the installation of a lift. It was agreed that the organisation of all this was 'well within the scope of the [Bank's] Maintenance Superintendent', and his Assistant, John Williams, was put in charge of it.[31]

The work was carried out successfully over the following four years, and was finally completed in early 1965. The demands made by the scheduling of the Branch in 1952 were met by obtaining written approval under the Town and Country Planning Act for the external alterations, which included some changes in the brickwork and windows at the back of the building and blocking up a doorway in Cook Street; internally, the work which was carried out did not, in the opinion of the Bank, affect the 'character of the building' and indeed in the Banking Hall, which was the only area to have any special architectural features, no alterations were made to the fabric. This did not, however, protect the Bank from criticism from the Victorian Society, whose Honorary Architectural Adviser, Peter Fleetwood-Hesketh, was Deputy Lieutenant of Lancashire.* In the summer of 1964 he wrote to Sir Harry Pilkington† expressing the considerable anxiety of the Society about what it understood was to be the modernisation of the principal rooms of the Branch, and he was subsequently shown round by the Agent. This visit resulted in a lengthy memorandum to the Governor critical of the fact that the work carried out 'irrespective of any intrinsic merit, pays

---

* Fleetwood-Hesketh, Peter, TD, 1905–85. Architect. Founder Member of Victorian Society, Sec. 1961–3, Hon. Architectural Adviser, 1963–85.
† Pilkington, Sir Harry, see chapter 5, p. 185n.

unnecessarily scant regard to Cockerell's original design, style and character'. The Society deplored much of the interior work, lamented the demolition of Cockerell's Bank Chambers and expressed its opinion that the whole scheme should have been supervised by a qualified architect. The Victorian Society itself 'would be only too glad to offer free advice and consultation in cases of this kind'.[32] A copy of the letter was sent by the Society to Liverpool Corporation, and a meeting with their representatives took place at the Branch. The Chief of Establishments, C.H.H. White, was deputed to answer the Society's criticisms in detail, and did so with firm but polite refutation of most of them, acquiescence on some minor points and the remark that 'many of the statements in the report are opinions which, although sincerely held by the Society, are not shared by others, including the Bank'. After this the work proceeded smoothly and was completed on schedule.*[33]

In Newcastle the Branch, opened in 1828, had moved ten years later to premises in Grey Street where it remained. Newcastle had never been high on the list of priorities either for rebuilding or modernisation: in 1954 it was scheduled as a building of architectural interest. As with all the other Branches except Southampton, its difficulties centred on shortage of space in the Treasuries and note counting areas, which were alleviated by extensive alteration and replanning, including the Banking Hall, completed in 1959. Access to Newcastle's Bullion Yard also caused problems, owing to the narrowness of the surrounding streets. Nothing could be done in this respect beyond the request of the Agent to the local corporation that, when the surrounding area was redeveloped in the 1970s, plans should include a proper service road to the Bullion Yard and the possible extension of the Yard itself.[34] Little work other than enlargement and improvement of the Treasuries was carried out at Leeds; like Newcastle it was low on the list of priorities, but the premises were, as Sir George Bolton† noted after a Director's visit, 'out of date, uninviting and only partly used'.‡[35]

By 1946 there were only two Branches with a resident Agent, Newcastle (where he was not obliged to live on the premises) and Law Courts Branch in the Strand, London, where the 1937 Committee had decided that the Agent must continue to live. The Agent's house at the Law Courts, towering above the Branch building, consisted of twenty-seven rooms including two bathrooms and three lavatories, and recog-

---

* Liverpool Branch closed in November 1986. The premises were sold to the Trustee Savings Bank.           † Bolton, Sir George, see chapter 3, p. 86n.
‡ Newcastle and Leeds Branches were both later rebuilt, in buildings opening for business in May and June 1971 respectively.

Plate 8.3   Leeds Branch – the main entrance in South Parade, with Park Row to the left. The building was designed by P.C. Hardwick in 1865 for the Bank, which occupied it until 1971

nition of its size and general awkwardness led to a new examination in 1949 of whether it was necessary, from the security angle or otherwise, for the Agent or Sub-Agent to continue to live in it. This was primarily because a new Agent would have to be appointed on the retirement of J. Wedgwood in May of that year, and it was felt that any possible successor might be discouraged from acceptance of the post if taking over the house was obligatory. The Chief Cashier and the Secretary came to the conclusion that residence at the Branch should cease to be a condition of appointment and that the house itself should be converted into flats, one of which could be offered to the Agent or Sub-Agent and others let to Directors or senior officials of the Bank at the discretion of the Governors. The cost of the conversion, estimated at about £25,000, led to the abandonment of this plan, which was succeeded by the idea of letting at least part of the building to commercial tenants.[36]

While this was under consideration the Chief Cashier, P.S. Beale, suggested the possible transference of all the work of the Law Courts Branch to Head Office, thus making the whole of the premises including the Agent's house available for sale outright. The essential difference between the work of Law Courts Branch and that of the other Branches

Plate 8.4   Law Courts Branch, occupied by the Bank from 1888 until 1975 when its work was transferred to Head Office

lay in the fact that its receipt of notes and coin was by this date very small, owing to a change made in 1948 whereby the Branch's main customer for currency, the Paymaster General, was supplied instead direct from Threadneedle Street. This gave substantial economy in handling as well as increased security. The Branch no longer had a great commitment to what was elsewhere one of the principal Branch activities, and Beale was in no doubt that 'purely from the point of view of economy, the present banking activities of the Branch could with advantage be transferred to Head Office, and it is likely we should encounter little customer opposition to such a move except in the case of the Supreme Court'. Costings of the Branch operation were subsequently made by the Secretary, which showed that it was currently incurring a loss of £20,000 – running expenses amounted to some £65,000 a year, while return on deposits (at 1 per cent) was bringing in an annual revenue of about £45,000. It was eventually decided, however, not to close the Branch and by 1960 costings showed a negligible loss 'more than offset by rentals from the offices' which had been provided by the conversion of the Agent's house.*[37]

Another Branch whose closure was seriously debated during the 1950s was Southampton. In 1952 the Directors Sir George Bolton and Andrew (later Sir Andrew) Naesmith† reported that it 'serves as a model for a modern Bank of England Branch... its staff are better housed and more comfortable than in any other Branch – perhaps with the exception of the Exchange Control office in Glasgow. Unfortunately, they have little to do...' The generous amount of first-class security accommodation was scarcely used: the fears of the Bank that war conditions would necessitate heavy use of the vaults for gold storage had not been realised. Gold movements, inwards from South Africa and outwards to New York, were still taking place via Southampton (later gold was almost exclusively flown in and out of London Heathrow), but the Branch was rarely required to play any part as the gold was moved directly to London by means of road and/or rail transport. It was only during rail and dock strikes that the spacious Branch vaults were used.

In 1955 the town of Southampton was still partly derelict from its heavy war damage and the Bank, examining the case for Branch closure, could detect 'little evidence of local initiative' towards rebuilding. Only the large-scale development of Fawley by the Standard Oil Co. of New Jersey (Esso) and the planned dock expansion gave promise of renewed vigour. The Branch, operated by about twenty staff, held just sixty-two accounts, twelve of which were government, six bankers, and the rest internal, and its deposits were normally under £1m., so it seemed that the local banks would not be seriously inconvenienced should the Branch be closed. However it was finally decided that, although not essential, it did serve a useful purpose as a currency centre: business might well expand because of Fawley, and Branches 'are part of our service to government and to the community and Southampton should not be judged, and indeed was never intended, as a purely commercial proposition'. By March 1955 the Governors had decided to keep it open, but asked for economies to be practised where possible; the chief of these was to allow the post of Deputy Chief Clerk to lapse, a Principal Clerk being appointed in his stead.[38] The increase of note work in the following two

---

* The work of the Law Courts Branch was transferred to Head Office in 1975.
† Naesmith, Sir Andrew, Kt. (1953), CBE, 1888–1961. Director, Bank of England, 1949–57.

Plate 8.5   Bristol Branch in Broad Street, designed by Charles Cockerell and occupied by the Bank from 1847 to 1963

years – 20 per cent for the Branches overall – was reflected at South-ampton, and a tentative suggestion in 1957 for a further review of the Branch's usefulness was met by the Governor's preference for review 'either in 1960 or when we are considering plans for Bristol rebuilding, whichever is earlier'.*[39]

The decisions of the Premises Committee when it met again after the war had, as described above, resulted in Bristol's advancement to third place in the league table of Branch rebuilding. It was regarded as one of Cockerell's best works, designed in the Greek Doric style: its schedule as an Ancient Monument early in 1949 precluded the idea of rebuilding on the same site, and also meant that it would be hard, if not impossible, to sell. The Agent was constructed to 'keep his eyes and ears open' for a suitable site for a completely new building, but for a long time was unsuccessful, and in 1954 work on extension of the Treasuries was undertaken, after which Heal planned the complete modernisation of the Branch to include the provision of much extra space in the Banking Hall.

* Southampton Branch was closed in 1986.

This work was deferred because of the credit squeeze of 1955; meanwhile delivery of notes proved a continuing problem because of the constrictions of the site.[40] Closure of the Plymouth Branch gave the Branch extra work, and it served a large area which included Somerset, Dorset, Devon, Cornwall, Gloucestershire and South Wales.

It had always been recognised by the Bank that any scheme for a new or rebuilt Branch in Bristol would have to fit in with the ideas of the city's Post-War Town Planning Committee; its site in Broad Street was in the centre of the banking district and had escaped bombing and fire damage to a remarkable extent when compared with neighbouring areas. Early in 1956, the Agent drew the Bank's attention to a possible site on the corner of High Street and Wine Street, forming part of a large bomb site currently in use as a car park.[41] By 25 January 1956 the Governor was able to tell the Committee of Treasury that he had agreed that enquiries could be made of the Bristol Corporation as to their willingness to give the Bank first refusal of the lease of the site, which had an area of around 30,000 square feet. The following month it was 'tentatively reserved' by the Bank.

When the planning stage for the new building was reached in 1957, the Bank's choice of architect for the project was Sir Howard Robertson,* who had so successfully designed the new Printing Works at Debden. Heal, when he learnt that Robertson had been down to Bristol to report on the suitability of the site, was unhappy, and wrote to Abell to say that although the pre-war agreement had been waived by mutual consent 'I assumed that the spirit of the Agreement would follow automatically as and when Branches were remodelled or rebuilt. A definite departure from this particular appointment, which is known in the Profession, would be damaging and embarrassing whilst I am in active practice – a period of not less than five years I hope!' 'It would be a rash man who would guarantee that the Bristol project will be finished within the next five years' replied Abell, and after a talk with Heal he noted that the architect 'accepts that the appointment for the rebuilding of the branches is no longer operative'.[42]

Robertson reported favourably on the site, which he described as being 'a sort of sunken pit, 4–5′ below road level', with the foundations remaining from the previous department store; it would present problems and the building would be a 'snug fit', but he recommended its acquisition. Robertson's firm, Easton & Robertson,† was commissioned to carry out the project in April 1959, but even at this date there was still

---

* Robertson, Sir Howard, see chapter 5, p. 178n.
† Later Easton & Robertson, Cusdin, Preston and Smith.

some doubt as to the form the building should take, because of the uncertainty as to whether the note work was to be done at the Branches or at Debden. Robertson affirmed that he would make the front elevation 'an harmonious whole with the building being erected for the Norwich Union on the adjacent site', but his first ideas for a triangular shaped Treasury were considered by Noakes 'revolutionary and unlikely to be acceptable'. At the end of 1959 the Bank entered a formal agreement with Bristol Corporation to pay £100 a year for a five year option to build on the site. During the development period of the building a peppercorn rent would be payable; on completion the Corporation would grant the Bank a lease of the site for 200 years at an annual rent of £7,750, reviewable after 100 years.[43]

Detailed planning in the Bank, and liaison with the architect on every aspect of the interior of the building with particular emphasis on security, continued throughout 1960. In September of that year there was the first hint of forthcoming trouble when the Bristol Civic Society asked to see the plans: 'a somewhat saucy request' in Noakes' opinion, as they had not yet even been submitted to the Bristol Corporation, and in any case the Bank's architect was 'the eminent Sir Howard Robertson, who is not in the habit of building eyesores'.[44] By November, the local situation had become 'delicate and difficult'. The building was being designed by Robertson with careful attention to its relationship with surrounding buildings including the medieval church of St Nicholas and the post-war development in Wine Street itself, including the Norwich Union building which was at much the same stage as the new Branch. But opposition to both buildings was growing; there was a suspicion that, because both Branch and Norwich Union architects were from London, the pride of local architects had been hurt. The Bristol Architects' Forum was at the centre of the controversy, its principal complaint being that in the immediate post-war plan for the rebuilding of the blitzed centre of Bristol an area of just over four acres around Wine Street had been scheduled for public buildings. The intention then had been for some sort of cultural centre, with a museum and art gallery prominent among the plans. In the intervening years, however, the cultural focus of the city had gradually shifted up the hill towards the university, while two plots of land in the Wine Street area had been leased for non-cultural, non-public buildings.[45]

The Architects' Forum castigated the Corporation for its lack of candour in neither disclosing a change of intention nor applying for an amendment to the original development plans. The Wine Street area was held in 'high esteem' by Bristolians and its future was of direct public interest and should not be settled piecemeal behind the citizens' backs. The debate soon attracted national attention. Questions were tabled in the House of Commons asking the Chancellor of the Exchequer to ask the Bank 'not to proceed' with its plans, or alternatively to wait for 'discussion of proposals for comprehensive development of the site, perhaps the most important clear urban site in England'.[46] Sir William Holford* joined the chorus of protestors, and the Royal Fine Art Commission requested sight of the plans, which was granted.[47] The opinion of the newly appointed Agent in Bristol, A.E. Bilton, was plain: 'My own idea is that the Corporation have no firm idea as to how to develop the site as a whole nor where they would get the money from to do so.'[48]

At the height of the row, in May 1961, the Bank decided to exercise its option to enter into a building agreement,[48] but a few days later, before the necessary paperwork was complete, the Minister of Housing and Local Government, Henry Brooke,† wrote to the Governor:

> As you know, the Royal Fine Art Commission are greatly disturbed because no comprehensive scheme has yet been produced for the Wine Street/Castle Street area, and they fear that the buildings now proposed will spoil any chance of getting a really good scheme. They are strongly supported in this by local architectural opinion. I too am disturbed, for, in the light of a report I have just received from my Chief Architect on the whole of the area and the relationship to it of the proposed buildings, I feel sure that the Commission are right. I am almost certain to come under renewed pressure in the House to intervene, and I should find it very difficult to refuse.
>
> I have had a talk with representatives of the Bristol City Council, and I find that they now have an idea of putting a museum and an art gallery on the land adjoining that leased to you and to the Norwich Union, and laying out the rest as an open space. It seems to me that this might well prove to be a very fine idea, except that the two buildings as proposed would not fit in with it at all. Their backs would face the museum grounds, which probably ought to be laid out as a part of the whole great open space, whereas they have not been designed with any such idea in mind. It is not the fault of the architects; they did not know anything like this might come along, and the sites have cramped them. But I cannot help feeling that as soon as they know that the whole of the rest of the Castle Street/Wine Street area may be laid out as a great open space – with perhaps a museum and art gallery free-standing on part of it – they would very much want to start again...

* Holford, Sir William, see chapter 2, p. 72.
† Brooke, Baron (1966) of Cumnor, Henry Brooke, PC, CH, 1903–84. Minister of Housing and Local Government and Minister for Welsh Affairs, 1957–61.

> I know that it is very late. But this is so important, and the criticism is going to be so bitter if we do not get these buildings right, that I hope you will agree that, even now, the plans for the buildings should be reconsidered...

Brooke finished his letter by dark references to a possible 'Parliamentary storm akin to what happened over Piccadilly Circus where I had to intervene and insist on a comprehensive scheme being produced before any building went up'. He asked the Governor to come and see him, or arrange for somebody else to do so on his behalf, to discuss the whole matter.[50] The Bank decided to delay its exercise of the option and consulted Freshfields as to the powers of the Minister under the 1947 Town and Country Planning Act, learning that he could 'revoke or modify the permission already granted but the persons interested in the site can force a public enquiry to be held and after the recent incident concerning the chalk pit* I should not think he would relish such an enquiry'.[51] Shortly afterwards Brooke did indeed reject plans for a public enquiry, and eventually the Deputy Governor, Humphrey Mynors, went to see the Minister accompanied by Noakes. The meeting was also attended by representatives of the Norwich Union and Bristol Corporation; the Corporation had stood firm by its decision throughout and had no wish at all to reverse it.

After a long discussion at the Ministry, it was agreed that a further meeting should take place between the architects of all the interested parties – the Corporation, the Bank, the Norwich Union, the Ministry and the RFAC.[52] This was held in Bristol at the beginning of August. The Commission's architect made it clear that he would have liked to have been consulted at an early stage, but, in the face of the united stand made by the Corporation, Bank and Norwich Union, confined himself to some fairly minor criticisms of the design of the Branch: a request that the wall of Bullion Yard should be the same height as that of the main block, and that there should be some alterations in the treatment of the top storey which was 'unsatisfactory as viewed from the east'.[53] To these Robertson acquiesced; the Bank entered into the option agreement on 14 November 1961 and little more was heard thereafter of the 'Save Wine Street Campaign'.

The contract to build the Branch was awarded after tender to Sir Robert McAlpine and Sons who began work in February 1962; it proceeded on schedule, in spite of the freezing weather of the early

---

* The Ministry had come under fierce criticism for giving permission for the commercial extraction of chalk near a pig farm at Saffron Walden, after a public enquiry at which an inspector had submitted that the process would be harmful to the pigs.

Plate 8.6 The newly completed Bristol Branch, designed by Sir Howard Robertson in 1963

months of 1963. Robertson died in May of that year, and the project was taken over by his partner, Dr Preston. A slight flurry was caused by the demand of the local electricity authority to have a sub-station in the Bullion Yard, available for inspection at all times, as a result of the decision that the Branch should be entirely powered by electricity; this was quashed, but further difficulties over the conditions of supply were only settled after Abell appealed to the Board's Chairman.[54]

The old Branch in Broad Street was closed at 11.30 a.m. on Saturday, 23 November 1963 and Bilton and his staff carried out the move the following morning 'during matins'. They had run down the stock of notes as much as possible, but even so Bilton was greatly relieved to be able to telephone the Official-in-Charge in Threadneedle Street and report that 'all is safely gathered in'.[55] The Wine Street building opened for business at 10 a.m. the following Monday morning; it was formally opened by the Governor on 10 December and the occasion celebrated by a party at which he was presented with a pair of grape scissors by Dr Preston.[56]

The new Branch was of a conventional design, built of reinforced concrete faced with Portland stone and trimmed with black granite. Its smoothly curved facade had bold, convex glass windows in teak frames, and entrance doors of fluted silver bronze. The large Banking Hall, constructed with the minimum of sub-dividing grills and screens, was panelled in cedar of Lebanon and its handsome counter fronted with Persian walnut.[57] Innovations in the Branch included dial-operated locks – the first installed anywhere in the Bank – and solar-powered lighting in the Bullion Yard.[58] The former Branch building was sold to Bristol Corporation in November 1963 for £40,000.[59]

In Scotland, the Bank was represented by the Glasgow Office, opened in 1940 for the purpose of carrying out exchange control: there had never been a Branch in Scotland and only one outside England, Swansea. Established in 1826, Swansea lasted only thirty-three years before trading losses forced its closure and the business was transferred to Bristol. In October 1947 T. Courtis, Principal of the Glasgow Office, wrote to the Chief of Establishments, E.N. Dalton, urging the opening of a Branch in Edinburgh. Courtis noted that 'a year or so ago the Chancellor rejected such a suggestion on the grounds that it might cause controversy', but felt that the opposite would now be the case. A Branch to issue notes and coin throughout Scotland would be economical, and he added rather disingenuously that if London were 'blotted out overnight' by a bomb, it would be very useful if the Bank could carry on immediately and without interruption not only exchange control but also the work of issue banking from 'the less vulnerable Scotland'.[60]

This proposal did not meet with any great enthusiasm in Head Office. N. Redfern, Deputy Chief Cashier, replied that the Bank had been advised 'informally' in 1942 that the existence of an office in Glasgow might make them the subject of jurisdiction in the Scottish courts with regard to the management of stocks: 'The risk was considered slight, and so far as is known, no embarrassing situation has arisen. The position might be different if a Branch, i.e. a banking office of the Bank of England were established in Scotland. In any case this would presumably require legislation, since Section XV of the Country Bankers Act 1826, which gives the Bank authority to open branches outside London, refers only to England (and ? Wales).' And while defence considerations should not be ignored, the picture 'conjured up' by Courtis was not of itself a sufficiently good reason to advance his proposal.[61]

Nevertheless, there was confusion in the minds of the upper echelons of the Bank as to just what its powers might be to open a Branch outside England, and it was a question that continued to surface at intervals. The incident referred to by Courtis and Redfern had originated in doubts expressed at the time of the opening of the Glasgow Office as to whether the Bank was in fact acting *ultra vires*; in March 1942 a note on the matter was apparently handed 'informally' to the Treasury. A month later

Mynors informed Freshfields that 'it has been agreed to take no action, in spite of the expense and inconvenience that may be occasioned'. The question of incorporating in the Bank of England Act power to maintain offices in Scotland and Northern Ireland was raised in 1945, but Cobbold minuted 'Better to leave it alone, I should think'[62] and this advice was followed.

In November 1957 Sir Edmund Compton* of the Treasury wrote to O'Brien about the Country Bankers Act 1826. Parliamentary Counsel in charge of Statute Law revision wanted to know 'whether this Act is spent, and if so, whether it can be listed for repeal?'[63] Because of its relevance to the Branches, it was decided that the matter must be looked into carefully. After consulting Freshfields, the Secretary, H.N. Neatby, informed the Chief Cashier in February 1958:

> It has always been supposed in the Bank – or certainly in this Department – that a prohibition of Branches of the Bank of England *outside England* was implied in Section 15 [of the 1826 Act]... If Freshfields... are correct in saying that a body incorporated by Royal Charter has all the powers of an individual, unless they are expressly or impliedly prohibited by the Charter, we may have been wrong in thinking that Section 15 had the effect mentioned above. But if we were right in so thinking, we may run into trouble with the Scottish and Northern Irish bankers if the repeal goes through.[64]

Freshfields were asked to refer the question to Counsel in the persons of Geoffrey Cross QC and Lord McNair QC,† but before their Opinion was received, the Bank had intimated to the Treasury[65] that it was 'content to see the whole Act repealed',‡ and the wisdom of this decision was confirmed by the Queen's Counsel.

Their view was that there was nothing in the Bank's constitution to prevent it from opening Branches anywhere; also that Section 5 of the 1946 Charter specifically empowered the Court to delegate its functions, and this therefore superseded the previous explicit authority to delegate contained in Section 15 of the Country Bankers Act 1826. There was no reason to object to the repeal of this Act, and indeed there was a positive advantage in repeal, both to prevent a subsequent *ultra vires* doctrine being built up against the Bank, and to record the Bank's confidence in the extent of its powers under its Charters. While it was clear on the

---

* Compton, Sir Edmund, see chapter 1, p. 144.
† Cross, Baron (1971) of Chelsea, Geoffrey Cross, PC, Kt., 1904–89. KC, 1949; Judge of High Court, 1960–9; Lord Justice of Appeal, 1969–71. McNair, 1st Baron (1955) of Gleniffer, Arnold Duncan McNair, Kt, CBE, 1885–1975. KC, 1945; President of International Court of Justice, 1952–5.
‡ Repealed Statute Law Revision Act, 1958.

Bank's powers to operate outside England and Wales, the Opinion did not extend to the question whether local law or locally superior privileges, in, e.g. Scotland, would restrict or even preclude the Bank from conducting the business of banking there.[66] The opinion of Freshfields was that should the Bank wish to open a Branch in Northern Ireland or Scotland, the legal authorities there would have to be consulted in order to determine what limitations the 'entrenched rights of local banks and local laws' could impose on the Bank's activities.[67]

The discussion of these legal principles brought the whole question of the location of Branches into fresh consideration. A Branch in Wales was put on the agenda in the spring of 1958: the recent appointment of a Minister of State for Welsh Affairs was seen as giving the Principality 'an increased status', and it was thought that its growing industrial importance might perhaps warrant the re-establishment of a Branch. The industrial difficulties in Northern Ireland might also justify a move there.[68] In England, Governor Cobbold felt that East Anglia 'had a claim'.[69] A paper written in December 1958 by J.F.M. Smallwood,* a member of the staff of the Chief Cashier's Office working in Room 2,† summarised the possible value of a Branch in each of the three countries of Scotland, Northern Ireland and Wales and the work which each would be expected to handle.[70] The difficulties were seen as not insuperable but none the less formidable, especially in Northern Ireland where a Branch would involve the Bank not only in the problems of government banking arrangements in Ulster, but possibly in the removal of the Belfast and probably also the Dublin stock registers from the control of the Bank of Ireland. Smallwood went on to examine the desirability of establishing a Branch, or Branches, in other English locations; his conclusion was that a Branch, or, failing that, a note distribution and collection centre, might be justified in the Norwich/Ipswich/Cambridge area to cover East Anglia and afford some relief to London on note work. There was also a gap in the industrial Nottingham/Leicester area which a Branch could similarly fill. But there was no pressing requirement for any of these possibilities, in England or outside it, and the question was once more allowed to lapse.

---

* Smallwood subsequently became Auditor in 1969 and then First Deputy Chief Accountant in 1974.

† Staff in Room 2 of the CCO were principally occupied as 'Gimlets', preparing résumés of important issues for the Chief Cashier and Governors. See chapter 7, p. 231.

# 9

## OVERSEAS, ECONOMICS AND STATISTICS

It was not until 1927 that the Bank's inter-war preoccupation (stemming largely from Governor Norman's special interest in the topic) with the question of relationships between central banks was formalised by the establishment of the Central Banking Section within the Chief Cashier's Office. The Section had two main functions: to conduct the Bank's relations, both business and diplomatic, with other central banks, and to provide a 'nursery' in which selected members of the junior staff could be trained for the new responsibilities of a central bank.[1] Professor Sayers has described in some detail the Bank's activities in the 1920s and 1930s to promote and foster central banking in the Commonwealth and elsewhere, by the provision of advice (including participation in many financial missions, sometimes together with representatives from the Treasury), help in drawing up statutes and, quite frequently, personnel.[2] For example the Bank's Chief Accountant, W. H. Clegg,* became Governor of the new South African Reserve Bank in 1920 and Leslie Lefeaux,† an Assistant to the Governors and previously Deputy Chief Cashier, was appointed the first Governor of the Reserve Bank of New Zealand in 1934. This policy of what might be described as enlightened self-interest on the part of the Bank of England was one to which it adhered tenaciously: the desire to get the new banks established on the 'right', i.e. Bank-drawn lines, was combined with equally strong feelings about the importance of worldwide solidarity among central banks as a group whose centre of gravity was in London – and who were thus, inevitably, closely allied with sterling.

* Clegg, W.H., 1867–1945. Entered Bank of England, 1886, Chief Accountant, 1919–20. Governor of South African Reserve Bank, 1921–31. Director, Bank of England, 1932–7.
† Lefeaux, Leslie, 1866–1962, Entered Bank of England, 1904; Assistant to Governors, 1932; Governor of Reserve Bank of New Zealand, 1934–40.

In June 1932 it was decided, on the recommendation of the Peacock Committee,* to establish an Overseas and Foreign Department: this started work in November of that year, while the physical handling of transactions, such as the conduct of the banks' accounts with the Bank of England, remained within the Cashier's Department.[3] But already by that date, as H.A. Siepmann† (the Acting Head of the new Department) pointed out two years later, 'the Bank's business relations with other Central Banks had dwindled to insignificant proportions and practical co-operation, whether directly or through the B.I.S., was not a reality'. This was directly attributable to Britain's departure from the gold standard, which meant that monetary policy passed from the Bank to the government. Monetary policy, noted Siepmann, 'is the natural field of co-operation by Central Banks', and he thought it might be a long time before 'the opportunities for initiative are restored to us by a return to some international currency system'.

This placed a question mark over the future of the Overseas and Foreign Department, which Siepmann recognised as still on trial in 1935 but with little to justify its existence from the point of view of central banking relations: he felt that the field of active co-operation was by now limited to Scandinavia and the Empire, the latter fraught with problems of distance however direct and cordial the relationships themselves might be. Siepmann detested the notion that the Department should wither into a mere research centre (an idea he resisted strongly throughout his Bank career); on the other hand he had to concede that the opportunities for what he called 'outside jobs' were becoming less frequent and would almost certainly continue to wane. He also thought that with rare exceptions the responsibilities of conducting the foreign relations of the Bank could only be shared by the Governors with men whose earlier experience had been outside the Bank, such as Raymond Kershaw,‡ although this was in direct contradiction to what he had thought a few years before when the Department was first established.

Siepmann's long and detailed consideration of the future of the Department, which was prompted by a desire to overhaul its organisation, concluded with a survey of what work it could and should be doing. This included special jobs at home, such as the Secretaryship of the League Loans Committee, work at the BIS, preparing and presenting material for the Governors and their Advisers who dealt with central

---

* See chapter 10, p. 325.     † Siepmann, H.A., see chapter 3, p. 85n.
‡ Kershaw, R.N., 1898–1981. An Australian by birth, Kershaw entered the Bank in 1929 after spending five years with the League of Nations. Adviser, 1929–35; Adviser to the Governors, 1935–53. Chairman of London Board of Commercial Banking Co. of Sydney, 1964–6, and of Bank of New Zealand, 1963–8.

banking relations, and providing information for the Treasury. The latter was entitled to consult the Bank on foreign questions and frequently did so, often at very short notice. To a lesser extent the Department was also consulted by the Colonial Office and other government departments. In short its existence was justified, even if the purpose for which it had originally been designed no longer existed.[4]

Siepmann himself became an Adviser to the Governors on 1 March 1935, as did Cobbold who had previously been Deputy Chief of the Department: they were replaced by Frederick Powell* and M. McGrath. The work of the Department was redefined, with the emphasis on 'studying central banking developments abroad' rather than the actual work of co-operation, as well as providing the Governor, his Assistants and Advisers, with 'information of all kinds about foreign countries'. Foreign monetary, financial and economic affairs were studied, and future trends and movements anticipated as far as possible. Any potential criticism that the work of the Department was too theoretical and academic, or that its staff lacked 'practical experience of men and matters', was refuted by mention of the many outside activities on which its men had been engaged since 1932: conferences, missions to Brazil, Argentina and Salvador, the foundation of the BIS, Austrian Conversion, Brazilian, Chilean and other debt negotiations, German Clearing and League Loans Committee work. It was evident that, in spite of Siepmann's misgivings, there was the scope for men whose working experience had been confined to the Bank as well as for specially recruited outsiders like Kershaw. This was a tribute to the selection policies of the Department which had ensured a high level of intellectual (not always academic) qualifications, 'savoir faire...appearance and bearing, courtesy and tact'.[5]

For the few remaining years of peace the work continued on these lines. It was organised on a Group basis, each Group (originally six in number) being responsible for certain territories. Almost every man was proficient in at least one foreign language, and there was also a Translation Section, which worked primarily for the Department but did a certain amount of work, much of it highly confidential, on a Bank-wide basis. The chief translator, H.J. Guest, could and did work in fifteen languages including Polish, Czech and Icelandic. The Department was responsible for the production and up-dating of 'Washing Lists' (so called because of their narrow rectangular shape) which contained statistical profiles of particular countries in tabular form and

---

* Powell, F.J.J., 1890–1975. Entered Bank, 1910, Assistant Chief, O & F Dept., 1932–5, Deputy Chief, 1935–41; Adviser, Central Bank of Argentina, 1935–6. Adviser, Bank of England, 1941–6, Adviser to Governors, 1946–51.

which were provided for Committee of Treasury meetings every Wednesday. Sets of graphs illustrating the finances of the more important countries were also produced by a woman clerk. The growth of the business transacted by the governmental Export Credits Guarantee Department had brought in its train many problems associated with the credit risks of guaranteed trade with foreign countries, and Overseas kept a close watch on the risks assumed by the ECGD, giving advice as required to the Treasury on the credit ratings of the countries concerned. The Department also continued to fill the positions of the Secretary of the League Loans Committee and his assistant – as Governor Norman had undertaken at the time when the Committee had been established largely through his efforts and those of Sir Otto Niemeyer – and gave assistance and advice on defaulted debts via the Council of Foreign Bondholders (of which Niemeyer was a member). And, although the Bank was not very keen on the idea as a matter of principle, staff of the Department were occasionally lent for short periods to the Treasury.

The original concern of the Department, namely central bank co-operation, did have one remaining vestige in the production of the 'Empire Letters' and cables. A weekly communication, at first a letter and later a cable, was sent from Governor Norman to the Governors of the Empire central banks (in Australia, Canada, New Zealand and South Africa) and a few other recipients. This was supplemented by a weekly letter from the Chief Cashier and a monthly letter from the Governor, covering a wide range of financial and industrial information on the UK and, in the case of the monthly letter, comments on developments both at home and abroad.[6]

The sources of information regularly used by the Department, which included foreign newspapers and magazines, year books, annual reports, bulletins and statistical tables as well as information received privately or semi-officially from Departmental contacts abroad, numbered several hundred. All this called for a high degree of specialised filing and indexing, which was carried out by a team of seven women clerks.

The outbreak of war in September 1939 naturally swept the greater part of this orderly work aside. Many sources of information dried up, the post was unreliable or non-existent and travel became difficult and in many cases impossible. The 'research' side of the Department was necessarily reduced to a minimum – although it continued as far as possible to keep up a supply of accurate information – and its chief focus soon became the active participation in guiding the Treasury on financial policy and negotiating and implementing financial agreements with various countries. While many of its staff at all levels were of course in the

Services, several of the senior men spent long periods during the war on foreign missions. These were chiefly aimed at helping to preserve the EEA's gold and dollar reserves, preventing sterling paid to suppliers from accumulating unless there was no alternative, holding balances as securely as possible and encouraging overseas exporters to spend their sterling receipts in the overseas sterling area. Guy Watson, one of the two Deputy Principals of the Department, spent the war years in South America (he visited ten countries there and in Central America in 1943 alone, as well as the USA and, briefly, the UK), concerned with obtaining precious food and raw materials – maize, meat, tin, cotton and nitrates. J.B. Loynes (later de Loynes) and J.A.C. Osborne went to Canada, as did L.P. Thompson-McCausland and George (later Sir George) Bolton.* Others from the Department visited the USA, Spain, Russia (where a financial agreement was reached with the State Bank in late 1941), Portugal and Italy.[7]

At home, a diminished staff grappled with new problems. Many of these were inextricably bound up with those of exchange control, so much so that by the beginning of 1941 the Department seemed to Cobbold to be 'half in and half out of the Control': a few weeks later, on 1 March, it ceased to be a separate Department and became the Overseas and Foreign Office in the Cashier's Department (Exchange Control); it also absorbed the work of the former Exchange Economy Section. In charge of the Office was A.S.G. Hoar, joint Deputy Principal with the absent Watson.[8] One section of the new Office remained almost exclusively devoted to exchange control matters. This was the Group dealing with Dominion and Colonial foreign exchange regulations, which suggested measures for bringing these into line, where advisable, with the Bank of England's practice. Information was also made available to the Treasury, Colonial Office and banks in the UK as well as to the other Offices of the Control.[9]

The 1941 reorganisation, carried out for practical reasons at a time of intense pressure of work, was nevertheless much resented by many of the Overseas staff. Specially selected and trained, they regarded their work as more interesting and often more important than almost anything else carried out in the Bank: they had come to know and be known by

---

* Watson, G.M. 1905–. Entered Bank, 1924. Chief of Overseas Department, 1957, and of CBID, 1959. Adviser to Governors, 1963–5. de Loynes, J.B., CMG, 1909–69. Entered Bank, 1928; Adviser, 1955–65; Adviser to Governors, 1965–9. Thompson-McCausland, L.P., see p. 109n. Osborne, J.A.C., 1881–1971. Entered Bank, 1902. Secretary, June–November 1934; Deputy Governor, Bank of Canada, 1934–8. Adviser to Governors, Bank of England, 1938–45. Bolton, Sir G., see chapter 3, p. 86n.

Governors, Directors and Advisers, and indeed formed something of an elite both in their own estimation and that of many others. Being lumped together, no matter how expediently, with what they considered the *parvenu* activities of the Control, was a bitter experience.[10] This manifested itself in the adoption of an actively 'separatist' attitude, a variety of petty snubs and snobberies, and a quick leap to the attack when the Central Office, dealing purely with exchange control matters, was casually referred to as the 'senior office of the Control'. This prompted Hoar to a fierce rebuttal on the grounds that 'seniority should mean something. Experience, importance, responsibility...' and a demand that matters should be put right by 'public affirmation esp. through the House List'.[11]

However such irritations were not allowed to affect the quality of the work, whose volume increased steadily as the war progressed. It included liaison with exiled central banks such as Bank Polski, Norges Bank and the Banque Nationale de Belgique, relations with Allied Governments and problems arising out of British occupation of Axis or neutral territory. The War Office often asked for financial information for the use of military planning staff, requests to which the Bank acceded 'on the understanding that it would not be subsequently hashed about by other departments but that the Bank's approval would be obtained to the final shape in which it went out...'.

V.K. Bloomfield, who returned to overseas work in 1941 after an absence of five years, described his impressions of the differences from pre-war days in terms more picturesque than those usually encountered in the files:

> To me, who left O and F in 1936 and returned in 1941, the nature of the work of the Office appeared greatly changed. Then, for the most part, one's work was self-created, spun out of one's own resources, on one's own initiative, like a spider's web – one made it look as fine and symmetrical as possible, and time did not matter much, for the catching of flies was only a secondary consideration. Now, it is like nothing so much as that of a beaver left in charge of the dam during the spring floods. We have very little time to give our dam a decent finish, still less to speculate about the possible advantages of new dams of different materials, at other points, and none to spend on dam-philosophy; all we can do is to bung up the holes as well and as quickly as we can, sometimes even rebuild a section of it, and occasionally swim to the bank to get a hasty glimpse of the whole dam and make sure the river bed hasn't shifted...[12]

As the war progressed the work became increasingly focused on post-war problems, particularly in relation to central and south-east Europe. The

Plate 9.1   Overseas and Foreign Office, 1942

difficulties which would be faced by occupied countries when they were liberated were among the most pressing considerations and often involved the preparation of dossiers and handbooks such as the 194 foolscap pages on the economy of Yugoslavia written in 1944 for the War Office and the Treasury, which covered pre-war Yugoslavia and occupied Serbia and Croatia and was the only comprehensive survey of its kind ever to have been made. In the closing stages of the war there was much travel in connection with post-war reconstruction and the international meetings which led up to the formation of the International Monetary Fund and the International Bank for Reconstruction and Development.[13]

The end of the war brought various requests for staff for the Allied Control Commission in Germany, to which Hoar was seconded for a period in 1945; Loynes was lent to the Austria Commission for a year from March 1945, and was asked to extend his stay but refused. The Bank considered the Control Commissions to be extremely inefficient, and their calls on the Bank for information and assistance 'placed a heavy burden of responsibility on the Group concerned'.[14] The major preoccupations of the Office at this period were the problems of reconstruction, of safeguarding British interests, drawing up monetary agreements (eight were concluded between June 1945 and 1946, all with the active intervention of the Office, while another five were in the course of negotiation) and the policy of gradually restoring to sterling its 'erstwhile international character and availability'.

The demands of various government departments for Bank personnel also grew heavy immediately after the war – too heavy, in the view of Siepmann who deprecated the Bank being used as 'a reservoir of slave labour', and incidentally also disliked the 'linking of financial with commercial negotiations … [which] seems to involve us in a kind of tap-dance which wastes time and bespatters us with other people's dust'.[15] Siepmann personally kept a sharp eye on outside contacts, ruling who could and who could not speak on the telephone or write to named officials in the Treasury and elsewhere; letters were to be 'infrequent' and always submitted to a Principal before despatch. In contrast, the Office welcomed the possibility of travel on its own account, giving staff the ability to make personal contacts overseas, gain first-hand experience of the various countries and improve their language abilities. There was a corresponding increase in the number of visits from staff of overseas banks and financial institutions, for whom the Office arranged programmes of instruction and hospitality; in 1947 it received fifty-six such visitors, who stayed for periods of between three and forty-nine days. Much effort was also directed towards improving the supply of published information, which had suffered from lack of material (often unavailable for security reasons) and of time to collate it during the war years; several visits by senior Group men were made to the BIS during 1947 to review its sources of financial and economic data which at this date were acknowledged to be considerably superior to those of the Bank. Even so, the Filing Section of the Office numbered thirty-nine in that year.[16]

As soon as Sir Otto Niemeyer renewed his regular attendance at the monthly meetings of the BIS in Basle, the Office began once more to provide a 'bag-carrier', as it did to the Governor on many of his overseas visits. The brightest young men were selected for this task, which provided a good opportunity for assessing their potential. They were not required, except very occasionally, to take part in any meetings, but might be told to go and make contact with someone relatively junior from another central bank who happened to be present. The main area of responsibility was custody of the tickets and passports, and money to pay all the hotel and restaurant bills. (This gave rise to enjoyable but no doubt apocryphal stories of trains divided during the night, leaving a carrier who had sought more convivial company in another carriage separated from his seniors but in possession of all their travel documents.) Tips had to be bestowed according to a list, to the station masters at

Victoria and Folkestone, who also received turkeys each Christmas; they donned top hats to see off the distinguished party.

Niemeyer preferred to travel by boat and train and did so until a few years before he retired from the board of the BIS in 1965, and would give a talk en route to his bag-carrier on the origins of the BIS. Cobbold flew, which usually meant a less taxing journey unless aeroplanes were delayed or grounded, when it was the carrier's task to organise travel by the swiftest alternative route. Bag-carriers also accompanied Advisers on 'parish visits' to their particular territories.[17]

By the autumn of 1948 the future staffing policies of the office were under active consideration by Watson, who had returned to Threadneedle Street in March 1946 and been appointed an Assistant Chief Cashier (Exchange Control) with particular responsibility for the administrative transferability of sterling. He recognised two fundamental changes in the character of overseas work since pre-war days: firstly, largely owing to the pressure of work arising from UK exchange control questions, only the Empire Group had any 'real time to study and deal with the central banking subjects to which a great deal of attention was paid formerly'; and therefore few of the Group leaders had either the background or training of earlier days, and the junior staff were not getting adequate coaching or guidance. Secondly, the basic difficulty before 1939, the lack of practical work, was now completely reversed and there were so many calls on the Overseas side of the Bank that some could not be met. Watson predicted (correctly) that within the next five years there would be changes in the use of sterling, and a constant flow of negotiations with individual countries in the planning of trade interchange and means of payment, which would involve government missions with Bank representation. 'We are already called upon almost automatically to provide someone to go along and play second fiddle to the Treasury man.' International conferences and 'requests for assistance in the form of advice on central banking problems and seconding of personnel' were also going to put inevitable strain on the Office's personnel. Because the most important part of the work for the coming few years was likely to be changes in sterling availability, Watson felt that 'for the time being the Office must continue as part of the Exchange Control under the general direction of a Chief Cashier'.

Within this framework, it was necessary 'not only to have good knowledge and experience of overseas affairs but to know, and be friendly with, the people you are going to negotiate with... From this it follows that contacts must be kept green, there must be constant travel (preferably without specific object) and, broadly speaking, smooth running relationships with other central banks must be maintained (and in certain quarters the field extends far beyond our Central Bank friends).'

Watson envisaged a small group of Senior Advisers (like Siepmann before him, he felt that most of these would come from outside the Bank) and a larger group of Junior Advisers. O & F must be able to rise to fill these latter posts and the training given by the Office must be adequate if they were to go abroad as representatives of the Bank and meet people 'on level or unequal bargaining terms. Certain qualities must be developed in them at an earlier stage, not the least being complete self-reliance and self-confidence for abroad they stand alone and sometimes a long way away. It is of no help to them if during their training they are made to feel that they are merely cogs in a large machine...'[18]

These views coincided with those towards which Bolton and his Committee on Exchange Control Methods and Practice,* which was currently in session, were already inclining, and as a first result it was agreed that, in order to consolidate and co-ordinate the work of the Overseas and Foreign Office and to take account of the activities of the Office 'not directly related to Exchange Control', the Cashier's Department (Exchange Control) should be renamed Cashier's Department (Exchange Control and Overseas) with effect from 1 November 1948. A.P. (later Sir Anthony) Grafftey-Smith,† then an Acting Adviser, was appointed as an additional Deputy Chief Cashier in the new organisation. This was now expected to carry out not only its pre-war functions but additional tasks arising both out of the Bank's relations with Whitehall and its agency functions for the government with respect to UK membership of such international organisations as the IMF, the IBRD, the OEEC and the BIS. Grafftey-Smith was requested by Bolton to devote the whole of his time and attention to building up a team spirit, establishing these objectives and re-organising the Office.[19]

Since September 1946 the Bank had been recruiting 'special entrants' most of whom were Oxford or Cambridge economics or language graduates, young men with experience or qualifications considered to be potentially valuable to the Bank. As they were older than the usual intake, they were offered a slightly higher starting salary. These favoured candidates were usually, but not inevitably, destined for O & F and went round the Bank at three times the speed of the 'ordinary' entrant, taking

---

* See chapter 3, p. 112.

† Grafftey-Smith, Sir A.P., Kt. (1960), 1903–60. Entered Bank, 1923. Adviser to Governors (Acting), 1947. Deputy Chief Cashier (Exchange Control and Overseas), 1948–52. Governor, Bank of Rhodesia & Nyasaland, 1956–60.

nine months instead of the usual two and a half to three years to complete the tour. Other additions to the Office were men who possessed no special academic qualifications but who had shown more than average ability on practical, non-routine work in Exchange Control Offices. A new rank of Assistant was created at the end of 1948 for men appointed from within and outside the Bank and engaged on special work in the Office: Assistants were of equal status with Principals, but without the administrative responsibilities of the latter. Even with all this extra stiffening, however, the staff position was, and remained for some years, acute. A few women had been specially recruited in 1944 after application to the London School of Economics and Peterhouse, Cambridge, but the experiment had not on the whole proved a success, and there was no immediate attempt to repeat it.[20]

Groups were divided and sub-divided as different countries assumed importance: by 1953 there were twelve, ten of which were organised on a geographical basis and the others concerned with OEEC and Multilateral Sterling. Governor Cobbold kept himself well acquainted with the coverage and composition of the Groups: 'How well are we covered on Russia and Iron Curtain countries in O & F – language, knowledge and experience, please?' he asked Siepmann in May 1952, receiving in reply a list of eleven suitably qualified clerks and of three Advisers – J.StJ. Rootham,* J.M. (later Sir John) Stevens† and C.W.St.J. Turner,‡ – who had been in Russia or the Balkans during the war. Nonetheless it had to be admitted that 'our knowledge of what is going on in Russia and the Satellites is of course very thin by comparison with our knowledge of other countries'.[21] Two years later Cobbold asked for 'more attention' to be given to the Middle East, Latin America and the United States and Canada.[22]

'Washing lists' had disappeared during the war: they took up too much time in compilation and typing, quite apart from the scarcity of information. However in 1952 Watson decided to re-institute them, in a revised format, and excluding the Iron Curtain countries because no figures were available except those for foreign trade and travel, which themselves were 'sketchy and infrequent'. The lists were welcomed by

---

* Rootham, J.St J., 1910–90. Entered Bank, 1946; Adviser to Governors, 1957–62; Chief of CBID, 1963–4; Chief of Overseas Department, 1964–5; Assistant to Governors, 1965–7.

† Stevens, Sir J.M., 1913–73. Entered Bank, 1946; Adviser, 1946–54; Director, European Dept., IMF, 1954–6; Executive Director, Bank of England, 1957–64; Director, 1968–73. Chairman, Morgan Grenfell, 1972–3.

‡ Turner, C.W.St J., 1903–78. Entered Bank, 1922; Assistant Adviser (Acting), 1946–7; Adviser (Acting), 1948–58; Adviser, 1958–63.

Advisers and Assistants who found them of considerable use. At the same time the 'Red Books', which included all details of central bank returns, were also re-introduced after their wartime disappearance.[23]

The Bank had, as mentioned above, provided men for posts at various levels for new and developing central banks before the war. This was something which was to become much more frequent in the post-war years, as independence in India, Pakistan and Ceylon was quickly followed by nationalist aspirations in West and later East Africa. In the Caribbean, small British dependencies were equally eager for their freedom and Britain was not anxious to retain many of the more expensive ones. Countries acquired as spheres of British interest during the war, such as Iraq, Libya and Jordan, also wanted an end to foreign administration, as did Malaya, Singapore and Malta.

Thus freedom and independence for former colonial possessions was in the wind from the end of the war onwards, and the financial consequences of such emancipation was a subject of the very first importance to the Bank and to its Overseas and Foreign Office. As Eric Haslam,* author of the Bank's official history of this subject, noted, these consequences 'could be destructive if not controlled'. The finances of the Colonies were firmly rooted in the sterling system which itself came under considerable pressure after the war, and both the Treasury and the Bank were strongly committed to defend the rate and the reserves of sterling by means of co-operation with other members of the Sterling Area and with the Colonies as they attained independence. Exchange control, which was still generally accepted in the early post-war period, could hardly be expected to command indefinite support from sterling holders, and the possibility of spending, investing and trading outside the prescribed sterling system was obviously going to seem more and more desirable as the war receded into history. Sterling agreements with major holders – almost all of them orchestrated by the Bank as well as the Treasury – did secure the orderly release of the larger sterling balances accumulated during the war years, but the start of the Korean war in 1950 and the consequent upsurge in the prices of raw materials (including oil) and foodstuffs almost world-wide, meant that new sterling balances began to accrue in the hands of holders. Many of these were British colonies where independence was imminent.

These and allied problems were never far from the minds of the Governors and Advisers at this period, and Governor Cobbold's

* Haslam, E.P., 1912–. Commonwealth Bank of Australia, 1943–8. Entered Bank, 1948; Assistant Adviser, 1948–55; Adviser to Governors, 1965–72. Author of *Central Banks in the Making 1948–76,* printed at Bank of England in 1979 for private circulation.

determination that the Bank should be a prime influence in their solution found a ready reflection in the upper echelons of O & F. It was recognised that calls would be made on the Bank to supply a number of people for top or senior posts in new central banks; Governor Cobbold asked J.L. Fisher* in 1955 (apropos a draft by the latter of a paper on the imminence of the break up of the system of Currency Boards) to 'make sure we are doing everything we reasonably can to provide a reservoir of men for such jobs'. There is no doubt that one reason behind the anxiety of the Bank to fulfil any such requests was a desire to stave off possible intrusion on the part of the International Bank for Reconstruction and Development which, set up as a result of Bretton Woods like the IMF, was also like that institution in its freedom from any traditional respect for sterling.

To quote Haslam again: 'It was not, of course, a foregone conclusion that the Bank would be invited to tender help abroad; that had to be secured by skilful diplomacy, in the face of the power and prestige of the new Washington institutions and against other forces, some inimical, some merely toughly competitive, which pressed their services upon the new rulers.'[24]

In the event the strength of the old links did not weaken, and the Bank of England was almost invariably asked for help by British Colonies as they attained independence. In the first instance the need was usually for advice: whether a central bank was advisable (the Bank did not hesitate to say so when it felt that this was *not* the answer, but frequently had to bow to the determination of the country concerned to go ahead anyway) and if so, how its statutes should be framed. Here there were one or two tenets of doctrine that the Bank regarded as immutable, adhering to them during the years when growing experience of the problems of newly independent countries brought a more flexible attitude to some of the other 'ground rules'. One of the cardinal points was that of defence of an adequate cover for currency liabilities, such as had always been maintained by the Currency Boards. The Bank did recognise that some enlargement of the fiduciary backing of currencies would be inevitable, but remained firm on the need for adequate cover in the face of sometimes very strongly opposing views. The colonial currency mechanism came under fire for locking up too high a proportion of overseas reserves, which was held not only to be of unfair benefit to the UK but

---

* Fisher, J.L., CMG, 1899–1976. Entered Bank, 1921; Assistant Chief, O & F Department, 1937–9; Adviser to Governors, 1946–8; Deputy Chief Cashier, 1948–50; Adviser to Governors, 1950–9.

also to deprive the country of development opportunities. This view, in an over-simplified version, was considered by the Bank to be one of the chief dangers for new and inexperienced financial regimes, and the senior members of O & F who acted in a consultative capacity – men such as Loynes, L.F. Crick* and Watson among others – were at pains to emphasise the difference between long-term development capital and current income. Equally important to this necessity not to raid the reserves, in the Bank's opinion, was the question of the independence of the central bank from government (often difficult, if not impossible to achieve in practice) and the need for firm limitations on the power of governments to borrow from the central bank.

Once the statutes had been drawn up and accepted, often a lengthy process, the Bank was, as anticipated, frequently asked to supply staff for the new institutions, sometimes in the preparatory months before the doors were opened. Haslam's history lists nearly 300 overseas posts in new central banks and other financial institutions which were filled between 1945 and 1974 by men, and a few women, from the Bank of England. People of almost all ranks were supplied from Governor down to secretaries and filists, the bulk of them Advisers, Chief Cashiers (or General Managers) and Exchange Controllers. A high proportion of them came from ranks of O & F, after careful consideration of their suitability by their seniors. Many were given very little notice of what was to prove a major upheaval in their own lives and those of their families, sometimes because of hesitation on the part of overseas governments reluctant to commit themselves to a definite offer until the last possible moment. Forty-eight hours in which to say yes or no, followed by six weeks before departure, was not uncommon. Nor was it always an easy decision from the career point of view: a course had to be chosen between the hazards of refusal and possibly incurring a 'black mark' by so doing, and of accepting the post and perhaps losing ground at home. The Bank did however guarantee that seniority would be preserved even though promotion might not automatically follow from the fact that the overseas position was higher (sometimes considerably higher) than that held in Threadneedle Street. Wives, who played little part in their husbands' banking lives, now had to be considered too: few wives had their own careers in the 1940s and 1950s but attendant problems such as children's education, housing and perhaps elderly parents were manifold.

* Crick, L.F., 1908–85. Entered Bank, 1928; Assistant to Chief Cashier (Exchange Control and Overseas), 1948–50; Adviser, 1956–7; Deputy Chief, Overseas Department, 1957–9; Adviser, 1959–67; Adviser to Governors, 1967–8.

When the post was accepted, terms and conditions of service had to be agreed. Those appointed to senior positions such as Governor or Deputy Governor usually left the service of the Bank altogether, so that loyalty to the new institution would be undivided; however, their pension rights were preserved as was the unilateral right to re-enter the Bank at the termination of contract. Others were seconded to their new jobs for short periods and the Bank attempted to ensure that their financial status would not be impaired by the move – sometimes difficult as the new central banks could be parsimonious as well as understandably concerned that, as nationals of the country would eventually succeed to the posts, initial salary levels should not be set too high. When absolutely necessary the Bank did make some form of financial subvention, although against the practice in principle. The overall aim, modest enough, was that the Bank official who went abroad should return with a small nest-egg (of perhaps £500 in the early post-war years) of savings over and above what he might have expected to accumulate at home.

Before departure, he usually had an accelerated tour round the appropriate Departments and Offices of the Bank, and a briefing from the Advisers concerned with the country to which he was going. This, while useful in painting a broad political and financial picture, and providing introductions to, or at least character sketches of, the more important figures, was rarely able to fill in the actual details of daily life. Advisers had little firsthand experience of such hazards as tribal rivalries which could make for managerial difficulties, problems of climate, servants, water and electricity supplies and so on, and these were things which could only be appreciated on the spot. Working conditions bore little or no resemblance to those in Threadneedle Street, and Governors and Chief Cashiers were often called upon to roll up their sleeves and shift boxes of notes and coin or type their own letters, rather than being able to 'sit...apart from [one's] fellows, surrounded by highly trained subordinates, and playing a large part in certain aspects of policy'. Highly trained subordinates there rarely were, and not the least of the benefits conferred on the new banks was the training received from the Bank of England men, most of whom recognised quite clearly that their chief function, much more important even than the defence of sterling, was to pass on the banking lore and expertise that they themselves had gained in London.

*Central Banks in the Making* gives a vivid account of the successes, and occasional failures, of many of these appointees and of their relationships, conducted from a distance and usually by letter rather than by telephone or cable, with the parent Bank of England. These were almost always good, the Bank providing advice and practical help together with a realisation that the counsels were those of perfection and could not always be followed to the letter. For the most part the men were left to get on with their jobs without interference; and for the most part they proved well adapted and capable, surprisingly so when it is considered at what short notice they were pitched into completely alien surroundings. Occasionally there was an unhappy incident but these stemmed more usually from an impossible situation within the overseas bank than from inadequacy or temperamental unsuitability.[25]

Training for the staffs of the new central banks was also available in Threadneedle Street. The Bank received increasing numbers of requests to allow men from overseas to come to London and see something of its internal workings: as early as March 1947 Cobbold, then Deputy Governor, said he viewed the entertainment and instruction of members of overseas central banks as 'desperately important', and such requests were rarely if ever refused.[26] Cobbold had perhaps imbibed the importance of this doctrine from Norman before the war – certainly he never departed from it. This threw a heavy burden on the staff of O & F, who had to arrange programmes (involving the co-operation of other Offices and Departments) varying in length from a few days to six or more months for visitors some of whom proved to have only a rudimentary grasp of banking. The initiative for such visits was usually taken by the overseas bank, but occasionally when Advisers were visiting central banks they did issue invitations to send people to Britain 'to establish contact and to learn how London works'. Watson, however, felt that a more positive approach was needed.

In October 1956, by which time he was Deputy Chief Cashier (Exchange Control and Overseas), Watson put forward proposals for a 'Commonwealth Central Banking Summer School' for men who had reached or might soon reach junior administrative grade in Commonwealth Central Banks, Currency Boards and Banking Commissions. 'Education and propaganda (although not of an overt kind)' should be disseminated on such a course:

> The sterling area is a living entity with, we believe, a real value to all members. It is not, however, sufficient for us to preach this gospel, the other members must see the advantages in practice and we would hope hear it from fellow members. Part of this they can get at long distance but a true appreciation can only be obtained if their representatives come to London and see for themselves how the mechanism works and the wide variety of facilities which London has to offer. This is particularly true of the Colonies where there is a complete absence of adequately trained personnel

to man the new Central Banks. It is therefore essential to attract visits from good men in Central Banks – or in prospective central banking countries – and to have them with us when they are young and receptive.

Watson continued by describing a possible syllabus for such a course in considerable detail, including consideration of such aspects as suitable outside speakers, accommodation, length of course (once a year lasting, say, six weeks) and numbers: best limited to between twelve and fifteen candidates. 'If the School proved a success it would become known and we might have approaches from foreign Central Banks to join in... In addition it might be convenient for senior Group men from O & F and parallel people in the CCO to attend the school in order to acquire further background which might be useful in the event of their being seconded to the new Central Banks, to Currency Boards or Banking Commissions.'[27] The Governor evidently liked the idea, and shortly after receiving Watson's memorandum he mentioned the project in general terms at the first meeting of Commonwealth Governors, which took place in London later the same month. 'Welcomed with enthusiasm, particularly by India, Pakistan and Ceylon', noted the Deputy Governor, Mynors. 'Agreed that we should try an experimental course in the spring of 1957 and see how we got on.'[28]

One who was not so enthusiastic was Governor J.E. Coyne* of the Bank of Canada who said sharply that 'no Canadian would be interested in attending any course with a "Commonwealth" label'. The Deputy Governor told him that the Bank wished to begin with Commonwealth representatives anyway, but 'might widen later', to which Coyne replied that he hoped that representatives of the Federal Reserve System would be included from the start. 'I left it that we should regret the abstention of Canada, but that he could please himself', noted Mynors.[29] Subsequently Mynors suggested that a more acceptable name might be the Central Banking Course, and it was under this title that it came into being. Eric Crawshaw, an Assistant, was put in charge of the preparatory work for the first course and had much to do in a very short time as it was decided in November 1958 that it should take place from 24 April to 5 June the following year. This rapidity was not viewed with favour throughout the Bank: O'Brien, then Chief Cashier, said that the timetable 'frankly appals me'. O'Brien also queried the original idea of including a member of the Colonial Office on the grounds that it would then be difficult to oppose 'any Treasury request to allow their people to

---

* Coyne, J.E., 1910–. Assistant to Governors, Bank of Canada, 1944–9; Deputy Governor, 1950–4; Governor, 1955–61.

learn central banking here'. For this reason, and, because of shortage of space, it was ultimately decided not to invite a candidate from the Colonial Office. Invitations went out in early February offering one place each to Commonwealth central banks, including Canada, who declined: Coyne acknowledged that the new title was an improvement, but expressed doubts about the intended syllabus which he felt was too academic. He thought it should be a conference rather than a course of tuition. A few extra places, allotted after discussion with the Colonial Office, were offered to the Colonies.[30]

Despite the harsh deadline, the six-week course was duly held at the Bank, who paid for all administrative expenses while board, lodging and travel were the responsibility of the sponsoring organisations. The study of London as a financial and commercial centre, with special reference to the Bank of England, occupied a large part of the course, which also included sections on general principles, central banking in Commonwealth countries and related problems in territories without a central bank. The course was built round lectures, primarily by Bank officials but also by a few outside speakers, followed by periods for discussion and questions. Members were divided into small groups or syndicates, under the guidance of one of the three Bank men attending the course, for the preparation of questions and exercises. Visits to such places as the Royal Mint, the Stock Exchange, the Wool and Metal Exchanges and the Bank's Printing Works were arranged, and a weekend course at Ashridge Management College on the workings of the Treasury was also included. Additionally many of the O & F staff at all levels were involved in providing hospitality to the visitors, much of it in their own homes. This first course had thirteen members, including the three from the Bank: countries represented were Ghana, New Zealand, Malaya, Ceylon, South Africa, Pakistan, Singapore, India, Australia and Rhodesia and Nyasaland. The course was judged a success by participants and administrators, the main criticism of the former being that they would have liked more time for 'assimilation and private discussion', which last had proved the most valuable feature of the course for many. Discussion also revealed a persistent undercurrent of doubt about sterling as a currency reserve because of the steady decline in its value, the vulnerability of the UK economy and the imposition, for political ends, of restrictions on its use – the recent events in Suez being particularly cited in this respect.

With a few minor alterations – the Ashridge weekend, for example, was judged 'a failure' and not repeated – the pattern of this first course in 1959 was followed for what became a biennial event. It was evident that those members without previous banking experience, of whom there were a few, had been greatly handicapped, and the problem of the unevenness of participants' abilities and experience made the fine-tuning of the syllabus particularly difficult. At one time an annual course was considered, but the time factor weighed against it – it was too disruptive of the regular work not only of the course director, his assistants and the Bank participants but of the many others throughout the Bank who were involved in giving talks.[31] By 1963 Canada's scruples had been overcome and the third course was attended by a member of the Bank of Canada's Research Department; Watson's prediction that other countries would soon be applying to be included was quickly borne out and within a few years the Bank was hard pressed to accommodate the number of banks and institutions anxious to sponsor participants.

It was made clear to all the foreign banks that the courses did not preclude their own people coming to the Bank at other times, which indeed they continue to do. Many of the visitors from overseas subsequently rose to high positions in their own banks and elsewhere, and formed useful contacts for Bank of England staff who had met and worked with them in London.

In the same month that the Bank's first course began, April 1959, there was a meeting in Sydney of the Governors of the central banks of Ceylon, Pakistan, New Zealand and Australia, together with the Economic Adviser of the Reserve Bank of India. They discussed among other things a project to establish a joint course of training for 'potential Central Bank executives', with particular reference to conditions in South East Asia, New Zealand and Australia. This project, too, had arisen out of the discussions held in London the previous October by central bank Governors of Commonwealth countries, and was thus a direct off-shoot of Watson's original idea. The first SEANZA Central Banking Course began in September 1959 at the Commonwealth Bank of Australia Staff Training college in Sydney, and it was thereafter held in alternate years with the Bank's courses – by arrangement between Governor Cobbold and Dr Coombs,* Governor of the Commonwealth Bank of Australia. From its inauguration the Bank of England regularly sent one or more officers to attend in the capacity of 'Visiting Specialists', and to give papers on such topics as Transfer of Payments and the London Money Markets.[32]

Two months before the start of the first of the Central Banking

---

* Coombs, H.C., MA, Ph.D., 1906–. Governor, Commonwealth Bank of Australia, 1949–60; Chairman, Commonwealth Bank Board, 1951–60; Governor and Chairman of Board, Reserve Bank of Australia, 1960–8.

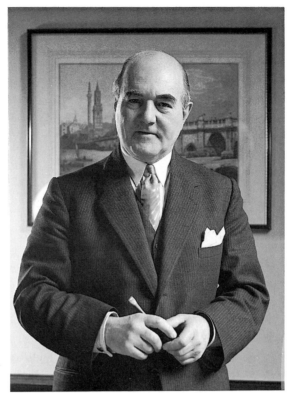

Plate 9.2   Guy Watson, Chief of Overseas Department, 1957–1959, and of Central Banking Information Department, 1959–1963

Courses, the complex structure of the Cashier's Department (Exchange Control and Overseas) had been unscrambled. Because of the dwindling importance of exchange control at this time and the simultaneous burgeoning of importance of the overseas functions, it was decided that the Department should cease to exist. The Overseas and Foreign Office was to be absorbed into an Overseas Department 'such as existed before the 1939/45 war': the Central Office and the remaining Control Offices were transferred to the Cashier's Department.[33] Guy Watson was appointed Chief of the new Overseas Department with L.F. Crick as his Deputy.

By this date the training available on the overseas side was among the most sophisticated in the Bank. From 1953 onwards there had been various attempts to implement advanced training schemes to discover men and women of promise who might ultimately be fitted for the higher administrative positions and to give them the opportunity to have a look at the Bank as a whole, to see something of policy-making and to understand how the different facets of Bank work fitted together. These efforts had been largely frustrated (particularly in the case of women) by staff shortages and recruitment difficulties. It was certainly true that the Chief Cashier's Office, and above all the work of Rooms 1 and 2 within the CCO, was recognised as the training ground that no high flier could afford to miss. But Overseas provided a wider field of opportunity. There were the visits and posts abroad already referred to, including as well as central banking posts the chance of a year spent at the BIS (working on European Payments Union matters), or one or two years as assistant to the UK Alternate Executive Director of the IMF in Washington. Overseas had also been successful in having a course on Industrial Development Finance instituted at the London School of Economics, to the first of which a man was sent in 1958, and Watson at this juncture was in the midst of supervising arrangements to send young men on a series of courses on development finance with the IBRD – a subject which was obviously going to be of increasing importance as the Colonies became independent. Special short courses at the School of Oriental and African Studies, Chatham House and the annual International Banking Summer School were also attended by clerks from Overseas.[34]

Governor Cobbold, however, was not satisfied with the state of training within the Bank and in May 1958 he had instituted a Committee under Sir Cyril Hawker's* chairmanship to consider the subject, with particular reference to Cobbold's long-felt desire for 'some form of Staff College training which [had] never met with much support or got under way'.[35] From the work of this Committee there emerged the Advanced Training Scheme which was operative from 1959 onwards. It was not, and was not intended to be, exclusive to the Overseas staff, but the Department was intimately connected with its design (A.E.G. Payton, a Principal in Overseas, drew up the outline plan) and provided a good proportion of its candidates.

As the Bank saw more of the world outside during the 1940s and 1950s, and indeed provided, via the Central Banking Course and hospitality to overseas bankers, glimpses of its own workings to an admittedly narrow section of that world in return, there was a continuing demand for more information about the Bank. It had long been notorious for the paucity of information in its annual reports: the evidence required of the Bank by the Radcliffe Committee made it clear that the traditional secretiveness, much of it for its own sake and a direct legacy from Governor Norman, could not be sustained for much longer. Naturally there could be no

---

* Hawker, Sir C., see chapter 2, p. 64n.

breach of the confidentiality preserved between banker and customer, but it was beginning to be appreciated at the highest levels within the Bank that there was much that could be disclosed without harm and perhaps with positive benefit.

The report of the Radcliffe Committee was published in August 1959. It recommended *inter alia* that more financial statistics should be collected by the Bank and other banks and institutions, that there should be more research into financial matters and that the Bank should provide more 'public exposition'. The areas which needed particular reinforcement, in the Committee's view, were the total flow of short-term credit and fixed capital investment in industry, but there were many other lacunae 'where we are still too much in the dark and where day-to-day decisions have to be taken with only a limited perception of the relevant factors'.[36] The tenor of the Committee's questioning and the unpalatable fact that the Statistics Office had found it very difficult and in some cases impossible to produce the figures requested by the Committee had forced the Governors to acknowledge that one of the prime needs was for a greatly strengthened statistical capacity. Before describing how this was achieved, and how the statistical, economic and overseas functions of the Bank were briefly welded into one Department, it is necessary to trace the evolution of statistical and economic work within the Bank.

Although statistics had been collected and analysed in a rudimentary way from the beginning of the Bank's existence, the first formal acknowledgement of their importance was in August 1921 when a tiny 'Economic Section' was formed within the Chief Cashier's Office. The Section was responsible for producing charts and tables of figures required by the Governors and senior officials. In January 1922 the first monthly report on the British economy, the banking system and public finance, the foreign exchange and other financial markets, balance of payments and comparative prices at home and abroad, was compiled and circulated in the Bank; soon afterwards it was sent to a limited number of overseas central banks. The Section expanded slightly, was renamed the Statistical Section, and in 1925 the employment of an economist was considered. Should he be a follower of Keynes? 'A man chosen from the Cambridge School, if under the influence of Mr. Keynes, might perhaps have acquired this desirable aptitude [i.e. of being able to apply economics to practical affairs]; but if he had also followed this Economist in his progressive decline and fall, dating from the *Tract on Monetary Reform*,* he would be worse than useless.' Perhaps the danger seemed to be too great – no economist was then employed, but the work continued

* Published 1923.

to expand and in 1926 the charts supplied to Court were replaced by a typewritten *Statistical Summary*. A year later this was printed by the Bank's Printing Works at St Luke's.

In 1928 Dr Walter W. Stewart,* a former director of the Research and Statistics Department of the Federal Reserve Board, was appointed Adviser to the Bank and from this date onwards the Section was progressively strengthened. The Bank did not recruit clerks for more than two years from August 1930, but the first to be appointed after the gap was James Selwyn,† especially selected by Sir Henry Clay‡ and J.A.C. Osborne, the Principal of the Section, as an outstanding statistician. In this the Bank was somewhat ahead of its time – there was no qualified statistician in any of the major government departments at this date except in the Board of Trade which compiled trade figures. Even so the Section remained something of a 'Cinderella' and the enterprise and initiative of Osborne was frequently frustrated by the 'dead hand of precedent – everything should be done as it had been done for generations past. Even the use of diagrams and charts was regarded as new-fangled, and thus frowned upon by the Chief Cashier's Office.' The work was occasionally enlivened by esoteric problems set by Siepmann, such as checking the mathematics in a book on extra-sensory perception, calculating the probability of being run over by a car on a wet night in London or estimating, 'if a skull is taken as lasting for 100 years, how many there are in Britain'.[37]

In 1933 the Section was re-named Economics and Statistics: a 'piece of bluff', as Osborne remarked, 'which was to be justified by the advent of a real economist'. This was Humphrey Mynors,§ who joined the Bank in August of the same year from Corpus Christi College, Cambridge, where he had read economics and become a Fellow. He was a nephew of the Deputy Governor of the time, Sir Ernest Harvey,‖ and came in as joint Deputy Principal with R. Allport at the suggestion of Oliver Sprague¶ of Harvard, an Adviser, who wanted some economic assistance.[38] The arrival of Mynors coincided with an expansion of the work of the Section which had been prompted by the recommendations of the Macmillan Committee; statistics of foreign balances were collected

---

* Stewart, Dr W.W., 1885–1958. Director of division of Research and Statistics, Federal Reserve Board, 1922–5; Economic Adviser, Bank of England, 1928–30.

† Selwyn, J.B., entered Bank, 1933; Principal of Statistics Office, 1957; Deputy Chief of CBID, 1959; Adviser, 1964–70.  ‡ Clay, Sir Henry, see p. 37n.

§ Mynors, Sir Humphrey, see chapter 1, p. 37n.

‖ Harvey, Sir Ernest, see chapter 6, p. 205.

¶ Sprague, O.M.W., 1873–1953. Professor of Banking and Finance, Harvard University, 1913–31; Economic and Statistical Adviser, Bank of England, 1930–3.

and regular studies of the national debt instituted. Collection and tabulation of retail trade statistics was undertaken by a specialist in this field, Miss Jessie Douglas, supervised by Clay. The *Statistical Summary* was sold commercially from 1932 onwards, again at the suggestion of the Macmillan Committee.

In the summer of 1934 Osborne was promoted to be the Secretary of the Bank, and for convenience the Section was transferred from the Cashier's to the Secretary's Department. Mynors took over as its Principal, leaving it when he became Deputy Secretary of the Bank at the end of 1938. The Section remained in the Secretary's Office and was still there at the outbreak of war. By then the staff numbered twenty-five: the work was still more compilation than analysis, and although its volume had risen its range remained quite narrow. It answered an increasing number of questions from within the Bank and from government departments, banks and occasionally individuals in this country and from overseas banks. The monthly *Statistical Summary* had a circulation of 1,700, compared with about 450 when it was first offered to the public, but was still concerned only with the presentation of statistics, with no commentary or discussion.[39]

When war broke out the embryonic research side of the work of the Section was greatly reduced as figures became inaccessible or withheld for reasons of security, and government departments also began to build up their own statistical services. However two statistical units developed within the Bank which were of vital practical use to a country at war. The Foreign Exchange Section, which had existed within the Cashier's Department since 1931, was attached to Exchange Control in 1940. It began to analyse and interpret the huge flow of information which became available from the UK control and similar authorities in overseas sterling countries. UK banks had, for example, to report disbursements of foreign exchange and transfers of sterling to non-residents: in 1940 the Bank received approximately 5,000 of these forms per month and analysed them by purpose of payment and residence of transferee. This work was tabulated not in ledgers (the Bank's traditional method) as this would have required a very large number running concurrently, but by use of the Hollerith system of punched cards which was already in use in the Bullion Office. A new Section was the Exchange Economy Section, first set up as part of the Overseas and Foreign Office. This had the responsibility of forecasting the UK balance of payments with overseas countries, particularly the USA and Canada, in order to work out how Britain's limited foreign exchange assets should best be employed. The preparation of these highly important figures (in a form later known as the 'Dossier') was helped by the Section's links with O & F, which provided information about the overseas countries, but was hindered by its separation from the FE Exchange Section and from the Economics and Statistics Section. It was in the latter that the knowledge of balance of payments technique in the Bank had developed and it was soon realised that there was a wasteful and unsatisfactory duplication of records and of effort. Accordingly in March 1942 the three units were combined in a new Statistics Office, the bulk of whose work – carried out by a staff of fifty-three – was in the field of exchange.[40] Departmental responsibility remained with the Secretary of the Bank, Mynors. He felt that an additional advantage of the reorganisation was the 'abolition of the absurd name "Economics and Statistics"'.[41]

The work on balance of payments was assisted by L.P. Thompson-McCausland,* who was recruited into the Bank as a Temporary Clerk from Moody's Economy Service. The Bank's analyses coupled with information from the Forces about the amount of dollars needed in the near future for armaments bought from the US (which had to be paid for from the 'G' Account at the Federal Reserve Bank of New York before shipment) enabled forecasts to be made of imminent dollar requirements. Likely receipts from exports and miscellaneous sources were deducted to give an indication of the shortfall. Decisions were taken by a joint Bank-Treasury Committee on Dollar Requirements as to how this should be met.[42]

After the war some of the statistical work handled by the Bank was transferred to the government. The *Statistical Summary* ceased publication at the end of 1945, in anticipation of the first number, in January 1946, of the Central Statistical Office's new publication the *Monthly Digest of Statistics* which contained all the series previously provided by the Bank plus several new ones.† The Bank considered for a time keeping the *Summary* going, and there were even fears that its disappearance might be seen as 'connected with nationalisation – possibly a clipping of the Old Lady's wings', but the Principal of the Statistics Office felt that the Bank 'should not compete for public favour'.[44] In 1947 the Bank handed over its responsibility for the retail trade statistics to the then Board of Trade (but retained the task of collection of figures relating to the wholesale textile trade, initiated by Clay in 1935, until 1958).

---

* See p. 109n.

† In 1939 a Central Economic Information Service had been set up in the Cabinet Office, with a small staff of economists and statisticians. In early 1941 this was divided into two new offices, the Economic Section of the Cabinet Secretariat and the Central Statistical Office.[43]

The importance of the Bank's intelligence gathering functions was emphasised in August 1947 when a run on sterling precipitated the suspension of convertibility. At an emergency Cabinet meeting on Sunday 17 August doubts were expressed about the adequacy of the arrangements for collection and analysis of financial statistics, 'particularly those relating to the dollar drain'. Harold Wilson, then a junior minister at the Board of Trade, was commissioned by the Chancellor at the request of the Cabinet to enquire whether exchange information at their disposal could be made 'less inadequate than it had proved to be in the matter of convertibility' and whether the crisis could have been foreseen from the figures which had been available.

Wilson was introduced to the Bank by Sir Wilfrid Eady of the Treasury, who regarded him as 'one of the most coming young men of this Government'. Mynors gave Wilson a general résumé of the material collected by the Bank, and where it came from, and Wilson's technical assistant, a Miss Mitchell, then spent several days in the Statistics Office looking at the work in detail. Mynors was relieved to learn that Wilson was 'entirely sympathetic to the idea that not all figures were always available immediately' – those from the sterling area of the Commonwealth were often particularly late. The report, made in October (by which time Wilson had become President of the Board of Trade), specifically cleared the Bank and the Treasury from any blame in not foreseeing the rate of the dollar drain from the figures available to them, and made several suggestions for tightening up the linkage of statistical information with policy-making. Both the Treasury and the Bank, he felt, should have more freedom of access to individual government departments. His account of the 'efforts made to collect material and the uses made of it within the Bank' was in general very favourable. The Treasury for its part took active steps to make the flow of figures from the Colonies both fuller and more prompt, and noted, in a letter to Cobbold, that a small statistical section was being formed under Professor Roy Allen* to work primarily for the Treasury and the Ministry of Economic Affairs, which would need 'to establish and maintain very close relations with your people'.[45]

The decade following the end of the war was an unhappy time in the Statistics Office. While it was busy in a routine sense, particularly with work for the Treasury, it was generally seen by its own staff and by the rest of the Bank as the poor relation of the more vigorous and thrusting O & F. This stemmed partly from the fact that it remained for

---

* Allen, Sir R.G.D., Kt. (1966), CBE, 1906–83. Statistical Adviser, HM Treasury, 1947–8; Professor of Statistics, London School of Economics, 1944–73.

administrative purposes within the Secretary's Department, under Secretaries who had little or no interest in its work which fell outside their long-established field of activity. Mynors, who might perhaps have rectified matters, was as Deputy Governor fully occupied in a sphere of wider influence. The undoubted talent in the Office was scarcely used, enterprise and initiative stifled, delegation almost unknown (no new file could be opened, for example, without permission from the Principal) and contact with other Departments of the Bank, and still more with commercial banks, continued to be restricted. 'Departmental walls within the Bank at this date were very thick and high' recalled one who worked there in the early 1950s, 'and none thicker and higher than those round the Statistics Office'.[46] It was only with the Treasury and to a lesser extent with the Colonial Office that a measure of productive personal contact was maintained. About a hundred of the staff were concerned with balance of payments work (compared with around ten working on domestic developments) throughout the 1950s. The detailed estimates were sent to the Treasury and the CSO, and global estimates were published in the half-yearly White Paper on the balance of payments, the first of which, relating to 1946, appeared in 1948.[47]

Morale in the Office slowly improved as the 1950s progressed. There was more movement of staff between Statistics and Overseas, and the views of those who favoured analysis and economic research, which would be valuable to the operational side of the Bank and hence to government as monetary policy took on a new importance after November 1951, began to prevail. New fields of work, such as sector finance, were introduced and proved valuable analytical instruments used by both Bank and Treasury in surveying, for example, the gilt-edged market.[48]

In this freer atmosphere, and stimulated by the obvious trend of the Radcliffe enquiries, as mentioned above, as well as by the increasing amount of information made available by other banks and financial institutions, it became evident that the Bank, too, would have to step up its research – and make the fruits of that research more accessible. By the early months of 1959 serious thought was being given by W.M. Allen* to the best ways of achieving this.[49] Various organisational schemes were considered, including the transfer of the Statistics Office to the Cashier's Department, but it was finally decided to set up a completely new Department which would combine overseas functions, economics and

---

* Allen, W.M., 1908–88. Fellow in Economics, Balliol College, Oxford, 1931–48; Assistant Director of Research, IMF, 1947–9. Entered Bank 1950; Adviser, 1950–4. Adviser to Governors, 1954–64, Executive Director, 1964–70.

statistics. Not the least of the problems involved was to find a name for it; a first suggestion was the Research and Overseas Department, but this idea was short-lived. The old dislike of the word research surfaced once more: in the words of Watson

> I should deplore [the] regular work or indeed 'special investigations' being *called* 'research', even though a lot of it will be 'search'. But it all should be directed towards assisting operations, whether operations are thought of as policy formation, management, or influencing public opinion. From the standpoint of the government of the Bank, people in the Department and in other Departments, and of public opinion, there should be no suggestion that these people are 'ivory tower' or 'outside the main stream'.

He went on to advance the cause of the word 'intelligence' – 'a perfectly good English word – I think of "research" as American!'[50] However the name finally chosen was the Central Banking Information Department, or CBID.

The new Department, whose Chief was Guy Watson, began work in October 1959. It was divided into four Offices. The Overseas Office consisted of some eighty people from the former Overseas Department and was headed by Roy Heasman,* an Assistant Chief of that Department. Its work continued on a geographical Group basis as before. The 'Home Affairs' side of the work, headed by Selwyn (who had been Principal of the Statistics Office for the previous two years) was subdivided in two. The Home Intelligence Office incorporated the domestic side of the old Statistics Office while the Balance of Payments Office, around a hundred strong, dealt with the external side. A new departure was the General Office which formed a bridge between Home and Overseas. This was run by John Fforde,† an Oxford economist who had been specially recruited to the Bank two years earlier: it was to be responsible for economic studies for the use of the Governors and Advisers, and also for any new publications which the Bank might choose to launch in the wake of the recommendations of the Radcliffe Report.[51]

The Deputy Governor, Mynors, gave interviews to the City and financial correspondents of the more serious newspapers and magazines on the formation of the new Department, warning them not to look for 'eye-catching disagreements with Government' in the expanded Annual Report or any other new publications.[52] Governor Cobbold took

---

\* Heasman, R.E., 1914–76. Entered Bank, 1932, UK Alternate, EPU, 1954–5, UK Alternate Executive Director IMF, 1956–8. Adviser (Acting), 1958, Assistant Chief Overseas Dept., 1958–9, Deputy Chief CBID, 1959–64, Chief Economic Intelligence Dept., 1964–7, Chief Accountant, 1967–70, Chief Management Services Dept, 1970–3.

† Fforde, J.S., see chapter 1, p. 38n.

Plate 9.3 Sir Humphrey Mynors, painted on his retirement in 1964 by Lawrence Gowing RA. Mynors was Deputy Governor from 1954 to 1964

advantage of the Lord Mayor's Dinner for 'the Bankers and Merchants of the City of London' on 12 November to allude to the reorganisation in his speech. Referring to the Radcliffe Report he said:

> The one fundamental criticism, of financial institutions in general and the Bank of England in particular, is that we should go further and faster in the assembly, and more particularly in the publication, of financial information, and in the business of explaining to the public what we are about. I can only say at once that the Bank of England accept the Committee's general conclusions on this subject.
>
> In the matter of talking about what we are doing and why, we can claim over the past decade, to have moved a long way from our old habits. Our economic advisory services have also been much developed in recent years and are well integrated with the operational side of the Bank. And in forming the broad picture which we need as a background for policy we are greatly helped by our close relations with the banking system at home and

with Central Banks overseas. The more complete the picture of statistics and information, the better – though it will not necessarily tell you what is going to happen next month or next year, which is always the sixty-four dollar question.

But I fully agree that our work on financial statistics can be much further expanded, in co-operation with the other main financial institutions, to the advantage of ourselves and others. I see much force in the argument that, in modern conditions, the Bank of England should develop research and information, as a service to the public, in a way which would have been quite foreign to our earlier traditions. We have already undertaken to produce a more detailed annual report, and we shall hope in due course to supplement it with some other form of publication.

All this will put a lot of new work on the Bank. We have already made some organisational changes to prepare for this extra load; the formation of a new department bringing together our various services concerned with overseas relations was announced last month and we shall strengthen it progressively as required. I would only ask the forbearance of our friends and our critics if we continue to advance a little gradually, preferring quality to quantity of output and avoiding waste of manpower by unnecessary duplication of statistics...[53]

The new departmental structure lasted just under four and a half years. The main area of growth was in the Home Intelligence Office, which expanded from a staff of less than twenty at its inception to nearly seventy. Radcliffe's recommendations for the increase in statistics collected from banks and other financial institutions were largely implemented, and as well as this there was more analysis of domestic financial developments and the economy as a whole. The study of sector finance was greatly developed and flow of funds analysis was begun. The Balance of Payments staff remained at about 100. The responsibility for the official balance of payments figures was transferred from the Bank to the Central Statistical Office in 1960, largely because the estimates were by this time drawn much more from inquiries undertaken by government departments and less from exchange control sources; when the transfer was made the underlying work went on in the Bank, but the Office was reorganised by subject instead of geographically – Groups were concerned with trade, invisibles, oil transactions and so on. New groups were also set up as required, such as commodities in 1961 and energy, including oil, two years later. The Bank remained the prime source for much of the raw data such as the sterling holdings of overseas countries and the foreign currency assets and liabilities of London banks.[54]

Staff numbers in the General Office increased to about a dozen during the life of the Department. In spite of its name, the work of this Office was in fact highly specialised, and it recruited a number of special entrants, mostly economics graduates; it was largely concerned with the enhanced Annual Report of the Bank and a new publication, the *Bank of England Quarterly Bulletin*, which was first published in December 1960 under Fforde's editorship. This contained commentary on recent financial and economic developments, articles and notes on relevant topics and a statistical annex.[55] Other studies were also undertaken by the General Office, usually covering the work of more than one Office or Department. The Office was significant, apart from the intrinsic importance of what it produced, for another reason: it signalled the first occasion when senior economists were properly integrated in the departmental structure of the Bank as opposed to their largely extra-departmental status before this date.

In practice the organisation of the CBID proved unsatisfactory in many ways; it was unwieldy, and continued to give too much emphasis to overseas finance while it became clear that domestic developments needed much more attention; and the way it had been structured tended to create barriers between the different parts of the Department. J.StJ. Rootham took over as Chief of Department in September 1963 when Watson was appointed Adviser, and almost at once began to plan its reorganisation. The CBID was disbanded at the end of February 1964 and its work divided between an Overseas Department (the third in the history of the Bank) and a new Economic Intelligence Department, headed respectively by Rootham and Heasman.[56]

# 10

# THE ESTABLISHMENT DEPARTMENT

The original organisation of the Bank in three Departments – Cashier's, Accountant's and Secretary's – remained undisturbed for two hundred years until the institution of the Auditor's Department in 1894 as the result of the indiscretions of a Chief Cashier, Frank May, which had come to light the previous year. There was no special Department to look after the interest of the staff, but their welfare and the maintenance of the premises in which they worked had always been an important aspect of the policy of the Bank. The Deputy Governor had an overall, if largely undefined, staff responsibility – 'You cannot think what it means', said Norman of his own Deputy Governorship, 'to be father and mother to five thousand souls'[1] – but necessarily had many other pressing concerns. A Staff Committee was formed in 1918 by the amalgamation of six Committees* some of which had been in existence since the eighteenth century: its members were all Directors and it met regularly every month except August to discuss details of staff policy and practice. In July 1919 the Advisory Council of Directors and Staff was formally constituted as a result of growing discontent on the part of the clerks about their treatment during and after the First World War. A Director was Chairman, five others, at least two of whom were Directors, were appointed by Court, and five selected by the staff by secret ballot and representing different grades. There were also a series of Clerks' Committees, again representative of various groups – such as Clerks, Principals, Women Clerks – with a somewhat nebulous relationship to the Advisory Council. A Staff Representative on the Council was *ex*

---

* Committees for the Examination of Clerks; Branch Banks; House and Servants; Appointments and Promotions of Staff; Inspection for the Accountant's Office; and Inspection for the Cashier's Office.

*officio* a member of the relevant Committee, and would certainly be aware of what it was doing; but he or she was not bound to represent its views to the Council, although in practice this was usually done.[2]

Each Department was concerned with the recruitment, training and promotion of its own clerks, and the importance and complexity of this work grew rapidly after the First World War in the period of heavy post-war recruitment. The Secretary's Department took an increasing role in those parts of staff administration which could be centralised, such as recruitment, payments, income tax, insurance and loans to staff, and various aspects of the work were carried out by the Comptroller*, the Staff Superintendent and the Superintendent of Women Clerks. In 1931 Governor Norman asked E.R. (later Sir Edward) Peacock† to chair a Committee which undertook the most wide-ranging investigation into the organisation of the Bank of the inter-war period. From the tenor of its questioning of the Heads of Department and others, it was evident that the Committee saw that one of its prime objectives must be to relieve the Secretary of the majority of his staff responsibilities, which by this date accounted for more than three-quarters of the work of his Department.

The Committee's Report was approved by Court on 23 June 1932. It made several important recommendations as to the functions of Directors, including the advice that two Executive Directors should immediately be appointed, one with responsibility for the money market and one for the staff, the latter to be chairman of the Staff Committee. The formation of two new Departments was recommended: an Overseas Department, as described in chapter 8, and an Establishment Department. The Head of the latter should be called 'Chief of Establishments' and work under the new Staff Director: he would be responsible for 'the whole domestic organisation of the Bank, other than St Luke's Printing Works', which would include everything to do with buildings, staff and welfare work. The relevant work to do with the Branches should also be transferred to the new Department. The Chief of Establishments should attend the meetings of the Rebuilding Committee and 'shall submit proposals for appointments etc. to the Staff Committee in collaboration with the other Heads of Departments'.[3]

Immediately after approving the Report, the Court appointed William Clegg‡ to be the Staff Director. A previous Chief Accountant of the

---

* The post of Comptroller was created in 1918 'to manage the internal affairs of the Bank and to co-ordinate the two sides [i.e. Cashier's and Accountant's] and generally to assist the Governor'.

† Peacock, Sir E.R., GCVO, 1871–1962. Director, Bank of England, 1920–46.

‡ See note, p. 293.

Bank, Clegg had recently returned to England after serving as the first Governor of the South African Reserve Bank for ten years, followed by a year as Chairman of the Hong Kong Currency Commission. He had been appointed to the Court in the previous April while the Peacock Committee was still in session. Clegg was soon immersed in discussions with the Heads of the existing Departments about the way the new one should operate. It began work on 7 November 1932; the Secretary of the Bank, Ronald Dale, was additionally appointed Chief of Establishments as a temporary measure in order to undertake the necessary reorganisation, which it was appreciated could not all be done at once.[4] The position of Comptroller, which had recently been vacated on the retirement of Cyril Mahon,* was allowed to lapse, and was shortly afterwards abolished.

The institution of the new Department effected a radical change in the way the sizeable Bank staff was organised, and not all the fiefdoms were absorbed without at least a token struggle. The Principal of the Branch Banks Office, in particular, fought gamely to retain some of his major staff responsibilities and functions. It had never been intended that every aspect of staff work would or could be transferred to Establishments, and most Offices retained a staff 'Corner' which continued to deal with minor, day-to-day matters. On the subject of appointments, however, the Department was to suffer a seemingly small but in fact crucial erosion of the position which the Peacock Committee had envisaged for it.

On 6 January 1933 the Heads of Department, including Dale who was still operating in his dual capacity, submitted to Clegg a memorandum suggesting modifications in the duties of the Chief of Establishments. The main one was that, although the Peacock Committee had recommended that all promotions should be 'submitted to the Staff Committee by the Chief of Establishments in collaboration with the Heads of Departments', it was now proposed that for the *higher appointments* the position should be reversed and that they should be submitted 'by the Heads of Departments in collaboration with the Chief of Establishments'. This subtle change of emphasis was seen as essential to safeguard the rights of Heads of Departments with regard to appointments and promotions. Clegg, after what seem to have been some initial misgivings, eventually agreed, and so did the members of the Peacock Committee; it was decided that the alteration was so slight as not to need submission to

---

* Mahon, Cyril Patrick. Entered Bank, 1901; Chief Cashier, 1925–9; Comptroller, 1929–32.

Plate 10.1    Edward Holland-Martin, Director from 1933 to 1948

Court.[5] Before long, the term 'higher appointments' was construed to mean all appointments above the rank of Grade 2.†

By the time the new Department had been in operation for a year, it had assumed all the work in connection with rebuilding and maintenance, all the staff duties formerly discharged by the Secretary and a considerable amount of staff work from the Chief Cashier and Chief Accountant, such as the recording and classification of reports on the Permanent Male Staff and subsequent interviews, medical reports and sick leave, disciplinary cases, investigation of cases of 'financial embarrassment' and the arrangement of loans. Two Offices which had remained outside its sphere until November 1933 were those of the Staff Superintendent and the Superintendent of Women Staff. The former

† At this date and until 1947 the male Classed Staff was composed of two Grades: Grade 2 of Probationary Clerks, Assistants, 3rd, 2nd and 1st Class Clerks, Grade 1 of 2nd Division and 1st Division Clerks. Above Grade 1 were the administrative grades.

dealt with all staff, both men and women, in regulating movements between Offices in collaboration with Principals. He also kept records such as daily attendance returns, leave and absence ledgers, addresses, overtime, costing returns and various cash payments. His Office was abolished in November 1933 and an Attendance Section created in the Establishment Department to carry out its work. The Superintendent of Women Clerks dealt with 'discipline and all feminine matters' including dress, medical affairs, report cards, resignations and marriage gratuities; she was henceforward to be 'primarily responsible to the Chief of Establishments through whom recommendations affecting Women Clerks should be taken to the Staff Director'.[6]

John Mackenzie was appointed Chief of Establishments in June 1934. The Heads of all the Departments began to meet at irregular intervals in December 1936 to discuss staff matters, chaired at this date by the Chief of Establishments.[7] Their meetings were attended by the Staff Director: Clegg ceased to be an Executive Director in 1935 (although he remained on the Court for a further two years) and Holland-Martin replaced him as Staff Director in that year. Two years later, in 1937, most of the staff work relating to the Branches was finally relinquished by the Branch Banks Office and undertaken by Establishments.[8] The Department was divided into three groups, with Offices dealing respectively with management and training, payments and premises. There was also a Welfare Office, which embraced the social and recreational side of staff management; the General Welfare Officer* acted as the connecting link between the officials of the Bank and the numerous Bank clubs and societies. These included the Bank of England Operatic, Dramatic and Orchestral Society (BEODS), all sections of the Sports Club (see below), Rifle Club, Horticultural Society, Arts Society and the Library and Literary Association. The latter, as well as running the Clerks' Library (a lending library established by the Directors in 1850), provided a sub-committee which supervised the production of *The Old Lady of Threadneedle Street*, a quarterly publication of impressively high standard with, from 1935, a full-time editor.[9]

By 1939 the Establishment Department was in charge of a total staff of 4,120 men and women, clerical and non-clerical. Until the First World War the Bank had grown slowly: in 1914 it numbered only 1,004, of whom sixty-four were Women Clerks. During that war the work increased considerably and large numbers of Temporary Clerks were

---

\* Sydney Belsham held this post, which also involved confidential counselling to members of staff with problems they did not wish to take to their own superiors or to the Establishment Department, from 1934 to 1957.

engaged to deal with it and to replace men released to the Forces. Soon after the Armistice it was decided to increase the Permanent Staff, and between 1919 and 1927 1,515 Probationary Male Clerks were admitted, as well as many women. Few of the men appointed before the Second World War were graduates. Most of them were school leavers from public and grammar schools, who needed a nomination from a Director to be considered for employment and who had to pass the Bank's own examination in Orthography, Arithmetic, English Composition and either General Knowledge or a foreign language. A handwriting certificate from the London Chamber of Commerce was also required, and for many years those who wrote with the left hand were disqualified.

The traditional recruiting policies had produced a largely homogenous male clerical staff of similar outlook and capabilities, a body of good all-rounders rather than specialists or men of first-class ability. After the probationary period (which lasted for three years before the Second World War), if all went well a clerk was admitted to the Permanent Male Staff and began his progression up the classes. Above the Classed Staff were the administrative ranks of Assistant/Deputy Principal, full Principal and finally departmental positions. Men were allocated to the Cash or Stock side shortly after permanent appointment and once 'fixed' most of them stayed there for the rest of their careers. Training was not particularly systematic. Clerks were moved round from Office to Office at approximately six monthly intervals, progress being determined by excellence in the routine work of the Bank. Those who did well in this were given a trial in one of the 'Special Offices', of which the most important was the Chief Cashier's and to which extra salary was attached.

Probationers were reported on every three months or on leaving an Office; the permanent staff usually once a year by the Office Principal.* Promotions and annual increments of salary were normally made on the third Thursday in February, known as Black Thursday (or the Feast of the Passed Over). Promotions to fill vacancies were also made throughout the year. Accelerated salary rises, sometimes as many as six or seven in a year, were possible in Special Offices and there was keen rivalry among the more able and ambitious and especially among those of the same 'election' or date of admission to the Bank.

---

* The reporting system in the Bank is one of the earliest. Clerks were reported on to the Court by the 'Committee of the house' which was in existence by 1695, and by the superior officers to the 'Standing Committees of Inspection' from 1801. By 1867 reports were extremely detailed and by an Order of the Governor covered 'the general character, disposition and ability of each of the Clerks ... their fitness for the duties which they have to perform, and any special circumstances affecting them, including their health, during the preceding year'.

The regular work of the Establishment Department was greatly increased by its close involvement in the preparations for the removal of the Accountant's Department at the outbreak of war in 1939, as well as for those remaining in London and for the often extremely complex arrangements for the men and women who joined up. Because the Accountant's Department at that time employed over 50 per cent of the total staff of the Bank, and Establishments' essential books of record were felt to be vulnerable to bomb damage in its offices on the fifth floor of Threadneedle Street, seven men and twenty-five women under Leslie Gash, the Deputy Chief, were removed to Hurstbourne, where new Sections had rapidly to be formed to deal with a range of problems quite outside their experience. By March 1942 the Establishment Department staff in Hampshire numbered 381, including 106 domestic staff and a Works Department of fifty-eight. Mackenzie, himself based in London, felt at this juncture that his Department could function more efficiently if all its activities except those immediately concerned with location affairs were concentrated in Head Office, but it was decided for the moment, because of the possibilities of air raids, to leave everyone in position.[10]

Eric Dalton was appointed joint Chief of Establishments with Mackenzie in August 1943, and shared the post with him until Mackenzie's retirement in 1945. Dalton's appointment coincided with the beginning of intensive post-war planning, and in the same month an Assistant to the Chief of Establishments, Stuart Ellis, addressed himself to 'a list of 116 questions which will have to be decided either before or soon after the end of the war'. One of the questions was 'whether it was considered desirable that "Establishment Officers" should be allocated to the Departments of the Bank to act as a connecting link between them and the Establishment Department and if so, under whose control would they be?'.[11] Ellis noted the modifications to the original remit of the Department, which he felt had seriously vitiated its authority, and cited a recent White Paper on the Organisation and Control of the Civil Services, where Establishment Officers had been appointed shortly after the end of the 1914–18 war in response to the recommendations of the Haldane and Bradbury Committees.* The White Paper stated:

> In spite of the growth of centralising tendencies the control of each department over its own staff is still a vital, vigorous and salutary principle. Of all the witnesses who have been heard none has emphasised the

---

\* Committees on the Machinery of Government (1918) and the Organisation and Staffing of Government Offices (1918–19) under the chairmanship of Viscount Haldane and John (later Baron) Bradbury respectively.

importance of maintaining the doctrine of departmental responsibility more strongly than the representatives of the Treasury itself... Departmental independence must continue, but it is an independence which must be exercised within a framework common to all departments. The provision of such a framework is, however, only one of the functions of the central authority. There must be close study of modern methods of management and organisation and wise and constructive guidance in the application of those methods to the individual administrative machine ...[12]

It was for 'such reasons', a final report on the subject by the Establishment Department stated, 'that the Heads of Department have each decided to nominate a Departmental Establishment Officer'. Laverack, the Inspector of Offices and Branches, who was strongly in favour of this move, pushed also for the institution of Office EOs, but was defeated by the combined opposition of the Secretary and Chief Accountant, who maintained that 'only the Principals of an Office could properly be an OEO'.[13]

The newly appointed Departmental Establishment Officers (DEOs) were soon playing an important role in the study of post-war problems, assessments of future numbers of staff, recruitment policies and the future of women staff, all of which they discussed in their own regular meetings and with members of the Establishment Department.*[14] The Heads of Departments, who had met monthly from July 1941 onwards and were now under the chairmanship of the Chief Cashier, focused mainly on senior appointments, promotions and disciplinary questions.

During the war the number of women rose as that of men fell but despite the mushroom growth of exchange control (which was employing 960 men and women by May 1944) the overall total staff at work in the Bank at that date numbered only 351 more than in September 1939.[15] The end of the war was obviously going to bring a need for more clerks. The seniority and prospects of the men and women joining the Forces had been safeguarded to some extent by a promise to re-appoint them 'to the rank and with the seniority they would have attained had they not been absent'. It was realised that, in order to maintain the staff in both size and vigour, recruitment of younger men would be necessary; what haunted all those concerned was the spectre of the 'Hump'. The effects of the engagement of so many men after 1919 were all too obvious. There were too many moving together 'up the ladder' with lack of promotional

---

* The chairmanship of these meetings was the subject of some contention. Until 1970 it was usually assumed by the DEO of the Cashier's Department: after that date by the Chief of Establishments.

opportunities for themselves while at the same time they blocked the paths of their younger colleagues. By the time they had reached the position of First Class Clerk, for example, the majority could only expect to continue to do the same sort of work as they had been doing in the Second and Third Classes, and a corollary of this was that the cost of doing the routine work of the Bank was and would remain abnormally high. By 1944 there were altogether too many men aged thirty-six to forty-two; and, in the future, the numbers of retirements during the ten years beginning in March 1958 would be around 1,000 – quite out of proportion to the numbers of men in the younger age groups.

To avoid repeating such a position was vitally important, but an accurate forecast of the numbers of clerks required for the post-war years was difficult to make because of the uncertainties of the future of exchange control. There had been no recruitment to the permanent staff during the war, but numbers of Temporary Clerks had been recruited. Between 200 and 300 Uncovenanted Clerks* were also working in the Bank; these were usually young men awaiting call-up, at which time their employment ceased (as it did on marriage), but a good proportion of them might be offered permanent appointments when recruitment started again. Finally, after hours of deliberation, in the spring of 1944 the Heads of Department made a tentative estimate of a post-war requirement of 1,824 male clerks, which would necessitate – to allow for wastage by 'quitters' – the appointment of some forty-five Probationary Clerks a year, including as many as possible of the younger age groups.[16]

The question of Women Clerks in the post-war years was inextricably entangled with that of the Hump and equally fraught with uneasiness and uncertainty. Women had successfully risen to the challenge of doing 'men's work' during the war, handling, in spite of initial misgivings on the part of many of the older men remaining in the Bank, work such as appearing on counters and some of the routine banking functions in the Offices. They had done especially well in the CCO, notably on the Issue and Governor & Company Posts. Many women had found opportunities for work which was much more to their taste than the traditional 'women's work' of typing, filing, operating office machinery and the soulless drudgery of bank note counting. It was accepted that women, who since early 1940 had outnumbered men in the Bank, would probably continue to do so. Outside Threadneedle Street there was 'a growing

---

* The rank of Uncovenanted Clerk – which had also been used during the nineteenth century and again in the First World War – was instituted in November 1939 and abolished in December 1955 when National Service was about to come to an end.

agitation for equality' as Deputy Governor Bernard acknowledged: the Royal Commission on Equal Pay for Equal Work for men and women was set up in the spring of 1944. Bernard felt that 'we must be prepared to cater for women who are able to and desire to do more important work than had been allotted to them hitherto. It is a grave reflection on the organisation of the Bank that there is no scope for really intelligent women in any capacity other than administration.'[17] The reverse of the coin was the inescapable fact of the high wastage rate among young women (who since the beginning of the war had been recruited from the age of sixteen), and their presence was certainly seen in many Offices as the loss of a training ground for men destined for higher posts. The marriage bar was still officially in operation although suspended during the war. Twenty-five per cent of women left the Bank within five years, and only 30 per cent reached pensionable age (fifty at this date for women), whereas, allowing for deaths and early retirement because of ill-health, 99 per cent of the male clerks did so.[18]

The memorandum by the Bank to the Royal Commission spelt the position out unequivocally:

> It is ... mainly in the simpler clerical and repetitive operations that men and women are engaged on the same work. These are the normal duties of women: men are engaged on them only as part of their initial training.

On the question of how far men and women received the same pay, the memorandum stated:

> Apart from fixed salaries for the higher posts, there is in the Bank no 'rate for the job'. The bulk of the clerical staff receive salaries according to scale, that for women being appreciably lower than that for men. Salaries are determined by (i) length of service (ii) the degree of efficiency and rank attained.* From the emphasis placed on length of service, it follows that even where only men are employed on a specific type of work, their salaries may vary considerably. In the few cases where it arises, women may receive more or less than men for doing the same work.[19]

The Bank realised that if equal pay for equal work were introduced for women in the Civil Service 'it might be difficult, on political grounds, for the Bank not to follow suit'. But, if women were paid on the same scale as men, the increased cost of salaries would be significant – and what if the Bank's charges to government were challenged? Then it might be

---

* This was the Bank two-column salary system: Ordinary Salary, based on age, and Class Salary, based on attainment.

difficult to justify the employment, on routine work, of men whose scale of salaries 'rise as high as £600 a year excluding wartime allowances'.[20]

Bernard, who in addition to being Deputy Governor had taken over the job of Staff Director from Holland-Martin in April 1943, asked the Chief of Establishments to comment on all these points in December 1944; a canvass of the views of Principals elicited, in addition to a few lame jokes about Governesses and Deputy Governesses, a variety of responses ranging from the opinion of the Principal of the $3\frac{1}{2}\%$ War Stock Office that 'men are not good judges of women, particularly where the women resort to tears or wheedling' to that of his colleague in the Bank Stock Office who felt that women were underpaid, had a full knowledge of the work in his Office and that their judgements were 'ready and reliable': a wider field of opportunity should be open to them.[21]

The women themselves were tactful, but firm. The Representatives of Women ranking above Grade 1 noted: 'It is realised that men returning from the Forces will naturally displace some of the women who have been doing their work during the war. But it is urged that women who have been tested and have proved their worth should have special consideration when final positions are being allocated. In particular we should be glad to have the assurance that sections developed and ably run by women over a period of years should be retained by them and not transferred to male control.'[22] The women also asked for more training.

The end of the war and the gradual return of the Bank's servicemen and women and the staff from the Hampshire locations meant a great deal of work for the Establishment Department, now reunited in Threadneedle Street. Recruitment to the Permanent Staff was swiftly begun: an Order of Court of 26 July 1945 abolished the requirement for candidates to obtain a Director's nomination and pass the Bank examination, for which School Certificate in four subjects was substituted.

The staff returning from the Forces were reinstated with little disruption in spite of earlier fears that some might have 'caught the spirit of restless radicalism which is unmistakable in all the Services and is likely to colour the life of the country after the war [and] ... will probably show itself in readiness to criticise faults in "Organisation and Method" and in staff management'.[23] Bank men had done well in the war – of the 700 servicemen, three-quarters had been commissioned, 230 reaching the rank of major or above. The return to office life thus gave rise to the occasional absurdity such as a brigadier being 'qualified' or trained in some routine by a girl of eighteen, but this was usually taken in good part.

In practice, however, the attempts to safeguard the career prospects of the servicemen which the Bank had so honourably made did not prove completely successful; it is hard to see how they could have done. Those who had remained in Threadneedle Street did in many cases advance their careers – especially in exchange control – to an extent which caused an undercurrent of resentment, slight but perceptible, on the part of men returning from the war.

By the summer of 1946 male Probationary Clerks were joining the Bank at the rate of about forty a year, and the probationary period had been cut from three to two years. A decision was now taken to appoint graduates. This was done very tentatively, initiated by the Order of Court of 26 September 1946 which sanctioned the recruitment 'of a certain number of young men who have experience or qualifications considered to be potentially valuable to the Bank' and could thus be up to three years older than the normal intake. All or part of the time spent acquiring such qualifications was allowed to count as service 'for all purposes other than calculation of pension'. The 'certain number' was treated with caution – at first six graduates were recruited per year and later, from 1955, eight. Graduates, known as 'Special Entrants', did an accelerated tour of the Bank's Offices but were warned that they would take little responsibility for many years. Until the end of 1950 they were recruited mainly, but not exclusively, for the Overseas side and the Statistics Office. There was keen competition for the graduate vacancies and the Bank was in a position to be 'highly selective'.

An immediate preoccupation post-war had been the urgent need for a new salary scheme. Before the war Schemes of Classification, which prescribed ranks and salary scales, had been updated every five years with intermediate adjustments when necessary; the most recent dated from March 1936. The steep rises in the cost of living during the war years had been dealt with by a series of special wartime allowances. A framework for a new scheme was drawn up in outline in 1944 but needed considerable adjustment before it emerged as a finished article in 1947. The work in producing the Classification Schemes was laborious. A Special Committee of Directors worked on each one for some six months, inviting evidence and suggestions from Heads of Departments and others, aided by a team in Establishments; each new amendment or provision was submitted for agreement by the Advisory Council of Directors and Staff. The 1947 Scheme of Classification, as well as providing for the necessary salary increases, abolished 'fixing' in Special Offices, placing all clerks under the new rank of Senior Clerk on an unallocated basis, in accordance with the Deputy Governor's express wish that there should be maximum interchangeability of promising clerks of all ranks. There were also alterations in the titles of the various grades of the Classed Staff which now progressed from 4th to 1st and then to new ranks of Senior and Principal Clerks which replaced the earlier Grade 1, and were themselves later reclassified as Deputy Superintendents and Superintendents.[24]

In the early post-war years the growth of the non-clerical staff which had begun pre-war with the rebuilding programme, continued steadily. In 1939 they had numbered about 600, compared with a clerical staff of over 3,000. They formed a number of different groups, each with its own well-defined hierarchy: Porters and Messengers (most of them attached to specific Offices), watchmen, liftmen, women cleaners and floorkeepers, at all the Bank's premises including the Branches, and all under the Head Gate Porter; the staff of the Maintenance Superintendent, and of the Chief Engineer; the banknote posters, prickers and stampers, as described in chapter 4; and others including chauffeurs, telephonists, medical staff* and the staff of the Directors' kitchen. The Head Gate Porter, responsible for 200 staff in 1939 and over 300 in the 1950s, had what was in fact one of the major managerial jobs in the Bank, although it is doubtful if many people outside Establishments realised it.

The Head Gate Porter and his Deputy had lived in the Bank until 1927, and later in Bank Buildings or Finsbury Circus: the incumbent Head Gate Porter, William Bentley, was badly injured in the raid which damaged Bank Buildings in 1944. They were among the handful of senior staff who were paid salaries as opposed to wages, tended to be rigid disciplinarians and were called 'Sir' by their subordinates. All the non-clerical staff clocked in and out, ate in separate canteens from the clerks, and had their own library and a sports club, St Christopher's, which shared grounds at the Forbanks Club in Beckenham with the messenger staff of other City banks. Messengers and Porters, whose duties were more or less interchangeable except at the senior end of the scale, had to stand at least 5 feet 8 inches in their socks although this requirement was occasionally waived, unofficially in London but officially at the Glasgow Office, if otherwise suitable candidates were slightly under height. The title of Porter was dropped in 1958; below the Porters came the Oddmen, none of whom were recruited after 1945.

* The part-time services of a doctor had been employed by the Bank since the early nineteenth century, and a nursing sister since 1918. By the mid-1950s there was a sister in charge plus two assistants. The implications of the Hippocratic oath were apparently not always appreciated by the senior Bank officials, one of whom accused the current MO, in 1952, of confusing 'the interests of the "patient", which is not his major concern, with the interest of the Bank, which is'.

Plate 10.2   The Doorkeeper receiving a message in the entrance to the Parlours. A painting by Sir Thomas Monnington RA, one of a series painted during the rebuilding of the Bank in the 1930s. On the left is Samuel Barnetson, First Parlour Messenger, centre, W.J. Strong, Doorkeeper, and on the right, H. Gardner, a Parlour Messenger

The duties of the Messengers were varied, including tidying the offices in the early morning after the floorkeepers and women cleaners had done their rounds; inkwells on every desk were filled daily and washed weekly long after the use of ball-points, at first deplored and often forbidden, had become widespread. During the day they did 'whatever was necessary to help the smooth running of the Office': an important task was receiving visitors who had been escorted from the Front Hall and showing them into waiting rooms until the Principal or Head of Department was ready to see them, when the Messenger took them into his room. 'A very important part of the Office furniture was the Messenger's seat, situated outside the Principal's office or at the end of a corridor in a suite of offices.' Those working in the Bullion, Issue and In-Tellers' Offices (the latter reckoned to be the hardest job of all) had, as described in earlier chapters, to be physically strong as did the men responsible for getting out and putting away the huge ledgers. Hernias and back injuries were an occupational hazard.

The ten or so Parlour Messengers, an elite group, personally attended Governors, Directors and Advisers, took messages, received their visitors and waited on them at lunch and when necessary at dinner, which they also served to the Officer of the Picquet and his guest* at night. About a third of the Messengers wore the Bank livery of black trousers, pink tail coat, scarlet waistcoat and silk top hat, which is possibly but not conclusively derived from the personal livery of the household of Sir John Houblon, the first Governor of the Bank in 1694. Throughout most of the 1950s they were given a new tailor-made suit every eighteen months or so. Gatekeepers usually had at least ten years' service in the Bank before they were allowed to wear the 'Gold Band' of ribbon round their silk hat. Three were on duty in the Threadneedle Street entrance, two at each of the Princes Street and Bartholomew Lane entrances (both these doors were later closed permanently for security reasons), and two or more at the entrance to the Bullion Yard. The Lothbury, or 'Works' gate, was manned and used by the works staff. The Gatekeepers were qualified to take visitors on a tour of the Front Hall to see what was for many years the longest cantilevered staircase in Europe, the Roman mosaic pavement at its foot (found during excavations for rebuilding), and the fine modern mosaics by Boris Anrep. They could also deliver a short history of the Bank from its foundation.[25]

The other Messengers wore tweed or whipcord suits, also tailor-made and replaced regularly, with black bowler hats. (The Chief of Establishments feared that if they wore brown ones they 'might be mistaken for bookmakers or distillers' vanmen').[26] The bowlers were disliked by the Messengers, who usually took them off as soon as they were out of sight of the Bank; they prided themselves on their intimate knowledge of the City and ways through its buildings, rarely getting rained on as they went about their work. Similarly it was possible for other City workers in the know – and recognised by the Gatekeepers – to take a short cut right through the Bank from Princes Street to Bartholomew Lane.

In the early days of the twentieth century many of these men had been recruited from the personal staffs of Directors and their friends; later there was a good admixture of ex-Servicemen after both World Wars. Airmen were particularly acceptable in 1945, thought to be more adaptable and less imbued with the 'Prussian attitude to discipline' fostered by the Guards.[27]

* See chapter 1, p. 13. The Officer was allowed to invite a guest to dine with him.

The Maintenance Superintendent was responsible for the upkeep of the Bank's buildings and for many of the structural alterations, the workings of safes and keys and the preparations of drawings and plans. His staff included plumbers, carpenters, draughtsmen, a scalemaker, marble polishers, storekeepers, window cleaners (for the Bank's 85,000 square feet of window glass) and labourers. The Engineering Department dates back to 1932, when a Chief Engineer for the new Bank was appointed with a staff of seven – two for generating and five for heating and ventilating: his staff numbered nearly forty by the outbreak of war and about 130 by 1959, including nearly sixty electricians. They were responsible for the heating, lighting, ventilating plant, domestic water supply (some from the Bank's own artesian wells, of which there are nine on the premises), electrical installations and lifts and the internal telephone system. The pay of the Maintenance staff and the Engineers was related to union rates rather than the Bank's own Messenger scale: none of the non-clerical staff were represented on the Advisory Council of Directors and Staff but formed their own small in-house associations, sometimes sub-divided such as the 1951 Association of Electricians on the Engineering Staff which was a breakaway from the 1948 Engineering Staff Association. By the end of the 1950s there were just over 1,000 non-clerical staff, over a sixth of the total numbers employed by the Bank.[28]

The historian of the early years of the Advisory Council of Directors and Staff, I.A. Estridge, remarked on the way the 'spirit of staff representation within the Bank has been patiently nurtured in an atmosphere of mutual confidence and respect to the benefit both of the Court of Directors and of the staff'.[29] In 1946 Holland-Martin noted that the seating arrangements during meetings of the Council had led to 'the Representatives of the Court and the Staff being referred to as sides...[which] tended to militate against the Council's operating as a consultative body and he suggested that they should be altered at future Meetings. Council agreed.' Thereafter instead of the two 'sides' sitting opposite each other they alternated round the table, and at the end of the quarterly meetings tea was served with the presence, when possible, of either the Governor or the Deputy Governor to share it.[30]

This essentially civilised approach did not preclude some tough negotiations, notable for the high standard of presentation of argument on the part of the elected representatives. In 1948 an appointment was made to the senior ranks of the Bank which provided them on occasions with a formidable opponent, but whose gift for negotiation and conciliation, and real feeling for staff problems, were to prove of immense value to employers and employees alike. This was Sir George

Plate 10.3    Sir George Abell on his appointment as a Director in 1952

Abell,* an Olympian figure who had gained a double first and triple blue at Oxford in the 1920s, subsequently joining the Indian Civil Service where he had served as Private Secretary to the last two Viceroys, Wavell and Mountbatten. Abell joined the Bank in January 1948 as an Adviser, and two months later the Governor authorised the Deputy Governor and Staff Director, Bernard, to delegate to Abell his functions 'in connection with all matters relating to Establishments, the Audit Department and St Luke's Printing Works'. A year after that, in March 1949, at the same time as Mynors took over from Bernard as Staff Director, Abell became an Assistant to the Governors responsible to them, under the general direction where appropriate of the Chairman of the Staff Committee, St Luke's Committee and the Standing Committees of Court, for internal organisation and administration and for the work of St Luke's, the Audit Department, the Inspector of Offices and Branches and the Supervisor of Expenditure. He was appointed by the Court to sit on the Advisory Council in 1949, became a Director in 1952, and remained on the Council until his retirement in 1964.[31]

The Bank was a generous and considerate employer with rates of pay significantly above those obtainable in the clearing banks on whose scales a sharp eye was kept. This did not prevent the Bank Officers' Guild (later

* See note, p. 66.

the National Union of Bank Employees, NUBE) making some determined attempts to gain a foothold in the Bank. Having failed during the war, they returned to the attack in September 1946, when the Secretary, T.G. Edwards, wrote to ask for an interview with the Governor 'on the subject of the Bank's attitude' towards the union. Governor Catto duly met the Secretary who said that he thought that 'now the Bank was in public ownership they should recognise his union, and also that he thought that some members of the Staff feared discrimination if they were known to be members of his union'. The Governor pointed out in reply that 'only a very small number of the Staff were members of the union and he had every reason to believe that they were contented and had no wish to have their terms of service negotiated by an outside body...[and] there was not, and never had been, any objection to members of the Bank's staff joining the union, nor had there been any discrimination'. He added that he would bring the whole question to the notice of the staff and that, if any member of the staff had an individual grievance which he or she preferred to be taken up with the Bank by the union, there would be no objection; if, however, the individual's complaint related to a large section of the staff, 'the approach would have to be considered from that aspect'.

A week after this interview the Governor was not best pleased to receive from Edwards a draft of an article about it which he proposed to publish in the union's magazine, *The Bank Officer*. Catto did not feel he could prohibit publication, but did point out 'that it was most unusual for an intimate talk with him to be given publicity'; undaunted, Edwards returned to the fray a few months later with the bold request for distribution of a circular he proposed to send to the staff of the Bank. 'I am afraid you are asking too much' was Catto's rejoinder;[32] Governor Cobbold refused a similar request a few years later, the Advisory Council being kept fully informed of the position and repeatedly affirming the fact that their constituents were satisfied with the representational position as it was.[33]

In June 1950 the Council received a new constitution. Its name was shortened to the Council of Directors and Staff; more importantly, the Court agreed to omit the word 'substantial' from its undertaking that no final decision would be taken regarding proposals for any 'substantial change in the terms and conditions of service of the clerical staff' without prior reference to the Council. Two years later, in March 1953, the Deputy Governor, Bernard, remarked that the younger women were 'becoming very representation-minded', and the Council was subsequently enlarged to allow another woman to represent the Third Class

Clerks of whom by that date there were nearly 1,700. There were now eighteen members in all, nine appointed by the Court and nine by the staff. In 1957 a committee was appointed by the Council to consider a staff memorandum which had expressed 'an unprecedented amount of criticism of staff representation in the Bank'.[34] There was disappointment at salaries paid since the war, in face of the 'continual rise in the cost of living', combined with a mistrust on the part of many clerks of the whole system of representation, which was viewed as 'unduly ponderous and secretive and does not move with the times'. Yet it was difficult to get clerks to undertake the time-consuming duties of representation. Many believed, rightly or wrongly, that promotion was often 'frozen' during a period of representation, and some Principals were known to be actively hostile to the involvement of their own staff, despite the explicit wish of the Governor that 'utmost facilities should be given to carry out their duties'. It remained something that the most ambitious were unlikely to undertake. A particular grievance of the staff was the lack of communication: they made known their views to members of the representative committees, and then heard no more until a decision was reached one way or another. It was felt that the committees should have more say, rather than just advising the Council, and this position was improved by the agreement of the Governors, in July 1958, that elected members of Council 'could consult not more than three members of appointed principals of clerks committees on any relevant matter'.*[35]

While the topics of most importance to the staff, and hence to the Council, were naturally those of pay and conditions of work, the Council was also much concerned not only with the regular pension scales but also with the various special pension offers which were made with the aim of flattening the Hump by encouraging early retirement. There had been two before the Second World War (in 1935 and 1938) and one in 1944; these three led to a reduction of 147 men. In 1949 the Hump consisted of 810 men between the ages of forty-one and fifty, constituting 42 per cent of the Permanent Male Staff. Several different schemes were introduced during the 1950s in further efforts to bring the numbers down. These included compulsory retirement at age sixty, introduced in 1955 on a temporary basis but never rescinded, the acceptance in 1956 (after years of discussion) of service in the 1914–18 war to rank for pension, dismissal of the Temporary and Supplementary Staffs in 1951 and 1956 respectively, and the offer of early pensions in certain circumstances. Men

---

* The Council of Directors and Staff was replaced first by the Bank of England Staff Association and then, in 1975, by the Bank's internal but independent trade union, the Bank of England Staff Organisation (BESO).

aged fifty and over and not above the rank of Principal Clerk (later, on the reintroduction of the rank of Superintendent, above that rank) were allowed to retire on a scale pension less 1 per cent for each year or part year in advance of earliest normal retirement date. The scheme was first adopted by Order of Court on 26 March 1953 on the recommendation of the 1952 Special Classification Committee, and remained in force for a year. The offer was re-opened on the same terms for two years from December 1954 and subsequently extended for a further two year period from December 1956; by November 1958 a total of sixty men had taken advantage of it. The Staff Representatives valued the concession, and it was again extended until December 1960. A slightly more favourable special offer was also made in 1959, largely because of reduction in the work of exchange control offices. In all these offers reduced the Hump by about eighty men, or approximately 10 per cent.

The schemes, as well as necessitating an immense amount of preparatory work within the Bank, and particularly in Establishments, had also to be approved by the Inland Revenue. Throughout their preparation the Bank was careful to emphasise that the granting of such concessionary pensions was primarily to ensure that the Bank's work was done in the most efficient and economical way: they were not offers made on compassionate grounds.[36]

All the Bank's pensioners were paid from a Superannuation Fund which had been established in 1934 (replacing a previous system under which pensions were granted 'at the pleasure of Court' – although in practice they were hardly ever withheld or discontinued, but occasionally diverted from a retired member of staff and a lesser amount paid to 'some dependent or member of his family'). The report of the 1933 Special Committee on Economy recommended 'a scheme for a trust fund on an actuarial basis ... which ... would in the course of time effect a very large economy for the Bank', and the Committee of Treasury and Court agreed. The first trustees of the Fund were Clegg, Holland-Martin, Catterns and the Chief Accountant, Augustus Walker.[37]

Members of the Permanent Male Staff were also required to insure themselves with the Bank Provident Society, which had been established in 1854 with the dual purpose of providing whole-life assurance for the staff and a means of accumulation for their savings.* Provision for widows and dependants, although never regarded by the Bank 'as being more than a supplement to the provision made by the Clerks themselves',

---

* Because of its small size the BPS gradually became uncompetitive with the Life Offices. It was closed to new members in March 1967 and wound up in February 1983.

was made under a Widows' Annuity Scheme introduced in 1920 and itself a successor to various schemes dating from 1764. The 1920 scheme was reconsidered in 1947, when its annuity of £150 was considered 'altogether inadequate because of the substantial rise in the cost of living'; as a result the Widows' Annuity Fund was formed, taking into account the provisions for dependants made by the 1946 National Insurance Act and based on an internal fund. This made rather more generous payments including payments for children, and came into effect in March 1948. It was available to all categories of staff, and remained in force until the inception of a new scheme, the Widows' Fund, in 1965.[38]

Cases of genuine hardship among the staff during their working lives were occasionally helped by a grant from the Samaritan Fund, instituted in 1854 and administered by the Governors. The circumstances of each case were investigated personally by a Director. The Bank made it clear that the existence of the Samaritan Fund did not in any way imply 'that the Authorities have relaxed their attitude towards those who through their own imprudence have become financially embarrassed' – and who were bound by the rules to report in writing to the Chief of Establishments the circumstances which had brought about such difficulties. (Recourse to moneylenders for many years meant instant dismissal if detected.) The Fund's usefulness was several times questioned and reviewed, but it survived and continued to make small grants. In the year 1957/8, for example, it helped thirty-one members of staff, mostly faced with unexpected costs owing to illness, and disbursed a total of £1,292.[39]

More important financial benefits administered by the Establishment Department included house purchase and educational insurance schemes. The former, briefly alluded to in the previous chapter, was one of the most valuable – and valued – of the 'fringe' benefits available to the staff of the Bank. Mortgage lending was first introduced, via the Bank Provident Society, in 1876, and continued until the introduction of the Housing Loans Scheme in 1945.

This was instituted because of the serious difficulties faced by the staff, on return from the wartime Hampshire locations and from the Forces, in setting up home in the London area. It was almost impossible to find a house or flat to rent, and the type of house the staff had bought pre-war had virtually doubled in price since 1939 and was beyond the resources of most of them. The Bank received many applications for assistance, and in September 1945 the Governors decided to grant 'adequately secured loans up to a maximum of £2,500 to members of the Permanent and Auxiliary Male Clerical Staff' for house purchase. Interest was charged at $2\frac{1}{2}$ per cent per annum; the terms of the scheme were gradually amended, both as to categories of eligible staff and the maximum loan. On occasion loans were made in excess of the current maximum at slightly higher rates of interest, usually $3\frac{1}{2}$ per cent. Women were later included in the scheme, comprehensive reviews were carried out at intervals, and by 1959 the 'normal' limits for housing loans had reached £2,750 for clerical and £2,500 for non-clerical staff, still at a rate of $2\frac{1}{2}$ per cent.[40]

The question of loans for the education of children was less straightforward. A handful of clerks had been granted such loans just before the outbreak of war in 1939, and in 1942 the Clerks' Committee at Whitchurch submitted a possible scheme to their opposite numbers, the Clerks' Committee in London, 'who advised Whitchurch not to proceed with it'. The idea was that the Bank should make loans at a low rate of interest on the security of endowment policies to be issued by the BPS. Holland-Martin, in particular, was worried in case the repayments might prove burdensome to the majority of family men, but the Bank did make interest-free loans in cases of particular difficulty because of the shortage of suitable schools in the Whitchurch area. Governor Norman, however, was personally interested in the idea and asked Bernard to examine and report on it, along with the question of sabbatical years, in connection with the Bank's 250th anniversary in 1944.* Norman suggested some form of scholarship, either open to the public or exclusively for Bank staff. The subject was examined exhaustively from many angles including the moral and philosophical – Siepmann noted with regard to one suggested version that he could never endorse 'the implication that all human infants were equally worth educating'.[41]

Nothing had been decided by the time of the anniversary, and when at last, in 1945, a scheme acceptable to all parties had been drafted, it was realised rather belatedly that the Bank's contributions might be subject to tax 'in the hands of the recipient'. This suspicion was confirmed by the Inland Revenue. However the idea was finally dropped in that year not for that reason but because the passing of the Education Act implied that it should be possible 'for every child to receive the education it merits at a cost within the means of its parents'; and the staff, both clerical and non-clerical, although not averse to the idea in principle, had by this time become critical of the war-time allowances paid by the Bank and made it plain that they would prefer 'that a man should be paid for the job he was doing and not in relation to his family affairs'. There the matter rested until it was re-opened in 1951, and another six years

* See chapter 1, p. 35.

elapsed, in which further detailed examination took place, before a scheme was introduced in August 1957, available to members of the permanent Male Clerical Staff with not less than ten years' service. The initial limit of £750 for one child was based on half the approximate cost of sending a child to boarding school for five years. The scheme was subsequently widened, like the housing scheme, with regard both to those eligible, the amount that could be borrowed and the inclusion, in addition to fees and even where fees were not payable, of the cost of clothing, books, meals, travel and extras such as music and dancing lessons.[42]

Among the post-war problems considered by Ellis in 1943 had been the question of training. In an attempt to answer the query: are the present systems adequate? Ellis had found little positive. 'So far as the present writer is aware, there is no standardised system of training in the Bank. The Attendance Section sees to it that junior men do not stay too long in one Office but it is left to the Principal of each Office to train men as he thinks fit. This "training" is believed in many cases to amount to little more than qualifying under the other Clerks. In the writer's experience this qualification is often desultory and rarely intelligent...' The theory was that 'as soon as promising men become apparent' they were noted and moved within the smaller circle of central or departmental Offices, where they were sometimes fixed. Even this process had during the war been 'to a great extent, if not altogether, restricted', and it was realised that in the post-war period there would have to be signal improvements. The Principals of all the Offices were asked for their views, during which the old debate as to the quality of Bank recruits was aired again. One Principal noted: 'it seems that the Bank in building its "army" recruited only from the Officer class and, after a long spell of barrack-square drilling followed by prolonged courses on every subject encountered by the military profession, relegated the unsuccessful majority to permanent service in the ranks. The seeds of frustration were sown, and, although promotion from the ranks was tolerated, opportunity was rare.'[43]

This was a clear echo of the views of one of the most articulate pre-war critics of the Bank's recruiting policies, Reay Geddes.* Geddes, son of the Sir Eric Geddes famous for the 'Geddes axe' policy of salary cuts during the Depression years, had entered the Bank in 1933 at the late age of twenty-one – an exception being made in his case because he had been travelling with his father. He had made the rounds of six Offices before

---

* Geddes, Sir A. Reay M., KBE (1958), 1912–. Chairman, Dunlop Rubber Co., 1968–78; Deputy Chairman, Midland Bank, 1978–84.

he wrote a lengthy document addressed to the Chief of Establishments in which he described his very adverse impressions of what happened as a result of the Bank recruiting nothing but 'A' class men, most of whom would spend their working lives doing work well below their capabilities. 'Unless the authorities present to a boy a blunt and pessimistic picture of his early years in the Bank, he will start work in a fool's paradise, and become a prey to lowering forces when disillusionment comes...the boy either becomes discontented, when the Bank pays a high wage for a trouble maker, or else leaves, in which case the Bank is less merely a year's probationary pay, less the value of twelve months' work of messenger boy standard'.

Geddes continued in his analysis of what happened when the initial 'pride in work – loyalty and accuracy and quickness' are subjected to the hard truth of years of routine work far below the standard of the entrance examination. His own suggestions for a solution to the problem, which included the 'war block' (i.e. the Hump), were given in detail and included special pension offers and a totally new attitude to recruitment, drafting in ten trainees every two years specifically to fill 'A' posts, plus a less well qualified 'B' and 'C' intake as cheaper labour for routine work. Even a 'sharp' accent would be tolerated by the public at the Bank's counters 'if it went with a less reluctant manner', and 'the difficulty of taste in dress could easily be overcome by enforcing a black coat and striped trousers (three years grace to be allowed after any notice to this effect was published)'.[44]

No reply to this broadside is preserved in the files, and Geddes, who had received outstandingly good reports in all his Offices, left the Bank the year after writing it. The problem, however, remained.

By the end of the war no real conclusions had been reached on this tricky question other than the recommendations of the Special Committee on the Accountant's Department, chaired by Holland-Martin, which stated *inter alia* 'That the policy laid down in the 1936 scheme of salaries of interchanging Staff between the Departments, which was interrupted at the outbreak of war, be fully implemented and extended to cover the first twelve years of a Clerk's service'.[45]

A new training scheme was introduced in 1946 which 'aimed at giving a general training in elementary work in four to five years', eighteen months to be spent in the Accountant's Department and a similar length of time in the Cashier's Department and in Exchange Control, but within a year it was proving necessary to make alterations to speed up the training of 'promising older men', most of them ex-servicemen. Plans to improve the lot of women by giving them experience in different

" *Satisfactory . . . Satisfactory . . .*
*Satisfactory—look here this isn't*
*satisfactory . . .* "

Plate 10.4    A drawing by Basil Hone from *The Old Lady of Threadneedle Street*,
June 1963

Departments and Offices, making a woman clerk 'more useful to the
Bank and Bank work more interesting to her' were much discussed from
1947 onwards, but frustrated by shortage of candidates and the reluctance
of Offices, once a woman had proved useful in some capacity, to part with
her. By 1949 the problems of recruitment of women, which were to prove
so intractable during the 1950s, were looming: 'The Bank are in the very
unenviable position of having to offer girl entrants a choice of routine
jobs, none of which is inherently popular and all with a common
denominator of monotony.' It was not until this year that the 'marriage
bar', which enforced resignation on women on their marriage in all but

a handful of exceptional cases, was lifted, nearly three years after a similar restriction had been removed in the Civil Service.[46]

There was a lot of movement at the top of the Establishment Department between 1949 and 1955. In the earlier year, Michael McGrath took over as Chief when Dalton retired, and Howard Askwith became his Deputy. McGrath died suddenly in 1953, and his successor, Donald Randall, fell ill and retired early only two years later. Askwith was then appointed Chief of Establishments and instituted a complete overhaul of the processes of training, selection and reporting, which were gradually made much more professional and systematic. Throughout the 1950s the Department continued its attempts to balance the expectations of entrants with the needs and desires of the Office Principals and Heads of Department with varying success; a major difficulty was the voracious appetite for the best young men of the flourishing Overseas side and of the CCO, whose requirements when voiced by the Chief Cashier were difficult to withstand. For both sexes interchangeability tended to remain 'a desirable theory... rather than a live practice'.[47]

By 1958, however, training had been largely standardised and the normal practice was as follows. Ordinary, i.e. non-graduate, entrants spent (not necessarily in this order) a year in the Accountant's Department, of which two weeks were in the Departmental School and one week in the Central Mechanisation Office School; the balance of the year was passed in a Transfer Office or, 'if better than average progress is made', partly also in a return-making Office, e.g. Stock Returns, or in the Dividend Office. A further year in the Cashier's Department comprised practical work in two or three banking Offices and included four weeks in the Cashier's Department School. After this, some of the men spent some months in Exchange Control Offices. Then according to ability and promise shown the clerk was given a trial either in one of the more specialised Offices for periods of up to eighteen months, or added experience in a series of Offices where the work was of a more routine nature, or in one of the Branches, for a period of about two years. The programme for the graduate Special Entrants involved three to six months in a Transfer Office, including normal periods in the Account- ant's Department and Central Mechanisation Schools, plus four weeks in the Cashier's Department School followed by a month each in the Bill Office and the Drawing Office. The majority of Special Entrants then spent up to a year in the CCO after which they either remained there for a further year or moved for an extended trial to the Overseas Department or Statistics Office. Throughout this period of initial training every graduate was reported on quarterly by the Office in which he was serving, and on each occasion subsequently interviewed in the Establishment Department and his progress discussed with him.[48]

In addition to Bank training, there were a variety of external courses. Attendance at some, such as those at the London School of Economics, Henley and Ashridge, was sponsored by the Bank. A few clerks undertook evening classes for Institute of Bankers' and foreign language examinations, and were rewarded by small gratuities from the Bank if successful.

The Governors, and Governor Cobbold in particular, had remained not wholly satisfied with the position: Cobbold stressed on many occasions his conviction that promising young men should have an early opportunity to have some sort of 'overview of the Bank and its functions and the relation of one Department to another'. His wishes were largely frustrated by a combination of a general shortage of recruits and the passive resistance of the more conservative of the senior officials, who genuinely and unshakeably believed that there was no substitute for an early and prolonged apprenticeship in the established Office routines, such as most of them had undergone themselves (but which Cobbold, recruited specially by Norman at the age of twenty-nine, had not).

In response to Cobbold's ideas an Advanced Training Scheme had been implemented in 1953, under which the Heads of Departments and DEOs reviewed each year nominations for advanced training chosen from the more promising young men, and two lists, 'A' and 'B', were prepared. 'A' was composed of men of the rank of Principal Clerk or Senior Clerk aged between twenty-eight and thirty-five regarded as possessing 'outstanding potentiality'. 'B' was of men of junior rank thought to be likely future candidates for 'A'. Individual training programmes for 'A' men were planned by Establishments in consultation with DEOs, with a view to broadening their all-round experience in preparation for senior positions in the Department for which they seemed best suited. They were given the chance to come into direct contact with Heads of Department (a rare occurrence for most clerks), and to be 'qualified on duties which would normally be undertaken by men of more senior rank'. Special reports were prepared for each man and considered annually, and a regular progress report was submitted to the Governors.[49]

Cobbold remained unconvinced. In May 1958 he wrote to the Deputy Governor, Executive Directors and Heads of Departments:

> I have looked through various papers dating from 1951 and from 1953/54 about advanced training. We seem to have made some progress with ideas then put forward about training of promising men outside the Bank, both in the UK banks and overseas with B.I.S., I.M.F. etc and also

Commonwealth Banks. We have also, I should think, done a little better than previously on interchange between Departments for training purposes, though I am not certain that this ought not to be more systematic. I am still, however, quite unrepentant about various suggestions which I have put forward for some sort of 'Staff College' training which have never met with much support or got under way. I just flatly disagree with those who say that it is neither possible nor of real interest to give the most promising people around age 30 a broader look at the Bank and some acquaintance with what the whole Bank is trying to do and with the people who are doing it at the top. I believe it would be perfectly possible, and both interesting and useful, to have a short course for not more than 16 people lasting, say, a month or a bit more, putting somebody like Mr Rootham/Mr. Fforde (with the help of e.g. an Assistant Chief Cashier) in charge as Director of Studies, and making sure that they had a good all-round look at what was going on. I believe that if we had two or three courses over a year or two run by different people, we could get ideas and build up something really worth while. If, after a couple of years, this all proved negative, I would admit that I was wrong; but not before that.[50]

It was clear that further action was now necessary, and the project was encouraged by the vigorous moves in a similar direction already under way in Overseas where the Central Banking Course was in preparation. A Committee was appointed by the Governors to carry out a general review of training from the routine level upwards, and in particular to make recommendations as to the desirability and feasibility of making the broader view available to promising men of about thirty as the Governor wished. Sir Cyril Hawker, Jasper Rootham and James Keogh formed the Committee which made a thorough examination of all Departments and their training programmes. They also visited ICI, then recruiting upwards of 500 graduates a year, mostly with degrees in chemistry but also arts graduates, Shell and Barclays Bank which had two-tier recruitment to a limited extent. Evidence was invited from the Advisers: Allen and Thompson-McCausland were both uncompromisingly in favour of academic studies both in and outside the Bank.

The interim report of the Committee, which was produced in January 1959, found little to criticise in routine training but deficiencies at a higher level.[51] As a result the Governor proposed, subject to the agreement of the Committee of Treasury, to set up a body under the chairmanship of the Chief of Establishments to put into force a specific programme of advanced training under the regular supervision of Abell and Hawker. This was the so-called Committee of Advanced Training, consisting of Askwith plus a member of each of the five Departments. It was executive and not advisory, and proceeded immediately to formulate plans for selection and programmes of training within the Bank plus increased training outside it at commercial banks, the Administrative Staff College at Henley, the International Banking Summer School and Oxford University Business Summer School plus work at other central banks, BIS and IMF. The duration of the training would be for not less than three years; women were specifically included although it was felt that not many in the immediate future would qualify as 'having or being likely to develop outstanding potentiality'. There was also a special Internal Course, known as the Governor's Course, which was drawn up as described in chapter 8 and 'designed to give [Advanced Trainees] insight into the problems of the Bank, primarily in the field of home finance, and, more generally, to enable them to meet the Governors, Executive Directors, Heads of Departments and Advisers'. The courses lasted about three and a half weeks, the first being held in October 1959.[52]

The remark about the lack of suitable women candidates for this new initiative highlights the problems besetting the employment of women in the Bank. Despite the pleas of their representatives for better jobs and more responsibility, women had emerged from the war with only a few crumbs thrown to them by the Special Committee which reviewed the 1936 Scheme of Classification. This recommended:

> (a) That when or wherever practicable the field of work for women be extended.
>
> (b) That from time to time the work in all Departments be reviewed by the Establishment Department in collaboration with the Heads of Departments and certain duties done by men as soon as practicable given to women; these duties would consist, *inter alia*, of those which, during the War, women had shown that they could successfully perform; subject to an adequate field being left for training the male Staff.[53]

The employment of women on more than typing, filing, operating office machinery and the most routine clerical work did advance slightly in the next few years, especially in the Accountant's Department, but the necessity to recruit and train men against the disappearance of the Hump prevented any large-scale extension. The high rate of turnover of women was another factor militating against them; a still greater one was imposed by the growth of the note issue.

Chapter 4 has described the increasing volume of used notes returning to the Bank and the processes involved in their cancellation and destruction, which included examination and counting by teams of women and girls in the Issue Office. This work, which could scarcely be described as clerical work and was tedious and uninspiring, was generally disliked and was a major factor in the difficulties that the Bank was experiencing in attracting and keeping women. After two years a girl, recruited at the age of sixteen, would be appointed to the permanent staff provided that 'she was consistently diligent' and had reached a satisfactory standard of work – which, in the Issue Office, 'would merely mean that she had demonstrated her ability to count 15,000 notes a day'.[54] She could ask for a move when she had been in the Office for five years, but during that time she was not required to use her brain and learnt virtually nothing about the Bank beyond her allotted task. Not surprisingly, headmistresses of the schools from which the girls were habitually recruited got to know about this and tried to dissuade their best pupils from entering the Bank.[55]

In 1952 the possibility of recruiting a special staff for this kind of routine work, suggested several times before, was examined once more but the plan foundered because it was 'considered undesirable for two different types of Women Staff to work together in the same building'.[56] Two years later a plea from the Women's Clerks' Committee for two different grades with separate terms of service was again turned down;[57] in October 1955 the Chief of Establishments, Askwith, suggested it once more. 'The City Youth Employment Bureau consider, and Miss Knight* concurs...that much of the Bank's routine clerical and machine work could be done efficiently by girls from secondary modern schools. But within the Bank, on present personal and scholastic grounds, few girls from these schools...are acceptable.' Yet there were 8,000 secondary school girls aged fifteen and over who were placed in jobs by the Bureau every year and 'it would seem unwise that the Bank should ignore a source of recruitment which could usefully be employed...'.[58]

The crux of the problem was the fact, mentioned earlier, that women had been brought in to cheapen the cost of labour because their rates of pay were lower and with the greater turnover fewer survived to an expensive seniority. This was considered preferable to employing two grades of male staff which would have altered the whole character of the Bank and increased the risk of 'difficult relations between the staff and the Court probably resulting in professional representation of certain sections of the staff which has mercifully hitherto been avoided'.[59] If two grades of men were undesirable, so were two grades of women. But the more the Bank did for its women, the less it could do for the men – and

---

* Knight, Joan. Miss Knight was appointed Deputy Controller of Women Clerks in 1945. After a spell as Assistant to the Chief of Establishments (Women) she became in 1953 Assistant Chief of Establishments (Women) – at that time the highest position open to a woman. The tag known as 'Women in Brackets' disappeared in the 1958 Scheme of Classification – see below.

by the mid 1950s it was becoming difficult even to get enough suitable men candidates. By the end of 1955, for example, it had proved possible to recruit only 169 men, over the past four years, out of the target of 220, and the Bank as a whole was short of 100 women. Some of the reasons were beyond the Bank's control, such as the declining birthrate in the 1930s. Britain was enjoying a period of full employment, and a five-day working week was becoming more common. This was not possible in many Offices in the Bank, which had a statutory obligation (as did the clearing banks) to be open to the public on Saturday mornings, although as many people were allowed Saturdays off as could be spared, under a system of 'worked Saturdays' by which extra time was done after normal hours during Monday to Friday. The possibility of work on Saturday mornings remained, and was a strong deterrent to many women. They also disliked working in the City, which at this date was still very much a male preserve and had few of the facilities such as shops for food and clothes which made life easier for working women.

In 1955 Sir George Abell, who had frequently expressed his disquiet over the position of women in the Bank, was asked by the Governor to chair a small Special Committee on Women's Work, of which the other two members were O'Brien and W.D. Simpson, respectively Chief Cashier and Chief Accountant. Their conclusion was that a 'gradual integration of the male and female staff of the Bank is practicable and desirable'. At last at the highest level there was public acknowledgement of one of the chief difficulties of recruiting, whether male or female, which was not primarily one of salary scales or other conditions of service all of which compared 'quite well' with those of most commercial undertakings.* It arose rather from the insistence on a relatively high quality of staff and from the fact that this staff 'in the main is required to do comparatively uninteresting work with practically no chance for women of achieving real responsibility and only a somewhat hazardous chance of doing so for the men... It is particularly the case that men of the type we should like to recruit are not prepared to run the risk of wasting many years as routine clerks when there are more certain and immediate opportunities elsewhere for advancement to interesting and remunerative work.'

The Committee envisaged the likely position in twenty years' time: 'men and women working on equal terms and perhaps with equal pay or

---

* Salary scales also compared favourably with those in the clearing banks, although the differential was gradually being eroded. Bank salaries were 24 per cent higher, on entry, in 1947, but only 16 per cent higher by 1957.

at any rate more nearly equal pay'. Before this could be achieved there would be a difficult transitional period, intensified because the Hump would not have 'run off' completely until 1967. But this must be faced and the Committee suggested an organisation which not only provided for the Bank's work to be done but also allowed that 'women should have the opportunity to graduate from [women's] work to the work done by men and be promoted in competition with men, after an initial period of five years of their service, until age twenty-one or twenty-two, employed on routine work as at present'.[60]

This report proved the trigger to a major reorganisation, brought in over a period of years, which ultimately affected the whole staff of the Bank. The Heads of Departments' Committee immediately signified its acceptance in principle of the main conclusions and referred the matter to the DEOs for study in detail.[61] The Council of Directors and Staff also discussed the question at length.[62]

The DEOs suggested that the more promising women should be given the option to transfer to a 'common list' entailing the acceptance of conditions of service common to both sexes. It was agreed that the next stage should be an assessment of all the work done throughout the Bank by both men and women, and the appropriate rank for the job decided in each case. This was carried out by Thomas Neylan, seconded from his work as Principal of the Bank Note Office. It took Neylan ten months of much painstaking work, consultation with senior officials throughout the Bank and detailed comparison with the administrative and executive classes of the Civil Service. He reported to the Governors in July 1957; he concluded that there were, in round figures, 3,880 jobs in the Bank (excluding those of shorthand typists) done by clerical staff below administrative rank, 500 on which men only should be employed, 1,900 on which women only should be employed, and 1,400 which could be common to either men or women. Seventy-nine per cent of the 'common jobs' were currently held by men, thus demonstrating quite clearly that there was ample scope for 'women of the right quality' to be more widely employed on the clerical work of the Bank.[63]

As an interim measure the employment of a temporary staff of part-time women was sanctioned by Order of Court in October 1957.[64] Many of the women were ex-Bank employees who returned to work mainly in the Dividend Payments Office and the Issue Office. A year later, in September 1958, five years of almost continuous examination of the problems of the relative positions of men and women in the Bank resulted in the provisions of the 1958 Scheme of Classification, the first step towards complete integration of the sexes. The Scheme divided the bulk of the staff into three distinct categories, Classed Staff, the Staff of Women Clerks and Shorthand Typists. The Classed Staff would consist of men and women working alongside each other under similar conditions of service. The more simple work would be carried out by Women Clerks, any one of whom would be able to transfer to the Classed Staff (after the age of twenty) if and when she was 'deemed capable of performing work which is generally more exacting and responsible than that normally allotted to Women Clerks'. The women's salaries were increased slightly (including a rise of around £40 to compensate for the loss of the free lunches they had previously enjoyed) with more emphasis on incentives. The system of two column salaries, Ordinary based on age and Class based on attainment, was replaced, for those below administrative rank,* with single column salary scales based on age, for each class or rank. Salaries of the women staff were to be not less than 75 per cent of those of men of the same age and seniority.[65]

The most painful aspect of this quite revolutionary scheme was the fact that the translation of many of the Women Classed Staff to the new Staff of Women Clerks meant a down-grading by two or three ranks of all the current women Senior Clerks, Principal Clerks, Assistants and Assistant and Deputy Principals. This was necessary in order to bring their ranks, titles and responsibilities into line with those of men, but it was felt keenly by many of the women as a loss of status and resented as such.[66]

The new proposals brought about a slight problem for the Governor. It had been the custom since the very early nineteenth century for him to read what was known as the Governor's Charge to men on their election to the permanent service of the Bank after the probationary years. This was a brief homily on obedience, the dangers of 'pecuniary embarrassment', the necessity for secrecy in the affairs of the Bank, and general conduct both at work and during the hours of leisure. The reading ceremony took place two or three times a year to groups of clerks after a sitting of Court on a Thursday, in the presence of the Directors. The wording had been revised at various dates, most notably by Mynors in 1939 when Governor Norman had felt that his audience was either 'bored or frightened' by its current form.[67] In 1958 Mynors addressed himself to the question whether the charge should in future be given to women. He proposed a few alterations which might make it more suitable for their inclusion, but Cobbold demurred: 'I just cannot read this sort of lecture to a mass of women who have been in the Bank for a number

---

* i.e. up to and including the new rank of Superintendent which replaced that of Principal Clerk.

of years. Frankly I think the charge is less suitable to young women than young men anyhow, and if we could have avoided bringing women in I would have preferred it. But I see no advantage in trying to amend the charge which should either remain in about its present form or be abandoned. So if we must we must. The question must go to Court before decision.'[68]

All the Directors were therefore asked their opinion, and although some expressed 'a chivalrous distaste for subjecting women to a parade', the majority were in favour of retaining the ancient ceremony in its present form for men, with perhaps 'some sort of interview with the Governor' for the women. It was already the practice for women clerks and shorthand typists appointed to the permanent staff to be seen by Sir George Abell, and this remained unchanged, but from June 1959 the Governor decided that 'he will see...those women who are appointed direct to the classed staff or above, or an equivalent rank in the staff of shorthand typists, personally. At this interview he will, for their information, hand them a copy of the historic charge that is formally delivered at Court to the men.'[69]

The Bank's recruiting difficulties, although far from completely solved, did begin to lessen towards the end of the 1950s. The 1958 Classification Scheme was a major step forward as far as women were concerned, as was the gradual transfer, from that year, of note-counting to Debden. In 1958 too the number of young people of school leaving age began to rise. Discussions had begun at the end of 1957 as to whether to advertise for women staff – something the Bank had never done for either sex except for a teacher of shorthand and typewriting,* although career brochures, beautifully printed and illustrated, had been published since 1954 for men and 1955 for women. One school of thought held that to advertise in the press would mean a 'loss of dignity', a particular advocate of this theory being J.B. Rickatson-Hatt,† Adviser to the Governors on public relations and other related matters (there was no Press Officer as such at this date). It was refuted by Aphra Maunsell,‡ Senior Assistant to the Chief of Establishments (Women), who declared robustly that 'we must go down into the market place and compete with the other banks who do not hesitate to make the best of what they have to offer'. Her views prevailed. There followed much drafting and re-

---

* The Bank standards of typing were of the highest. Those trained elsewhere had to undergo re-training in the Bank's methods, which at this date in the late 1950s were still taught from a typing manual dated 1918.
† Advisor to the Governors 1941–58.
‡ Miss Maunsell later became Deputy Chief of Establishments from 1967–74.

drafting of the actual wording of the advertisements, and anxieties about whether to emphasise the excellent facilities such as the Sports Club at Roehampton, which it was feared might revive the old animosity which the Beaverbrook press had shown towards the Bank in pre-war days. The final result appeared in the three London evening papers – *The Evening News*, *The Evening Standard* and *The Star* – in February 1958, and produced a total of nearly 600 applicants: 'exceeding our wildest dreams' according to Askwith.[70]

The Bank had no difficulty in recruiting graduates, still referred to as Special Entrants in the late 1950s and early 1960s, despite a resolute refusal to join the so-called 'milk round' in which 'some industrial or commercial firms are visiting the Universities and signing up men of their choice forthwith over a glass of sherry ... we clearly cannot indulge in tactics of that sort' as Askwith noted firmly. The problems were rather in keeping them: they produced a much higher proportion of what the Bank called 'quitters' than the ordinary run of candidates. Of the 114 graduates appointed since 1946 only seventy-seven were still in the Bank in November 1957. Their expectations were naturally higher than those of school-leavers and they chafed against the lengthy period with little or no responsibility. Sir George Abell had much contact with the Oxford and Cambridge University Appointments Boards who were concerned by the number of young men who approached them 'in despair in the early years of their services'. Abell emphasised that 'there is no quick way to stardom', and the graduates were warned that 'the best can expect to reach their first administrative appointment within six to seven years'. In 1960, efforts were made to attract economics graduates with first-class degrees for the newly formed Central Banking Information Department, over and above the regular graduate intake, which was raised the following year from eight to fifteen: five of these were women, who were recruited directly to the Classed Staff.[71]

The emphasis placed by the Bank on all staff matters, together with the increasing complexity of such things as National Insurance, income tax, recruiting and training changes, meant that the staff and payments sections of the Department were constantly expanding. Once the post-war building and rebuilding programmes got under way, the Premises Section also began to grow in size.

Some of the major building projects have been described elsewhere, including the new Printing Works at Debden, the premises for the Accountant's Department at New Change, the new Branch in Bristol and various rebuilding schemes in other Branches. An immediate problem, almost on the Bank's back doorstep, was posed by Numbers 1, 2 and 3

Bank Buildings and the adjacent building at 19, Old Jewry, on the corner of Princes Street and Gresham Street. These had been built for the Bank by Arthur Blomfield* between 1902 and 1906 on sites acquired in the first half of the nineteenth century. Before the war Bank Buildings accommodated the Loans Office, Dividend Pay Office, Dividend Accounts Office and the Head Gate Porter's flat as mentioned above. The building at 19, Old Jewry was leased to the Ministry of Works and occupied by the National Debt Office and the Public Works Loan Board.

The buildings were badly damaged by a flying bomb in July 1944 and two-thirds rendered unusable. In 1945 Number 1 Bank Buildings, which had survived without much damage, housed Freshfields (whose premises at 31 Old Jewry had been destroyed by enemy action) on its upper floors, and Professor Sir William Holford† who worked there for a short period on the City Plan for post-war reconstruction. The Governors were anxious to rebuild entirely rather than just patch up the old structure; Heal, the Bank's architect, was instructed in 1945 to prepare a design for a new building. His plans provided for seven storeys and two underground floors, one of the upper floors being designed to 'accommodate distinguished visitors in a series of private rooms' (a scheme which was later abandoned) and another to house the National Debt Office.

Demolition of the damaged portions began in 1948; Heal's plans had by this time been submitted to and approved by the City Corporation and the London County Council. Difficulties over building licences prevented the Bank from carrying out the work in one operation, and it was decided to leave Number 1 Bank Buildings standing while the remainder was rebuilt. Trollope & Colls were the general contractors; they started work early in 1949 and the first stage was complete in September 1951. The building is steel framed, all the street frontages being faced with Portland stone, and the ground floor window frames made of bronze. The ground floor banking hall has Travertine marble floors and counter front. Discussions as to who should move in had begun among the Heads of Departments back in 1947: none of them showed great enthusiasm for separating any Office from the main body of their Departments, but it was finally decided that the occupants should be Dividend Accounts Office, Dividend Pay and Loans Office, the Inspector of Offices and Branches, the Supervisor of Expenditure, the Welfare

---

\* Blomfield, Arthur Conran, FRIBA, 1863–1935. Architect to the Bank from 1899 to 1918, in succession to his father, Sir Arthur Blomfield, who held the position from 1883 to 1899. A.C. Blomfield was architect to King Edward VII at Sandringham, and was responsible for Barclays Banks in Fleet Street and Pall Mall East as well as many country houses and City buildings.                    † See p. 72n.

Office, the Probationary Typists Office and the editorial office of *The Old Lady of Threadneedle Street*. The Ministry of Works continued to lease part of the new building, the tenants being the National Debt Office and the Public Works Loan Board.

While Stage 1 was in progress, the Bank sounded the Ministry of Works on several occasions about the possibility of getting a supplementary licence to carry straight on and complete the rebuilding in one operation. This would have been much more economical, but it was made clear that licences could not be given to demolish habitable buildings.

Licences were finally abolished in November 1954, and the question of Stage 2 was raised with the Governors from time to time, but because of the government's request for economy the project was continually shelved. However the Governor told the Committee of Treasury in January 1959 that 'future projects included the completion of Bank Buildings Stage 2... which... it seemed desirable to put in hand'. After referral to the Committee on Bank Premises the plans were approved. Lengthy negotiations took place with Freshfields during the rebuilding on the subject of the amount of office space they would require. Some of the floors were finished and occupied in October 1962, the final completion being made in January 1963; there was a general shuffle of Offices and tenants throughout the building, and Freshfields took over the third and fourth floors of the newly completed section, together with storage room in the basement, in March 1963.[72]

A large bronze statue of William Pitt had been in the entrance hall of the original building at 19 Old Jewry, placed there in 1823 by the wish of the National Debt Commissioners and with the agreement of the Bank. It was the work of Sir Richard Westmacott,* and was 8 feet 6 inches high including the plinth; in 1948 it was removed by the Ancient Monuments Division of the Ministry of Works who thought it might be erected temporarily in one of the London parks, but this was not done and it remained in a store-yard in Hyde Park. The Comptroller of the National Debt Office, Norman Young,† was anxious that the statue should find a permanent home in the rebuilt Bank Buildings, but Heal felt that it was 'much too big in scale' and that to create a special space for it in the building would be 'difficult, uneconomical and most probably very unsatisfactory'. Heal also rejected the idea of siting it in New Change,

---

* Westmacott, Sir Richard, RA, 1775–1856. His numerous statues and monuments include some of the reliefs on Marble Arch and the British Museum and the bronze statue of Achilles at Hyde Park Corner.

† Young, Norman Egerton, CB, 1889–1962. Comptroller General, National Debt Office, 1951–4.

and later the Committee on Bank Premises agreed that there was no suitable place for it in any of the Bank's buildings.[73]

Among the many building projects with which the Bank was anxious to proceed after the war was the Luncheon Club in Tokenhouse Yard. The original Club was built in 1926; when the rebuilding of Head Office was nearing completion in 1937 it was decided that the accommodation must be increased in order to make provision for the Staff of the Accountant's Department which at that stage was still destined to move into Threadneedle Street. In March 1938 the Bank leased Numbers 1 and 2, Tokenhouse Buildings, King's Arm Yard, from the Mercers' Company, with the object of pulling them down and erecting an extension to the Club on the site. Demolition was complete and the site cleared by the end of June 1939. Rebuilding plans were based on the assumption that a clerical staff of 3,000 would be working in Head Office: that number of lunches would be served daily in three sessions of forty-five minutes each.

In January 1940 a building tender was accepted. By this time the pressure on the existing premises was severe, and some 1,450 lunches per day were being provided, in five thirty minute sessions (men and women ate separately and the first session, for women, started at 11.30 a.m.). Despite the rise in material costs brought about by the war it was still hoped to go ahead, but a licence for the steel proved unobtainable and by May 1940 the project was abandoned 'for the duration'.

In 1948 the position was again unsatisfactory. Over 2,100 lunches were served every day, and about 650 women had to eat elsewhere. Heal drew up a new set of plans for an extension of five floors above ground and two below: the combined buildings, the existing Club plus the new extension, would be able to serve 5,000 people daily. However the building licence again proved elusive, and by the end of November 1955 the Establishment Department had decided that a better plan would be to put up an entirely new building on the King's Arms Yard site. The Tokenhouse Yard premises were grossly overcrowded, staffing them was becoming increasingly difficult, and the kitchens and storage facilities were at best out of date and in many particulars unhygienic. Noakes, Assistant Chief of Establishments, noted that service in the new Club 'would, of course, have to be a cafeteria system if only because of the increasing difficulty – which the whole catering industry is experiencing – of attracting and keeping waitresses. Segregation of the sexes would in all probability cease and we ought so to arrange our affairs that it is no longer necessary for anybody to be compelled to take luncheon before noon ...'.

The change from extension to completely new purpose-built Club was soon agreed, but while Establishments was preoccupied with the physical details, there was a groundswell of discontent from some sections of the staff. The chief object was to the end of segregation. The Principals' Committee was especially disgruntled: it had learnt with dismay of the Governors' decision that it would not be possible, in New Change, to provide for Principals and other senior officials 'such accommodation as would avoid the necessity of their queuing for their food'. They now, in January 1957, deplored the prospect that both at New Change 'and presumably in an extended Tokenhouse Club, they and their successors will be expected to join the broad mass of the Staff, both men and women, in queuing for their food', and stated that they would be prepared, if necessary, to pay more for their lunches if they could eat separately and with waitress service.

After much pained debate it was decided to provide at both locations a separate room, but without separate service, for those of the status of Assistant Principal and above, 'women to be "integrated" into this arrangement from the start'. The project still hung fire, partly because of all the many other building projects in which the Bank was involved, but in 1957 the Medical Officer of Health of the City of London made some serious criticisms of the existing Club and it was clear that rebuilding really must proceed as soon as possible. In October of that year Peter Ednie, ARIBA, of the firm of Troup & Steel, was appointed architect for the new project, as Heal was already fully occupied with work on New Change and elsewhere. The tender of Trollope & Colls was accepted and work on Phase 1, the erection of the new building, began in December 1958. Progress was slow, because of the restricted area, and it was not finished until January 1961. The new Club in King's Arms Yard was designed on eight floors, with a facade of Portland stone and Belgian blue pearl granite; an unusual feature was the Paternoster lift, a series of ten open-fronted cars each for two passengers which circulated continuously between the ground and fifth floors. The sexes ate together, and a room was set aside for the Principals (two of whom were women): even so this arrangement failed to find favour with some of them on the grounds that 'for half a century privilege at the Club has been unknown', and a few refused to avail themselves of their special quarters. There was a quick luncheon counter on the ground floor, and coffee rooms on the fourth and fifth floors.

As soon as the new building was ready work began on modernising the old Tokenhouse Yard premises, and was finished in September 1962.

The two buildings then formed a cohesive whole, with seats for 672 and capable of serving 2,260 lunches a day 'with ease'.[74]

Building licence problems were the main reason for the delay in making good the war damage to the Bank Sports Club in Priory Lane, Roehampton, in south-west London. This had been founded in 1908 at the initial suggestion of a clerk in the Private Drawing Office, and a substantial Record Office was built on the same $18\frac{1}{2}$ acre site which was purchased by the Bank from the Clarence House Estate. The Record Office, cottages for Club Steward and groundsmen and a sports pavilion were all designed by Blomfield, and the Club provided facilities for all major sports and many minor ones such as squash, fives and badminton. The Women Clerks had their own, inferior pavilion in the grounds; a new one was built for them to the design of Sir Herbert Baker and opened in January 1937.

During the Second World War the opportunities for games at Roehampton were much diminished as they had been during the previous war. About 100 staff were transferred from Head Office to work in the Record Office at the end of 1940, much of the land was taken over by Barnes Council for allotments and various precautions, such as trenching, were taken to prevent the landing of enemy aircraft. Air raid shelters (open to the public as well as to Bank staff) were constructed under the Club premises. The Forces, local ARP services and Army Cadets were given access to what remained of the sports facilities, and a limited amount of cricket, tennis, hockey and netball was played. In November 1940 the cottages were destroyed and the men's pavilion almost completely flattened by eleven incendiary bombs – only the long tea-room extension, built in 1922, remained usable – and the men accepted the offer of hospitality of the women's pavilion, which they were to continue to use for more than fifteen years.[75]

When Foxdown Camp at Overton was dismantled at the end of 1945 it was thought that some of the wood might be used to build a new Club House, but the London County Council scotched this idea by its insistence on the use of 'prohibitively expensive materials'.[76] The Club was granted the use of part of the ground floor of the Record Office, where a bar (for men only) was constructed with a counter made of a huge piece of Indian padauk wood first brought to England for the 1925 Wembley Exhibition and later installed in a Transfer Office in Finsbury Circus. Tea continued to be taken in the women's pavilion, but, despite the inconvenience of changing in one building, having tea in another and drinking in a third, the Club flourished at this period. Applications for the necessary licences were made at regular intervals, and were as regularly refused, although permission for a temporary cloakroom block was given in September 1948. At last, in 1953, the licences were obtained; Heal was anxious not to undertake the work and it was given to H.R. Steel, also of the firm Troup & Steel, who had designed an extension to the Record Office just before the war and who 'leaped at the opportunity' of this new commission.

A pair of semi-detached cottages was built in 1952 to replace the three destroyed during the war, as it had been decided that a third was no longer necessary. The new ones were occupied respectively by the Head Groundsman and the Chief Engineer. Troup & Steel also modernised Clarence Farm, one of the original buildings on the Clarence House Estate, for the Bank's gardener – the Bank had bought the additional twelve acres of the farm in 1920 and had leased the stabling to a series of riding clubs, whose unsatisfactory finances had caused many problems. The Sports Club Committee said that it would like the new pavilion to be 'outwardly the replica of the one destroyed': construction work began in November 1954 but was much hindered by excessive water in the foundations, the severe weather of early 1955, rail and steel strikes and the drain of labour to 'more lucrative employment' on less inconvenient sites. The Club House was in partial use by October 1955 and was finished by 1 April 1956; Governor Cobbold formally declared it open in July. It was very much like the old one in appearance, but was considerably larger and much better equipped, with new features which included a minstrels' gallery, a skittle alley and a shower for visiting women's teams. Two years later the Club celebrated its fiftieth anniversary with a dinner at Plantation House in the City on 28 March 1958, attended by nearly 400 past and present members; a Jubilee ball was also held in the new pavilion.[77]

Because of the rebuilding of the Threadneedle Street premises, which was not finished until 1941, there was little need for any structural work at Head Office in the post-war years, although much painting and decorating and interior maintenance was necessary in order to bring the building and its contents back to the high standards which had existed up to 1939. In 1945 the Bank commissioned a statue of Governor Norman from Charles Wheeler. The sculpture, which showed him in his peer's robes, was referred to as 'Monty-in-his-splendour' by Sir Herbert Baker, who was consulted as Bank architect; he graciously waived his fee for the consultation because he so much enjoyed working with Wheeler and this occasion 'puts in a friendly way a crown to my work for you at the Bank, which has always been such a pleasure to me'. The Portland

Plate 10.5   The newly built sports pavilion at Roehampton, 1956

stone statue was placed in a niche on the north side of Garden Court 'balancing the statue of Montagu'.* A bronze portrait bust based on the head of the statue was made by Wheeler for the Parlours (a second casting of it was made for Lady Norman) and was exhibited at the Royal Academy in the spring of 1946.[78]

The arrangements for Norman's statue were made by the Court, but Governor Catto was anxious that all members of the Bank staff should be able to express their views on the subject of a memorial to those of their colleagues who had lost their lives during the war. The Advisory Council of Directors and Staff suggested the formation of a War Memorial Committee, which was set up in June 1947. Chaired by Bernard, it had ten members: six representing the clerical staff, three the non-clerical staff, and Reginald Papworth, Assistant Chief of Establishments, representing the Heads of Departments.

As Bernard pointed out at the Committee's first meeting, the current situation was quite different from that after the First World War. In 1914–18, 414 men were on national service: in the recent war, apart from the 2,209 men and women who had joined the Forces, almost every member of the staff, men and women, had served in some capacity. A subscription list opened in 1919 had raised just over £2,000 which had

---

\* The statue, also sculpted by Wheeler, of Charles Montagu, Earl of Halifax, 1661–1715. Montagu was Chancellor of the Exchequer from 1694, when he adopted Paterson's scheme for a national bank which led to the foundation of the Bank of England, until 1699.

Plate 10.6　Governor Catto at the ceremony of unveiling the War Memorial, October 1948. Standing behind him is J.M. Humphry, Secretary of the War Memorial Committee and later Deputy Secretary of the Bank, 1968–1970. On the right are the Bishop of Stepney, the Rt Rev. R.H. Moberly, and the Bishop's Chaplain

been spent on the endowment of a bed in Guy's Hospital and the erection of a memorial in the Garden Court. This was a bronze statue of St Christopher sculpted by Richard Goulden, with the names of all the dead Bank staff engraved on a bronze plate on the pedestal. Some years later the names of all who had served were recorded on a temporary panel, and when the ground floor in Threadneedle Street had been rebuilt these names were carved in stone panels in the inner entrance hall, those who had died being marked with a small gold cross. The 1947 Committee, after wide discussion and canvassing of views throughout the Bank, decided that the names of the sixty-three dead should be inscribed on similar panels in the hall. Wheeler designed a bronze wreath to be placed in front of the St Christopher statue. The original inscription read:

> To the comrades who at duty's call crossed the dark waters to the further shore – 1914–1919

Alex Scott, a partner in the firm of Sir Herbert Baker & Scott, designed a new plaque to be placed under this, reading:

> To the memory of those who crossed the same waters – 1939–1945

Plate 10.7    Statue of Governor Norman by Sir Charles Wheeler, erected in the Garden Court in 1946

A War Memorial Fund was opened to which all members of the Court, the staff and pensioners were invited to subscribe, with individual subscriptions limited to 10s., and it was decided that any funds remaining after paying for the memorial would be given to the Star and Garter Home for Disabled Sailors, Soldiers and Airmen. The memorial was unveiled by Governor Catto on 20 October 1948, after which a service of dedication was held in Garden Court by the Bishop of Stepney. Lord Norman was present (it was his only public appearance at the Bank after his retirement in 1944), and two buglers of the Welsh Guards played the Last Post and Reveille at the conclusion of the service. As had been done after the First World War, a memorial issue of *The Old Lady* was published, in March 1949, and individual memorials were erected at the Branches where staff had lost their lives (their names were, of course, also included on the Threadneedle Street memorial panels).[79]

The care of the fine and valuable furniture in the Parlours and elsewhere in the Bank was officially consigned to Reginald Turner on his appointment in July 1945 as the Curator of Furniture. Turner, who had worked in 'high class interior decoration' before the war, joined the Bank as a Temporary Clerk in 1939 and since October 1944 had been occupied in examining and cataloguing the furniture, supervising its repair and purchasing additional pieces. He searched diligently for high quality antiques and, when new pieces were under consideration, made sure that 'the timber used and the finishings provided' were up to the Bank's standard – not easy in the days of Utility* specifications and difficulties in obtaining wood and other materials. By 1949 Turner's field of work had been considerably extended and included much furniture previously under the custody of the Clerk of the Works; he also looked after the Branches and the houses of the Agents and Sub-Agents and was later responsible for selecting furniture for the rebuilt Club House at Roehampton, New Change and the new Printing Works. When he retired in 1961 the Bank had spent an average of £1,000 a year on antique furniture since 1946, and the value of the pieces under his control was estimated at about £250,000.[80]

In 1952 the Deputy Governor, Bernard, expressed his dissatisfaction with the decoration of the Court Room; other members of the Court agreed with his criticisms. When Sir Herbert Baker designed the Court Room in his rebuilding of the Bank, he modelled it closely on its predecessor, the work of Sir Robert Taylor, but, with the agreement of Court, made certain alterations, in particular the redesign of the wall opposite the windows. Here Baker substituted a new central fireplace (transferring the old one to the Deputy Governor's room) surmounted by a panel of carved marble showing Jupiter awarding the apple to Minerva, and an elaborate twenty-four hour clock ornamented with figures representing the Empire, which was designed by his son Henry Baker. The whole centrepiece was disliked, and the Bank's Fine Arts Committee suggested that the Earl of Crawford and Balcarres[†] was 'probably the most suitable person to be consulted in the first place'. The Governor invited him and Sir Kenneth Clark[‡] to lunch to view the offending articles. Both recommended that Professor Albert Richardson[§] should be asked to give his opinion: 'They thought it would be possible, under his guidance, to restore completely the feeling of the

---

*   The Utility mark was instituted by the Board of Trade and used during and after the war to designate clothes and household goods made to an approved standard in accordance with official allowances of materials.
†   Crawford, 28th Earl of, and Balcarres, 11th Earl of, David Robert Alexander Lindsay, KE, GBE, 1900–75. Chairman of Royal Fine Art Commission, 1943–57.
‡   Clark, Baron (1969), Kenneth Mackenzie Clark, OM, CH, KCB, 1903–83. Chairman, Arts Council of Great Britain, 1953–60.
§   See note p. 72.

former Court Room, but there should be no question of reverting to an exact copy of the original style.'

Richardson approached the task with relish, proposing to replace both fireplace and clock with the originals. He also suggested putting basket grates in all three Court Room fireplaces. All this work was duly carried out, and for the Deputy Governor's room an eighteenth century fireplace was purchased, which had come originally from a house called Nuthall Temple* near Nottingham. The Empire clock was later installed in the Lecture Hall at New Change.

While Richardson was supervising these arrangements he suggested the redecoration of the Court Room to restore the varied colours of its pre-1887 appearance 'in the Cockerell tradition'. The Directors, however, did not like the idea, and when the room was repainted at the conclusion of the work on the fireplace it was done more plainly, reproducing the pale stone colour to which the mustard yellow of Baker's design had faded.[81]

* Nuthall Temple was built *c.* 1740 and demolished in 1929.

# 11

## THE SECRETARY'S DEPARTMENT

The reorganisation of the Secretary's Department along the lines recommended by the Peacock Committee Report in June 1932 proved in some respects a more exacting task than the institution of the Establishment Department as described in the previous chapter. The post of 'Secretary and Sollicitor' was one of the original triumvirate of the most senior officials in the Bank at its foundation, and the style remained the same until 1706 after which the word Sollicitor was dropped, although the appointment continued to be held by the same person. His Office appears to have been a fairly independent part of the Cashier's Department, and a separate Secretary's Department is not shown in the House List until 1851. His prime responsibilities were to act as Secretary to the Court and to the Committee of Treasury: additionally either he or one of his immediate deputies acted as Secretary to 'all standing or special committees of Directors'. A natural extension of this work was the attention 'to all matters in general connected with the Directors'. To these functions, and in the absence of any designated staff Director or Department, there had gradually been added a large body of staff matters; in his evidence to the Peacock Committee the current Secretary, Ronald Dale, estimated that these took up about 75 per cent of the time of his staff, consisting at that date of himself, a Deputy, an Assistant and six clerks. They also dealt with enquiries and claims on account of lost or stolen bank notes, and with 'any internal matter not falling specifically within the province of the Chief Accountant, Chief Cashier, etc.'.

Dale felt, and told the Peacock Committee, that although his Office was 'theoretically included in the general promotion scheme of the Bank...the former idea that the Office was a "backwater" has prevailed to a considerable degree'.[1] The men in the Office were above the average in ability and chosen for special qualifications, but these were admittedly different from those required in, for example, the Chief Cashier's Office, and their career prospects were thus rather limited. As Clegg later described it, up to the time of the Committee 'the Secretary was living, as he had probably always lived during the two and a half centuries of the Bank's history, a more or less secluded life, out of touch except in a purely formal way with the general business of the Bank, and maintaining only an occasional contact with any but the juniors of the Staff'.[2]

By creating an Establishment Department, the Committee took away the bulk of the Secretary's work, ostensibly leaving him little beyond the task of providing secretarial services to the Court, the Committee of Treasury and other Committees, but they indicated that being free of the routine staff duties meant that he would be able to perform some more important ones. His work 'as suggested in our recommendation will now bring him and his Department into more intimate contact with the main activities of the Bank'.

As envisaged by the Peacock Committee his duties were as follows:

> He shall be the Secretary of the Bank, but shall be relieved of all Staff duties.
> He shall be Head of the Secretariat and must work very closely with the Assistant to the Governors.
> He shall act as Secretary to the Court and the Committee of Treasury and shall not leave the Court during its deliberations unless requested to do so.[3]

The Assistant to the Governors was a new post recommended by the Committee, whose report stated:

> We consider that the Governors should be provided with an Assistant who would be in their confidence and would be capable of undertaking on their behalf any work with which they might entrust him. This position should be regarded as of the highest importance, free from departmental duties and to be held only by an Official of great experience and outstanding ability.[4]

As described in chapter 10, Dale was appointed Chief of Establishments as well as continuing to act as Secretary for the period of reorganisation, and the Establishment Department was soon implemented and operating efficiently. Within Dale's other Department, however, there were several important points which proved very difficult to resolve.

One of the first was how Ernest Skinner* was to be fitted into the new organisation. Skinner was Private Secretary to Governor Norman, the

---

* Skinner, Ernest Henry Dudley, CBE, 1892–1985. Entered Bank, 1911, Assistant to the Governors, 1935. General Manager of Finance Corporation for Industry (FCI), 1945–8.

first to hold the position in its enhanced form as suggested by a Committee reporting on the Conduct of Foreign Business in 1926:[5] he was transferred from the infant Central Banking Section. Before this date Norman's secretaries had usually been junior officials who did not stay in the post for very long. Skinner's evidence to Peacock as to his own duties ran to four typed foolscap pages, starting with the disclaimer that 'owing to the fortuitous nature of the post the duties have never been defined (and perhaps can never be fully defined)'. They included keeping himself as widely informed as possible over the various fields of the Governor's activity: 'much of the information acquired is of course never used but it is necessary, if only for the feeling of self-protection which it gives, to be fully prepared'. The Governor's Private Secretary (GPS) was responsible for the daily press summary, originally intended for the Governor but by 1932 circulated to some ninety-five people, travel arrangements for the Governors,* and virtually all the Governor's correspondence including the highly confidential telegrams warning central banks of probable changes in the Bank Rate. Further duties included arranging Governor Norman's numerous appointments (Norman continually complained of how wearing he found them), acting as a liaison between Governor and Advisers and 'as a centre for the rapid circulation of information and for the collection of miscellaneous information'.[6]

Whether the Private Secretary should be incorporated into the reorganised Secretary's Department was a matter for much discussion, and the position was further complicated by the new post of Assistant to the Governors. Who this should be, whether or not *he* should be within the Secretary's Department and what his relationship should be with Skinner, were all matters which continued to revolve for several months and elicited a vast amount of complex papers setting out the different possibilities.[7]

By September 1932 it was settled that Skinner should be Deputy Secretary to Dale; this incidentally brought connections with industry to the Secretary's Department, because Skinner was Secretary to the Securities Management Trust which had been set up as a wholly owned subsidiary of the Bank at the end of 1929 to help in the reconstruction and reorganisation of British industry. However this arrangement only brought further problems in its train: 'the existing Deputy Secretary

---

* Governor Norman regularly travelled under the name Skinner, a disguise which was easily penetrable and became well known to the press. It occasionally gave rise to complications, as when reporters besieged the cabin of an irate American professor whose name really was Skinner.

[Skinner]…is unfamiliar with most of his new duties and will have no opportunity of learning them while he continues to act as the Governor's private secretary'. If he were to continue in this capacity then an additional Deputy Secretary should perhaps be appointed 'who can take control of the Office in the Secretary's absence'.[8] More work would follow, it was noted, when the Assistant to the Governors had been appointed.

It appears that Percy Beale was at one time a candidate for this new position but in the event Leslie Lefeaux* was appointed at the end of 1932. He noted his functions and relationship with the Secretary's Department in January 1933: the Assistant should relieve the pressure on the Governors by undertaking on their behalf any special work they may require to be done, and by, wherever practical, interviewing people on their behalf. 'His appointment is personal and nobody will act as an alternate in his absence; but the Secretary's Department will act as his staff and all papers and records will be obtainable from that Department. The Secretary must be in a position to carry on the threads in his absence.' The Governor's Private Secretary would continue to deal with correspondence, and with appointments to see the Governors.[9]

A year after Dale's appointment in his dual capacity he was so anxious about the lack of progress in establishing an effective working relationship between these various elements that he addressed a personal letter to the Governor expressing his disquiet. Skinner's duties as GPS left him little or no time to begin to take over a substantial role in the Secretary's Department, yet Dale himself was hoping to retire 'perhaps in August 1935 but in no case later than February 1936'. Despite the good intentions of the Peacock Committee, the Secretary's Office was now 'little more than a machine for recording decisions of the Court and for carrying out the secretarial duties of the various Committees, so that the staff of the Office are thus more than ever in a backwater with little or no prospect of promotion'.[10]

Skinner in his turn noted that the Governor did not consider Skinner's work to be 'capable of being combined with the Committees etc. (except the Committee of Treasury). In his view the statutory duties of the Bank should receive the sole attention of the Secretary; yet he recognises that the man who looks after him is the best qualified as regards knowledge of current events to be Secretary of the Committee of Treasury.'[11]

In 1933 Leslie Lefeaux was appointed the first Governor of the Reserve Bank of New Zealand; the post of Assistant to the Governors

---

* See note, p. 293.

lapsed while the circular discussion as to the overlapping functions of the Secretary and Skinner – whose services Norman could not or would not dispense with – continued. In 1934 Dale retired and J.A.C. Osborne was appointed for a five month period from June to November. At the beginning of Osborne's term of office the Staff Director, Clegg, decided on some new measures in an effort to fulfill the Governors' explicit wish 'that the Secretary should be brought back into the Bank'. Three sections were transferred to his Department which, as Osborne noted, 'may claim to be *Banking* Offices' – the Bank Note Office, the Economics and Statistics Section (obviously concerned with banking and transferred from the CCO) and Accounts and Costing, transferred from the Audit Department. The old Secretary's Office with its legal and statutory obligations became the General Section.[12] This dealt with the work of the Court, Committee of Treasury and special and standing committees, all questions relating to the Charters, By-laws and Statutes in force, 'procedure and precedents generally and all matters of historical interest to the Bank' plus the needs of Governors, Directorate* and other members of the staff travelling abroad on official business.

Despite the extension of the Secretary's responsibilities Osborne was still concerned because, with the exception of the Economics Section, it remained a department of record rather than an executive department and 'unless further connecting links can be constructed...[might] fade gradually *out* of the Bank'.[13]

After Osborne's appointment as Deputy Governor of the Bank of Canada at the end of 1934, Skinner took temporary charge of the Secretary's Department, doing the work connected with Court, Committee of Treasury and other committees as well as the Governor's work. Early in 1935 Edward Stapley, who had earlier spent seven years as Assistant Chief Accountant, was appointed Secretary, a post he held until he became Chief Accountant jointly with A.M. Walker just before the outbreak of war, when he was succeeded as Secretary by Mynors. The difficulties of Skinner's position were resolved, greatly to his disappointment as he had hoped to become Secretary, by his appointment as Assistant to the Governors, the post which had been vacant since Lefeaux' departure: the Governor had no new Private Secretary so

---

* This sometimes led down curious byways, such as the Secretary's responsibility for the distribution of venison from the cull in the royal parks. Before the Second World War the Office of Works provided the Court with two bucks in the summer and two does in the winter, for which the fee was 13 shillings per doe and 26 shillings per buck, plus a few shillings for carriage. Those Directors who liked venison 'often take a quarter', but the arrangements were suspended because of meat rationing during and after the war, and seem not to have been resumed.

these positions were in effect amalgamated. Walter Nevill took over Skinner's job as Deputy Secretary at the same time, and the work for the Governor was thus confirmed in its position as a 'cell' loosely attached to the Secretary's Department, much as it had always been.[14]

This arrangement, with minor amendments, remained in force over the next thirty years. During the war the Economics and Statistics Section grew in both size and importance, as described in chapter 8. Its Principal was R.E.H. Allport; the Deputy Principal, Daniel Jones, was seconded to the Statistical Office of Exchange Control; in March 1942 all the various statistical units within the Bank were amalgamated, remaining in the Secretary's Department with the unhappy results outlined elsewhere.

Accounts and Costing had by 1941 split into two separate sections. The function of Accounts was to keep the accounts of the Banking and Issue Departments with a view to the preparation of the Bank's half-yearly profit and loss statements and the balance sheets, and to check the compilation by the CCO of the weekly Bank Return. The General Ledgers and other relevant journals were posted daily and 'a close check is imposed on all receipts and payments passing through the General Cash Book': interest on advances, bills and securities, management charges, commissions and fees on the one hand, and payments of salaries, wages and pensions, stationery, bills and rates and taxes on the other. The work connected with the Bank's costing system, introduced by Deloittes in 1920, was undertaken by the Costing Section.*[15]

The work of the Bank Note Office was described in chapter 4; it remained in the Secretary's Department and in 1958 was amalgamated with the Accounts Section and named the Accounts and Bank Note Office. In 1963 its bank note responsibilities were transferred to the Printing Works. Mynors became an Adviser to the Governors in 1944 and was succeeded as Secretary by his Deputy, Walter Nevill, who remained in the post for the next four years. This was a particularly demanding period because it covered the nationalisation of the Bank in 1946. The Treasury kept closely in touch with the Bank throughout the period of drafting the Bill and its passage through Parliament: the bulk of the work within the Bank was carried out by Mynors and Cobbold, with Nevill on hand for consultation on the legal and statutory aspects of the provisions of the Bill and of the new and simpler Charter which was necessary to replace those of 1694 and 1896. The new Charter, like its predecessors, was largely concerned with domestic organisation, and was

---

\* See chapter 6.

deliberately couched in fairly general terms. 'One of the advantages of working on a Charter 250 years old', as Holland-Martin noted during discussions on the wording of the new one, 'is that modern problems have not been dealt with in the [1694] Charter, which gives complete freedom to the Bank in most directions to deal with current matters as they arise'.[16] Once the Act was in force it was necessary for the Secretary's Department to familiarise itself swiftly with its provisions, and be ready to answer questions on them from all over the Bank with recourse to Freshfields where necessary.

The emphasis on records which was a concomitant of the work of the Secretary had led naturally to its housing of the Historical Records Section. The original terms of reference by which this was in effect constituted were contained in an Order of Court dated 13 February 1930, when William Marston Acres, author of *The Bank of England from Within* which was to be published the following year, was appointed an Assistant Principal attached to the Secretary's Office. His work was to include the compilation and maintenance of a general card index of 'the decisions of the Governors, Court, Committees etc.', a special card index for the Committee of Treasury, and a catalogue of the Bank's valuable collections of silver (much of it dating from the period of the Bank's foundation at the end of the seventeenth century), furniture, paintings, bank notes, coins and archives. Acres was also entrusted with general supervision of the Reference Library and the Directors' [lending] library, and of the silver and furniture,* and the preparation in conjunction with Freshfields of a new edition of the Charters, By-laws and Statutes in force.[17]

Acres and his assistant John Giuseppi, who succeeded Acres on his retirement in 1936, set about the lengthy and complex task of compiling the indexes to the Orders of Court and Governors, and to the minutes of the Committee of Treasury, back to 1694. They were also responsible for dealing with queries relating to the history of the Bank and of its Directors and Staff which were 'consistently numerous' and often involved a considerable amount of research. Further work was occasioned by the Section's direct links with various committees both internal and external. Giuseppi held the Secretaryship of the Reference Library Committee from the date of Acres' retirement until his own in 1960; he was also Secretary of the Bank Fine Arts Committee, which was set up in September 1944 with the object of reviewing items suggested for the Bank collections, including furniture and carpets, and advising on the best disposition of objects already acquired. The first members were

* A Curator of Furniture was appointed in 1945. See chapter 10, p. 367.

George Booth,* Holland-Martin and Mynors; by an Order of the Deputy Governor, Bernard, the Secretary of the Bank was added as an *ex officio* member of this Committee in March 1951.

In 1938 the Heads of Departments Committee had decided that a Bank Archives Committee should be formed. This was to consist of a Deputy Chief Cashier, a Deputy Chief Accountant, the Deputies to the Secretary and the Chief of Establishments and the Principal of the Branch Banks Office; later in the same year a representative from St Lukes' Printing Works was added. Its function was 'to decide upon the preservation of the records which would be likely to be of historical interest in the years to come'. It held only two meetings before the outbreak of war in 1939, and Giuseppi acted in an advisory capacity until it was reconstituted in 1949, after which meetings were held fairly regularly every six months. The Committee was itself advisory only and the final decisions concerning records were taken by the Head of Department concerned, who retained physical possession of them.

Giuseppi was also a member of various external bodies such as the British Records Association (established and maintained by the Public Records Office); the Council for the Preservation of Business Archives, set up in 1934, and the Roman and Medieval London Excavation Council established in 1946 by the Society of Antiquaries, of which Giuseppi was himself a Fellow. Holland-Martin was the Honorary Treasurer of the Excavation Council for a number of years and Giuseppi was appointed its Secretary in 1949.[18]

It was a long-held ambition of Giuseppi's to institute a museum in the Bank to display part of its substantial collection of treasures. A temporary exhibition held in 1937 had been very successful, and work had started in 1939 in a hall in the Sub-Vault to prepare for a permanent showing. The plans were frustrated by the war, but were revived in 1949, only to be shelved the following year because of the need for economy. At the end of 1955 the project got under way once more, and an exhibition room was opened in the spring of 1956. It was situated in the Secretary's Office adjacent to the Parlours, and displayed a range of items from the Bank's collections together with Roman and medieval relics unearthed in the Threadneedle Street site. It was not open to the public, but a visit to the exhibition was included in the weekly tours of the Bank available to the visitors who had a personal introduction.[19]

One Section of the Secretary's Office was devoted to the production of

---

* Booth, George Macaulay, 1877–1971. Director, White Drummond & Co., Municipal & General Securities Co. Dir. Gen. Min. of Munitions, 1914–19. Director, Bank of England, 1915–47.

a daily News Summary. This was started by the Governor's Secretary in about 1925, solely for the Governor's benefit, to give at a glance the outstanding items of financial and industrial news; its circulation and scope gradually increased until by September 1939 two men in the Secretary's Office were producing, normally by noon, fifty roneod copies based on information from *The Times, Financial Times* and *Financial News*, supplemented by occasional items from the more popular press. During the war years production was speeded up and the Summary was issued earlier and covered a wider range of papers, and its staff increased to a Principal Woman Clerk and nine others. An associated development was the appointment in 1941 – mainly because of the demands of exchange control – of Bernard Rickatson-Hatt, previously editor-in-chief of Reuters, to the position of Adviser to the Governors on all matters to do with the Press. He was always careful to emphasise the fact that he was not the Bank's Press Officer and that no such position existed, but his extensive journalistic contacts did prove useful to Norman and subsequently to Catto and Cobbold. Rickatson-Hatt assumed responsibility for the News Summary, and continued to expand and improve it. Cobbold's attitude to the press, although reticent, was far less Machiavellian than that of Norman, and he was also more willing to learn from it. He read the News Summary carefully and in June 1955 asked Rickatson-Hatt: 'Do you think my cuttings could be a little less respectable? What I really want to know is what Herald, Mirror, Worker and Tribune are saying about industrial troubles and other things which concern us. If you think this selection would cause alarm and despondency around the Parlours, send it to me in a plain van!!!' Rickatson-Hatt immediately issued instructions that these and 'other left wing journals in London and the provinces' were to be scrutinised daily and news items from them included in the News Summary where appropriate.[20]

To the Secretary of the Bank there also fell the overall supervision of the Bank's charitable giving. The first recorded gift was of £1,000 in 1745 to the Fund for the Relief, Encouragement and Support of His Majesty's Forces. The Bank was in constant receipt of requests for aid, usually financial, in a vast range of cases many of which were genuinely deserving. Until the 1930s there were no rules laid down as to how appeals were responded to: a memorandum from the Secretary's Office in October 1933 noted that 'it is in most cases extremely difficult, if not impossible, definitely to say what could have influenced the final decision of the Court or the Committee of Treasury' in their response to an appeal from any particular public charity. In general, however, it added, 'it can be said that applications for assistance on behalf of charitable organisations which are made by, or at the instance of, a Director or any other person of influence closely connected with the Bank always receive the most favourable consideration'.[21] An appeal sponsored by Buckingham Palace or the Mansion House was always supported; the Bank also made donations in certain instances for the purposes of obtaining an admission to an institution of a candidate in whom the Bank was interested, such as various schools of charitable foundation. It gave regularly to a good number of causes and institutions from which the staff could benefit, including the Bank Clerks' Orphanage, many of the London hospitals, convalescent homes, the City of London Truss Society and the Royal Surgical Aid Society. Single donations were also made to large national and international disaster funds, including 250 guineas to the Titanic Relief Fund and £2,100 for 'relief of distress in the mining areas' in 1928.[22]

Early in 1934 Dale was pleased to learn of the existence of 'an organisation of the Clearing Banks set up for the purpose of exchanging information concerning charitable appeals'. This was the Charities Committee of the London Clearing Banks, to whose weekly meetings the Bank sent a representative, co-ordinating its gifts carefully with those of the Big Five.

In June of the same year the whole question of giving was aired thoroughly in Court because of dissension among the Directors about the amount to be given to the Tower Hill Improvement Scheme. This had recently been launched with the object of buying up and demolishing 'unsightly buildings' in the vicinity of the Hill and converting the sites into open spaces. A Grand Council was formed under the patronage of the Prince of Wales, and six Directors of the Bank, including Cecil Lubbock,* were invited to become members. The Bank, in line with four of the Big Five, decided to give one hundred guineas to the appeal (the fifth bank gave £250).

Lubbock called this decision 'unsatisfactory and undignified'. The undesirability 'of giving away the shareholders' money' was cited against him, but Lubbock felt that the stockholders would not raise any objection to donations being made and wanted the question to be put to the General Court† with a view to getting permission to give away perhaps £10,000 in all annually. 'The Governor was against consulting the stockholders and thought that donations made to objects of *imperial*,

---

* Lubbock, Cecil, see p. 169n.
† A meeting of the Bank's Proprietors (stockholders) normally held in March and September each year.

*international* or *national* importance were legitimate because they were of a kind which would appeal to a Proprietor living in Edinburgh as much as one living in London and this should be the criterion.'

It was learnt that the Committee of Treasury 'had stated that they would be relieved if an understanding could be come to among the Directors that the Bank would not consider appeals if they were sponsored by individual Directors' and this was eventually agreed, although there was still strong feeling among some of the members of Court against such a proposal.[23]

In 1935 a Deed of Covenant was made with King Edward's Hospital Fund for London, who made annual subscriptions on the Bank's behalf to certain specified hospitals and used its own discretion as to how to apportion the balance of the covenanted yearly sum. Towards the end of the war the Secretary, Walter Nevill, decided to undertake a rationalisation of the Bank's charitable donations, and Deeds of Covenant were made with the National Council of Social Service by which the Bank set aside annual sums to be expended on specified donations.[24] This was obviously satisfactory from the points of view of both administration and tax effectiveness, and there was some discussion as to whether the bulk of the Bank's giving could be organised in a similar fashion. However because of the unpredictability of the size and nature of calls on the Bank's generosity in any one year, it was decided that such a plan was impracticable.

The smaller irregular payments were later put into the hands of a Charitable Appeals Committee which reported quarterly to the Committee of Treasury and Court. It was set up in January 1946, under the initial chairmanship of Sir Albert Gladstone;* the other members were Holland-Martin and Mynors, and the Secretary *ex officio*. This Committee had authority to grant on behalf of the Bank any amount under £1,000 in response to appeals, and to review annually the donations previously reviewed by the Committee of Treasury. Donations of £1,000 and above continued to be sanctioned by Court as before.[25] These arrangements continued in force, with increases in the amounts available for distribution, throughout the 1950s and 1960s. Policy, too, remained the same: the Bank continued to support appeals sponsored by Buckingham Palace and the Mansion House; institutions which offered some benefits to the staff; 'well-sponsored institutions, national in flavour, coming within the orbit of the City'; occasional provincial

---

* Gladstone, Sir Albert Charles, 5th Bt, MBE, 1886–1967. Chairman, Income Tax Commissioners for General Purposes, City of London; Director, Bank of England, 1924–47.

appeals in order to maintain the prestige of the Branches, and no denominational appeals unless in respect of 'buildings of a national and unique character'. Political causes were always eschewed.* The rule that appeals would only be considered when not sponsored by individual Directors also continued in force, although this occasionally gave rise to slight difficulties which were usually solved by letting the final decision be taken by the Committee of Treasury.[26]

A further concern of the Secretary's Department was protocol and the arrangements, in collaboration with Establishments, for visits by royalty and other distinguished visitors. King George V and Queen Mary came to the Bank in December 1917, the Duke and Duchess of York in 1934, and Queen Mary brought the young Princess Elizabeth in November 1937. Shortly after her accession, Queen Elizabeth II accepted the invitations of Governor Cobbold to come to luncheon at the Bank with the Duke of Edinburgh; the date was fixed for 4 December 1952, which gave the Bank six weeks in which to prepare for the visit.

The Secretary, A.W.C. Dascombe,† was responsible for all liaison between the Palace and the Bank, luncheon arrangements, Directors and Staff attending the luncheon, and an exhibition of archives in the Committee Room in the Parlours; the Chief of Establishments undertook everything relating to premises, arrangements for a tour of the Bank by the royal party and for the brief speech which the Queen agreed to give to the staff.

Dascombe was in constant communication with the Queen's Private Secretary, Sir Alan Lascelles,‡ about every detail of the arrangements including dress: the Palace pronounced that ladies should wear hats and gloves, and that short coats were correct for men. The lunch was to be attended by the Directors and chief officials of the Bank, making a party of some thirty in all. The compilation of the menu, supervised by Siepmann, gave rise to some anxiety. It was known that the Queen preferred quite plain and simple food (Deputy Governor Bernard noted for Siepmann's attention extracts to this effect from an article entitled 'A Day with the Queen' in *Everybody's* magazine), and there was no desire to provide too lavish a meal. But, although more than seven years had passed since the end of the war, some items of food were still rationed;

---

* The propriety of the Bank in making donations to a Mansion House fund for the defence of property in Ireland in 1882, and to a fund being raised to establish the Imperial Institute in 1887, was criticised in General Courts of those years by Proprietors on the grounds that the gifts 'indicated a political bias'.

† Arthur Dascombe was Secretary from 1949 to 1959.

‡ Lascelles, Rt Hon. Sir Alan Frederick, PC, GCB, GCVO, CMG, MC, MA, 1887–1981. Private Secretary to King George VI, 1943–52; to Queen Elizabeth II, 1952–3.

Plate 11.1    Governor Cobbold greeting H.M. Queen Elizabeth II on her visit to the Bank in December 1952. The Head Gatekeeper, J.A. Watson, in full dress, is on the right.

cream would be needed, which might prove difficult, and green beans had eventually to be obtained from France via an acquaintance of Siepmann's in the French Embassy in London.

The visit passed off most successfully. The tour of the Bank included the Issue Office, CCO, Drawing Office, Bill Office and Bullion Office as well as the small exhibition of Bank treasures laid out in the Committee Room in the Parlours. The Queen made a short speech from the balcony on the first floor to members of the staff (chosen by ballot) assembled in the Garden Court, and she and the Duke of Edinburgh signed the Distinguished Visitors Book, one of a series of leather bound books, nowadays containing partly printed £1,000 notes in the style of the old black and white £5, which are signed by the distinguished guests in the space normally reserved for the printed signature of the Chief Cashier. The inkstand given to the Bank the previous year by the Directors* was used, and two silver pens were specially made and later engraved to commemorate the occasion.[27]

* See chapter 1, p. 39.

The Coronation took place in June the following year, and numbers of foreign rulers and heads of state came to London to attend it. Several of them visited the Bank, including Crown Prince Akihito of Japan, the Sheikhs of Bahrein and Qatar, the Ruler of Kuwait and Queen Salote of Tonga.[28]

The work of the Secretary's Department, and consequently the numbers employed in it, expanded steadily in the late 1940s and the 1950s. In 1957 its responsibilities included, in addition to those already mentioned, a large and heterogeneous mixture including the provision of administrative or secretarial assistance to the Dollar Exports Board, the Council of Foreign Bondholders, the Securities Management Trust, the Governor's trusteeships, several internal and external funds and the preparation of the Annual Report. By 1958 staff in the Department numbered just over 100, excluding the members of the Statistics Office; but the fragmentary and specialised nature of the work meant that opportunities for promotion remained limited.[29]

# APPENDIX

## Governors, Deputy Governors, Directors and Senior Officials, 1930–1960*

### Governors

| | |
|---|---|
| Montagu Collet Norman | 1920–1944 |
| (Baron Norman of St Clere, 1944) | |
| Lord Catto of Cairncatto | 1944–1949 |
| Cameron Fromanteel Cobbold | 1949–1961 |
| (Baron Cobbold of Knebworth, 1961) | |

### Deputy Governors

| | |
|---|---|
| Sir Ernest Musgrave Harvey | 1929–1936 |
| Basil Gage Catterns | 1936–1945 |
| Cameron Fromanteel Cobbold | 1945–1949 |
| (Baron Cobbold of Knebworth, 1961) | |
| Dallas Gerald Mercer Bernard | 1949–1954 |
| (Baronet, 1954) | |
| Humphrey Charles Baskerville Mynors | 1954–1964 |
| (Baronet, 1964) | |

### Directors

| | |
|---|---|
| Lord Hyndley of Meads | 1931–1945 |
| William Henry Clegg | 1932–1937 |
| Patrick Ashley Cooper (Knight, 1944) | 1932–1955 |
| Edward Holland-Martin | 1933–1948 |
| Basil Gage Catterns | 1934–1948 |
| (Deputy Governor, 1936–1945) | |
| James George Weir | 1935–1946 |
| Dallas Gerald Mercer Bernard | 1936–1949 |
| (Deputy Governor, 1949–1954; Baronet, 1954) | |

* For previous appointments see Sayers, Vol. 3, Appendix 39.

| | |
|---|---|
| Laurence John Cadbury | 1936–1938 |
| | 1940–1961 |
| John Colbrook Hanbury-Williams (Knight, 1950) | 1936–1963 |
| John Martin | 1937–1946 |
| Evelyn James Bunbury | 1937–1938 |
| Sir Otto Ernst Niemeyer | 1938–1952 |
| Cameron Fromanteel Cobbold | 1938–1945 |
|   (Deputy Governor, 1945–1949; Governor, 1949–1961; | |
|   Baron Cobbold of Knebworth, 1960) | |
| Lord Catto of Cairncatto | 1940 |
|   (Governor, 1944–1949) | |
| Isaac James Pitman (KBE 1961) | 1941–1945 |
| John Maynard Keynes | 1941–1946 |
|   (Baron Keynes of Tilton, 1942) | |
| Hon. Josiah Wedgwood | 1942–1946 |
| Basil Sanderson | 1943–1965 |
|   (Baron Sanderson of Ayot, 1960) | |
| Harry Arthur Siepmann | 1945–1954 |
| Ralph Ellis Brook | 1946–1949 |
| George Gibson | 1946–1948 |
| Lord Piercy | 1946–1956 |
| Arthur George Wansbrough | 1946–1949 |
| Charles Dukes | 1947–1948 |
|   (Baron Dukeston of Warrington, 1947) | |
| Hon. Hugh Kenyon Molesworth Kindersley | 1947–1967 |
|   (Baron Kindersley of West Hoathly, 1954) | |
| Lord Braintree | 1948–1945 |
| George Lewis French Bolton (KCMG 1950) | 1948–1968 |
| Michael James Babington Smith | 1949–1969 |
| Sir George Chester | 1949 |
| | (March 1–April 21. |
| | Died in office) |
| Sir Kenneth Oswald Peppiatt | 1949–1957 |
| Humphrey Charles Baskerville Mynors | 1949–1954 |
|   (Deputy Governor, 1954–1964; Baronet, 1964) | |
| Andrew Naesmith (Knight, 1953) | 1949–1957 |
| Geoffrey Cecil Ryves Eley (Knight, 1964) | 1949–1966 |
| Sir George Edmond Brackenbury Abell | 1952–1964 |
| Frank Cyril Hawker (Knight, 1958) | 1954–1962 |
| Hon. Randal Hugh Vivian Smith | 1954–1966 |
|   (Baron Bicester of Tusmore, 1956) | |
| William Johnston Keswick (Knight, 1972) | 1955–1973 |
| Sir William Henry Pilkington | 1955–1972 |
|   (Baron Pilkington of St Helens, 1968) | |

| | |
|---|---|
| Sir Alfred Roberts | 1956–1963 |
| Maurice Henry Parsons | 1957–1970 |
| (Deputy Governor, 1966–1970; Knight, 1966) | |
| John Melior Stevens (KCMG 1967) | 1957–1965 |
| | 1968–1973 |

### Assistants to the Governors

| | |
|---|---|
| Leslie Lefeaux | 1932–1933 |
| Ernest Henry Dudley Skinner | 1935–1945 |
| Sir George Edmond Brackenbury Abell | 1949–1952 |
| Maurice Henry Parsons | 1954–1957 |
| John Melior Stevens (KCMG 1967) | 1956–1957 |

### Advisers to the Governors

| | |
|---|---|
| Oliver Mitchell Wentworth Sprague | 1930–1933 |
| Sir Henry Clay | 1933–1934 |
| Cameron Fromanteel Cobbold | 1933–1938 |
| Charles Bruce Gardner | 1935–1938 |
| Gilbert Edward Jackson | 1935–1939 |
| Evelyn James Bunbury | 1935–1937 |
| John Arundel Caulfield Osborne | 1938–1945 |
| Sir George Lewis French Bolton | 1941–1948 |
| John Bernard Rickatson-Hatt | 1941–1958 |
| Humphrey Charles Baskerville Mynors | 1944–1949 |
| John Stewart Lithiby | 1946–1955 |
| Frederic Francis Joseph Powell | 1946–1951 |
| Sir George Edmond Brackenbury Abell | 1948–1949 |
| Lucius Perronet Thompson-McCausland | 1949–1965 |
| John Lenox Fisher | 1950–1959 |
| Frank Cyril Hawker | 1953–1954 |
| William Maurice Allen | 1954–1964 |
| Hon. Arthur Maxwell Stamp | 1954–1958 |
| Sir Laurence James Menzies | 1957–1965 |
| (seconded to ECGD 1958–1962) | |
| Jasper St John Rootham | 1957–1963 |

### Secretaries

| | |
|---|---|
| Ronald Clement George Dale | 1927–1934 |
| John Arundel Caulfeild | June–Nov. 1934 |
| Edward Maitland Stapley | 1935–1939 |
| Humphrey Charles Baskerville Mynors | 1939–1944 |
| Walter Howard Nevill | 1944–1949 |
| Arthur William Charles Dascombe | 1949–1959 |
| Howard Mossforth Neatby | 1959–1968 |

## Chief Cashiers

| | |
|---|---|
| Basil Gage Catterns | 1929–1934 |
| Kenneth Oswald Peppiatt | 1934–1949 |
| Percival Spencer Beale | 1949–1955 |
| Leslie Kenneth O'Brien | 1955–1962 |

## Chief Accountants

| | |
|---|---|
| Augustus Merrifield Walker | 1921–1945 |
| Edward Maitland Stapley | 1939–1948 |
| Frank Cyril Hawker | 1948–1953 |
| William Douglas Simpson | 1953–1962 |

## Chiefs of Establishments

| | |
|---|---|
| Ronald Clement George Dale | 1932–1934 (Secretary and Chief of Establishments) |
| John Drysdale Mackenzie | 1934–1945 |
| Eric Neale Dalton | 1943–1949 |
| Michael McGrath | 1949–1953 |
| Donald Murray Randell | 1953–1955 |
| Howard George Askwith | 1955–1963 |

## Overseas and Foreign Department

| | | |
|---|---|---|
| Harry Arthur Siepmann | Chief (Acting) | 1932 |
| Cameron Fromanteel Cobbold | Acting Deputy Chief | 1933 |
| Frederick Francis Joseph Powell | Deputy Chief | 1935 |

Overseas and Foreign Department was absorbed into Cashier's Department (Exchange Control) under title of Overseas and Foreign Office – Order of Court 27 February 1941

## Deputy Chief Cashiers (Exchange Control and Overseas)

| | |
|---|---|
| Frank Cyril Hawker | 1943 |
| John Lenox Fisher | 1948 |
| Anthony Paul Grafftey-Smith | 1950 |
| Lawrence James Menzies | 1951–1957 |
| Maurice Henry Parsons | 1952–1954 |
| Guy McOlvin Watson | 1954–1957 |
| Cyril Robert Parke Hamilton | 1955–1957 |

The Court of 21 February 1957 decided that from 1 March 1957 the group of Offices known as Cashier's Department (E.C. & O.) should cease to exist as a separate organisation and that:

(a) The Overseas and Foreign Office should be absorbed in a Department to be known as Overseas Department;

(b) The Central Office should be abolished and the remaining Offices of the Cashier's Department (E.C. & O.) should be transferred to the Cashier's Department.

### Chief of Overseas Department

| | |
|---|---|
| Guy McOlvin Watson | 1957–1959 |

Overseas Department and Statistics Office in the Secretary's Department merged in a new Central Banking Information Department by Order of Court 29 October 1959.

### Chief of Central Banking Information Department

| | |
|---|---|
| Guy McOlvin Watson | 1959–1963 |

### Auditors

| | |
|---|---|
| John Douglas Spencer Dean | 1925–1931 |
| Walter Howard Nevill | 1931–1935 |
| William Axten | 1935–1938 |
| Alexander Stewart Craig | 1938–1941 |
| Ronald Clapham Thomas | 1941–1949 |
| Alexander Stewart Craig | 1949–1952 |
| Howard Mossforth Neatby | 1952–1957 |
| Stanley Lamb | 1957–1959 |
| Kenneth James Stuart Andrews | 1959–1963 |

# NOTES

## 1 The Bank at War

1 M5/533–9 Bank of England, 1939–45, volumes 1–7. This is a history of the war years in the Bank, compiled for internal use by J.A.C. Osborne, an Adviser to the Governors, and R.E.H. Allport between 1943 and 1950. Volume 7 is entirely concerned with staff matters and includes full details of all wartime salaries, wages, pensions and allowances, etc., as well as a description of the locations written by L.A. Gash, the Deputy Chief of Establishments, 1938–45.

2 ADM 2/4 Bank of England, 1914–21, vol. 4, pp. 79–83. Another internal history, written in 1926 by several people in different Offices.

3 M5/539, p. 1657.

4 *The Old Lady of Threadneedle Street* (hereafter OL), December 1942, *Air Raid Precautions at Head Office*, by A.C.H. 81/26, vol. 7, p. 1645. 5, June 1940, *Blitzkrieg at the Bank*, by Donald Norris, MD, FRCS, the Bank's Medical Officer.

Mackenzie, A.D., *The Later Years of St Luke's Printing Works*, Bank of England, 1961, pp. 37–8

6 G 15/16, Bank of England War Book, 1939–45, section I.

7 ADM 24/25 E. Holland-Martin's Correspondence 1939. Letters to J. Wedgwood, nos. 169, 190, 194, 199, 239.

8 AC 13/9, The Accountant's Dept. during the Second World War, 1950, f. 33.

9 M5/539, p. 1658.

10 ADM 24/25 Letters to P. Donner, nos. 62, 63, 67, 82, 90, 116, 121, 187, 191, 218, 257, 324.

11 M5/539, pp. 1658–60.

12 AC 9/6, Records, Accts Dept., 25 August 1939; 9068 Trentham Hall Correspondence, 1939–45, 28 August 1939, et seq.;
AC 10/17 DAO Barlaston Hall, 1939–44.

13 M5/539, pp. 1660–7. Descriptions of the early days at the locations,

based on diaries and letters, are given by Ted Bellamy, OL, December 1972, *Something in the country*; J.A. Mulvany, OL, Autumn 1979, *Whitchurch Diary*; and J. Fyson, Letters OL, Winter 1979.

14 Orders of Court, 7 September and 9 November 1939.

15 Order of Court, 12 June 1940. For a summary of the different leave arrangements throughout the war, see 81/26, vol. 7, pp. 1593–5.

16 M5/539, pp. 1709–12.

17 For further discussion of the 'Hump', see chapter 10.

18 ADM 24/4 Letter to H. Parker, 17 October 1939, no. 328.

19 Wartime amendments to Rules and Orders for Clerks, Rule I. For summary of amendments see 81/26, vol. 7, p. 1614.

20 M5/539, *Table*, Numbers of Staff 1939–46, p. 1590.

21 Orders of Court, 30 May and 1 August 1940.

22 E9/2 Bank Picquet, 1941–6; 81/26, vol. 7, p. 1641.

23 AC 2/4 Emergency Measures–Evacuation of Head Office, DPO to Barlaston, Arrangements in the event of further evacuation, 1939–42.
Information from Derrick Byatt.

24 ADM 10/6 Anniversary, f. 103.

25 OL, December 1986. *Looking Back*, by Lady Pamela Davis, who as Pamela Louch worked in the Drawing Office during the war.

26 OL, Winter 1975, obituary notice of Venting Gibbs, by W.D.T.

27 M5/539, p. 1649.

28 ADM 20/29 Governor Norman's Diary, 1940, 9 and 10 September.

29 G I/510 Governor's Correspondence, Norman to J. Martin, 18 September 1940.

30 G I/510 Norman to J. Martin, 24 October 1940.

31 M5/539, p. 1646.

32 Information from Derrick Byatt.

33 OL, December 1940.

34 OL, December 1942. *Air Raid Precautions*.

35 Mackenzie, *The Later Years*, pp. 44–5.

36 OL, December 1942, *Air Raid Precautions*.

37 M5/539, pp. 1606–7.

38 C 7/2, 3 and 4 Annual Reports from Branches to Chief Cashier, 1943–8.
C 56/43 Work of Offices–Branches, 1937–49.
E 5/70 Branches General, 1938–61.
E 5/74 Liverpool Branch, 6 October 1959.

39 M5/539, p. 1610. By the end of the war twenty-three members of staff and sons of staff had been taken prisoner.

40 Framed copy of Beaverbrook's letter to R.C. Kidd, Secretary and Treasurer of the Bank of England Staff Spitfire Fund, hangs (1991) on wall in Financial Accounts Office on 6th floor, Head Office. History of the aircraft, Spitfire No. P8509, obtained by Secretary's Office from Air Historical Branch, Ministry of Defence, in 1967.

41 OL, Spring 1943.

42 G 15/283, Expenditure Committee Meetings – Matters Arising, February 1936–February 1962. Hampshire Locations, 1939, 1940.
ADM 20/30 Governor Norman's Diary, 1941, 7–9 August.

43 Administrative arrangements at the locations, covering blackout, Camp Police and many other facets of life in Hampshire, are contained in the following files:
AC 10/7 Hurstbourne Camp Police, 1940–2,
AC 10/9 Camp Site, Mansion, 1939–40,
AC 10/10 Camp Site, Mansion, 1940–45,
AC 10/11 Whitchurch Notices, 1939–45,
AC 10/13 Hurstbourne Correspondence, July 1941–June 1942,
AC 10/16 Overton Administrative Arrangements, 1939–44.

44 M5/539, pp. 1685–6.

45 ACD/B, 703/5, May 1945. War-work at the locations was organised by R. Peake, who was responsible for the cinema – see note 53 below.
G/3 170 Advisers Duplicate letters, 1943–4.

46 M5/539, pp. 1692–6.

47 AC 10/16, 23, 24 and 25 September 1940.

48 G 1/510 Norman to J. Martin, 30 June 1940.

49 M5/539, pp. 1686–90.

50 *Andover Advertiser*, 15 November 1974, quoted in OL, Spring 1975.

51 OL, December 1964, retirement notice of A.F. Coldicott.

52 The Editor of *The Old Lady* from 1939–46 was Beryl Langford, who had been secretary to Leslie Bonnet, the previous editor, who left for war service shortly after the outbreak of war.

53 ACD/B 703/1–5. These papers give a full account of the history of the Film Society in Hampshire, including films chosen and shown, finances, organisation, etc.
87/49, Commentary by A.F. Coldicott on film of life at Hurstbourne made by Peake Brothers.

54 OL, June 1946, *A Temporary Takes Stock*, by E.B. Mumford.

55 Boothroyd, B., *A shoulder to laugh on*, Robson Books, 1987, pp. 77–8.

56 G 15/209, Special Committee on Accountant's Dept., 1940–5, 7 January 1942.

57 M5/539, p. 1650.
ADM 30/36 Gifts to the Bank.

58 Boyle, Andrew *Montagu Norman*, Cassell, 1967.
Sayers, R.S., *The Bank of England, 1891–1944*, vol. II, Cambridge University Press 1976.

59 ADM 24/4 Letters to Sir John Clapham, no. 42.
ADM 24/5 Letters to Sir John Clapham, nos. 250, 264.
For further material re. administrative arrangements for Clapham's History see G 15/567–572.

60 G 15/45 250th Anniversary Special Committee.

G 15/227 250th Anniversary-General.

ADM 10/6 Anniversary.

61 Court, 1 June 1944–quoted in G 15/45.

62 ADM 10/6, ff 58, 61, 67.

63 ADM 10/6, ff 111–18.

64 ADM 10/6, ff 147.

65 EID 14/4 Houblon-Norman Fund General, 1943–51. 30 May 1944.

66 EID 14/4 Niemeyer and Mynors to Governor, 2 June 1944.

67 G 15/227 Memo by Mynors, 7 July 1944.

68 G 15/227, 28 July 1944.

69 ADM 10/6 Texts of speeches at lunch, f. 131; menu, f.129; Governor's broadcast, f. 138.

70 Boyle, *Montagu Norman*, pp. 325, 328.

71 ADM 30/123 Plate Modern: Individual Makers: Durbin, L.
   Bank of England Museum Catalogue, Plate, Accession no. P178.

72 AC 10/17 March 1944.
   M5/539, p. 1706.

73 G 15/209 Catto to Bridges, 30 April 1945.

74 M5/539, p. 1699.

75 G 15/283 Reports on expenditure at the Hampshire Locations, 1939–45.
   M5/539, p. 1713.

76 M5/539, pp. 1706–7.

77 G 15/283 Bank's Hostels in London and Glasgow 1948–51.
   G 14.20 Committee of Treasury Files 1945–50.

78 M5/539, pp. 1588–90, 1599–1600.
   For details of War Memorial in Head Office, see chapter 10.

## 2 The Accountant's Department

1 Acres, W.M., *The Bank of England From Within*, vol. I, Oxford University Press, 1931.

2 Ibid., p. 111. Chief Cashier at this date was Thomas Madockes, Chief Accountant was Thomas Mercer.

3 P.G.M. Dickson, *The Financial Revolution in England: a study in the development of public credit*, Macmillan, 1967, pp. 78–9.

4 *Bank of England Quarterly Bulletin* (hereafter QB), March 1963, The Bank of England as Registrar, p. 22.

5 AC 4/1 A short history of the development of the system of transfer of British government stocks by instrument in writing. Compiled by G. Blunden Sen., November 1952, pp. 1–6.

6 AC 13/283 A history of Inscribed Stock and the payment of dividends. Compiled by J.M. Luce and others, 1957.

7 24 Vic cap 3, Section 7.
   Court Minute Ic 8/9, 17 April 1861.

8 Bank of England Museum Catalogue Access nos. 187 and 818.
   No 818 is a smaller version of 187. At least one other copy is thought to exist.

9 AC 13/283.
10 Dickson, *The Financial Revolution*, p. 459n.
11 Stockdale, E., *Bank of England in 1934*, Eastern Press, 1934, p. 91.
12 AC 4/1, pp. 11 and 25.
13 AC 4/1, p. 44.
14 OL, Spring 1976, R.N. Goodman, Correspondence, pp. 83–4.
   OL, September 1963, R.N. Goodman, *The Drawing Office Kipper*, p. 165.
   Stockdale, *Bank of England*, p. 91.
15 OL, Spring 1981, *An editor looks back*: L. Bonnet, p. 28.
16 OL, Spring, 1976, M.H.Browning Correspondence, p. 13.
17 *The Bankers' Magazine*, December 1981, N. Craik, *How the Bank looked after its evacuees*.
18 AC 2/1 Mechanisation, September 1928–May 1939. See also AC 2/2, Mechanisation, 1939–42. Much of the work of mechanisation in the Accountant's Department in the 1930s was planned by H.V. Such, who retired as Deputy Chief Accountant in 1939.
19 M5/539, p. 1744.
   AC 4/1, pp. 49–50.
20 M5/539, p. 1745. The Logograph seems never to have been used.
21 M5/539, pp. 1746–7.
22 AC 4/1, p. 65.
23 AC 4/1, p. 73.
24 AC 4/1, p. 73.
25 G 15/16 Bank of England War Book, 1939–1945.
26 AC 13/279 Abolition of Inscribed Stock, 1939–1943. Norman to Hopkins, 21 December 1939.
27 AC 13/279.
28 AC 13/9 The Accountant's Department during the War, 1939–45.
29 ADM 15.10, Establishment Department Papers, 1941–57, Section A318.1 Inspector of Offices and Branches. Order of Court, 19 February 1941.
30 AC 13/10 Accountant's Department: Inspector of Offices' Reports, March–September 1943.
31 G 15/209 Special Committee on Accountant's Department, General.
32 G 15/206 Special Committee on Accountant's Department, 1943.
   G 15/209.
33 G 15/206, 9 September 1943.
34 G 15/209, 7 May 1943.
35 E 5/5 Accommodation, Royal Exchange, section P803.127.
   G 15/206.
   AC 10/10 Camp Site, Mansion etc., 2 October 1944.
   G 15/206, September 1944.
36 G 15/206 Chancellor to Governor, 10 October 1944.
37 G 15/209.
38 Giuseppi, J., *The Bank of England*, Evans Bros., 1966.
39 G 15/209 Catto to Bridges, 30 April 1945.

40  E 5/46 Regent Arcade House. Governor's Note, 26 March 1947.

41  E 5/46 Eady to Emmerson, 30 June 1947.

42  E 5/46 October 1947–February 1948.

43  AC 13/543 Electricity Nationalisation, December 1946–March 1948 C 7/6 Agents' Meetings, May 1938–March 1972. Statement by Hawker, February 1949.

44  QB, March 1963, p. 23.

45  E 5/46, 1948–53.

46  AC 13/2 Report on Work of Accountant's Dept. ('Abell Committee') Documents and Minutes. Terms of reference: Committee of Treasury Minutes, 28 July 1948.

AC 1/5 Report (final version), June 1949.

47  AC 13/451 Mechanisation, 1934–73, 27 September 1945.

48  AC 13/455 Hollerith Scheme, 1945.

AC 13/456 Hollerith Scheme, 1947.

49  AC 1/5, p. 9.

50  OL, Spring 1980, p. 10.

51  *The Times*, 11 February 1890.

52  ADM 6/30 Stock Management – Accumulative Dividend Scheme, 1935–77.

53  AC 13/457 USA and Canada – Mr. Hawker's visit, 1950.

AC 13/458 Accountant's Department – Visits, 1948 and 1954.

AC 13/459 Accountant's Department –Mechanisation. Visits to USA, 1949 and 1954.

AC 13/460 Mechanisation. Visit to USA, 1955.

AC 13/295 Visit to North America, 1956.

54  AC 15/18 Accountant's Department – Permanent Home. Paper by W.D. Simpson, 18 October 1948, summarises steps taken, 1943–8.

55  G 3/35 Governor's Duplicate Letters, April–June 1947. Cobbold to Bamford, 26 June 1947, f. 906.

56  AC 15/18 Report on possibility of staff recruitment outside London, July 1951.

57  AC 15/18, 18 October 1948.

58  E 5/55 Friday Street Site-Press Cuttings. *Evening News*, 4 May 1950.

59  E 5/49 Friday Street Site, October 1949–July 1953. January 1951.

60  E 5/48 Friday Street Site, February 1949–February 1957. Bamford to Cobbold, 18 January 1951.

61  AC 15/18, 17 and 18 September 1951.

62  E 5/48, October 1952–February 1953.

63  The member of Establishments most closely concerned with the building of New Change was Geoffrey Noakes. Noakes moved to the Department to oversee the Premises Section in 1947, and became Deputy Chief of Establishments, under H.G. Askwith, in 1956.

64  The Special Committee on Branch Premises, set up in October 1937, was renamed the Special Committee on Bank Premises in November 1947.

65  E 5/55 *Daily Telegraph*, 21 June 1954.

66  *The Times*, 4 and 13 May 1953.

67 Pevsner, N., *The Buildings of England-London, Vol. I*, Penguin Books, 1957, pp. 164, 199n, 256n. Pevsner described New Change in this volume as 'shockingly lifeless and reactionary'.

68 E 5/53 Friday Street Site, December 1956–April 1964. 27 February 1958.

69 E 5/50 Friday Street Site, August 1953–March 1962. Negotiations for lease and building.

70 E 5/53 Mynors to Watkinson, 8 March 1955.

71 E 5/53, May–August 1955.

72 E 5/41 Governor's Note, 24 February 1953.

73 E 5/51 Friday Street Site – Governor's Flat and Living Quarters.

74 E 5/54 Friday Street Site – Suggestions by staff.

75 E 5/52 New Change Building, February 1950–April 1965.

76 E 5/55 *Financial Times*, 28 June 1954.

77 E 5/53, April 1954–September 1955.

78 Paterson, William, entry in *Dictionary of National Biography*, Smith, Elder & Co., 1895.

79 E 5/53, 9 September 1955.

80 E 5/59, Statues and Busts, New Change, 1956–9. Enclosure to 16 March 1959 gives details of all statuary.

81 ADM 30/51 Premises General, 1927–1960. 22 December 1976.

82 E 5/53 Correspondence re mosaics, July 1955, July 1957 and April 1959.

83 E 5/59 *The Scotsman*, 28 June 1957.

84 E 5/59, April 1956–May 1957.

85 E 5/53 Enclosure to 27 February 1958.

86 E 5/59, 14 January 1958.

87 E 5/59.

88 OL, September 1955 Editorial Notes, The Demise of the Power of Attorney Office, p. 148.

89 AC 13/465 Mechanisation, 1956–7.
AC 13/467 Mechanisation, 1957–64. Chief Accountant's Report to the Governors.
AC 13/471 Mechanisation – Powers-Samas Experiment.
AC 13/472 Powers-Samas Scheme Progress Meetings, 1957–9.
Powers-Samas and British Tabulating Machine Co. merged in January 1959 and became International Computers & Tabulators Ltd.

90 AC 13/467, 4 March 1957.

91 OL, June 1958, New Change, pp. 61–7.

92 AC 13/18 Move to New Change.
OL, September 1958, Photographs opposite p. 145.
A detailed description of stock management procedures at the time of the move is given in AC 1/6 Stock Management at the Bank of England, 1958.

93 E 5/56 Friday Street Site Tenants, 1950–5.
E 5/57 Friday Street Site Tenants, 1955–6.

## 3 Exchange Control, 1939–1957

1 M5/534, pp. 274 ff.
2 G 3/216 Deputy Governor's Letter Book 1937, no. 235, 8 July 1937.
3 81/26, vol. 2, pp. 274 ff.
   EC 4/92 Authorised Dealers and Depositaries, 1939–41.
4 Sayers, *The Bank of England*, vol. II, p. 571. Siepmann's notice is located
   (1991) in the Officials' Dining Room on the fourth floor, Threadneedle Street.
5 M5/535, pp. 549 ff.
6 EC 6/25 Exchange Control Work of Offices: Engagement of Temporary
   Staff. Note by Bolton, 17 September 1942.
   EC 6/30 Sub-Exchanges. The original four Sub-Exchanges were:
   Harlow & Jones Ltd, 16 Coleman St, EC2;
   Edward Meyer & Co., Kent House, Telegraph St, EC2;
   M.W. Marshall & Co., 1 Royal Exchange Avenue, EC3.
   Souch Jefferys & Spillan Ltd, 2 Great Winchester St, EC2.
7 EC 6/25.
8 See for example the UK exchange control: a short history: QB, 1967,
   pp. 245–60; EC 3/1 Exchange Control. An internal history, 1939–45, by
   E.T. Ruddle, a former member of the EC Staff; The evolution of exchange
   control in the UK, 1939–49: *Midland Bank Review*, February 1949.
9 EC 1/1–4 contain Minutes of Exchange Control Conference, 1939–45.
10 E 4/35 Redundant Staff. Note by Siepmann, 7 August 1953.
11 Lord O'Brien, personal communication to author, July 1987.
12 Order of Court, 2 November 1939.
13 C 94/60 Securities Registration – Gifts and Loans, 1940–2.
   EC 6/20 Securities Control and Registration Offices, 1940–56.
14 M5/535, pp. 565 ff.
   Reports to the Chief Cashier: EC 6/1 Acceptance Credits; EC 6/7
   Regulations General; EC 6/9 Trade Control and Investigation.
15 EC 6/9, 30 June 1941.
16 M5/535, pp. 585 ff.
   EC 6/1.
17 EC 6/17 Central Office. Note on origins of Staff Register Office, 25 July 1950.
18 M5/535, pp. 622 ff. gives detailed account of operations of Control Filing
   Section throughout the war.
   EC 6/17.
19 G 3/218 Deputy Governor's Letter Book 1939 no. 664, 1 December 1939.
20 M5/535, p. 578.
   EC 6/4 Reports to Chief Cashier, Export Permits Office
   Order of Court, 30 May 1940.
   EC 6/8 Securities Control Office including UKSD, 1941–62.
21 EC 6/23 Exchange Control Work of Decentralisation: General Memoranda.
22 EC 5/99 Glasgow.
   EC 6/5 Glasgow Office.

EC 6/10 Glasgow Local Control Dossier.

M5/535, pp. 635 ff. Review of the first three years of the Glasgow Control.

23  M5/535, pp. 604 ff.

EC 6/20.

A dramatic but substantially accurate account of the removal of the gold and securities to Montreal is given in 'The secret voyage of Britain's treasure', Stowe, L., *Reader's Digest*, November, 1955.

24  G 14/130 Committee of Treasury-Exchange Control 1940–69. Minutes of 13 November 1940 and 5 February 1941; Dalton's report, 16 December 1940.

G 15/53 Cashier's Department–Exchange Control and Overseas, 1939–57

EC 2/1–9 Minutes of Defence (Regulations) Committee, 1941–7.

25  M5/535, pp. 612 ff.

26  A copy of the report of the Post-War Committee is filed in EC 6/15 Committee to review Exchange Control Practice 1942. No record of any formal minutes of the Post-War Committee appears to exist in the Archive but many of its policy papers and documents are filed in EC 4/307 Post-War Committee Preliminary Papers, 1942–6, EC 4/413 Exchange Control Post-War Planning – Siepmann's papers, and EC 4/414 Defence (Finance) Regulations and Exchange Control Policy Post-War – Bolton's personal file.

OV 164/19 League Loans Committee Annual Reports, 1933–50.

27  G 14/130, 3 July 1942.

28  ADM 15/5–7 Inspector's Office Investigations, nos. 15–28.

29  EC 6/14–15 Evidence, Minutes, Conclusions and further papers – Committee to review Exchange Control Practice, 1942–3.

EC 2/10 Committee to review Exchange Control Practice, 1942–3.

30  M5/535, p. 598.

EC 6/17.

31  EC 6/7.

32  EC 6/4.

33  EC 6/9.

34  E 5/99.

OL, March 1976, p. 21, *Early recollections of the Glasgow Office*, R. Stevenson.

35  M5/535, p. 649.

*Midland Bank Review*, February 1949.

36  E 5/99.

37  G 14/130, 3 July, 6 September 1945; Letter from Chancellor to Governor, 28 September 1945.

38  Exchange Control Bill Memoranda, 1946, HMSO Cmd 6954.

39  EC 4/308–318 relate to drafting and revision of Bill which became 1947 Exchange Control Act.

40  G 14/130 Catto to Hopkins, 9 January 1945.

41  The Bank does not possess a complete set of Minutes of the FECC, 1945–79, but many extracts from them are in the files, especially those on outward

remittance. Early volumes of Treasury copies of the Minutes are in the Public Record Office at Kew.

42 EC 6/13 Costs of administration of Exchange Control, 1953–61. Note dated 2 February 1953.

43 Inspector's Final report filed in EC 2/11 Committee to review Exchange Control methods and technique, 1948.

44 EC 2/11, 30 March 1945.

45 EC 2/11 Final report, 1948 December.

46 G 14/130 Note by Cobbold, 11 October 1948.

47 G 14/130 Bridges to Cobbold, 4 January 1951.

48 Grafftey-Smith to Cobbold, 16 January 1951.

49 Acres *The Bank of England*, vol. II, p. 438.

50 E 4/27 Supplementary Staff, 1949–52.

51 G 14/130 Bernard to Bridges, 2 February 1951.

52 EC 6/18 Central Office, Commodities Section, 1951–4.
    EC 6/3 Reports to Chief Cashier – Commodities Office, 1954–62.

53 EC 2/12 Exchange Control Liaison Committee 1952. Kindersley to Siepmann, 14 August 1952.

54 EC 2/12 Draft reply, Siepmann to Kindersley, 20 August 1952.

55 EC 2/12 Governor's Note, 7 October 1952.

56 EC 2/12 Report of Liaison Committee, 24 December 1952.

57 EC 6/1.

58 EC 6/4.
    EC 6/9.

59 EC 6/17.

60 EC 6/7, July 1954.

61 G 14/130 Note by Deputy Governor Mynors of arrangements reported at Committee of Treasury, 2 January 1957 and at Court, 3 January 1957.

62 Extracts from Minutes of Exchange Control Conference, 1942–3, are filed in G 1/45.

## 4 The note issue

1 For the early history of the Bank of England note see A.D. Mackenzie, *The Bank of England Note: A History of Its Printing*, Cambridge University Press, 1953.

2 Clapham, John, *The Bank of England 1694–1914*, vol. II, Cambridge University Press, 1944, pp. 106–7.

3 Ibid., pp. 126–8.

4 Ibid., pp. 183–4.

5 QB, June 1969 *The Bank of England Note: a short history*, p. 214.

6 Mackenzie, *The Bank of England Note*, pp. 139–40.

7 QB, June 1969, p. 213n.

8 Sayers, *The Bank of England*, vol. I, pp. 291–3.

9 C 12/65 Britannia, 1952–63.

10 C 12/52 Note by Fortin, 6 April 1960.
    C 12/51 New Issues, 1 March 1960–31 March 1960, f247.

11 M5/533, p. 223.
12 Mackenzie, A.D., *The Later Years of St Luke's Printing Works*, Bank of England, 1961, p. 37.
13 Currency and Bank Notes Act 1939, 2 and 3 George VI c 7, section I.
14 M5/533, pp. 235–7.
15 M5/533, pp. 231–4.
    Pirie, A., *Operation Bernhard*, Cassell & Co. Ltd, 1961.
    Burke, B., *Nazi Counterfeiting of British £ Currency During World War II*, Franklin Press, USA, 1987.
16 G 29/28 SLC-Notes-War Printing BMA Free French and 'Baby Notes', 1939–49.
    M5/533, pp. 237–8.
17 G 29/28.
    M5/533, pp. 246–8.
18 EC 6/15 Committee to Review Exchange Control Practice, 1942, contains copy of Interim Report of Post-War Committee.
19 C 12/37 Bank of England Notes – Withdrawal, December 1942–March 1944.
20 C 12/39 Bank of England Notes – Withdrawal, May 1945–March 1961.
    M5/533, p. 226.
21 M5/533, p. 229.
    C 12/42 New Issues, June 1944–October 1948. Herbert Brittain to Catterns, 5 April 1945.
22 M5/533, p. 217.
23 ADM 15/7 Inspector's Office Investigations. No. 27: Reports on Bank Note Office, November 1942 and March 1945.
24 QB, September 1963, *Mutilated Notes*, pp. 199–201.
    C 12/26, 27, 28, 29, 30 Lost Destroyed and Mutilated Notes, April 1929–December 1961.
25 C 12/9 Bank of England Notes: Sundry Subjects, 1948–50.
    C 29/22 Notes: Destruction and De-Inking, 1927–73.
26 C 40/881 Currency and Bank Notes Act 1954, 28 July 1945.
27 C 40/881, 26 August 1949.
28 C 40/881, 9 September 1949.
29 C 40/881, 13 September 1949.
30 C 40/881, Draft Bill, 4 October 1949.
31 C 40/881, Draft Bill, 2 March 1950;
    Chief Cashier to Mynors, Peppiatt and Governors, 15 March 1950.
32 C 40/881, Chief Cashier to Mynors, Peppiatt and Governors, 20 March 1950.
33 C 40/881 Note by Mynors, 24 March 1950.
34 C 40/881 Trend to Beale, 22 April 1950.
35 C 40/881 Treasury to Beale, 22 June 1951.
36 C 40/881 Beale to Peppiatt and Governors, 27 November 1951.
37 Draft Bill, 21 December 1951.
38 C 40/881 Governor's Note, 17 October 1952.

39 *Hansard*, 3 December 1953.
   Currency and Bank Notes Act, 1954 2 and 3, Elizabeth II, c. 12.
40 C 12/20 Store, supply and re-issue, 1859–1940. Issue Office Note, 3 June 1937.
41 C 56/58 Work of Office – Annual Reports from Offices, 1949, Issue Office.
42 C 12/23 Store, supply and re-issue, January 1952–December 1956.
43 QB, March 1966, *The growth in demand for new bank notes*, p. 37.
44 OL, September 1980, J. Deacon: *In search of Stephen Gooden*, p. 114.
45 C 12/43 New Issues, April 1949–December 1954. Houblon note: Deputy Governor's Note, 28 June 1950.
46 C 12/43 Cobbold to Bridges, 26 January 1954.
47 C 12/125 New Issues, March 1949–December 1972. 16 March 1949.
48 C 12/43 Beale to GM, St Luke's, 10 February 1950.
49 C 12/43 Gooden to Beale, 29 May 1950.
50 C 12/43 Gooden to Beale, 29 September 1950.
51 C 12/44 New Issues, January 1955–March 1956. Memoranda by O'Brien, 27 January, 1 April, 7 September 1955.
52 C 12/44 O'Brien to Tong and Fortin, 29 December 1955.
53 C 12/44 O'Brien to Peppiatt and Governors, 11 January 1956.
   C 12/44 Fortin to O'Brien, 23 January 1956.
   C 12/44 Fortin to Tilley, 24 January 1956.
54 C 12/44 Fortin to O'Brien, 13 February 1956.
55 C 12/44 Note for Record, 7 March 1956.
56 C 12/44 Cobbold to Adeane, 27 March 1956.
57 C 12/45 New Issues, April 1956–September 1956. Fortin to O'Brien, 14 May 1956.
58 C 12/45 Fortin, note re sitting at Buckingham Palace, 1 May 1956.
59 Fortin to Governors, 16 April 1956.
   Press Announcement, 27 July 1956.
60 *Hansard*, 3 December 1953.
61 C 12/45 Fortin to Tong, 22 June 1956.
   Further discussion on this topic is in C 12/47, New Issues, March 1957–June 1958, May and June *passim*.
62 Hewitt, V.H. and Keyworth, J.M., *As Good as Gold : 300 Years of Bank Note Design*, British Museum and Bank of England, 1987, p. 123.
   C 12/57 Public comments on new issues, 1957–9.
63 C 12/47 O'Brien to Governors, 26 November 1957.
64 ADM 6/79 Bank Notes – Registers 1934–73.
65 C 12/47 O'Brien to Governors, 29 April 1958.
66 C 12/48 New Issues, July 1958–September 1959. Adeane to Cobbold, 22 October 1958.
67 C 12/48 O'Brien to Governors, 10 September 1958.
   Minutes of Committee of Treasury, 8 October 1958.
68 C 12/125 Makins to Cobbold, 6 August 1959.
69 C 12/125, November 1959 *passim*.

C 12/49 New Issues, October–December 1959. November 1959 *passim*.
Cabinet Memorandum, 13 November 1959, and Minutes, 17 November 1959: Public Record Files CAB 128/33 and 129/99.

70 C 12/49, 19 November 1959.

C 12/50 New Issues, January–February 1960 *passim*.

C 12/51 New Issues, March 1960 f 118 ff.

71 *Hansard*, 1 April 1960.

72 C 12/52 New Issues, April–December 1960. 22 April 1960.

*Daily Telegraph*, 31 March 1960.

73 C 12/51 P. Reilly to Cobbold, 24 March 1960.

C 12/51 Cobbold to Lord Bridges, 28 March 1960.

74 C 12/53 New Issues, January–September 1961. Russell to O'Brien, 24 January 1961.

75 C 12/52 ff 53, 61, 68, 86, 114.

C 12/54 New Issues, September 1961–March 1962. Meynell to O'Brien, 3 November 1961.

76 C 12/53 Note by O'Brien, 3 February 1961.

77 C 12/54 Austin to O'Brien, 13 October 1961.

78 ADM 6/84 Paid Notes–Destruction–General

79 C 12/10 Bank Notes Sundry Subjects, October 1950–January 1954. January 1953; November 1953.

80 C 12/12, 13, 14, 15, Bank Notes Sundry Subjects, 1955–61 *passim*.

81 C 12/137 Reproductions, 1926–65. Peppiatt to Bamford, 19 July 1946; Bamford to Peppiatt, 2 August 1946. Summary, Note by Issue Office, 21 May 1954.

82 C 12/127 Reproduction notes, legal opinions etc., July 1959–May 1960. *The Times*, *Financial Times*, 9 August 1959.

83 C 12/127, ff. 124c, 125a/c, 134b, February–March 1960.

## 5 The Printing Works

There are three histories of the Bank of England Printing Works. Two were printed in limited editions by the Bank: *The St Luke's Printing Works of the Bank of England*, by H.G. de Fraine, 1931, and *The Later Years of St Luke's Printing Works*, by A.D. Mackenzie, 1961. The third is in typescript in the Bank's Archive: *The Further History of the Bank of England Printing Works*, by M.J.S. Cubbage (Archive reference PW 6/9–11). This covers the years 1956–1981.

1 Mackenzie, A.D. *The Bank of England Note: a History of its Printing*, Cambridge University Press, 1953, pp. 36–46.

2 De Fraine, H.G. *The St Luke's Printing Works of the Bank of England*, Bank of England, 1931.

3 G 29/1 Printing Works: organisation and administration 1919–49, f 1a 6 June 1919.

Committee of Treasury, 11 May 1921.

C 40/305 St Luke's Refinery.

4 G 29/1, f 3a October 20 1921; Report, 8 February 1922.

5 G 29/1, 8 February 1922.
6 De Fraine, pp. 59–63.
7 De Fraine, pp. 66–8.
8 G 29/1 Memorandum on Committee on St Luke's, 10 April 1931 Court, 16 April 1931.
9 G 29/35 Bank Note Paper: Metallic and Non-Metallic Thread.
10 *Britannia Quarterly*, February 1961: Obituary of S.B. Chamberlain by J.R. Dudin, pp. 3–4.
11 Mackenzie, *The Later Years*, pp. 20–6.
12 Ibid., p. 28.
13 Ibid., pp. 15–19, 30–2.
14 PW 13/4 Minutes of Committee on St Luke's, 17 June 1938.
15 M5/539, pp. 1724–32.
16 M5/539, pp. 1725–6.
17 G 29/49 Staff: Direction of Women to St Luke's, 1945–9.
18 G 29/1 ff 78 ff., January 1949.
19 G 29/1, f. 90, Memorandum by Sir George Abell, 10 March 1949.
20 C 56/28 St Luke's Printing Works – 1949 Security Committee.
21 G 29/1, f 93, 16 March 1949.
22 G 29/2 Printing Works: Organisation and Administration, 1950–5. Report of Committee, f. 30, 28 April 1950.
23 G 29/62 St Luke's Committee: Premises, 1949–51, ff. 1–10.
24 G 29/62, ff. 15 ff.
25 G 29/62, f. 8, 31 October 1949.
26 PW 13/6 Minutes of Committee on St Luke's, 24 August 1950.
27 G 29/62, ff. 59 ff.
28 G 29/62, f. 100, 14 November 1950.
29 G 29/62, f. 46, 19 July 1950.
   PW 13/6, 13 July 1950.
30 G 29/62, f. 112d. 11 January 1951.
31 PW 13/6 Special Meeting of Committee, 15 January 1952.
32 G 29/63 St Luke's Committee: Premises, 1951–3, f. 9a, Braintree to Abell, 1 February 1952.
33 G 29/63 MS note by Abell and Governor, 11 February 1952.
34 G 29/63, f. 111, 22 January 1953.
35 G 29/14 St Luke's Committee: Notes: General, 1924–55, 11 November 1949, 10 December 1953.
36 Mackenzie, *The Later Years*, pp. 66–7.
37 G 29/14, 9 May 1952.
38 G 29/14, Report, 16 July 1952.
   G 29/107 St Luke's/Debden Research Section, ff. 1–9.
39 G 29/107, ff. 10–15.
40 PW 13/6, 9 November 1950.
41 PW 13/6, 5 June 1952.
42 G 29/2, ff. 80 ff.

43 G 29/2, ff. 87, 88, 89, 91, 101.
44 G 29/2 Memorandum by Sir A. Anderson, December 1925, quoted in f. 86, p.4.
45 G 29/2 Memorandum by Mynors, f. 89, 3 November 1954.
46 G 29/2 Mynors to Pilkington, enclosure to letter 19 May 1955.
47 PW 13/6, 11 August 1955.
48 *Architectural Review*, June 1956, pp. 229–307, Bank of England Printing Works, Debden.
   OL, June 1956, pp. 68–9, *The New Bank Printing Works*: A.F.J. Davies.
49 G 29/65 St Luke's/Debden Premises, 1955–7, Whitworth to Abell, 12 July 1956.
50 G 29/66 St Luke's/Debden Premises, 1957–61, ff. 19–41, 63, 84.
51 G 29/86 St Luke's/Debden Finance: General, 1950–8.
   Cadbury to Abell, 21 February 1958.
52 G 29/86 Abell to Cadbury, 27 February 1958.
53 G 29/20 Notes: Costs of Production and Charges to the Issue Department, 1930–60.
54 G 29/14, 16 July 1952.
55 PW 7/6 Handling of Paid Notes: Special Committee. Memorandum by Beale to Peppiatt and Governors, 11 November 1954.
56 PW 7/6 Governor's MS note, 12 November 1954.
57 PW 7/6 Report, 16 February 1955.
58 PW 7/6, 28 October 1955.
59 PW 7/6 Report, 22 February 1956.
   Committee of Treasury, 2 May 1956.
   Court, 3 May 1956.
60 G 29/68 Debden: Premises: Paid Notes Building, 1956–7.
   Report by Personnel Administration, f. 13, October 1956.
61 G 29/69 Debden: Premises: Paid Notes Building, 1957–8, f. 29b, 22 January 1958.
62 PW 13/7 Minutes of Debden Committee, 1958–66, 13 February 1958.
63 *Britannia Quarterly*, May 1959, Hall, Derek, *The Shape of Things to Come*, pp. 84–6.
64 PW 13/7 Minutes of Debden Committee 1958–66, 5 September 1963.
65 G 29/71 Debden: Paid Notes Building, 1960–2, Committee of Treasury, 9 November 1960.
66 E 5/42 Sale of St Luke's, 1957–64.

## 6 The Banking Department

1 EID 7/3 Bank of England History, 1937–62. Information disclosed to nine Parliamentary Committees between 1797 and 1875 is summarised in f. 5, October 1937.
2 EID 7/3, f. 27.
3 Mackenzie, *The Later Years*, p. 27.
4 Leaf, Walter, *Banking*, Thornton Butterworth, 1935, pp. 47–8.

EID 7/5 Bank of England General, 1928–52, ff. 4 and 5.

5 ADM 6/89 Bank's Accounts General, 1845–1959, 28 January 1934.

6 G 15/244 Special Committee on Bank's Profits and Increase in Capital, 1918–19, January 1919.

ADM 6/89, 29 January 1934, 15 September 1944.

DB (File No. not yet assigned) The Bank's Accounts, Profits and Profitability. A paper compiled by David Best as background to this chapter.

7 Order of Court, 2 February 1965.

Minutes of General Court, 15 December 1694.

Minutes of General Court, 16 September 1869.

ADM 6/90 Bank's Accounts General, 1960–5, f. 9, 2 May 1962.

8 ADM 19 Stock Estimates &c, 15 vols. 1806–1970. Original entries consisted of Stock Accounts (summary of assets and liabilities), the Profit and Loss Account and an 'Estimate of the State of the Bank as it is supposed it will be' (on Dividend Days, 5 April and 10 October). The Estimates were discontinued following the formation of the Issue Department in 1844.

9 ADM 6/89 Memo by Mynors, 15 September 1944.

10 ADM 11/2 Charters, Statutes and By-Laws, Bank of England Act, 1946. Passage through Parliament. Reference to Norman's broadcast (reprinted in *The Listener*, 23 March 1939), Mynors to Sir H. Brittain, f. 5, 18 October 1945.

11 Sayers, *The Bank of England*, vol. I, pp. 17–27.

12 ADM 11/2, f. 34a, 15 November 1945.

13 ADM 11/2, f. 34, 10 November 1945, Mynors speculates on 'what conclusions on the size of "hidden reserves" could an outsider derive from the Bank Return?': he arrives at a figure of £50 m.

14 ADM 6/91–6 Bank Accounts – Half-Yearly Accounts, 1911–66.

15 G 15/244 Correspondence between Bank and HMT *passim*.

ADM 6/136 Costing – Deloittes' Original Proposal for the Costing System, 1920/1.

OL, December 1983, *Gentlemen, The Firm—Deloitte's, The Bank's Auditors*: Roger Woodley.

DB, pp. 3–4.

16 Order of Court, 13 April 1933.

G 15/281 Expenditure Committee – General.

17 G 15/281 Interim Report of Special Committee, 19 July 1933.

Final report of Special Committee, 13 December 1933.

18 G 15/281, 15 January 1948.

19 Order of Court, 8 March 1934.

G 15/281.

20 G 15/281, 28 July 1934, ff.

21 DB.

22 ADM 6/89, 30 June 1936.

G 14/1 Committee of Treasury–Accounts of the Bank General, June 1936–October 1960, 24 June and 8 July 1936.

23 Evidence to the Committee on Finance and Industry (Macmillan Committee) 1929–31, HMSO Cmd No. 3897.

24 G 14/1, 29 June 1937.

25 G 14/1, 1 July 1937.

26 G 14/1, 13 February 1939.

27 G 14/2 Committee of Treasury Accounts of the Bank – Banking Department Investments, 1921–69. October 1939 and February 1940.

28 ADM 6/57 Exchange Control Cost of Administration – Claims to HMT, 1940–53.
81/26 Bank of England, 1939–45, vol. 6, pp. 1364–8.

29 G 15/285 Expenditure Committee Reports, 1935–52. 26 June 1941.

30 G 14/4 Committee of Treasury Accounts of the Bank – Management Charges and Remuneration for Agency Business. 10 June 1942.

31 *Hansard*, 5 and 26 February, 15 March 1926.
*Annual Register*, 1926, pp. 24–5.
EID 7/4 Bank of England General 1930–1. f. 6a, 5 February 1926.
G 15/122 Charters Statutes and By-Laws General, 1918–33. ff. 2f. and 2g.

32 ADM 11/1 Charters Statutes and By-Laws Bank of England Act, 1946, Drafting the Bill. Note of Governor's speech in Court, 1 November 1945.

33 *Hansard*, 29 October 1945. Bank of England Bill 2nd Reading.

34 ADM 11/1 Note of discussion in Court, 11 October 1945.

35 Minutes of Proceedings of Select Committee on the Bank of England Bill plus Minutes of Evidence, HMSO, November, 1945.

36 *Hansard*, 17 December 1945.

37 ADM 6/89 memo by Cobbold, 19 September 1945.
ADM 6/90 3 March 1961. A detailed note by J.B. Atkinson on the subject of the half-yearly payment to the Treasury.

38 Minutes of Proceedings of Select Committee.

39 *Hansard*, 17 December 1945.

40 EID 7/6 Bank of England Annual Report Policy and General, December 1945–August 1954.

41 EID 7/6.

42 EID 7/6 f. 91a, 27 May 1953.

43 The lecture is reprinted as 'The Bank of England in 1953' in R.S. Sayers, *Central Banking After Bagehot*, Oxford University Press, 1957.

44 EID 7/6, f. 101, 4 January 1954, et seq.

45 G 15/125 Charters Statutes and By-Laws General, 1947–61, 3 April and 25 May 1948.

46 G 15/285.

47 Minutes of Court, 15 January 1948.

48 G 15/281, 20 February 1948.

49 G 15/281, 29 June 1948.

50 G 15/285.

51 Order of Court, 28 October 1948.
G 15/281, 28 October 1948.

52 G 15/327 Administration-Miscellaneous, 1930–51. 15 March 1949, et seq.

53 ADM 11/3 Charters Statutes and By-Laws Bank of England Act, 1946. After Appointed Day, 1946–56. Mynors to Governor, 11 March 1948.

54 G 15/288 Expenditure Committee – Economy-General, 1935–65. Report on Meeting held by Deputy Governor on 17 February 1950.

55 G 15/286 Expenditure Committee Reports, 1962–4.

56 ADM 6/89 Governor's Note, 17 March 1950.

57 G 31/1 Committee on Permanent Control of Expenditure Minutes, 27 August 1942.

58 ADM 6/54 Exchange Control Cost of Administration General, January 1949–September 1954. f. 58a, 12 November 1951, et seq.

59 ADM 6/49 EEA Management General – Review of basis of charges for administration.

60 *Hansard*, 7 November 1951.

61 ADM 6/95 Governor's speech to Committee of Treasury and to Court, 24 and 25 September 1952.

## 7 The Cashier's Department

1 QB, September 1970, *The Work of the Cashier's Department*, pp. 285–94.

2 C 40/39 Chief Cashier's Office, Work of Office, 1945–8, Inspector's Report on CCO, October 1945.

3 C 40/39–43 Chief Cashier's Office, Work of Office, 1945–60.

4 C 40/40 Chief Cashier's Office, Work of Office, 1949–52, Annual Report of Correspondence Post, October 1952.

5 C 40/39 Inspector's Report on CCO, October 1945.
  C 40/39–43.

6 C 40/39 Inspector's Report on CCO, October 1945.
  C 40/39–43.

7 C 40/39 Inspector's Report on CCO, October 1945.

8 C 40/39–43.

9 C 40/39–43.

10 E 21/5 Committee on Advanced Training, 1959–61, 20 June 1959.

11 C 40/39–43.

12 *Hansard*, 7 November 1951.

13 C 56/58 Annual Reports to Chief Cashier 1949–1953, Report of Discount Office, 1951.

14 H.S. Clarke to author, February 1990.

15 C 40/39–43.

16 QB, September 1970.
  QB, December 1968, *The Exchange Equalisation Account*, pp. 377–87.

17 C 56/57 Annual Reports to Chief Cashier, 1940–8, Report of Drawing Office, 1947.

18 C 56/59 Annual Reports to Chief Cashier, 1954–6, Report of Drawing Office, 1954.

19 C 56/59 Report of Drawing Office, 1955.

20 C 56/58 Report of Drawing Office, 1950.

21 C 40/1049 Crown Jewels, 1945–70, papers, 1945–7.
C 56/57 Report of Drawing Office, 1947.

22 *Report of the Select Committee on Dormant Bank Balances and Unclaimed Securities Bill, HMSO, December* 1919. Filed in C 40/75 Unclaimed Balances, 1908–40.

23 C 56/58 Report of Drawing Office, 1952.

24 C 6/5 Cashier's Department General, 1953–60, 1 March 1955.

25 C 56/60–62 Annual Reports from Offices 1957–1959, Reports of Drawing Office.

26 C 40/103 Clearings, 1941–50.
C 40/104 Clearings, 1950–8.
C 56/59 Reports of Bill Office.
C 56/22 Work of Office – Bill Office, 1939–75.

27 C 40/106 Clearings, January – June 1960.

28 C 19/6 Securities Office Reports, 1935–72.

29 C 56/4 Work of Office – Treasury, 1903–42.
C 6/10 Treasury, 1903–74.

30 C 56/8 Work of Office – Bullion Office, 1936–9.
C 56/9 Work of Office – Bullion Office, 1939–53.

31 G 15/205 Special Committee on Organisation, 1932, Report as approved by Court of Directors, 23 June 1932.

32 C 56/10 Work of Office – Bullion Office, 1953–8, f. 12, 12 May 1954.

33 C 43/238 Gold Set Aside for Bank Customers, 1940–69.
C 56/57 Annual Reports from Offices, 1940–8. Report of Bullion Office, 31 December 1940.
C 56/9 Work of Office – Bullion Office, 1939–53.

34 C 56/57 Reports of Bullion Office, November 1946 and December 1947.

35 C 56/57 Report of Bullion Office, September 1948.
C 43/169 and 170 Tripartite Agreement for the Restitution of Monetary Gold, 1948–52 and 1952–57.
Smith Jr, A.L., *Hitler's Gold : the story of the Nazi war loot*, Berg, 1989.
C 40/370–77 Restitution of Looted Gold – Dollfus Mieg et Cie, 1947–58.

36 C 40/58 Annual Reports from Offices 1949–1953, Report of Bullion Office, November 1950.
C 43/238.

37 C 56/10, 19 March 1954.

38 C 56/10 P.S. Beale, Note for Record, 11 March 1954.

39 C 56/10 V.C. Tong to O'Brien, 9 December 1954.

40 C 56/10, January–June 1955.

41 C 40/894 Silver Withdrawal, 1947–51, f. 56, 20 October 1948.

42 C 56/60 Annual Reports from Offices, 1957, Reports of Dealing and Accounts Office, November 1957, and Bullion Office, September 1957.

43 C 56/63 Annual Reports from Offices, 1960, Report of Bullion Office, 1960.
B. Kettell, *Gold*, Graham & Trotman Ltd, 1982.

44 Acres, *The Bank of England from Within* vol. 1, p. 32.
45 C 53/1 Work of Office – In-Tellers' Office, 1921–58, f. 49, 2 February 1954.
   C 56/16 Work of Office – In-Tellers' Office, 1903–7.
46 C 53/1, f. 194a, 16 January 1951.
47 C 53/1, f. 83, 7 November 1947.
48 C 40/893 Silver Shortage of Supplies, 1948–56.
   C 40/894.
   C 40/895 Silver Withdrawal, 1951–7.
   *Annual Reports of Deputy Master and Comptroller of the Royal Mint 1949–1959*, HMSO.
49 C 6/12 In-Tellers' Office, 1935–57, November–December 1947.
50 ADM 15/7 Inspector's Reports, 1942–56, Report on In-Tellers' Office, 1956.
   Order of Court, 16 May 1957.
51 56/23 Work of Office – Loans Office, 1904–49, Note on the History of the Sub-Treasury, 2 April 1937; Note by Principal, 2 May 1939.
52 C 56/57 Report of Dividend Pay and Loans Office, October 1944.
53 C 56/23 Papers relating to mechanisation, 1934–7.
54 QB, September 1964, *The Treasury Bill*, pp. 187–8.
55 C 56/58 Annual Reports from Offices, 1949–53, Report of Dividend Pay and Loans Office, October 1951.
56 C 58/60 Annual Reports from Offices, 1949–57, Reports of Dividend Pay and Loans Office.
   C 6/13 Dividend Pay and Loans Office, 1913–77.
57 C 56/60 and 61 Annual Reports from Offices, 1957 and 1958, Reports from Dividend Pay and Loans Office.

## 8 The Branches

1 Sayers, *The Bank of England*, vol. I, pp. 255–7.
2 E 5/68 Special Committee on Branches, 1937–47.
3 G 14/21 Committee of Treasury, Branch Premises, 1930–1969: 22 September and 20 October 1937.
4 C 56/43 Work of Offices, Branches, 1937–49.
5 C 56/43, 14 April 1938.
6 E 32/2 Salaries, Agents, Sub-Agents and Chief Clerks, 1906–54.
7 G 14/21, 14 September 1938.
8 E 5/94–98, Premises General: Southampton, 1938–62.
   OL, vol. XVI, June 1940, pp. 96–7.
9 G 14/21 Notes of meetings between Bank and members of Hull Corporation, July 1938.
   OL, vol. XV, March 1939, pp. 79–80.
10 E 5/68 Extracts from Minutes of Special Committee, 1939.
11 M5/539, pp. 1733–40.
   C 43/263 Gold held at Bank and Branches, 1940–3.
   C 56/43, 29 October 1945; October 1946.

12 C 6/16 Branches: Memorandum by Branch Representative, Advisory Council, 28 May 1945.

13 C 7/1 Annual Reports by BBO to Chief Cashier, 1935–75: Reports 1946, 1947, 1948.
C 56/50 Reports by Inspector of Offices and Branches, 1943–9: Country Branches Reports September 1946 and January 1947; BBO Report, February 1947.

14 C 7/2 Annual Reports by Agents to Chief Cashier, 1943–8: Plymouth, 1945; Bristol, 1947.

15 C 7/6 Minutes for Agents' Annual Meetings at Head Office, 1938–72: 18 December 1952.

16 A.E. Bilton to author, 5 May 1988.

17 E 5/70 Branches General, 1937–65: Premises Committee, 6 June 1945.

18 Order of Court, 20 November 1947.

19 C 79/57 Closing of Plymouth Branch, 1948–55.
C 56/43, 21 May 1948.

20 E 5/70, 1 July 1949.

21 C 7/6, March 1950.

22 E 5/70, 1 July 1949.

23 E 5/71 Premises General: Branches: Manchester, 1938–65: 28 March 1952.

24 E 5/71, 15 July 1952.

25 E 5/71, Committee of Treasury, 21 November 1956.

26 E 5/71, 13 September 1957 et seq.

27 Court, 1 April 1954.
E 5/70, 15 September 1953.
E 5/72 Premises General: Branches: Birmingham, 1885–1965: see papers for 1955, 1959, 1961.

28 E 5/73 Premises General: Branches: Liverpool, 1937–61: 1 July 1949, August 1952.

29 E 5/73 Agent to Noakes, 7 July 1954.

30 E 5/73 Note by Noakes, 21 July 1954.

31 E 5/74 Premises General: Branches: Liverpool, 1959–62.

32 E 5/77 Premises General: Branches: Liverpool, 1964–5: Victorian Society to Governor, 2 September 1964.

33 E 5/77 Chief of Establishments to Victorian Society, 8 October 1964.

34 E 5/92 Premises General: Branches: Newcastle, 1959–64.

35 E 5/91 Premises General: Branches: Leeds, 1952–64.

36 E 5/93 Premises General: Branches: Law Courts, 1938–65.
C 7/12 Branches, 1951–68: Closing of Law Courts Branch considered, 1951.

37 E 5/93 O'Brien to Abell, 4 August 1960.

38 C 7/13 Branch Banks Office General, 1919–70: February and March 1955.

39 C 7/13 Governor's Note, 17 October 1957.

40 E 5/79, Premises General: Branches: Bristol 1954–9: January–September 1955.

41 E 5/79, January 1956 et seq.

42 E 5/70 Correspondence, Heal and Abell, November 1957.

43 E 5/80 Premises General: Branches: Bristol, 1959–60.

44 E 5/81 Premises General: Branches: Bristol, 1960–1: Noakes, 27 September 1960.

45 E 5/89 Premises General: Branches: Bristol Press Cuttings: *Architectural Review*, February 1961.

46 E 5/81 February and March 1961.
*Hansard*, 23 March 1961.

47 E 5/81, 21 February and 3 March 1961.

48 E 5/8 Agent to Noakes, 25 April 1961.

49 Court, 25 May 1961.

50 E 5/82 Premises General: Branches: Bristol, 1961–2: Minister of Housing and Local Government to Governor, 31 May 1961.

51 E 5/82 Freshfields to Noakes, 5 June 1961.

52 E 5/82, 10 July 1961.

53 E 5/82, 3 August 1961.

54 E 5/82, August 1961.
E 5/84 Premises General: Branches: Bristol, 1962: Abell to Chairman, South Western Electricity Board, 30 August 1962.

55 A.E. Bilton to author, 5 May 1988.

56 E 5/87 Premises General: Branches: Bristol, 1963–4: November–December 1963.

57 E 5/89 *Bristol Week-End*, 17 July 1963.
OL, vol. 40, March 1964 *The New Bristol Branch*: A.F. Scannall, pp. 23–4.

58 A.E. Bilton to author, 5 May 1988.

59 E 5/90 Premises General: Branches: Bristol, 1963–5: November 1963.

60 G 15/125 Charters Statutes and By-Laws General 1947–60: Courtis to Dalton, 2 October 1947.

61 G 15/125 Redfern to Courtis, 7 October 1947.

62 G 15/125 Note, JMH to Secretary, 6 February 1951.

63 G 15/125 Compton to O'Brien, 5 November 1957.

64 G 15/125 Neatby to O'Brien, 14 February 1958.

65 G 15/125, 5 March 1958

66 G 15/125 Opinion of Counsel, July 1958.

67 G 15/125 Freshfields to O'Brien, 14 July 1958.

68 G 15/125 Paper by Smallwood, 8 December 1958.

69 G 15/125, 1 August 1958.

70 G 15/125, 8 December 1985.

## 9 Overseas, Economics and Statistics

1 OV 21/4 Administration of work, 1927–59. Historical note, 4 September 1958.

2 Sayers, *The Bank of England*, vol. I, 1, Section 1D, Fostering Central Banks in the British Dominions, 1920–30; vol. II, Section 20C, Promoting central banking in the Commonwealth and other countries, 1931–9.

3 Order of Court, 23 June 1932, with effect from 1 November 1932.
4 OV 21/10 Administration of work 1932–57. Memorandum by Siepmann, January 1935.
5 OV 21/4 Memorandum, 10 July 1935.
6 OV 21/10 Manual of Procedure, O & F Dept, 18 April 1939.
7 OV 21/21 Annual Reports on Overseas and Foreign Office, 1941–8.
EC 6/6 1941–56 Half yearly reports to Chief Cashier, Overseas and Foreign Office.
OL, December 1987, *The Bank Archive: Missions Abroad 1939–1945*: A.F.A. Carlisle, pp. 156–8.
8 Order of Court, 27 February 1941, with effect from 3 March 1941.
OV 21/10 Memorandum on Exchange Economy Section, 3 March 1941.
9 OV 21/10 Memorandum prepared for wartime history of Exchange Control, 8 February 1944.
10 E 35/7 Administration – Organisation of Offices, 1932–65.
Memorandum by A. Payton, 19 October 1951.
11 OV 21/10 MS note by Hoar, 20 February 1943.
12 OV 21/10 Quoted in memorandum, Hoar to Siepmann, 14 July 1943.
13 OV 21/1 Administration of work, 1941–50.
OV 21/21.
14 OV 21/1 Visits Abroad.
15 OV 21/1 Siepmann, 8 April 1948.
16 OV 21/1.
OV 21/21, 19 February 1947.
17 A.F.A. Carlisle to author, 23 July 1987.
18 OV 21/10 Memorandum by Watson, 11 October 1948.
19 Order of Court, 21 October 1948.
OV 21/1 – Memorandum Bolton to Deputy Governor, 26 October 1948.
20 OV 21/3 Staff – Women, 1941–71, March 1944.
21 OV 21/10 Cobbold to Siepmann, 13 May 1952, et seq.
22 OV 21/10 Governor's note, 25 January 1955.
Memoranda, September 1955.
23 OV 21/4 Memorandum by Watson, 17 March 1952 et seq.
24 OV 18/2, 3 and 4 *Central Banks in the making: 1948–1976*: E.P. Haslam.
Printed at Bank of England, 1979, for private circulation.
25 OV 18/2.
R.E. Barber and D.A.H. Byatt to author, November 1989.
26 EC 6/6 Annual Report, July 1946–June 1947.
27 OV 21/26 Administration of work – Central Banking Courses, 1956–74.
Memorandum by Watson, 1 October 1956.
28 OV 21/26 Memorandum by Mynors, 4 October 1956.
29 OV 21/26 Memorandum by Mynors, 19 October 1956.
30 OV 21/26, December 1956–January 1957.
31 OV 21/26 Reports on First Course, June 1957.
32 OV 21/44 External banking courses, 1957–68. SEANZA Courses.

33 OV 21/14 Administration of work 1966–69. Historical note, 21 February 1967.

34 E 21/4 Advanced Training: Sir Cyril Hawker's Committee, 1958–60.
Memorandum on training in Overseas Department, 18 July 1958.

35 E 21/4 Governor's note, 2 May 1958.

36 *Report of Committee on working of Monetary System*: HMSO Cmnd 827, August 1959, chapter X, Statistics, p. 280.

37 EID 8/1 Statistics Office, Organisation, Policy and Staff, 1923–44.
QB, December 1976, *The Work of the Economic Intelligence Department*, pp. 436–7.
OL, March 1970, Retirement Notice, J.B. Selwyn, p. 52.
EID 8/5 Description of work of Economics and Statistics Section, 1939.
J.B. Selwyn to author, 1 July 1987.

38 OL, March 1964, Retirement Notice, Sir H. Mynors Bt., pp. 6–7.
OL, September 1980, *Sir Humphrey Mynors: A City Squire*: R. Woodley, pp. 101–2.

39 EID 8/1.

40 EID 8/1.
OV 21/10, 4 September 1941.
Order of Court, 19 February 1942.

41 EID 8/1 Memorandum by Mynors, 5 December 1941.

42 EID 8/1.
EID 8/2 Statistics Office Organisation, Policy and Staff, 1945–54.
J.B. Selwyn to author, 1 July 1987.

43 Bridges, Rt Hon. Lord, *The Treasury*: George Allen & Unwin, 1964, p. 91.

44 EID 3/5 Dossier General, 1942–9, October 1945.
EID 2/20 Summary General, 1927–44.

45 EID 1/1 Harold Wilson Report, 1947.

46 M.J. Thornton to author, 18 January 1988.

47 QB, December 1976.

48 EID 8/2.
EID 8/4 Statistics Office General Administration, 1953–61.

49 ADM 12/6 W.M. Allen Duplicate Memoranda 1959. 25 February 1959.

50 OV 21/11 Overseas Department Administration CBID, 1959–60, f 8, 11 September 1959.

51 OV 21/11 f 39, 28 October 1959.

52 OV 21/11 Deputy Governor's notes for seeing the Press, f 39a, 29 October 1959.

53 OV 21/11 Governor's Speech at Lord Mayor's Dinner, f 81, 12 November 1959.

54 QB, December 1976, pp. 440–1.
OV 21/12 Administration of Work, 1963–6.
EID 8/10 Central Banking Information Department Work of Department: Policy, 1959–64.
J.S. Fforde to author, November 1989.

55  EID 5/24 Bank of England Quarterly Bulletin Policy and General, 1958–60.

56  OV 21/13 Overseas Department Organisation, 1963–6, ff 1–36, November 1963.

QB, December 1976, p. 440.

Order of Court, 13 February 1964 with effect from 1 March 1964.

## 10 The Establishment Department

1  Clay, Sir Henry, *Lord Norman*, Macmillan, 1957, p. 481.

2  E 15/1 *A short history of Staff Representation in the Bank of England*: I.A. Estridge. Privately printed by the Bank of England, 1954.

3  G 15/201–205 incl. Special Committee on Organisation, 1931–4.

4  E 35/2 Formation of Establishment Department, 1932–44.

5  E 35/2 6 January 1933 et seq.

6  E 35/2 Sections 316.12 and 316.13.

G 15/628 Establishment Department, 1932–1976. Note on origins of position of Staff Superintendent, 31 January 1944.

7  E 13/1 Heads of Departments' Meetings, 1936–41.

8  E 35/2.

9  E 33/32 Welfare – General, 1921–65.

10  E 36/2 Reports on Staff – General.

E 35/2.

E 4/22 Future Organisation of Staff, 1943–5.

81/26 Bank of England, 1939–45, vol. 7.

11  E 14/1 Departmental Establishment Officers' Meetings, 1938–46.

Paper by E.S. Ellis, 3 August 1943.

12  E 14/1 3 August 1941.

13  E 14/1 Note by F.W.R. Laverack, 17 September 1945.

14  E 14/1.

15  E 14/1. Notes on the future constitution of the Clerical Staff of the Bank, June 1944, f. 59.

C 6/27 Staff Requirements of Department, 1943–55.

16  E 13/2 Heads of Departments' Meetings, 1941–5. 1943 et seq.

E 4/22.

17  E 14/2 Departmental Establishment Officers' Meetings, 1946–52, memorandum by Bernard, 14 February 1944.

18  G 3/237 Governor's Duplicate Letters, January–March 1944.

Letter from Catterns to Capt. Rt Hon. Sir D. Hacking Bt., 19 January 1944.

19  C 6/3 Administration of Work – General, 1943–9. Memorandum to Royal Commission, June 1945.

20  E 14/1, 26 May 1944.

21  E 4/22, 28 December 1944, et seq.

22  E 4/22, June 1944.

E 4/23 Future Organisation of Staff, 1945–56. The Future of Women Staff, 14 September 1954.

23  E 14/1, 1 June 1945.

24  E 12/4, 1947 Reclassification Scheme, 1946–51.

E 12/25–34 incl. Special Committee to Review 1936 Scheme. Papers and Minutes, 1946–8.

25  E 37/1 Porters and Messengers and Oddmen, 1934–65.

E 37/2 Parlour Messengers and Doorkeepers, 1927–65.

E 37/3 Messengers and Porters, 1896–1948.

E 37/15 Bank Medical Officer 1877–1963. 13 March 1952.

OL, September 1989, *Servants of this House: The Technical and Services Staff*, A. Carlisle, pp. 114–17.

W. Thompson and K.W. Thompson to author, May–June 1990.

HR 13/1–2 Bank Picquet.

26  E 37/24 Uniforms, 1912–69.

E 17/1 H.G. Askwith Personal, 1950–5. 19 August 1954.

27  E 3/29 Porters Messengers and Oddmen, 1923–64.

28  OL, September 1989.

29  E 15/1.

30  E 15/1.

31  E 1/49 Personal File, Sir George Abell.

32  G 14/190 Committee of Treasury – National Union of Bank Employees, 1940–63. Papers, 1940–6.

E 15/1.

33  G 14/190, 30 June 1954.

34  E 15/1.

E 15/5 Council of Directors and Staff General, 1936–55. Note by Bernard, 5 March 1953.

E 15/6 Council of Directors and Staff General, 1957–60. 1 October 1957.

35  E 15/6, July 1958.

36  E 18/3 Superannuation Fund, 1942–47. 1944, Special Pension Offer.

E 18/4 Superannuation Fund, 1943–1957. 1953, 1954, 1956, Special Pension Offers.

E 18/5 Superannuation Fund, 1958–61. Special Pension Offers.

E 18/6 Superannuation Fund, 1959. 1959 Special Pension Offer.

37  E 18/29 Superannuation Fund – Formation, history and growth, 1933–65.

38  E 24/10 Bank Provident Society, 1910–65, Management.

E 18/14 Clerks' Widows and Children Annuity Scheme, 1919–52.

E 18/19 Widows' Annuity Fund, 1946–51.

39  E 18/2 Samaritan Fund, 1854–1963.

40  E 33/3 Housing Loans, 1945–69.

41  E 33/20 Educational Loans Bank Scheme, 1941–51. Note by H.A. Siepmann, 9 June 1944.

42  E 3/21 Educational Loans, 1954–68.

43  E 21/1 Training, 1943–45. Need for training postwar, 19 July 1944.

44  E 1/5 Staff Personal File A.R.M. Geddes.

45  G 15/206 Special Committee on Accountant's Department, 1943.

46  E 14/2, 4 February 1949.

Order of Court, 24 February 1959.

47 E 14/3 Departmental Establishment Officers General, 1953–7. f. 12, 27 October 1953.

48 E 21/3 Training, 1957–65. Memo by J.B. Reid, 9 May 1958.

49 E 21/2 Training, 1953–6.

50 E 21/4 Advanced Training. Governor's Note, 2 May 1958.

51 E 21/4, 8 January 1959.

52 E 21/5 Advanced Training – Chief of Establishment's Committee.

53 E 31/2 Future of the Women Staff, 1946–57. Interim Report of Special Committee to Review 1936 Scheme, 9 October 1946.

54 E 31/2 Minutes of Council of Directors and Staff, 23 September 1954.

55 E 3/24 Recruitment, 1953–62. Abell to Deputy Governor, 15 October 1954. Miss A. Maunsell to author, 11 June 1987.

56 E 3/24.

57 E 3/24 Note on future of women staff, 14 September 1954.

58 E 4/23 Future Organisation of Staff, 1954–6. 15 September 1955.

59 E 4/23 Note by O'Brien, 31 October 1955.

60 E 3/24, 6 October 1955.
E 31/2 Report to Governors, 14 July 1955.
E 34/6 Saturday Work, 1919–65.

61 E 31/2, February–May 1956.

62 E 31/2, July–August 1956.

63 E 31/2 Neylan's report to Governors, 18 July 1957.

64 Order of Court, 3 October 1957.

65 E 12/7 1958 Scheme of Classification.
E 12/47–55 incl. Special Committee on Classification, 1957–8.

66 E 14/4 DEOs Meetings, 1958–9. 19 September 1958.
E 15/18 Council of Directors and Staff, 1936–65. 14 October 1958.
Miss A. Maunsell to author, 11 June 1987.

67 E 34/1 Governor's Charge, 1812–1981. July 1939.

68 E 34/1 Note by Governor, 3 October 1958.

69 E 34/1, 1 June 1959.
E 3/3 Career Booklets, 1954–75.

70 E 3/17 Women Clerks; Sources of Candidates, 1954–65. Papers, 1958.

71 E 3/7 Special Entrants, 1953–64.
E 3/8 Economists, 1959–65.
E 3/13 Special Entrants, 1959–64.

72 E 5/43 Bank Buildings and 19 Old Jewry, 1931–65.

73 E 5/45 Bank Buildings and 19 Old Jewry Statues, 1948–63.

74 E 5/47 Tokenhouse Yard and King's Arms Yard, 1948–63.

75 E 5/60 Roehampton: Bank of England Sports Club, 1910–51.
E 5/62 Roehampton: Bank of England Sports Club, 1945–52.

76 E 5/62, April 1946.

77 E 5/60.
E 5/61 Roehampton: Bank of England Sports Club, 1953–8.

E 5/64 Roehampton: Record Office and Cottage, 1943–65.

E 5/65 Roehampton: Clarence Farm and Cottage and Clarence Lodge, 1907–65.

E 5/66 Roehampton: Clarence Farm and Stables, 1939–64.

Bond, A.J.N. and Doughty, M.O.H., *The House: A History of the Bank of England Sports Club 1908–1983*, Published by Bank of England Sports Club, 1984.

78 E 5/39 Statues and Busts: Head Office, 1943–62. Papers, 1945–6.

79 E 6/4 War Memorials, 1921–49

OL, Memorial Supplement, March 1949.

80 E 37/19 Curator of Furniture, 1941–64.

81 E 5/4 The Parlours, 1925–64. Papers, 1952–4.

## 11 The Secretary's Department

1 G 15/202 Special Committee on Organisation, 1931–4. Notes on Secretary's Office, 25 June 1931.

2 G 15/202 Memorandum by W.H. Clegg, 25 May 1933.

3 G 15/201 Special Committee on Organisation, 1931–4. Report, 23 June 1932. Recommendations III 4.

4 G 15/201 Report, para. 40.

5 G 15/253 Trotter Committee on the Government and Administration of the Bank 1926–7. File includes Report to the Governors of Foreign Business Committee, 2 December 1926.

6 G 15/202 'The Post of Governor's Secretary': memo. by Skinner, 6 January 1932.

Boyle, Andrew, *Montagu Norman*, Cassell 1967, p. 217.

7 G 15/202 Section 1.

8 G 15/202, August 1932.

9 G 15/202 Note by Lefeaux, 11 January 1933.

10 G 15/202 Dale to Norman, draft, ? August–September 1933.

11 G 15/202 Note by Skinner, ? October 1933.

12 G 15/202, 5 June 1934.

G 15/429 Secretary's Division, Work of Office, 1855–1960. 25 June 1934.

13 G 15/202, 5 October 1934.

14 G 17/62, Skinner, E.H.D., Personal File. See Skinner's letter of 25 March 1978 to current Secretary, detailing events of 1934–5.

15 G 14/429 Notes on functions of Accounts and Costing Sections, 6 and 7 October 1941, and on work of Secretary's Department, 10 October 1941.

16 ADM 11/1 Charters, Statutes and By-Laws, Bank of England Act, 1946; Drafting the Bill. Note by Holland-Martin, 27 August 1945.

17 G 15/429 Note on origins of Historical Records Section, January 1955.

18 G 15/429 January 1955.

19 ADM 30/87 Museum: Premises and Equipment, 1949–87.

20 ADM 10/2 News Summary: General Work of Section.

21 G 15/387 Donations and Charities: General, 1916–46. Note on Donations to Public Charities, 10 October 1933.

22 G 15/387.

23 G 15/387. Court, 14 June 1934; Committee of Treasury, 20 June 1934; Court, 21 June 1934.

G 15/389 Donations General, 1945–65. Note on Tower Hill Improvement Fund, 1 February 1955.

24 G 15/387 Draft note on Charitable Donations, 25 May 1945.

G 15/395 National Council of Social Service General, 1941–51.

25 G 15/394 Charitable Appeals Committee General, 1945–65.

26 G 15/390 Donations General 1956–57. Note on policy, 3 July 1957.

27 G 15/298 Royalty – Visits: Visit of the Queen and Duke of Edinburgh, 1952.

28 G 15/297 Royalty – Visits, 1937–68.

29 G 15/431 Secretary's Office Staff General, 1922–78, September 1957 and September 1958.

# INDEX